CW01239197

'Superbly researched and compellingly told'

James Holland

'Jack Bowsher has found a fresh story in a campaign that is itself often overlooked, with a book that explains as much as it reveals.'

Al Murray

'The employment of British armoured vehicles in Burma deserves to be better known. Jack Bowsher's story of ordinary tank soldiers doing extraordinary things in inhospitable terrain fills this gap admirably. I am sure that Forgotten Armour, of how tank troopers quite literally sped up allied success, will be standard reading for decades to come.'

Peter Caddick-Adams

"As we celebrate the 80th Anniversary of D-Day the attention is inevitably on Normandy, but we also need to remember and celebrate the war winning engagements by Slim's "Forgotten" 14 Army in the campaigns in Burma and NE India. This fascinating book by Jack Bowser does just that and the attention it brings to the armoured elements of that extraordinary campaign is to be warmly welcomed.

I have skin in this business because as a tank soldier by training and profession it is good to see a much needed focus on the vital contribution made to that Far East campaign by armour. I was also privileged to command the British Army's Second Division, the very division which relieved Kohima in 1944 and have visited the challenging terrain where so many of the described exploits took place. This well-researched book charts the development of doctrinal thinking and professionalism which enabled the Allies to meet Slim's advocacy, that the tank could be a battle winner in any terrain except swamp. It is a must read for anyone interested in the ubiquitous use of armour in conflict.

Finally as the President of the Kohima Educational Trust, this fascinating book makes a worthy contribution to one of our Trust's aims of keeping the flame of remembrance alive, for which I am very grateful."

Major General Robert Gordon, President of the Kohima Education Trust and former GOC 2 UK Division

'It is not widely known that the 7th Armoured Brigade fought with great distinction in the Far East after making its name as part of the 7th Armoured Division, "The Desert Rats" early in the war. An experienced fighting brigade, they brought much tactical nous and armoured punch with them. They brought the clever, quick thinking of armoured soldiers too and proved to be able to adapt swiftly. Changing their famous red rat symbol to a jungle green one, they genuinely re-energised the campaign. They overmatched Japanese armour time and again; they raised morale; they were "battle winners". Courage can be infectious and The Desert Rats have never lacked that vital quality. This book tells a very inspiring tale - and well.'

Major General Patrick Marriott CB CBE DL, Commander, 7th Armoured Brigade 2005-2007

Jack Bowsher has always had a passion for history. His grandfather did his National Service in the late 1940s driving Sexton self-propelled guns, under senior NCOs who were veterans of the Second World War. He passed on the stories of these men, alongside war films, model kits, and visits to historical places. One summer, Jack and his grandfather, inspired by A Bridge too Far, managed to drag the whole family to the Netherlands to drive Hell's Highway from Eindhoven to Arnhem.

Now a teacher, Jack is inspiring another generation of historians as Head of History in a secondary school in Hertfordshire. Alongside this, he recently completed a Military History Masters with Distinction, at the University of Wolverhampton.

FORGOTTEN ARMOUR

Tank Warfare in Burma

Jack Bowsher

Chiselbury

Copyright © 2024 Jack Bowsher

Published by Chiselbury Publishing, a division of Woodstock Leasor Limited 14 Devonia Road, London N1 8JH, United Kingdom

www.chiselbury.com

ISBN: 978-1-916556-38-6 (hardback/colour/dustjacket)
ISBN: 978-1-916556-52-2 (hardback/B&W/Case laminate cover)
ISBN: 978-1-916556-43-0 (ebook)
A CIP catalogue record for this book is available from the British Library

The moral right of Jack Bowsher to be identified as the author of this work is asserted.

This is copyright material and must not be copied, reproduced, transferred, distributed, leased, licensed or publicly performed or used in any way except as specifically permitted by the publishers, as allowed under the terms and conditions under which it was purchased or as strictly permitted by applicable copyright law. Any unauthorised distribution or use of this text may be a direct infringement of the publisher's rights and those responsible may be liable in law accordingly.

Chiselbury Publishing hereby exclude all liability to the extent permitted by law for any errors or omissions in this book and for any loss, damage or expense (whether direct or indirect) suffered by any third party relying on any information contained in this book.

To my wife Alex
who has gamely put up with my war parp for fifteen years,
to the men of all faiths and nationalities who fought, survived, and died
for something far bigger than themselves,
and
to my Grandpa, Bill,
the inspiration for my love of military history, and to whom I owe everything.

Table of Contents

Foreword by James Holland	1
Prologue	5
Introduction	11

Part I — 19
1 The Failure to Mechanise	21
2 The War against Japan	37

Part II — 47
3 7th Armoured Brigade arrive in Burma	49
4 The retreat from Burma	61
5 Laying the Foundations	92
6 Arakan: Lessons Learned	103

Part III — 131
7 'I felt no sorrow' - The Battle of the Admin Box	133
8 On Mountains and Plains: The Battle of Imphal	158
9 Clearing Kohima	200

Part IV — 233
10 Capital Investment: Engineering and Logistics	235
11 Combined Operations in Arakan	248
12 Crossing the Irrawaddy and the Road to Mandalay	262
13 Thunder Run to Meiktila	283
14 The Race to Rangoon	324
Epilogue	336
Acknowledgements	345
Notes	351
Image Acknowledgments	350
Notes	353
Bibliography	364
Index	371

INDIA
Kohima
Naga Hills
Imphal
Chindwin River
CHINA
Kalewa
Irrawaddy River
Chin Hills
Mandalay
Sinzweya
(Admin Box)
Meiktila
Donbaik
Arakan Yomas
Ramree
Island
Pegu Yomas
Sittang River
Irrawaddy River
THAILAND
Rangoon

Foreword
by
James Holland

It was late on the night of Wednesday, 9 February 1944, that twenty-year-old Norman Bowdler first heard a faint creak. He was exhausted after four days of intense and nerve-jangling battle and, if truth be known, had been unable to stop himself nodding off, even though he was on turret duty, keeping a watch for any enemy attack. The whole of C Squadron of the 25th Dragoons were lined up in leaguer on the eastern side of Ammunition Hill in the 7th Indian Infantry Division's administrative area, known as the 'Admin Box'. An otherwise insignificant area of the Arakan, this had become the scene of a do-or-die battle because Bowdler and the few thousand other defenders in this small corner of north-west Burma were entirely surrounded by Japanese – troops the Fourteenth Army had yet to defeat in battle. Ahead of him was open paddy fields, while around them were hills and the jungle-clad slopes of the Mayu Range.

Then he heard that creaking sound again and he was now suddenly wide-awake and conscious that what he was hearing was leather; and that the only leather that could be moving out there at night was from the webbing of Japanese soldiers. A moment later, and to his horror, he suddenly saw a line of enemy troops emerging from the night mist, no more than fifty yards away. 'The moment they appeared out of the mist like that,' Bowdler recalled, 'everybody in the unit seemed to open fire all at once and not just with machine guns and rifles but the 75s were going off, the 37s were going off and the din was terrible.'

Many of the attackers were slaughtered, the survivors slipping back into the jungle so that when dawn crept back over the Box, the paddy in front of the tanks was strewn with the dead. A number were found clutching magnetic mines: their target had been to destroy the thirty-ton Lee tanks of the 25th Dragoons, for the Japanese had rightly realised that it was these vital pieces of weaponry that held the key to success or failure in this battle.

A couple of days later, their failure to destroy the Dragoons' tanks really came home to roost as the British tankmen systematically cleared the larger Artillery Hill of a further enemy infiltration and doing so use newly developed techniques honed by the Dragoons' second-in-command, Major Hugh Ley. Using their high-explosive 75mm shells to clear the vegetation to reveal Japanese positions they then switched to very accurate solid shot shells until the infantry, advancing behind their fire, were within fifteen yards of the enemy. Grenades, small arms, and bayonet did the rest.

It was a devastatingly effective formula that helped win a stunning victory at the Admin Box, and was a method that would be tried and tested again and again - perhaps most significantly on Nunshigum Hill in late April that year in an action that saved the key town of Imphal in north-east India and helped turn the battle in Fourteenth Army's favour for good. As Jack Bowsher conclusively points out in this superbly researched and compellingly told new work, armour really was a key weapon that led directly to the Japanese defeat in South-East Asia.

The long three-and-a-half year Burma campaign has long been kept to the margins of the narrative of the Second World War. Not for nothing was the Anglo-Indian Fourteenth Army known as the 'Forgotten Army', and yet the role of armour in their story has remained even more forgotten. This book rights a significant oversight in the telling of their story – one in which, as he points out, too much emphasis has been placed on the narrative of the beleaguered infantryman fighting his way through the shadows of an impenetrable jungle. There was jungle, of course, and the experience of the infantryman has understandably captured our imaginations, but this focus has ensured a skewing of history. Rather, the war in south-east Asia was really one of immense logistical challenges, which, as Bowsher vividly demonstrates, were both gargantuan and overcome with barely comprehensible ingeniousness, vision, determination, skill, and titanic human endeavour. It was because of this determination to create functioning roads where there had been none, widen railway gauges, and continually think outside the box, that pioneers like the brilliant General Frank Messervy and Bill Slim, arguably Britain's greatest wartime general, were able to bring thirty-ton beasts like the Lee/Grant tank and later the Sherman to the front line and in enough numbers of make a truly decisive difference to the battlefield. The Japanese simply had no answer. Indeed, the final, brilliant battle in Burma – the outflanking of the Japanese by IV Corps with the armour leading the way – was a stunning operation: strategically, operationally, and tactically.

Forgotten Armour very effectively charts the story of the Anglo-Indian victory in South-East Asia, from the under-development of the 1930s through to the defeat in Burma and retreat back into India, and from the early failures in the Arakan to the turning point and brilliant victories that followed. Reading this epic story again – and here in one narrative – reminded me of just what an astonishing story it really is, and one made all the more remarkable by the incredible contribution by key enlightened senior commanders as well as junior officers, NCOs and crews who pioneered such devastatingly effective ways of using tanks in terrain that offered so many challenges to their employment. All too often, the British have been accused of lacking tactical and operational imagination in the Second World War; Bowsher has convincingly kicked such notions into the long grass. More than that, he has produced a work of genuine freshness and originality that deserves to significantly alter how future generations understand this enduringly fascinating, complex, and compelling campaign.

James Holland

April 2024

Prologue

The plan was already going wrong.

John Henslow, a 22-year-old lieutenant in 77th Field Company Royal Engineers, was summoned to Colonel Tom Wright, Chief Royal Engineer (CRE) at 7th Indian Infantry Division's HQ. All was set for the mighty assault across the Irrawaddy River by IV Corps. D-Day was set for eight days' time: Wednesday 14th February 1945. One of the most important weapons for the reconquest of Burma was the tank. The strategic plan relied on tanks' speed, their overwhelming firepower, and the Imperial Japanese Army's relatively poor anti-tank weapons. Tanks would therefore be the decisive weapon. There was one problem. A big one.

The crossing of the Irrawaddy, one of a number of great rivers that divide Burma[*], was never going to be easy. It is the largest river in Burma at 1,400-miles long with strong currents and shifting sands. In the low-lying central dry belt of Burma, the Irrawaddy fluctuates from over a mile wide to six miles in the monsoon. In December 1944, this was where the Japanese Burma Area Army commander General Heitaro Kimura chose to make his stand: from behind one of the most formidable natural obstacles in the world.

The plan was to make the Japanese think the main thrust would come from XXXIII Corps across the Irrawaddy near Mandalay, in the northern part of the central plain, and draw in Japanese reinforcements. Meanwhile, IV Corps would secretly shift south, where the 7th Indian Division would cross the Irrawaddy and create a beachhead. The 255th Indian Tank

---
[*]Myanmar since 1989.

Brigade and 17th Indian Division would then cross into the 7th Indian Division's beachhead before charging to the town of Meiktila in central Burma, the vital point for Japanese supplies. All major transit routes, and therefore supply lines, passed through on their way to the fighting fronts. By holding it, the Fourteenth Army would cut off the bulk of the Japanese forces in the north, forcing them to send reinforcements to reopen the supply lines. Once XXXIII Corps captured Mandalay, and when the timing was right, XXXIII Corps would push south. Between these two operations, Fourteenth Army would get a decisive battle on the central plain where their greater firepower, especially with armour, could be most effective. Fourteenth Army's commander Lieutenant-General William Slim, 'Uncle Bill' to his men, explained the protagonist's roles: 'XXXIII Corps [will be] the hammer from the north, against the anvil of IV Corps at Meiktila – and the Japanese in between'.[1]

Therefore, the rafts that would take the tanks into the beachhead at the earliest opportunity were crucial. The pontoons had been assembled. The Bailey bridge sections that would be attached on the pontoons were ready to go. The outboard engines were there too, capable of powering these class-40 and class-60 rafts[*] with a tank and its crew. Now the problem. Lost somewhere on the supply lines stretching hundreds of miles back to India, were the frames that had been specially made to attach the engines to the rafts. Or they were never ordered, no one could be quite sure. But one had been found, possibly the original mock-up. For something so vital, it was underwhelming, like a cheap wrought iron bedhead.

Without these engine frames, no tanks would cross the Irrawaddy any time soon.

The CRE's adjutant, Bill Baker, handed this one frame over to Henslow. He was to fly to India with the engine frame and instructions to get sixteen more made by the base workshops. He

---

[*] The number denotes the approximate weight in tons they can carry.

would need to be back by D minus-3 – three days before D-Day – on 11th February. It was the evening of the 6th.

'It was a challenge and responsibility to which I felt proud to be entrusted ... the whole success of the operation depended on it, and I felt very honoured that it was entrusted to me, a humble lieutenant; you cannot get much humbler in the chain of command'.[2] For the next few days, John Henslow would be the most important person in Southeast Asia. If only someone had told the rest of the army.

The next morning at a hot and dusty airfield hurriedly set up during the advance, Henslow and his engine frame were greeted like VIPs. Everyone knew he was on an important mission, and everything was ready and waiting for him. He was flown by Lysander to the nearest large supply airfield at Pagan, and thence by C-47 Dakota to Comilla, and finally on to Dum Dum Airport, Calcutta.

'No one showed the slightest interest in a scruffy lieutenant clad in jungle green battle dress carrying what looked for all the world like a metal bedhead, and with some unlikely story that it was vital for the success of the Irrawaddy crossing'. Henslow was about to be hit hard in the face by the bureaucratic base-wallah's world. 'Where was my authority? That was what mattered in their world. Without written authority you could get nowhere.'[3] He made his way, engine frame in hand, to the Grand Hotel in Calcutta, now used as a billet. The Indian Army would be 2.5 million men strong by August 1945. So, with no paperwork and a sketchy story about a job of vital importance that had been entrusted to a lowly lieutenant, Henslow probably did sound implausible. At worst it sounded suspicious.

Henslow did manage to get some sense out of the officer running the Grand Hotel, who directed him to the Army Group HQ at Barrackpore. He made his way there, and followed signs to the Royal Engineers HQ, along another road. After more directions, he passed the Chief Engineer's office, before he made it to a man driving a desk. On the wall was a map that took Henslow by surprise. Despite all of the secrecy of the latest movements in Burma, this map appeared to show, in great detail, the locations of engineer stores and bridging units for the secret southern Irrawaddy crossing. At no point that morning had he been asked for his identification. The map did at least suggest to Henslow this was the right place to be.

"Please be brief as I am very busy," said the man.[4] Henslow explained his task and the importance of getting tanks across the Irrawaddy for the whole plan to work. There was a long pause.

"Look old boy, you may not realise it but, I have got to find 50 thousand bricks for a Brigadier's mess by Thursday and you come in here expecting me to get you sixteen pontoon propulsion unit frames made up without any authority whatsoever."[5] Henslow was directed to another office, and retreated seething.

The next office had a sergeant in it, who explained the man Henslow needed was sick. Could Henslow come back on Thursday? Feeling desperate, Henslow went back to where he had seen the Chief Engineer's office. 'My only hope was to burst in on him before anyone could intervene to stop me … I took my chance and strode past him [the officer on duty] to the obvious door to the inner sanctum, gave a quick rap and without waiting for a reply entered and closed it behind me'.[6] Henslow found himself face to face with a general. He explained his situation, and the perplexed, but understanding general finally wrote a note that gave him the authority he needed. He was to go to Lieutenant-Colonel White at the army base workshops to get the engine frames made.

Henslow arrived at the base workshops and met Lieutenant-Colonel White as he was leaving his office to go home for the day. He passed the note from the Chief Engineer.

"Who does he think he is? Everyone thinks that their requirement is priority … who is your CRE?"

"Colonel Wright." Henslow replied.

"Not old Tom Wright?"

"Yes." Henslow had no idea if it was *his* Tom Wright, but it seemed like the right answer.

"Oh, that's different. I was at the shop with Tom. OK, I'll do it, but you tell old Tom that Colonel White did it as a favour to him."[7] He shouted something, and a Chinese technician appeared. After a brief conversation, Henslow was told the sixteen engine frames would be ready by 3pm tomorrow. He could stay at their mess, and White said he would arrange transport back to Dum Dum Airport once they were ready.

The sixteen engine frames were made, and whilst the paint was still tacky, they were loaded onto a 15cwt lorry, and taken to Dum Dum Airport. Henslow had more problems. It was now Saturday 10th February – four days to D-Day on the Irrawaddy. Many of the Royal Air Force (RAF) personnel were concerned about their evening plans in Calcutta. Without written authority he was in trouble again. After some hopeless wandering around the rapidly emptying airport, he found an American pilot on leave, who normally flew supplies to China. His date for the night had cancelled, with nothing to do, he agreed to help Henslow.

The next morning the pilot, and his more reluctant navigator, were waiting for him at their Dakota. They flew directly to 7th Indian Division's airstrip, using the Irrawaddy for navigation from the coast over enemy territory. Luckily the Allies had total air supremacy over the entire country by 1945. After a slightly rough landing, and a quick thank you to his American pilot and navigator, Henslow reported to the CRE, Lieutenant-Colonel Tom Wright. The crucial engine frames had been delivered. It would now be possible to get the tanks across as soon as the 7th Indian Division had secured the beachhead on the east side of the Irrawaddy without them. The grand plan to use tanks to spearhead the charge to capture Meiktila and trap most of the

Japanese army in the north around Mandalay, was on. What Henslow had done was clearly important. 'I had expected some recognition of what I had been through, to be back with my mission completed, but that was not quite the reception I got.'[8]

"Good show, what kept you so long?" Came the gruff reply. "Get them offloaded onto that 15cwt truck and sent off to the Field Park Company, who have been waiting for them for the last 24 hours."[9]

On the 15th February, D+1, 7th Indian Division's commander Major-General Geoffrey Evans watched the reinforcements being sent into the beachhead. 'Streams of rafts were going backwards and forwards across the river. The Indian Engineers, sitting nonchalantly beside the outboard motors driving the rafts carrying the huge tanks, looked as though they had been doing this sort of job for years.'[10]

The role that tanks played in Burma had come a long way since the dark days of the 1942 retreat. The reconquest of Burma had now begun, and tanks would lie at the heart of Japanese defeat.

Introduction

The excellent National Army Museum, in Chelsea, London, has a webpage titled *The Far East Campaign*. The first paragraph describes the British-Indian war against the Japanese as one in which 'fighting took place in malaria ridden jungles during drenching monsoon rains'.[1] This illustrates the stereotype, that of a soldier creeping through thick dripping jungle, barely able to see more than a few metres, fighting an enemy charging at them with bayonet or samurai sword. Elements of this are not wrong. Much of the fighting did take place in thick dripping jungle where visibility was down to a few metres. This does not, however, tell the whole story. Nor does it even reflect a true understanding of the reality of the war in India and Burma between 1942 and 1945.

The terrain in Burma and north-eastern India is much more varied than the NAM's website suggests. There *are* hilly or mountainous tropical and sub-tropical jungles. Although there are also large plains, open areas of cultivation, and even desert-like stretches in the central dry plain. Slim was clear though: 'tanks can be used in almost any country except swamp'.[2]

Yet the role of infantry has dominated narratives of the war against the Japanese. Partly this is because infantry made up the majority of the fighting troops. Thirteen infantry divisions, Indian, British and West African, fought in Fourteenth Army from its creation in 1943*. There were eight more assorted infantry brigades – East African, parachute, airlanding, commando and so on. Only three tank brigades served in

---

* The army fighting the Japanese in 1942-43 was called Eastern Army and was redesignated Fourteenth Army. This was done, at least partly, to create a distinction between the army that had come off so badly against the Japanese, and the vast new army being built.

Fourteenth Army, plus one more that served in the 1942 retreat. The focus on the infantryman's war is therefore obvious; the men and their commanders, and consequently the memoirs and official histories to whom tank brigades were attached, were written by soldiers who fought primarily on foot. The most prominent memories would fairly understandably be those that took place in horrific conditions such as thick dripping jungle, in those driving rains, whilst climbing muddy hillsides. The sources available are therefore overwhelmingly focused on the infantryman's experience.

This means that certain fundamentals are missed from the story, and one of those is the role of armour in the war against Japan. 7th Armoured Brigade were at their most effective during the 1942 retreat when they were used as a striking force in the central plain of Burma. They countered Japanese advances, holding them up long enough for infantry units to retreat in relatively good order. During the 1944 Japanese invasion of India, Slim's plan was to retreat to the Imphal Plain and 'fight the decisive battle there on ground of our own choosing' where Japanese logistics, such as they were, were overstretched across mountainous jungle tracks.[3] Once the Japanese troops were 'committed in assaults on our prepared positions, [they] would be counter-attacked and destroyed by our mobile striking forces, strong in artillery, armour, and aircraft'.[4] For the 1945 reconquest of Burma, Slim wanted to 'get as many divisions and as much armour as possible, and as quickly as possible, into the Shwebo Plain, and there fight an army battle'.[5] When the Japanese retreated beyond the Irrawaddy, the same idea was simply transplanted to the eastern side of the river around Meiktila and Mandalay instead of Shwebo. What has so often been forgotten then, is that the infantry slogging through jungle was just one part of a bigger war and was essentially a means to an end; get the army onto the plains and use Allied strengths in firepower and logistics to fight the Japanese there and destroy them in large scale decisive battles.

For the British-commanded Indian Army, the principle Allied force that fought the Japanese in this theatre, the war against the Japanese was fundamentally about the superior application of firepower against an enemy. The industrial base of the Western Allies, and their way of war, were led by technology in the name of saving Allied lives where possible. This can be seen across every theatre, where settlements from hamlets to cities could be flattened by artillery and air power, not always wisely, in the name of reducing friendly casualties amongst the infantry.

From 1943 the Allies were advancing most of the time in every theatre. A typical action involved troops moving forward until they came under fire from known or unknown positions. If possible, the troops would try to manoeuvre to a flank and use their unit's supporting weapons to neutralise the enemy to keep up the momentum of the advance. If this failed, they would call in heavier fire support of some kind to suppress or destroy the position, before making a new assault. This could happen at a platoon level on patrol, or at the army level in vast set piece battles. This was obviously very destructive, but the Allied aim was first and foremost to keep their own casualties to a minimum.

The tank was born out of the same desire; to use technology to provide protection and firepower to advancing infantry in the First World War. The technology was adequate, although not quite the revolution in its 1917/18 form that is sometimes supposed. The potential, however, was obvious. In Burma and India, tanks were mostly used roughly in the manner intended in 1917/18; methodically destroying enemy strongpoints as they broke through bunker complexes, rather than manoeuvre warfare popularly known as *blitzkrieg*. The final battles in the reconquest of Burma in 1945 saw the birth of a modern way of war, using all of the technological and logistical might of the Allies to deliver firepower into the heart and stomach of an enemy's army at speed.

There were three main tanks used by the British and Indian Army units in India and Burma. All were designed and built in the USA. The M3 Stuart was known by British troops in particular as the 'Honey'. There was the M3 Lee/Grant. The difference between the two was the turret: the Lee had the straight-sided US-designed turret, the Grant had one that curved inwards at the base. This was designed by the British for their radio equipment, and to reduce the crew from seven to six, sacrificing the radio operator. Finally, there was the M4 Sherman. Other tanks were used in small numbers, such as the British made Valentine in 1943. A bridge laying version of the Valentine was also used.

The Stuart was the main tank used by 7th Armoured Brigade during the retreat in 1942. Thereafter, it was used as armoured reconnaissance, for example with the 7th Light Cavalry. The Stuart was a small, slightly boxy, light tank, with a crew of four. Armed with a 37mm main gun in the turret, and two Browning machine guns. The armour was relatively thin, but it was fast at 36mph, and mechanically reliable.

The bulk of the tanks that fought the Japanese though, were the Lee/Grants. These tanks were sent to DUKE* forces in large numbers by Lend-Lease partly because the Sherman was scheduled for production, leaving the Lee/Grant obsolete. The US would mostly equip itself with the newer tanks and send the Lee/Grants to Britain whose immediate needs were greater. The Combined Chiefs of Staff considered the war in Burma to be 'a supporting operation, on a subsidiary front in the second priority war'.[6] When Britain started to receive Shermans, the Lee/Grants were sent to the Far East instead. Obsolescence is relative†, however; the Lee/Grant may have been outclassed by German armour and AT guns by 1943, it was more than a match for anything the Japanese had available.

---
*DUKE – Dominion, United Kingdom, and Empire
†Credit to the historian and comedian Al Murray who introduced me to this phrase.

The Lee/Grant is a strange looking design. Most tanks in the Second World War were built in the format recognisable today with the main gun in the turret. It had a crew of six or seven, decent armour, was relatively fast for its mid-war medium-tank designation at 26mph, mechanical reliable, and found to have surprisingly good hill-climbing ability. There were two Browning machine guns, a 37mm gun in the turret, and a 75mm gun in a sponson on the top-right hand side of the hull. This was a disadvantage in the desert when it first arrived in British hands, where its size and high silhouette made it an easier target. This was especially so if it adopted a hull-down position where the tank hid behind a hill or other feature with as little of the tank showing whilst allowing the main gun to be used. With the Lee/Grant this meant there was a lot more tank showing, and therefore a bigger target than a Stuart or Sherman. In Burma and India, however, this design gave a great deal of flexibility to the crew. Multiple targets could be engaged at once, in different directions. The 75mm could be used to destroy bunkers whilst the machine guns and 37mm kept enemy tank hunters at bay. The machine guns and 37mm firing canister shot[*] would not penetrate friendly armour, so they were used to shoot enemy soldiers approaching and even climbing onto friendly tanks. This was especially useful when tanks were used in small numbers or on narrow frontages.

The Sherman tank was more orthodox in design, with two Browning machine guns and a 75mm gun in the turret. The Lee/Grant and Sherman shared numerous design features, especially under the main hull. They had similar armour, top speed, and were both reliable, although the Sherman had a smaller five-man crew. These similarities helped; many spares for the Lee/Grants could be used on Shermans, and crews and mechanics needed less time to become accustomed to the newer tank.

---

[*] Similar principle to a shotgun round.

The Lee/Grant and the Sherman had one more very important similarity: their very accurate 75mm gun. This would prove to be one of the most important weapons in the war against the Japanese. The 75mm was a dual-purpose weapon, capable of using both high-explosive shells, and armour-piercing (HE and AP respectively). This gun was outclassed by many German tank guns, especially when more and more high velocity AT guns were put into their tanks. Early war experience had shown, however, that tanks did not usually destroy other tanks. That was done mostly by stationary AT guns. The 75mm was adequate against most tanks in the war if well-handled but was also very effective against soft targets like lorries, artillery, and infantry. An AT gun would send an AP shell through one side of a truck and out the other. If it didn't hit anything vital, the vehicle could keep going or be easily repaired. A 75mm firing HE would destroy it.

The 75mm gun in a tank in Burma was crucial because it provided the most effective way to destroy Japanese bunkers. Alan Jeffrey described the Japanese bunker as 'the single greatest tactical problem facing British Commonwealth units in Burma'.[7] A method of using tanks with their highly accurate 75mm guns to destroy bunkers was devised in the Arakan in January 1944. This solved the tactical problem, so long as you could get a tank in the right place. The after-action report from the Arakan in late January 1944 described how 'there is, indeed, no other weapon whose successful development is likely to have such a decisive impact on the whole course of the war against JAPAN as a medium tank armed with a 75mm gun'.[8]

This book begins with the interwar period. The armoured mechanisation of the Indian Army is not a straightforward issue. In essence, the attempts to mechanise the Indian Army's armoured forces failed. The role of the Indian and British armies meant they had different needs because they perceived different threats that required different solutions. This was exacerbated by the economic situation in the 1930s, which played an outsized role in decision making for both the British Army and the Indian Army. The fact that tank technology was subsequently underdeveloped created inertia. Expensive investments in new technologies that may not be needed before they become obsolete is a difficult sell to a government's exchequer.

The way that armoured units trained, and how they trained for cooperation with other arms is also important. The Indian Army was excellent at taking on board lessons and working out solutions, a key part of its culture. A culture of adaptability inspired by the nature of its varied roles. The Indian Army expanded hugely in the war; in 1939 it was just under 200,000 men, by the end of the war it was 2.5 million. Over the course of the war the Indian Army had to prepare its men for multiple roles, from desert warfare, jungle warfare, and modern manoeuvre warfare, not to mention its pre-war roles that had to continue.

There were huge logistical headaches to contend with too. The geographical features of the theatre have already been mentioned, but it should be emphasised how difficult they were to overcome. So much of this story is misunderstood though. This is best reflected by the emphasis on dropping supplies by air. This was no doubt dramatic, impressive, and significant to the success of Fourteenth Army. This also reflects the nature of the literature's focus on the infantry battle, whose equipment tended to be easy to drop as it had to be man portable. What is often forgotten is that every airfield was served by road-borne logistics; every item that was dropped or landed by plane in the forward areas, travelled hundreds of miles by rail and road to get to an airfield. Subsequently, the heavier logistics of armour is frequently taken for granted. There were immense engineering feats to build the roads for the logistical system, on which every tank had to travel to get to the front. Furthermore, the tanks had to be kept at the front, where new methods of forward maintenance were devised to ensure firepower was always available to the infantry.

Operationally, tanks fought from the 1942 retreat, through a poorly planned and disastrous first Arakan campaign, against the Japanese diversionary attack at Sinzweya and the Japanese invasion of India. They took part in combined operations in the third Arakan, and finally the epitome of modern warfare during the reconquest of Burma itself in 1945. *Forgotten Armour*, therefore, does not tell a comprehensive story of the war against Japan, or even of the entire Burma Campaign. This book is about the Burma Campaign from the cramped interior of a tank. From the Royal Engineers who built the roads that got tanks and other supplies to the front, how the tankies learned to fight, and how their tanks were maintained, and the infantry who fought beside them. From senior officers to crewmen and humble lorry drivers. Primarily though, this book is about the way that armour made a decisive impact on victory over Japan in Burma, and the brave men who fought inside them. The majority of the campaign is covered, almost all of the major battles, and many of the smaller ones, involved tanks in some way. Everywhere tanks were used, they provided the key direct firepower onto their targets. This is a history of the Burma Campaign, but through a tank-man's periscope.

Part I

"The 17th/21st Lancers soon showed that they could master the tank as well as they had mastered their horses: the pity was that they had not been set to the task ten years earlier."

Val ffrench Blake

1
The Failure to Mechanise

In November 1919, Major-General Sir Louis Jackson gave a lecture to the Royal United Services Institute, explaining "the tank proper was a freak … the circumstances which called it into existence were exceptional and are not likely to occur again. If they do, they can be dealt with by other means".[1] Just a few years later much had changed. In 1921, the Army Council agreed to disband four regiments of cavalry because of approaching mechanisation and did not want to disband from the other arms – artillery or infantry for example. On 15th March 1921 the Secretary for War Sir Laming Worthington-Evans told the House of Commons that these four regiments were chosen because they were the most junior on the Army List. The apparent ruthlessness of this was not helped when, rather tactlessly, he explained that he could use the savings to buy more tanks. Until recently, whether rightly or wrongly, tanks have been inextricably linked with the perception that mechanisation was a threat to the cavalry, and the existence of their regiments.

Val ffrench Blake arrived in Bombay as a fresh-faced 21-year-old lieutenant in 1934. He had spent most of the trip seasick: "I'm a very bad sailor, and I am always the first person on the ship to be seasick, and this was no exception to the rule".[2] An Old Etonian, keen horseman, and later in life an expert on dressage. He was posted to the 17th/21st Lancers.

The 17th/21st Lancers was an amalgamated* cavalry regiment, necessitated after the size of the army was reduced in the wake of the First World War in 1922. To help preserve the historical and corporate identities of two amalgamated regiments, the 17th and 21st Lancers, both numbers were carried over. The regimental system, with a focus on tradition, identity, and history, has always been important to the British and Indian armies. The idea was to give a sense of identity to the individual soldier and provide a history that had to be upheld. This fostered healthy competition, to make sure *your* regiment was the *best* regiment. To give examples of heroism that would inspire, or at worst, shame, the contemporary soldier into action to create their own chapter in their regiment's history.

ffrench Blake expected to be mechanised when he arrived in India. Horsed cavalry 'was extremely dull" he explained, "very, very boring … the training was stifling, we weren't really allowed to test our horses in any way, and they were not in any way capable of great endurance. The main object was to keep them fat, fit and shiny'.[3] His love of polo was the only thing that kept him in the army beyond his initial three years. When mechanisation finally began in 1938, he felt a release of tension.

Mechanisation did not match the hype. The 17th/21st Lancers were in Meerut, near Delhi, in 1938. The horses were gone by the 14th January, and the first vehicle, an open Ford touring car, arrived on the 6th February. On paper they were not yet mechanised, so had not been issued any petrol. The car arrived empty, so had to be pushed from the railway station to the nearest petrol station. When the first tank arrived, of late 1920s vintage, 'the commanding officer and adjutant led from the front and drove the first Mk II Tank that arrived the same month.

---

*Amalgamated units retain the suffixes in both numbers. In the large Indian Army, Indian and Gurkha units were written in a similar shorthand, as they will be in this book. It is important to understand the difference: for example, 1/10th Gurkhas (no suffix following the first number) would be the 1st Battalion, 10th Princess Mary's Own Gurkha Rifles, not two amalgamated units.

They had to walk four miles back to the barracks after the tank had shed its tracks. The turret fell of the second Mk II Tank'.[4] Confidence in the vehicles soon plummeted.

Along with the tanks arriving in early 1938 were members of the Royal Tank Corps (RTC) to help mechanise the cavalry units. They had to train 200 men across the various vehicles who would then be able to disseminate what they had learned to the rest of their unit. Training started with a six-week driver and maintenance course, which ran concurrently with gunnery training, meaning there were plenty of instructors for the regiment in the two fundamentals of tank warfare.

Not everything had gone well though. The lack of tanks and other vehicles meant what they were overworked, with little time for dedicated maintenance. There was also a lack of instructional equipment, like special teaching turrets, which would have allowed more people to be trained at once. There was a desire to become a driver or signaller because it came with extra pay, however, gunnery did not. This inevitably led to either the best rising into those roles, or for COs to play favourites. ffrench Blake led the gunnery training, and was starved of equipment, including ammunition. 'The only gun we had was a two pounder without any mountings, so it just lay on the bench, and we could open the breech, and that was about it. All that could be done to train the gunners was to take the gun apart and put it back together again'.[5]

The central question here is why did the Indian Army fail to effectively mechanise? For many years, this failure in both the British and Indian Armies was blamed on intransigent, traditionalist, cavalry officers, desperate to keep hold of their horses and regimental identities. The truth is far more complex, as ffrench Blake's experience suggests. The differing roles of the British and Indian Armies meant there was still a place for cavalry, especially for the Indian Army. Without armour that could outperform horses, and crucially the money to develop that armour, mechanisation would be a challenge to achieve.

Separating the British Army and Indian Army over mechanisation is sometimes difficult. Many of the problems that beset the former, affected the latter. The difference in roles exacerbated this problem too. The doctrine of the British Army at the time was for a small professional force that used technology as a way to preserve manpower. This was a reaction to the casualties of the First World War, so staff college taught its students to wear away their enemy. Subsequently, the emphasis of doctrine was around consolidating ground captured, much like the famous bite-and-hold tactics developed through 1916, rather than exploiting success, similar to the Hundred Days Offensive in 1918. The second of these was something that armour was more suited to carry out.

The British Army was also intended to police the empire, leaving strategic assets like the Royal Navy and Royal Air Force to deal with peer enemies through control of the oceans and trade routes, and the deterrent or real effect of aerial bombing. The Indian Army for most of the interwar period was for internal policing and defending the North-West Frontier from Afghan raiders. There was little interest in modernising the Indian Army because countries like Afghanistan were not considered to be a strategic threat; certainly, they were not considered peers to British and Indian units. The Garran Tribunal in 1933 added the imperial reserve role, where Indian units could serve overseas in a more conventional role if needed, supporting limited spending on the British Army.

The late 1930s saw a change in the role of the Indian Army. Between 1935 and 1936, operations in Waziristan and during the Mohmand Uprising saw some tanks deployed and used reasonably successfully. The now motorised logistical tail, however, was found to be problematic. Furthermore, the Indian Army was finding more modern weapons were beginning to appear in the hands of Afghan tribesmen, like machine guns. This led to the 1938 Auchinleck Committee, chaired by then Major-General Claude Auchinleck, which considered the modernisation, composition, and re-equipment of the Indian Army. Their recommendations became the basis of the Chatfield Committee in 1939. These redefined the roles of the Indian Army as frontier, coastal and external defence, internal security, and a reserve force for service overseas. The committee also accepted the possibility of a Japanese war, but effectively saw it as a concern for the Royal Navy based in Singapore – and therefore not the Indian government's responsibility. This explains the inertia behind modernisation and mechanisation. The enemies that the Indian Army was likely to face were rarely considered so-called 'first class' opposition, despite some minor scares in the mid-30s, and so there appeared to be a less pressing need for armour. Other British funded assets would take care of 'first class' enemies.

This created a problem when British units had to operate alongside Indian ones, an arrangement going back to the Indian Mutiny/Rebellion of 1857. British units were trained to fight using their greater number of vehicles and tanks in a different way to Indian units. For example, the splitting of tank roles in the 1920s – slower heavily armed infantry tanks for cooperation with foot soldiers, and fast, less armoured light tanks for reconnaissance and causing havoc in the enemy's rear. The light tanks made up the majority of cavalry units in India because the heavy infantry type was not considered necessary there. The two armies were only able to work alongside each other because they were flexible and fighting less well armed enemies when they fought together. There was significant doctrinal confusion that was survivable in the imperial policeman role because of classic British-led muddling-through. Muddling-through was simply not good enough, though, if the Indian Army were to face an enemy of similar technological abilities. The 1938-39 modernisation recommendations desperately needed to be enacted and done so quickly with the full economic and industrial backing of Britain and India. Time was running out in South-East Asia.

Attitudes to mechanisation, as suggested by ffrench Blake's experience, were more positive than was often supposed in the decades following the Second World War. Ralph Younger was a Captain in the British Army's 7th (Queen's Own) Hussars when mechanisation began. Younger was born in 1904, of Scottish descent. His father was the chairman of McEwan's Brewery in Newcastle. He went to Charterhouse School, and Trinity College, Cambridge, with the idea of following his father into brewing when he left. He failed an exam at the end of his first year at university, and this made him reconsider his options. He had always liked history, especially military history, so he switched courses, and joined the university's cadet corps.

Younger always liked horses and riding and knew some members of the 7th Hussars because they used to hunt near the family home. He liked the idea of joining the cavalry because he would get to ride most days, if he had a normal job, it might only be once or twice a week. After university he spent the summer of 1926 in Edinburgh on a six-week attachment with the 7th Hussars so they could "have a good look at me".[6] A week later he joined them.

He had no immediate concerns about the future of cavalry. Allenby's great Palestine Campaign that concluded with the capture of Jerusalem towards the end of the First World War, was still fresh in mind: it had been a big cavalry success. Younger's training at Tidworth was mostly grooming and riding the horses over autumn and winter. Each year there was churn amongst the other ranks to supply drafts to regiments in Egypt or India. Only in the spring did training pick up, with exercises at troop and squadron level. The training was mostly around reconnaissance, screening advances, and covering withdrawals.

Sometimes there was a regimental exercise in August, but not always because it was expensive to run. The annual routine reset with the latest drafts to Egypt or India in the Autumn.

Younger and his comrades did have a feeling of competition with the RTC, but the thoughts of a coming war in the 1930s focused their professional minds. The 11th and 12th Hussars took mechanisation well; "good regiments always take those things in their stride, and must, otherwise they're not good regiments" Younger reflected.[7] Professionalism was key to mechanisation, and the 7th Hussars took to it well. "It was bound to come sooner or later … [opposition came from] the very horsey junior ones … whose life was hunting and polo".[8] There was some bellyaching: a few threatened to leave if it happened, but they never did in the end. Most accepted it with slight regret, and when they were mechanised in Egypt in 1936-37 they had been away from hunting for a long time. A poll was taken at the time and under 10% of other ranks and non-commissioned officers were opposed. In the end the process was far less painful than they supposed, the fear of the unknown had probably played a big role in the initial reluctance. The fact was, the culture and a soldier's pride in their regiment meant that cavalry units undergoing mechanisation adapted easily to the change. Being the best on a horse or in a tank brought the same prestige. Whilst some regretted losing their horses, they soon just got on with their job.

Between the World Wars three issues converged to really stymie the armoured mechanisation of the Indian Army and slow the same process in the British Army. They were: the lack of a seriously considered threat to Britain and its empire, a poor economy, and underdeveloped technology. As mentioned earlier, the casualties of the First World War cast a shadow over the interwar period. There was a desire to limit casualties in a future war by substituting manpower with technology. The problem here was money. After the huge amounts spent winning the First World War, the Treasury wanted to regain control on military spending. In August 1919, the Cabinet instituted a policy that made two assumptions: that the world was now at peace for the medium to long-term future, and machines were cheaper than soldiers. Winston Churchill as Secretary of State for War agreed, despite the lack of forecasted costs to make a considered decision. The first assumption led to the Ten-Year Rule – essentially it was officially believed by the government that there would not be another European war for at least ten years. This was frequently rolled over and used to hold money back from defence spending. The 1925 Locarno Treaty promised to aid either France or Germany if either was attacked, thereby deterring aggression by either country. The Kellogg-Briand pact, where 65 countries agreed to guarantee international borders, increased the feeling that European wars were unlikely. Therefore, the General Staff had to contemplate policing the empire with a small army whilst trying to mechanise, and cut costs, all at the same time.

The lack of funding for mechanisation put the cavalry at a technological crossroads. They lacked the protection and firepower that was afforded to tanks and other armoured vehicles to break-in or breakthrough enemy positions. But armoured technology generally lacked the range, mobility, and reliability to perform cavalry roles, especially in the imperial policing role and on the Northwest Frontier of India. The lack of funding meant there was not enough experimentation with new designs through the 1920s. This was exacerbated by the financial crises of the late 20s and early 30s, which halted development on newer designs.

This economic crises were the moment the British Army lost its lead in tank design. By 1931 the value of exports had declined by 30%, reducing business profits and tax income for the Treasury. At the same time, unemployment rose from one to three million people. The Treasury simply could not cope with mechanisation and the economic crisis. The General Staff, for example, wanted a technological bedding-in period for mechanisation, where new tank and armoured car designs would come on stream alongside horsed-cavalry. This would allow a transition period, where those designs were tested and developed to allow improved armoured vehicles down the line. It would also be expensive. This was just not possible if public spending was to remain under control through the interwar period. There was never more than £1m spent per annum between 1926 and 1934 on new weapons. A couple of cavalry regiments were mechanised suddenly, the rest were left as they were for now.

Admittedly, the financial cost of mechanising wholesale was daunting. Basil Liddel Hart, the influential former soldier, military theorist, and journalist, said in his diary in 1928 'the main trouble in the way of mechanisation is the capital cost … that had frightened 'His Worthiness' [referring to Sir Laming Worthington-Evans, Secretary of War at the time]'.[9] Simply to bring the *existing* tank battalions up to strength and completing mechanisation of the artillery would cost £5-6m, that is £250-300m today. They didn't quote for expansion of the RTC or mechanising the cavalry perhaps because they already knew they couldn't afford it. This is before even considering the cost of converting the Indian Army's cavalry.

The pressure to expand the RTC or mechanise the cavalry therefore decreased. Horses were still considered better than armoured vehicle technology for most of its roles, there was no official threat that created urgency, and the money was simply not available. The knock-on effect of this with companies like Vickers, the vast arms conglomerate, was significant. The 1928 Staff Conference on rearmament outlined the importance of medium tanks after a series of trials. Brigadier RJ Collins, commanding 7th Infantry Brigade explained their findings on the composition of tank battalions: "It was laid down that a medium tank battalion was to be the basic unit ... the light [tank] group was therefore never more than one-fifth of the establishment accepted."[10] The army was clear that medium tanks were their desired vehicle, over light tanks.

Vickers, however, were reluctant to over-invest in tanks and armoured vehicles. There was not much incentive to provide what the army wanted, or even to solve their lack of vehicles in general. The 1931 Geneva Conference had tried to cap tank tonnage at twenty tons, thereby limiting manufacturing to light tanks. The conference even discussed banning tanks altogether. In the end it was never ratified, but it created a hesitant atmosphere for those deciding where to prioritise investment in case their choice was banned in international law. The government was focusing its investment on the Royal Navy and Royal Air Force because they were strategic assets, whilst the War Office was pressurising Vickers to keep prices down. They subsequently focused manufacturing on light tanks which were attractive to the foreign market, despite the army wanting medium tanks. This was a difficult time to be an arms manufacturer. The very nature and expense of heavy engineering and the need for long-term decision-making regarding factories, machine-tools, and manpower planning, meant they craved certainty. Vickers simply did not see a viable commercial opportunity in armoured vehicles compared to aircraft and prioritised accordingly. Vickers did not get the right commitments in the 1930s, and so the vehicles produced were inadequate in quality and quantity for the British, and therefore Indian Army's needs. This meant that, once the war with Japan broke out, and India could not rely on deliveries from Britain due its own shortages, there were not enough of the right tanks where they were needed in the Far East, and too little experience in using them across the expanding Indian Army.

What was actually wrong with the technology that was developed in the interwar period then? Or what was so good about horses? Sergeant James Randall had been a veteran of the Palestine Mandate as a horsed cavalryman. As a tank commander in the Second World War he reflected: 'you could go anywhere on a horse… up into these little villages dotted about up in the hills, in fact in horse days we used to ride these patrols all over the country… Tanks wouldn't have been any good, getting up these tracks in the hills on the sort of patrols that we did'.[11] Tanks in the 1920s and 30s did struggle off-road in hills and mountains, and could be held up by rivers and ditches. The Army Council set up a committee in 1926 to decide the army's requirements for cavalry. Three of the six members of the committee were cavalrymen. The outcome was support for mechanisation, but there could be no further reductions of cavalry regiments themselves. Priority should be given to manufacturing an armoured car that had good cross-country performance to eventually replace horses. Tellingly, this meant there would be no need to establish new RTC units. The final report included a veiled threat to the cavalry.

"The inevitable trend of the developments in methods of warfare, will readily adapt themselves to any necessary changes in organisation and equipment; and they [the committee] feel strongly that it is in the interests not only of the cavalry but also of the Army as a whole to retain the existing cavalry regiments, whose traditions and *esprit de corps* are an invaluable asset."[12]

If cavalry did not get on board with mechanisation for the main wartime role that remained for cavalry, reconnaissance, then new armoured cars and other technologies would go directly to the RTC. What future then for the cavalry?

As we have seen, two years later, the army superseded this committee anyway and recommended medium tanks. Interestingly the Indian Army was keener on light tanks. Some Carden-Loyd tankettes had shown they could cope with Indian terrain the previous year. The technology they represented might eventually match the ability of horses in speed, radius of action and manoeuvrability. Even in the 1930s though, tanks had reliability problems. The Mk III and IV light tanks of 1st Royal Tank Regiment during the 1935 Abyssinian crisis could barely make ten miles per day due to poorly made rubber on the bogey wheels, and brittle track pins. "You had to have five or six 3-ton lorries backing them up with spare parts."[13] The need for these lorries to come forward tied the tanks to the roads, or they would be stranded somewhere offroad. If the tanks were well looked after though, these problems could be overcome. The Indian Army did have some success with light tanks and armoured cars on the Northwest Frontier in the mid-30s. The Mohmand Campaign in 1935 included the use of tanks in a reconnaissance role, but also in the mountains supporting infantry almost as mobile pillboxes. They could ride with impunity into tribal positions forcing them to retire. But cavalry had done similar for centuries, the only change was the armour.

The problem seemed to come from the increasingly large logistical tail. There was a need for a large flat area well connected by roads not only for supply and maintenance bases away from the front, but also to the front itself. Some of these roads had to be constructed on the Northwest Frontier by the Royal Engineers. Consequently, light tanks, armoured cars, infantry, and cavalry had to patrol these roads because supply lorries were vulnerable to tribal raiders on horseback, or to snipers. This then tied the tanks even more closely to the road, and some of them to the supply lines, limiting the number on the main operation. Horsed cavalry did not need anywhere near the same amount of logistical support, and so more of its fighting power could be concentrated on the main tasks they were there to complete, rather than patrolling the lines of communication. Tactical flexibility actually declined in the forces deployed to the Northwest Frontier as the Indian Army modernised.

Horses were still ideal in towns too, for the internal security role. Armoured cars and tanks were impervious to rioters' rocks or similar missiles, and they could ram or crush barricades, but they could not pursue people into narrow alleys or side streets. Horses could do most of these things with little difficulty. Machine gun-armed armoured cars or tanks could risk another Amritsar Massacre, where hundreds, if not over a thousand, were killed by troops firing into a crowd. Most urban crowds are unused to horses too, so are more wary around them, and so cavalry is good for diverting or dispersing crowds, hence the continued use of mounted police into the modern day.

Despite the army acknowledging in 1929 that it wanted medium tanks, they also accepted they were not yet mechanically capable. They were too wide, unwieldy, and unreliable. In their view, light tanks might be useful, and armoured cars were no better than horses anyway. Their preference was also to use as many of the same designs as possible to help with logistical issues. The tanks and other vehicles should be simple, have similar top speeds and fuel consumption so that units could move at the same speed on a similar radius before resupply. Brigadier John Blakiston-Houston, a cavalryman it should be noted, pointed out "the armoured force is more sensitive to ground, very difficult to handle, is blind and is so noisy that it is very difficult to achieve tactical surprise. I lay the blame for this primarily on its basis – the medium tank ... I feel that the armoured force based on the light tank ... would produce very good results."[14] As the light tank was the closest available for their needs, and without the investment available for medium tank development or procurement, the British and Indian Armies continued to use them, despite their flaws. This is not to say there were no medium tanks, but the best designs were not being produced in the numbers required, and certainly not for the Indian Army.

Immediately before the Second World War began in Europe, the Indian Army was only just mechanising, and hardly with equipment it could rely on. When the Chatfield Committee in 1939 was redefining the roles of the Indian Army, they also acknowledged how it survived on British Army cast-offs. The modernisation programme led by Auchinleck had the added bonus of setting up the mechanisms for the rapid expansion of the Indian Army when the war began. The required speed of expansion from 1939, especially after early war setbacks, outpaced the ability to train, equip and even accommodate new recruits.

For eighteen months from May 1940, the 195,000-strong Indian Army exploded to 900,000 by the end of 1941. 300,000 were in the Middle East. There was a process of 'milking' existing Indian units of experienced non-commissioned officers, Viceroy Commissioned Officers*, and other officers, and assigning them to the new units. This was supposed to spread the well trained, professional, and in most cases, veteran soldiers to help raise and run the new units. The rush to train them, however, undermined the value of the recruits, and broke up high quality units at the same time.

The Indian Army, like the British Army, was seriously affected by the Dunkirk evacuation in May-June 1940. Until 1942, the British Army understandably took priority for production because of the threat of invasion. The decision was made in August 1940 to mechanise all Indian cavalry and set up a new training centre at Muttra. This was easier said than done in the circumstances, however. On paper there was the newly created 31st Armoured Division, but it would need British cavalry and new Indian cavalry units to actually man it. There would be a number of paper armoured divisions over this period, many of the units raised ended up being converted to other corps due to the lack of equipment. In October 1940, Major-General

---

*VCOs – authority was only over Indian soldiers. They were senior in rank to Warrant Officers, the most senior NCO, and subordinate to all commissioned officers – including Indian Commissioned Officers.

Thomas Hutton, the Deputy Chief of Staff of the Indian Army, went to the UK to get more men and supplies for the expansion. He got 10% of all production, but no anti-tank guns. The fear of *blitzkrieg* was clearly fresh in the minds of those in London. This was only a guide, though. Deliveries actually varied from month to month, and depended on shipping getting through unmolested, diversions to the Middle East, and damage to UK factories from aerial bombing. In the early days of lend-lease, supplies from the USA were often held up due to a lack of shipping to India. The main problem thereafter was the continued search for suitable instructors to continue expansion, and many of these would have to come from the British Army. The British Army was concentrating on its own expansion, and so instructors came only in small numbers.

The main Indian Army deployments in December 1941 were roughly this: two infantry divisions and one motor brigade[*] in North Africa. In Malaya and Singapore there were two Indian infantry divisions, and the 3rd Cavalry that had recently been equipped with armoured cars, alongside an Australian division. Reinforcements in January 1942 included the 100th Indian Independent Light Tank Squadron with twenty-three obsolete Carden Loyd Tankettes – similar in size to a Universal Carrier – armed with machine guns. In Hong Kong there were also two infantry battalions, with two infantry brigades, one British and one Canadian. Burma itself had two weak infantry divisions, the 17th Indian Division, and 1st Burma Division[†].

Indian Army expansion, and the mechanisation process continued. The rush between 1938 and 1942 was an attempt to make amends for the failure to mechanise sooner. Before the war in Europe, there had been a lack of funding for mechanisation. For much of the interwar period there was no clear threat to create impetus for increased funding, and relatively poor

---
[*] Infantry in lorries
[†] Approximate size of British and Indian Army formations in the Second World War: a battalion is 1,000 men, brigade 3,000 men, division 16,000 men.

technology for the roles required. This meant the Indian Army's failure to effectively mechanise immediately undermined its efforts when the war against Japan began. The failure to effectively mechanise does not explain the early defeats on its own. Earlier effective mechanisation may have made a difference, however, as the experience of the 7th Armoured Brigade suggests during the retreat of 1942.

Val ffrench Blake reflected: 'The 17th/21st Lancers soon showed that they could master the tank as well as they had mastered their horses: the pity was that they had not been set to the task ten years earlier'.[15]

2
The War against Japan

'When I first joined my infantry regiment from Sandhurst, full of young ideals, I thought forty years to be sufficient time to live ... I would be killed in action before I was as doddering and decrepit as I thought some of our majors were then'.[1] Miles Smeeton had just joined the Green Howards in 1925. He transferred to the Indian Army in 1936 and joined Hodson's Horse, a cavalry regiment. Hodson's Horse would eventually be mechanised in November 1942 when it was in the Middle East. An adventurous and restless soul, Smeeton threw himself into all-sorts whilst in India, where he met his wife, Beryl Boxer. Beryl and Miles were made for each other: shortly after marrying in 1939, they shared their first of many adventures mountaineering in the Himalayas.

Smeeton attended the Staff College at Quetta, near the border with Afghanistan*. The city is five thousand feet above sea level, and the air cold and clear. Snow capped the mountains and occasionally sunrise and sunset shone rose-red on the blue sky. Smeeton and Beryl kept fit riding, and with more climbing in the mountains around Quetta. Climbing was a new sport in the area, so many of the routes had never been completed before. They had a bull-terrier that loved every moment climbing and would leap into their arms when they called her for the next stage of an ascent. They went skiing, and even learned to fly in a month spare after Staff College. His callous attitude to death clearly concerned him after his marriage to Beryl. Shortly after the war against Germany started, he discussed pensions and wills with his new brigadier, who noticed his anxieties.

---

* Quetta is now in Pakistan, the Staff College is still in use for the Pakistani Army.

"You know, Miles, you're not bloody well going to get killed in this war. Only the best people get killed in war." Smeeton reflected on this, and it gave him confidence; perhaps the reason the brigadier said it. 'I never thought of being killed again, although I was often frightened and could jump for cover as quickly, if not quicker, than most people'.[2]

The six-month course at Quetta focused on operational exercises. The enemy was clearly the German Army in a repeat of the First World War. 'We fought an imaginary enemy across the plain … we fought on paper across the fields of France and moved rapidly into Belgium, but we never fought on the paper desert nor in the jungle'.[3] An oversight that would prove to be quite costly.

To understand how the Japanese ended up in Burma, a brief exploration of the context and series of events leading up to the invasion in December 1941 is required.

Japan missed out on the empire building and scrambles of the previous few centuries. To preserve Japanese culture, they had in fact kept themselves isolated under the *Sakoku* policy since the first Europeans arrived in the seventeenth century. Apart from China and, to a lesser extent Korea, trade with other countries was tightly controlled. Ordinary Japanese people were unable to leave the home islands, and access to foreigners was restricted. Just as European nations began to explore and colonise, Japan closed up. Japan was later coerced into trade relationships by gunboat diplomacy in the shape of US Navy warships in 1854. Over the following years Japan signed multiple trade and diplomatic treaties with various imperial powers. When Japan opened up, it mostly found itself surrounded by other large powers, or imperial possessions. Their immediate neighbours were China and Korea to the west, to the north Imperial Russia (Soviet Union from 1917), to the south the Spanish Philippines (surrendered to the USA in 1898) and the Dutch East Indies*. After the Russo-Japanese War, where Japan first showcased their growing naval power, Korea became a Japanese colony, in effect to prevent it falling under European control.

The issue for Japan, however, was a lack of resources. Japan's isolationism under *Sakoku* had impeded industrialisation. European influence on trade, industry, and the military, followed by the Sino-Japanese and Russo-Japanese wars helped kickstart and then accelerate industrialisation. The government and its armed forces were at the heart of this process. In the early 1880s government shipyards employed 10,000 workers compared to 3,000 workers for shipyards in private hands. The latter were still building wooden ships, whilst the government shipyards were building relatively technologically advanced vessels. By comparison, the textile industry that was of lesser importance to the military, had barely got started. The goal of industrialisation was 'weapon independence', and by the 1890s the Japanese were producing steel and military technologies on par with the Western powers.

This made Japan thirsty for raw materials, but it was not resource rich. Their reliance on imports of heavy machinery and raw materials like iron ore, meant the government helped subsidise industries, like steel, so they could expand their mills and increase output. These subsidies did not solve the problem though – they had no problem turning iron ore into steel in large quantities, but they still relied on imports of the raw material all the same.

Japan had received German colonial possessions in the 1919 Treaty of Versailles which illustrated the potential for war to grant territory. Japan's increased global power in the interwar period came from increasingly aggressive nationalism in the form of wars of expansion to get access to the raw materials it craved. Japan was soon on a collision course with China, the

---

*Mostly modern Indonesia

USA, and the European colonial powers. Naturally these countries were not keen on another rival power in Asia. For much of this period of growth, Britain was an ally of Japan as a counterweight to the USA's growing influence in the Pacific. When push came to shove in the 1930s, however, Britain sided with the Anglophone nation.

Just as the age of imperialism was about to come to an end, Japan acted more and more aggressively in its efforts to forge an empire of its own. This was initially done at the expense of China. Manchuria, in north-east China, is a resource rich region long disputed by Japan, China, and Imperial Russia/Soviet Union. Japan occupied the territory in 1931, specifically to gain access to coal, iron ore and timber. The entire local economy was eventually geared towards Japan's war economy, closing the market to everyone else. This signalled the beginning of a militarising economy, and by the end of the 1930s the free market had been replaced by government controls and central planning. Japan's economy modernised even further: industry grew rapidly, including for motor vehicles, shipbuilding, and aircraft. This was sustained by the army and navy's expansion, with their expenditure taking up an eyewatering 75% of the national budget by 1938.

This increased Japan's thirst for raw materials that Manchuria, or Manchukuo as Japan called it, could never provide. Two thirds of Japan's oil was bought from the USA. Rubber and tin from European colonies in Asia, such as Burma, was imported too. Japan expanded its Empire in China in July 1937, starting a full-scale war that brought the Communist and Nationalist Chinese into a fragile alliance. This expansionism meant patience from the other powers in the region started to run out. The infamous Nanking Massacre, and the less famous Panay incident – the bombing of a US Navy river-gunboat and three oil tankers – brought condemnation from the USA. There were a number of border disputes with the USSR, culminating in the Battle of Kalkhin Gol in Soviet Mongolia in the summer of 1939. This was a sobering incident for the Imperial Japanese Army (IJA), with 18,000 dead, that persuaded the government that they and their army could not fight in China and against the Soviet Union at the same time.

The IJA, as a consequence of its defeat against the Soviet Union and stalemate in China, lost some of its influence with the government and agreed to a southern plan, as advocated by the Imperial Japanese Navy (IJN). A first step, to help free Japanese soldiers for a wider conflict, was to avoid extending their own supply lines in northern and central China. Then they would cut the supply lines from European colonial powers and the USA to the Chinese Nationalist military. To do this, Japan advanced into southern China and northern French Indochina* in the summer of 1940. France was in no practical position to resist after its own defeat at the hands of Nazi Germany. This cut the supply routes running through the region from the European colonial powers. The following year they took southern Indochina as well. Crucially, this supply route would be replaced by the Burma Road, running from Rangoon†, southern Burma, through to Kunming, south-western China, after the invasion of northern Indochina. The southern plan, and the IJN, had their sights further afield.

The IJN had developed along British lines and had a strong reputation since the Russo-Japanese War in 1905, and the First World War. As Europe descended into war, and as diplomatic efforts with Nazi Germany and Italy produced the Tripartite Pact, Japan saw a developing opportunity to get its resources elsewhere. As early as 1935, the Dutch East Indies had been identified as a potential future source of oil and other materials. Malaya and the Philippines were highlighted as important targets as well. Borneo, Hong Kong, Guam, and others were also considered, either for their resources, or for strategic purposes.

*Indochina comprised of modern-day Cambodia, Loas and Vietnam.
†Now Yangon

Taking possession of these territories whilst the European powers appeared neutralised by the war with Nazi Germany was seen as a potential way to get everything the Japanese economy needed to finish the job in China. The biggest gamble was the USA, who controlled the Philippines and Guam. The USA was not yet distracted by Nazi Germany to the same extent as the European powers were at this time. In an attempt to challenge Japanese expansion in the region, the USA, Great Britain, and the Netherlands had cut off oil supplies to Japan after issuing an ultimatum demanding that Japan retreat from China and Indochina in the summer of 1941. This at least contributed to Japan's decision to initiate the wider southern plan, including the attack on Pearl Harbour, the Philippines and Guam, bringing Japan into the war rather than curbing its aggression.

The Japanese government felt that the pre-emptive strike on Pearl Harbour in December 1941 would cripple the USA's ability to retaliate or retake lost territory, at least in the short term. The USA would need to rebuild its Pacific Fleet, by which time Japan would have consolidated its gains, continued to build its own strength, and be too big a risk for the USA to take on, for territory that Japan perceived was of negligible value to the USA. The Japanese had failed to understand the mindset, and potential, of the USA, and the reaction of its people to what they saw as an unprovoked attack. The Japanese gamble failed to understand how such a fiercely democratic and anti-imperial country would consider the *principles* that Japan's attack represented, on top of its violence. To the Japanese, Guam, Wake Island, and others may have just been tiny islands with naval bases thousands of miles away from the USA, but many of them were formal US territory*. Hawaii was a US territory too and would become a state in 1959. It is an obvious point to make, but thousands of American lives were lost in these attacks;

---

*It should be noted that US ownership of these places, and the Philippines, essentially constituted an empire in and of themselves. American perception at the time is important in this instance.

as far as most Americans were concerned, their people, their homeland was attacked, regardless of the distance. Furthermore, Japan's actions were unacceptable, especially as they came without a formal declaration of war. Japan had made one of the greatest miscalculations in history.

To impose a similar shock to the British and Dutch, and seize access to resources, Burma, Malaya, Hong Kong, and the Dutch East Indies were to be attacked at the same time as the US possessions. The Burma Road, as mentioned, had replaced the Indochina route for supplies to China. Operations in Burma would therefore support the fighting there as well.

The sheer size of the theatre, and the overwhelming nature of the Japanese offensive in south-east Asia in early December 1941 meant the Allies in ABDA Command (American, British, Dutch, Australian) under General Wavell were spread thin. Hong Kong fell on Christmas Day 1941. The primary targets on Sumatra in the Dutch East Indies were captured by March 1942, although resistance on Borneo and Celebes continued on until October.

Malaya, with Singapore at its southern tip, was considered too thickly covered in jungle for a large-scale invasion. Many of the Indian troops garrisoned there were the newly raised units with NCOs 'milked' from more experienced units: they had received very rushed training and were poorly armed. The Australian, British, and Indian forces on Malaya were not well supplied with vehicles either, so they lacked manoeuvrability. The Japanese quickly took control of the sea sinking the battleships *HMS Prince of Wales* and *HMS Repulse*. The Japanese also took control of the air fighting against brave but outnumbered Allied pilots fighting in obsolete aircraft. Japanese units, veterans of the war in China, relied on outflanking tactics, either using the cover of the thick jungle or amphibious hooks to get behind Allied positions. The excellent roads also gave opportunities for Japanese tanks and even bicycle troops to move south at pace, exploiting the lack of mobility in Indian units. Singapore was not built to be defended from the landward side, although cost cutting meant many of the seaward defences were inadequate anyway. The surviving Allied units on Malaya retreated onto Singapore Island at the end of January 1942. The Japanese incursions onto the island signalled the beginning of the end, and after some brave counterattacks in places, the Allies retreated into Singapore city. On the 15th February, with the situation appearing hopeless on both military and humanitarian grounds, the garrison surrendered. The Japanese 18th Division took captured vehicles and began loading them onto transport ships. They then began their journey to Burma to help finish off the retreating British, Indian, and Burmese troops.

The invasion of Burma began on 14th December 1941 by the Japanese 15th Army* under Lieutenant-General Iida Shojiro. His opening move was to send 143rd Infantry Regiment†, of the 55th Division to capture the airfield at Victoria Point, just over the border from Thailand on the long strip of Burma that stretches down towards the Malayan peninsula. The main invasion followed on 19th January 1942, when the 55th and 33rd Divisions crossed the jungle covered mountains that mark the frontier between Thailand and Burma further to the north at Moulmein. The 17th Indian Division, after 1942 known as the Black Cats for their new shoulder patch, were responsible for defending the area.

The 17th Indian Division had been training in Dhond, India, in preparation for mobile desert warfare in the Middle East. They were not prepared for the jungles of southern Burma. They were not really a division anymore either, with only the 48th Brigade, and Divisional HQ. Two of its brigades, the 44th and 45th had been sent to reinforce Malaya at the end of December. They received the 16th Brigade when they reached Moulmein as a partial replacement. The division's original commander fell ill

---

* A Japanese army was equivalent to a British or Indian Army Corps.
† A Japanese regiment was equivalent to a British or Indian Army brigade

and was replaced by Major-General John Smyth. Smyth had been awarded the Victoria Cross in the First World War, and the Military Cross on the Northwest Frontier in 1920. Smyth was clearly physically brave. He took command despite being in significant pain from an anal fissure, with inadequate troops for the area he was defending, and against a larger force. Smyth had also appealed to his superior, Lieutenant-General Thomas Hutton, now commanding officer of Burma Command, that he did not have enough troops, and that this forward defence of Burma risked fighting the Japanese on their terms. Smyth wanted to withdraw to a place of his own choosing and fight the Japanese on *his* terms.

This was a difficult situation: they were essentially defending Rangoon to ensure the Burma Road remained open to the Chinese. Hutton wanted to defend as far forward as possible, not least to avoid Japan denying the use of Rangoon with aerial bombing from airfields in south-eastern Burma. Smyth wanted to use the various rivers across the likely route the Japanese would take advancing on Rangoon, and force them to make multiple, dangerous river crossings. This would, however, allow Japan access to the airfields at Tenasserim that were in range of Rangoon. Perhaps this reflects the different roles each man had, where Hutton had to consider the wider strategic problem of keeping the Burma Road open, whereas Smyth had to consider how to defend his corner of Burma most effectively.

Regardless of Hutton and Smyth's differing opinions (which would turn ugly in the aftermath), the 17th Indian Division was pushed back by Japanese infiltration tactics, under superior enemy artillery, and with 16th Brigade losing much of its transport. Morale was plummeting. Hutton allowed Smyth to abandon Moulmein before it was surrounded, with no reserves available to rescue them, at the end of January.

The 17th Indian Division were exhausted after close quarter fighting in the jungles around the Bilin river between the 14th and 19th February. Smyth said: 'The 17th Indian Division gave everything it had at Bilin and surrendered no ground to the Japanese; but as the pressure increased, every single reserve had to be thrown into the battle – and even then, we could not prevent strong parties of the enemy turning our flanks'.[4] The 17th Indian Division fell back towards the Sittang River in further rearguard actions. Hutton gave Smyth permission to withdraw his exhausted troops across the Sittang Bridge*. The bridge, a 550-yard-long iron railway bridge with hurriedly laid wooden planks to allow vehicles to cross, was prepared for demolition by the Royal Engineers on the 22nd February. In a horrific moment of poor radio discipline, one unknown British unit passed on the instructions for the withdrawal in clear language. The intelligence section of Japanese 33rd Division heard this and passed it on to their commander Lieutenant-General Shōzō Sakurai. He ordered his units to race for the bridge to cut off Smyth's depleted force, and then destroy it.

On the 22nd February Sakurai's men were pressing in on the bridgehead around the eastern end of the Sittang Bridge. Convinced he would not be able to hold it much longer, Smyth mentally prepared himself for the inevitable. After being woken up by an aid in the middle of the night of the 23rd, he was told the bridge was about to fall. He gave the order: "blow it."[5]

---

* As with many controversial moments in history, there has been significant argument ever since the events described over exactly what happened, by whom, at the Sittang Bridge. This is beyond the scope of this book.

Part II

"Without the 7th Armoured Brigade, we should not have got the army out of Burma".

Lieutenant-General Harold Alexander

3
7th Armoured Brigade arrive in Burma

"Rest fifteen minutes!" came the order, each exhausted man turned and whispered the message to the man behind. They were on another long night march, although this one did not afford them the same cover as earlier hooks through the jungle. Lance Corporal Umeo Tokita, of the 2nd Battalion of the 215 Infantry Regiment, took the opportunity to lay down and grab a few minutes sleep. Clutching his rifle, he looked up at the sky and saw the Southern Cross shining brightly in the night's sky. 'For a moment, I thought of my home country which lay beyond the far end of the sky'.[1] After midnight they heard the sound of rifles and machine guns firing, and saw flares blazing in the sky, far to their left. It was probably the 1st Battalion attacking Kokkogwa, thought Tokita. 'We were going to attack positions of a famous armoured corps'.[2]

The 7th Armoured Brigade had been in Burma for about 6 weeks. One of their regiments, the 2nd Royal Tank Regiment (2RTR), were near Taungdwingyi in the central plan, east of the Irrawaddy River, in a wood north of the main road at Thadodan. An area of paddy fields and dry *chaungs*, interspersed with wooded areas in the immediate vicinity. They had lost contact with the Japanese, who had been pursuing them northwards, so they sent out patrols to make sure there were no surprises and didn't find any. Tokita's battalion had managed to avoid these patrols.

'Our company came to the main road, our first target, without any resistance, and continued to advance along the lower edge of the road in single file'.[3] They heard voices on the far side and sent a single man across to find out who they were.

It was the enemy, one hundred metres beyond the road. 'The situation was not in our favour' reflected Tokita, 'the enemy had more men and better weapons, so we preferred a night attack. But time passed and the sun came up … an enemy sentry must have noticed us. Firing began at once'.[4] Tokita had earlier exchanged his rifle for a light machine gun, so dropped into a ditch by the road, and placed his gun on the road surface. He could see a tank at the entrance to the village that seemed to be pointing right at him. He fired towards some infantry near the tank, but everything was so frantic that he couldn't check if his shots were hitting anything. Enemy tank and mortar fire started to overwhelm Tokita's company, so they retreated to a dry *chaung* under cover of their own light artillery. The *chaung* was about two or three metres deep and wide, with a flat bottom covered in pebbles. They had already lost some men and had brought the wounded with them.

Someone cried out: "tank coming!"[5] Tokita went to the edge of the *chaung* and slowly peered over and could see a tank about 300 metres in front. Shortly after more followed. 'We were like mice in a trap! Nothing we could do; we had only rifles, machine guns and grenade launchers'.[6] The tanks approached but could not depress their guns enough to fire at the Japanese troops. The riverbed afforded them good cover, and the tanks could neither cross it, nor drop down into it without risking turning over. The tanks eventually pulled back a little, although the enemy sent small groups of infantry forward, which were pushed back. As the day wore on heat became a problem, and Tokita and his fellow soldiers ran out of drinking water. Tokita dug a hole and scooped muddy water into his canteen, after a while the mud settled in the bottom, and he could drink it.

Behind Tokita, a Type 94 37mm anti-tank gun was dragged forward to a clump of palm trees on the plain behind them and fired over his head.

'Its first shot pierced the tank's track but that was all. No more shells penetrated the armour. Most of our gunners were killed by the concentrated fire from the tanks, and the gun itself was run over by a tank and smashed. In order to use a petrol bomb, or *Chibi* bomb (glass container filled with an acid) in close range attack we had to leave the riverbed'.[7]

One man did try though, climbing out of the riverbed and out of sight. There was a hail of machine gun fire from the tanks. The man didn't return.

The situation in the *chaung* was getting desperate by the afternoon. 'I prayed that the sunset would come quickly'.[8] The tanks came forward again, and some more had found a way round behind Tokita's position. There were more casualties, with more and more wounded lying in agony on the hot pebbles. As tanks approached the *chaung* Tokita and the other able-bodied men would shift between the banks, getting themselves in the right cover depending on which side they were being fired on. Rumours circulated that they would be rescued by their own tanks. When they saw more tanks approaching from their own lines, they thought they were friendly and shouted "Banzai!"[9] The tanks near them must have heard and pulled back slightly to increase the distance in case the Japanese charged them.

The friendly tanks turned out to be more British ones. At this critical moment though, 150mm and 105mm artillery fire began to land amongst the tanks. The tanks pulled back, and their infantry went with them. The firing soon died down, and Tokita and his company breathed a collective sigh of relief. The invasion of Burma had been so easy up to that point. Whenever they met the enemy, they hooked behind them, and they panicked into withdrawing into ambushes. Tokita and his comrades were not really equipped to fight tanks. Even the 37mm anti-tank gun had proven to be weak. These tanks had changed the game.

Tokita's company carried their casualties away to a village about two kilometres away and cremated the dead. 'I would never again experience such a long day in my life,' thought Tokita. He then dragged his weary body with the rest of his unit as they continued their inexorable march west towards the Irrawaddy River.[10]

The experience of Umeo Tokita at Thadodan in early April 1942 illustrates a great 'what-if' for the retreat from Burma. The tanks, of 2RTR alongside 48th Indian Infantry Brigade, had managed to pin down, but not push back Tokita's battalion, and eventually had to pull back themselves. The developing Battle of Yenangyaung, where the main oilfields in Burma were, meant there were other Japanese incursions taking place elsewhere, and they needed the tanks' firepower. 7th Armoured Brigade could not be everywhere. This was to say the least, a shame. The Japanese did not have enough effective anti-tank weapons, so when the 7th Armoured Brigade arrived in Burma at the end of February, the tanks had an impact out of proportion to their size. If more armour had been available, then maybe things could have been different. But there were not more tanks. The reasons the Indian Army did not have armour in Burma have been discussed already, and the poorly trained and underequipped infantry in Burma at the time meant there were fundamental flaws that were essentially insurmountable. The situation in southern Burma was already practically lost when the 7th Armoured Brigade arrived, and certainly once Rangoon fell. They were firefighting from the moment they went into action.

The Brigade was raised in Egypt in 1938 and was made up of the 7th (Queen's Own) Hussars, 2RTR, with infantry support from the 1st Battalion, West Yorkshire Regiment, and the 414th Battery (Essex Yeomanry), Royal Horse Artillery. They also had various B echelon support units, providing the maintenance workshops, medical support, and so on attached as well. Some of these units, like the 7th Hussars, had been in Egypt since 1935. The Brigade was commanded by Brigadier John Anstice, who had been serving in tanks in battle since August 1916.

The 7th Hussars passed the New Year of 1941 into 1942 resting out of the line in relatively comfortable barracks near Cairo. They had no tanks at that time and were doing boring guard duties around Cairo and Heliopolis. They had a fine reputation from their time in the Middle East. Ralph Younger who had run the gunnery training when the 7th Hussars were mechanised in 1937, was now a Major and second in command of the regiment. He had led raids on Fort Capuzzo and had commanded his men in most of their battles in North Africa. Since the war in North Africa began the regiment had been part of the successful offensive at Sidi Barrani, assisted in the capture of Tobruk, and helped destroy Marshal Graziano's army at Beda Fomm. They had held the line successfully against an entire German armoured division at Sidi Razegh too. The 7th Armoured Brigade and the 7th Hussars were battle hardened veterans experienced in manoeuvre warfare. There were some gaps in the ranks after such hard fighting, but morale was high.

On the 5th January the 7th Hussars moved to Tahag near Tel el Kebir, where, among other things, there was a base specifically for maintenance and training on American tanks. The camp was far more isolated than the one they had left near Cairo, and the various entertainments the ancient city could offer. The base was cold, and there were frequent sandstorms that whipped through the mostly tented camp. They did, however, get some new toys. Stuart tanks, or "Honeys" as British crews often referred to them due to their smooth running, and reliability. The bulk of the regiment had not used Stuarts before, and they undertook a crash-course on them, getting out on the ranges every day for the next two weeks. The intensity of the training was because they were soon to embark for the Far East. They had seen the news of the Japanese attacks across the region and were to be sent to

Malaya, although the men did not know this until they were issued maps of Singapore and Sumatra on the troopship.

They started packing up on the 22nd January and headed for Suez over the next few days. They loaded the support vehicles and tanks onto transport ships before the men boarded the Blue Funnel liner *Ascanius*, requisitioned as a troopship. The long period they had served in Egypt meant many of the men had built roots there. The officers' wives, including Ralph Younger's wife Greta, came down to see them off, and gave them books and games to take for the voyage. They set sail on the 28th January, initially for Ceylon, before continuing to Malaya.

In early February General Wavell flew from Java to Rangoon, and visited the 17th Indian Division, shortly after they had retreated from Moulmein, and as they were setting up a defensive line on the Bilin river. Wavell wanted to impress on both Hutton, GOC Burma Command, and Smyth, GOC 17th Indian Division, they should try to retake lost areas like the airfields at Tenasserim. With Rangoon so close, defence in depth was impossible. Wavell reported after the battle that 'if ever there was a country where attack was the best form of defence it was Burma'.[11] One thing he saw were the dry rice fields – it looked like suitable tank country. If offense was the best form of attack, then armour could provide vital manoeuvrability and firepower to make that possible by countering any thrusts made by the Japanese. Wavell proposed to the Chiefs of Staff that the 7th Armoured Brigade should be redirected from its current destination to Burma. The garrison of Malaya had retreated across the Johore Strait onto the island of Singapore itself already, and the Japanese were preparing to launch an assault that would come on the night of the 8/9th February. The Chiefs of Staff approved Wavell's proposal. 7th Armoured Brigade would now go to Rangoon.

7th Armoured Brigade reached Ceylon in early February, and by the 12th an armed convoy had assembled to escort them to Rangoon. The men had been given a few days ashore in Colombo, and some met the local British community. The mood was gloomy, a feeling exacerbated by an oil fire sending plumes of black smoke into the sky. Across North Africa and the Far East, the military situation had deteriorated rapidly: Rommel was closing on Benghazi, Singapore was about to fall, and the 17th Indian Division had fallen back to the Bilin river. On the 14th February, the convoy and escort slipped their moorings and headed for Rangoon, arriving there on the morning of the 21st.

The land either side of the Irrawaddy estuary was flat paddy field, with oil refineries on the east bank. They passed a troopship with RAF personnel retreating to India, which hardly cheered the spirits of the men. They docked at 11:30am and found the area eerily quiet. Lend-lease equipment that was once destined for China was strewn all over the place, with no sign of any dock workers or guards. This was the aftermath of the air raids over Christmas 1941, where more than 2,000 people were killed, with much of the population fleeing to the countryside as a result. Subsequently, there was no one there to organise the unloading. There were a few figures on the docks, and the men of 7th Hussars soon saw it was Brigadier Anstice, commander of 7th Armoured Brigade. He had flown ahead and came aboard to explain the situation: the inexperienced and underequipped Indian Army troops were being pushed back towards Rangoon, 7th Armoured Brigade were there to stiffen the resistance and would be needed in active operations immediately. They were to be unloaded over the next two days and would assemble at a rubber plantation fifteen miles north of the city near Mingaladon airfield.

The lack of labourers was a problem for unloading the tanks and support vehicles. Luckily one trooper had been a crane operator before the war. He and the ship's crews helped train some more of the troopers on the cranes, and soon the process was in full swing. While the tanks waited to be unloaded, other men cleaned them and made sure they would be ready for action. The men worked through the night without breaks and fuelled by a case of beer for each team, they finished just as the sun rose. By 8am on the 22nd the first tanks began to arrive at the rubber plantation. They had their first contact with the human misery of the Japanese invasion; the endless stream of refugees. A sight they would become accustomed to over the next few months.

Once the 7th Hussars had assembled in the rubber plantation, they moved forward to Pegu, about 27 miles west of the Sittang Bridge. As the dust and debris settled after Smyth's order to blow the Sittang Bridge, the remnants of his 17th Indian Division trudged west, many without their equipment, some half-naked after swimming the river. They had lost around 5,000 men, half their strength, and were desperate for a rest. They had taken the brunt of the Japanese offensive so far, along with the 1st Burma Division. They would be re-clothed and re-armed at Pegu*, before rejoining the fray. Ralph Younger saw some of them whilst on a patrol east of Waw. 'They had no arms and looked helpless to a man'.[12] In the meantime, 7th Armoured Brigade would move forward to the north and northeast to be prepared to counterattack Japanese advances over the Sittang River in the area north of Payagyi and Waw. This also put the brigade between the Japanese and 17th Indian Division, giving the latter the time they needed to recover. The Japanese 33rd and 55th Divisions started crossing the Sittang River on 3rd March to exploit the gap between 7th Armoured Brigade and 1st Burma Division 35 miles north at Nyaunglebin. Most of the 55th Division would attack Pegu, while 33rd Division would cross and cut the Rangoon-Toungoo road north of Payagyi. They would then cross the low jungle-clad hills further north of Pegu, cut the

---

*Now Bago.

Rangoon-Prome road, and turn south to attack Rangoon from the north-east.

The Sittang Bridge disaster prompted a reshuffle over the following weeks in the organisation of the forces now in Burma. Major-General Smyth, commanding 17th Indian Division, took the blame for blowing the bridge with half of his men on the far side, and was replaced by the newly promoted Major-General David 'Punch' Cowan. As the 7th Armoured Brigade arrived in Rangoon, Smyth's immediate superior Lieutenant-General Hutton told his boss General Wavell that he was preparing for the evacuation of Rangoon, and the associated demolitions of the port, and oil facilities. Wavell, 2,000 miles away in Java and slightly out of touch with the situation, lost confidence with Hutton. Between Wavell, the Chiefs of Staff, Prime Minister, and the Viceroy of India, Hutton was replaced by General Alexander. Hutton was, rather humiliatingly, made 'Alex's' chief of staff. The final part of the reorganisation was the creation of Burma Corps (Burcorps) on 19th March 1942 under Lieutenant-General William 'Bill' Slim, who had been flown in from Iraq. Burcorps was made of 17th Indian Division, 1st Burma Division and 7th Armoured Brigade.

There was much confusion owing to the military situation, and the reorganisations now taking place. Before the axe fell on Hutton, his plans were set in motion, before they were countermanded by Wavell whilst Alexander was on his way to the theatre. This meant preparations were made for the 1st Burma Division to retreat north to cover the deployment of the 5th Chinese Army at Toungoo. Meanwhile 17th Indian Division and 7th Armoured Brigade would cover Rangoon until it was evacuated and any demolitions were complete, before heading north for Prome. In preparation for this, the 7th Hussars moved south to Hlegu, north of Rangoon, whilst the rest of the Brigade remained in the Pyagyi-Waw area. A dumping operation by C Squadron of the 7th Hussars also started where stores were placed in supply dumps on the planned route north towards India via the oilfields at Yenaungyaung and Mandalay. Wavell gave Alexander orders to be more aggressive, to try and hold onto Rangoon, but if that was not possible, then to retreat into central Burma, all the while keeping contact between friendly forces, including the Chinese. The 2RTR patrolled towards Waw on the 2nd March, and found it occupied, losing 2 tanks to anti-tank fire. They put in an attack with some attached infantry of the 1st Battalion, Cameron Highlanders, who took casualties, before they pulled back and allowed the RAF to bomb the village. The ferocious Japanese attacks in the area, and on Pegu in particular, culminated in a final withdrawal through Hlegu on the 6th March, which led Alexander to conclude Rangoon could not be held. He gave orders for the city's final evacuation, to be complete by the following day.

2RTR had now been in contact with Japanese units for a number of days. Along with local reconnaissance, they soon discovered that the rice paddies that Wavell thought would be so good for tanks had one obstacle. To control irrigation, the single-acre fields were often separated by one-foot-high earth bunds, just big enough to force a tank to slow down to 4mph every 100 yards. This increased fuel consumption and were an irritation for the crews being bounced around as they crossed them. On the 4th March the 7th Hussars would relieve 2RTR, who were struggling to shift a Japanese position in Kyaikhla and a roadblock at Pyinbongyi due to the lack of infantry and artillery. They could engage and suppress an enemy position, but they could not clear it, especially if they came up against anti-tank guns.

The 7th Hussars were due to relieve 2RTR at 6:45am on the 4th March. The 1st Cameronians would come under the 7th Hussars command at the same time. At 5:45am, the regiment moved off with B Squadron in the lead. One troop of A Squadron was detached from the main column and ordered to patrol towards Pyinbon to reconnoitre a reported roadblock, the rest moved up to Payagyi. The men of the 7th Hussars were veterans, most had seen action plenty of times before against both the Italians and Germans. In the dim pre-dawn light and thick mist, in the completely new environment of southern Burma, there must have been some trepidation amongst the crews as they prepared to face a new enemy in the Japanese. 'By the time we were approaching Payagyi', Lieutenant Geoffrey Palmer, one of the troop leaders in B Squadron, noted 'the dawn light was just breaking and there was a thick mist with visibility down to ten yards'.[13] Further ahead, the lead troop commander, Lieutenant Stanley Evans, was standing with his head out of the open turret hatch, straining his eyes through the thick heavy mist hanging in the air in front of him. As they approached their objective, a number of lorries emerged from the murk along the narrow road.

7th Armoured Brigade's fighting retreat 1942

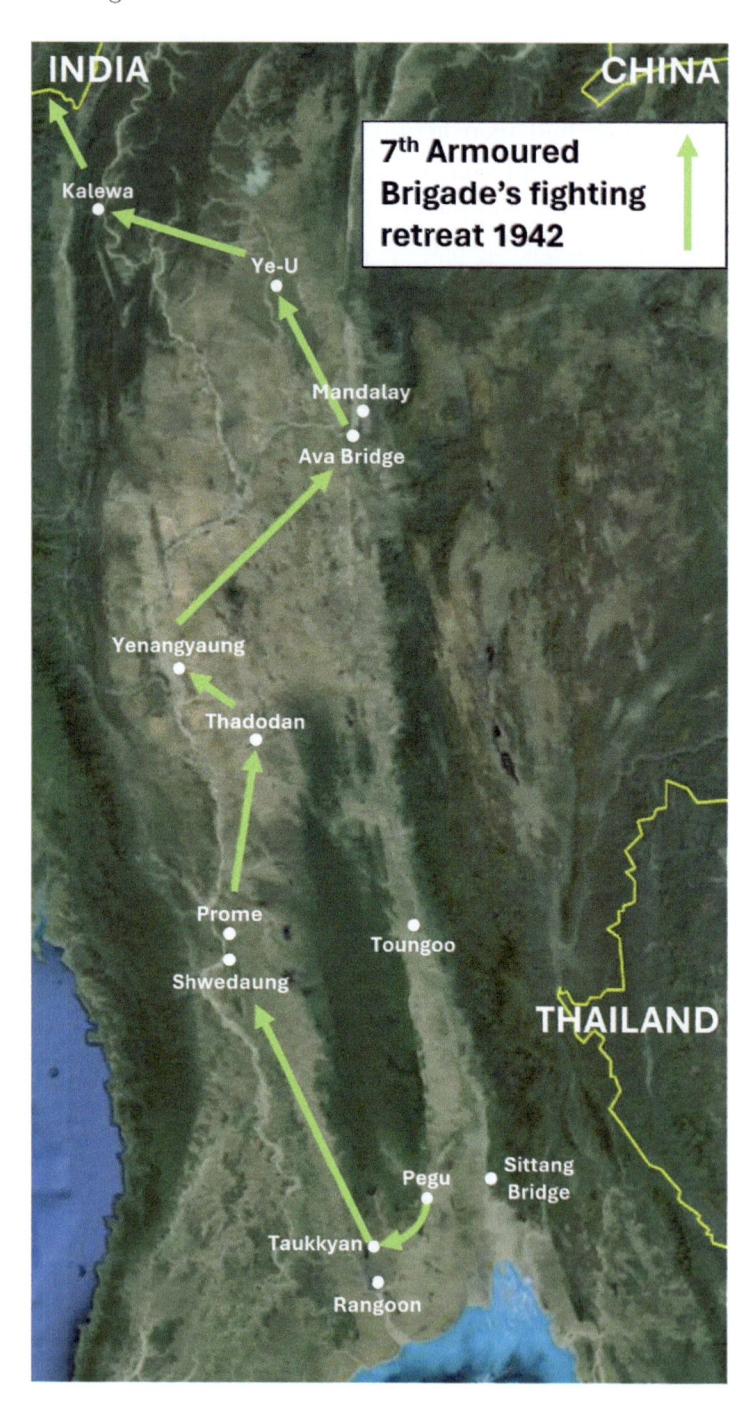

4
The retreat from Burma

Rangoon was beginning to fall into a state of panic. 5,000 prisoners and mental health patients had been released from prisons and psychiatric hospitals by accident, although basic infrastructure like water and electricity was generally still working. Major Tony Mains was the recently appointed head of the Field Security division in the city and was mostly worrying about looting, fires, and potential fifth columnists. 'The Civil Police just melted away. Many of this force were not Burmese but Indian; the Rangoon City Police was mainly Punjabi, Moslems and Sikhs, and they were in mortal terror of the Japanese'.[1]

After Hutton had started the evacuation plans on the 20th February, Mains had been sent to Rangoon station to help the local railway authorities organise refugee trains. 'I am a "Rail Buff" and have been since I was about nine' confessed Mains.[2] They also supervised the departure of supply trains to Pegu with equipment and uniforms for the recovering 17th Indian Division. Along with his security team of around twenty mixed British and Indian soldiers armed with pump-action shotguns and *lathis** headed into the vast Victorian station.

The railway line ran north through Pegu, Toungoo and on to Mandalay, worryingly close to where the Japanese were approaching since the Sittang Bridge disaster. 7th Armoured Brigade was patrolling the area immediately north of Pegu at the time, but beyond that there were concerns it could be cut at any time. Most of those in Rangoon station did not know this, their

---
* A 60-100cm bamboo stick, used for crowd control by police and other security forces, especially for riot control since the Mughal period to the present.

panic was caused from earlier air raids, and the general threat to the city itself. 'Every now and then there were disputes or even fights which had to be quelled ... [one] man was so panic-stricken that he had lost all sense of reason and was even trampling on other people in his anxiety to get into the train'.[3]

Generally, the evacuation and loading of trains was orderly, despite the scale of the operation: Rangoon was a city of half a million people, roughly half of whom were Indian – the group most likely to want to evacuate before the Japanese arrived.[4] There was also an unknowable number of refugees from outside the city who arrived from all directions looking to escape north. Mains wanted to avoid dangerous overcrowding, and to see that the trains were loaded with people not baggage, so they only allowed one bag per person. 'Many tried to move their entire household, or stock in trade, and heart-rending appeals were made to us that their abandonment would mean financial ruin'.[5] The noise of a tense and even panicking crowd was far above the normal rumble of voices at a busy station, making organisation difficult.

On the second day of the evacuation over one hundred Indian constables of the Rangoon City Police arrived in the station forecourt and demanded passage to Mandalay. There were rumours that the Japanese had severely mistreated, even tortured, Indian police in Burma. They claimed they were under orders to head for Prome and be reformed for service elsewhere. No one had informed the authorities, the railway staff, or Mains' security team. The policemen threatened to storm the barriers. Mains worried the situation was about to get out of hand. He had only five men with him, armed with their *lathis* and pump-action shotguns. '[I warned] the police that should they attempt this [storming the barriers] they would be fired upon'.[6] The threat had little effect. The policemen still threatened to force their way through, prepared to call Mains's bluff. Luckily, the Deputy Commissioner of Police arrived and used a megaphone to diffuse the situation, partly by shaming them for their behaviour. He had given them their word they would be taken to Prome, and as policemen, they should have behaved accordingly. They were placed under Main's control and were to obey his orders. Any who disobeyed could be shot.

Mains began loading the policemen after the latest Mandalay train departed. They were now behaving, but it seemed every man was carrying a bolt of cloth. They had looted the nearby cloth market, causing another altercation with Mains' security team as they forced them to give up their loot. When the Commissioner of Police arrived to see this and complain, Mains lost his temper. 'I replied hotly, regardless of his high rank, that I should like to know why he had sent the police to the station without prior warning, why they had become a disorderly mob and why they had looted the cloth market. I added for good measure, that he should be thankful I had not opened fire on them'.[7] The Commissioner backed down, and Mains was able to continue the evacuation, including the police train to Prome.

After five days, the evacuation was going smoothly enough that Mains' security team were sent into the city to monitor law and order, which was breaking down in the rapidly emptying city. He spent the next few days chasing looters, and after a near miss where he almost opened fire on 17th Indian Division personnel, he gave permission to loot abandoned clothing and equipment to help them recover after the Sittang Bridge disaster. Mains even had the grim job of clearing up some corpses caused by two rival gangs arguing over loot in a warehouse. After this, his team were given orders to head north to Maymyo. They received their orders on 7th March, and in a few requisitioned vehicles, made their way out of the city after dark. They joined up with the main column, alongside the final evacuees that included the Army HQ and local officials and headed along the road north towards a town called Taukkyan.

Back at the approach to Payagyi, the lorries emerging from the mist towards Evans's A Squadron tanks turned out to be Cameronians pulling out of the village. Just as they realised the road was too narrow for the lorries and tanks to pass, Japanese infantry appeared from the woods and village and opened fire. Evans's Stuart tanks returned fire, as did the rapidly dismounting Cameronians. B Squadron was nearby and engaged some Japanese infantry in a paddy-field. Ralph Younger was keeping a close eye on B Squadron's engagement, when he heard reports crackling over the radio that there were twenty tanks approaching. Younger questioned the report, before a rather sheepish troop commander conceded they may have been elephants. A mistake he never lived down among his comrades.

They decided to pull back and monitor the village. The mist was clearing, and the Essex Yeomanry were able to bring their 25 pounders into action, whilst arrangements were made for an RAF raid with the few Blenheim light bombers that were available. This turned out to be a complete shambles, as only one bomber came over, and missed the entire village. Another attack went in and the Cameronians cleared the area. They set the buildings on fire, and retired again, reporting 63 casualties on the enemy, and checking their advance on this road.

The next morning, the 5th March, B Squadron moved up to observe the village. At about 9:30am. Captain Marcus Fox then spotted a tank and two lorries. 'They appeared to be very lonely and untrained, and obviously did not know what to do, remaining stationary in the middle of an open field. They were knocked out immediately before they knew we were there'.[8] The tank turned out to be 'a small two-man tank on the lines of the Italian CV/33*.[9]

---

*The reader should note that in Bryan Perrett's Tank Tracks to Rangoon, Marcus Fox's testimony suggests the tanks (two of them) were Type-95s – a 3-man turreted tank. Both the 7th Hussars official history and the 7th Hussars war diary say there was only one, and that it looked like an Italian CV/33. This is a smaller Universal Carrier-sized 2-man tankette, with no turret. It may have been a 2-man Type 94 TK tankette, inspired by the Carden-Loyd

A Squadron and a company of infantry continued to clear some nearby woods. There were warning signs that the Japanese were trying to get in behind the brigade: to the south and west 2RTR were fired on by unseen AT guns, and some lorries were also shot at in the area. Confusion from the changes to the command structure did not help. First Hutton's order to withdraw from Pegu came, before what were clearly the newly appointed Alexander's orders to hold the town. Much of the town was burning at this point, and the jungle that closed in on their positions was potentially full of Japanese infantry encircling them.

The next morning, 6th March, there was another dense mist in the air, and the vehicles were huddled in together. The men had dismounted and were brewing the British soldier's ubiquitous tea. As breakfasts were being cooked a shell landed in the leaguer* followed by intense scurrying by the crews back to their tanks. The Japanese 55th Division had moved through the hilly jungle to the north of Pegu, before 143rd Regiment attacked from the west, and the 112th Regiment built a roadblock on the road to Hlegu at Payathonzu. This split the 17th Indian Division and 7th Armoured Brigade HQs from some of their units fighting in and around Pegu, a distance of 20 miles. The 7th Hussars spent the rest of the morning clearing the woods either side of the road to allow a fighting withdrawal.

Lieutenant Evans was assisting in one of these operations, firing into Japanese positions before the infantry went in to clear. He shifted round behind the wood to try and catch the retreating Japanese in the open. He was about to repeat another of these

---

Vib - the Italian CV/33 was based on imported Carden Loyds. Fox's testimony compares the tanks to his own Stuart; the Type 94 did have a small turret but is significantly smaller. Fox's description of the behaviour of the tanks matches the action of the 5th March, rather than the action the following day against Type 95s. They could well be Type 95s from the same unit faced on the 6th March, as the war diary admits they did not get a close look at the tank destroyed on the 5th.
*The name used for the area tanks parked overnight.

operations at 11am when the call came in – tanks were attacking another troop where he had been earlier. Three Type-95 *Ha-Go* tanks from the Japanese 2nd Tank Regiment were supporting the attack on Pegu. Evans moved his troop to the area they had been seen, but the messages through the radio were not enough to pinpoint the exact location of the enemy. Evans could see three tanks near some haystacks, with some of the crews dismounted. He got on the radio, and checked with Lieutenant Barton, who had made the initial call. None of Barton's men were out of their tanks.

The 7th Hussars experience of the desert now shone through. Evans and Barton made their plan: Barton would move into a hull-down position to the flank of the Japanese tanks, whilst Evans would advance on them from the front. Evans put his troop into an arrowhead formation and charged, in true cavalry tradition. Soon the Japanese tanks saw the advancing Stuarts charging towards them. The Japanese tanks opened fire first, Barton's followed suit. At 800 yards Evans halted his troop and fired. Too far. They moved up another 100 yards. Evan's gunner, Trooper Clare fired the 37mm at two dismounted men who had not returned to a tank, forcing them into a bushy gully. There seemed to be more fire coming in from nearby AT guns, but they couldn't see them – perhaps the dismounted men were from these guns. At about 300 yards there was a shattering clang as Evans's tank was hit on the frontal armour, momentarily blinding his driver, Trooper Bridges.

The interior of any tank is tight, but with the Stuart being so small, the driver's face is almost pressed against the inside of the armour. Luckily, the Type 95's 37mm gun, the same size as Evans's main gun, was quite ineffective even against the thin armour of a Stuart. As Bridges put his hands to his face the tank ran on out of control. Trooper Clare continued to fire at the Japanese tanks, as did the rest of the troop. This somewhat reckless charge, without reconnoitring the area, or with infantry support, was at risk of falling apart. After what was probably barely more than a moment, and realising he was not badly hurt, Bridges recovered his composure and regained control of the tank. The three Stuarts continued their charge and closed on the enemy. They pulled up to the now disabled tanks: the Type-95s were a mess. Two were on fire, the other abandoned and there were several Japanese bodies lying about nearby. Some of the men dismounted. As they were inspecting their prey they came under rifle fire, and again scrambled to the safety of their Stuarts. The Japanese did not risk their armour against 7th Armoured Brigade again during the retreat.

The 7th Hussars had shown one aspect of their cavalry tradition*, and the occasionally poor armoured tactics from the Western Desert. On numerous occasions 7th Armoured Brigade, and other units, had charged German AT gun screens, rather than wait for artillery and infantry to assist them. This was a shortcoming of their interwar training, where combined-arms operations were rarely practised. That would have been far too expensive. The 7th Hussars and later tank units were able to be so effective in the Burma Campaign because the Japanese never really developed a truly comprehensive system of effective AT weapons and tactics. The 7th Hussars got away with these tactics against the Japanese.

The situation in Pegu was declining rapidly. With the roadblock two miles south at Payathonzu, the town was effectively surrounded, and the 48th Indian Infantry Brigade holding it had been out of radio contact for some hours. The sound of fighting was constant, and the town ablaze. In the afternoon, the 7th Hussars were sent from their position northeast of Pegu into the north of the town itself to make contact with the 48th Brigade. One tank had been sent to their

---

*This is not to say they trained to charge, rather it happens to fit the traditions of the cavalry. Cavalry training since the First World War had focused on reconnaissance and force protection. Even before this, they had been expected to fight dismounted, rather than from the saddle.

HQ to act as a radio vehicle with the higher command at Hlegu 20 miles south of them. With little experience of the new, longer range, no. 19 wireless set, they were still effectively out of contact. The roadblock also meant the 63rd Indian Infantry Brigade that was coming up to reinforce Pegu could not get through, although some of their senior officers had gone through before the roadblock as a reconnaissance party.

This is when Alexander changed his mind after realising Rangoon could not be held. The 7th Hussars and 48th Brigade were to withdraw to Hlegu. One troop of 2RTR, who had also been cut off in Pegu, brought the 63rd Brigade's reconnaissance group out in the morning. In forcing the roadblock, all of the 63rd Brigade's officers were killed or wounded whilst riding in soft-skinned vehicles. Ralph Younger caught up with 48th Brigade's HQ to plan the withdrawal. Evans's troop was sent out on a patrol to find a way to avoid the roadblock, but none was found. Evans then pushed his patrol south to the roadblock and came under mortar and AT gun fire. It was getting too dark to fight through the roadblock without infantry support, so they moved off the road into a jungle clearing. The jungle to the north and east was blazing, to the south was the roadblock, and there was no infantry to dig in around the tanks. There was firing throughout the night, making the crews jumpy for the only time in the campaign, with the constant worry of the Japanese emerging from the treeline. Lieutenant Palmer recalled 'As a night attack was expected we had to stay in the tanks and spent one of the most harassing nights I can remember in the war. Dawn was most welcome'.[10] What little sleep was possible was taken in short bursts, curled up as best they could in their seats, for most of them this was just a small, round fold-away seat. They were mostly disturbed by occasional mortar fire landing nearby.

Back in Pegu, the 7th Hussars and 48th Brigade made their final preparations for a frontal assault on the roadblock.

There was the usual heavy mist on the morning of the 7th March. Just north of Rangoon, Tony Mains and his security team were amongst the convoy now evacuating north to Prome, via Taukkyan, where there were rumours of another roadblock. Alexander's staff were there, along with the remainder of the Rangoon garrison and assorted other units. 17th Indian Division, and 7th Armoured Brigade HQs were still at Hlegu.

At the Payathonzu roadblock the morning was quite still. At 8:10am the Essex Yeomanry's eight 25 pounders broke the early-morning quiet, firing a 400-round barrage at the roadblock. The main obstacle across the road were two burnt-out lorries parked nose-to-nose, with infantry dug in on either side. The 48th Brigade's transport vehicles were brought up and were mixed in with the 7th Hussars behind the leading troop so protective fire was available along the entire column. Infantry started to make their way forward to clear the jungle on either side of the road. Once everyone was through, they would regroup at Hlegu.

Lieutenant Palmer was old for a subaltern at 33-years-old. He had enlisted in the ranks and bounced around various units before showing his promise whilst serving with the Honourable Artillery Company in France, until he was evacuated from Dunkirk, before attending Sandhurst. His troop had been chosen to lead the attack to clear the roadblock and had the Essex Yeomanry's Forward Observation Officer (FOO) observer with them. Sergeant Davis was the lead tank, and as he approached the two lorries everything remained quiet. They inched forward, every man straining to see through their periscopes, commanders with their heads out the turret hatches. Davis's tank reached the lorries and tried to push them out of the way. 'We succeeded in partly moving the lorries with the tanks' Palmer recalled 'and immediately came under a hail of small arms fire'.[11] The rest of his troop took up fire positions as best they could on the narrow road, the thick jungle took away any chance of outflanking the position. The infantry were clearing the jungle either side of the road, but its density meant the tanks had moved ahead of them. Palmer's troop plastered the area for ten minutes with machine gun fire from their Brownings, two in each tank. The infantry now caught up, and a stonk* landed on the Japanese positions.

'In the middle of all this I suddenly saw a bottle hit the side of Davis's tank and burst into flames – some kind of Molotov cocktail. No damage was done, and we shuffled forward'.[12] Thankfully, the flames did not ignite anything vital in the tank. Another tank was hit and this time it did real damage. 'Corporal Barr's tank [was] knocked out, again by a Molotov cocktail, although he and his crew got clear'.[13] Davis now forced a way through the roadblock this time, everyone aware that the longer this operation took, the more likely the whole of the 7th Hussars and 48th Brigade would be destroyed. The infantry successfully cleared the immediate jungle around the block, and the column started to pass through. Palmer's troop now raced ahead to check the route was clear. Apart from an HE shell exploding on the outside of the tank and destroying his belongings, they made it through unscathed. There was still the odd sniper pestering vehicles as they passed, but the road was now effectively open.

48th Brigade were out, and the 7th Hussars had punched the hole for them to escape. The operation lasted just a couple of hours, but was not without cost; Major Stephen Francis of the West Yorks, part of the infantry support in the jungle, died of wounds a few days later. Trooper AP Clarke had been killed, and two men were wounded in the B echelon vehicles. These were, however, far fewer than could have been expected in the circumstances.

The column now moved through Hlegu and rejoined the rest of 7th Armoured Brigade and 17th Indian Division, before moving on a lateral road east to Taukyyan, 20 miles north of

---
* British slang for concentrated artillery fire

Rangoon. They were to rendezvous there that afternoon with the evacuating Rangoon garrison under Alexander before clearing the now confirmed roadblock north of the town. This group consisted of over 1,000 tanks, armoured cars, lorries, and various sorts of civilian transport. Alongside the administrative units and Alexander's HQ staff, there was a great mass of human misery escaping the threat of Japanese occupation. There were men, women, children, animals, food, baggage, and even furniture piled haphazardly on cars. There were refugees on foot, some with hand carts pulling their belongings or family. This column was stretched over miles and came with the din of thousands of people walking and talking.

The head of the column found the roadblock three miles north of Taukkyan around 11am on the 7th March. Everything behind soon began to pile up bumper to bumper, but still stretching back for miles down towards Rangoon. The 7th Armoured and 48th Infantry Brigades arrived from Hlegu about an hour later, having broken through from Payathonzu. The local area around the roads were mostly rubber plantations: the regular rows of trees with cleared undergrowth gave tanks the chance to bypass the traffic jams and get forward to clear the roadblock. The jam was problematic, and there on the dusty road at the Taukkyan crossroads were two lieutenant-generals in Alexander and Hutton, directing traffic to ensure the vehicles carrying the men and equipment got through for the coming battle.

The roadblock had been hurriedly created by 214th Regiment of 33rd Division by felling trees across the roadway just after an advanced guard that included C Squadron of the 7th Hussars had passed through. Japanese infantry were behind the roadblock and in the jungle either side. They were also supported by at least one 75mm mountain gun. B Squadron, 7th Hussars was first to arrive at the head of the vast column and were put straight into the attack to clear it. The narrow road meant only one tank could advance at a time. Lieutenant Young nosed his Stuart round the corner of the bend before the Japanese position, when he received a direct hit from the 75mm, damaging his main gun without penetrating the armour. Some 25 pounders from the Rangoon garrison were organised to lay down some fire, before repeated frontal attacks by various infantry being called up from the column: 1st Gloucesters, Duke of Wellington's Regiment, King's Own Yorkshire Light Infantry, and the Frontier Force Regiment. They were each supported in turn by B Squadron, but they could not shift the stubborn Japanese position. B Squadron had led the assault on the Payathonzu roadblock earlier that morning, and the men were exhausted. By late afternoon A Squadron of 2RTR took over for another attempt but fared no better.

During the day's fighting, Tony Mains had made his way forward. Around 9pm, after the fighting had died down for the night, he found Army HQ. The atmosphere was gloomy. 'The most unruffled man in the whole set up appeared to be the Army Commander himself' referring to Alexander, 'he was sitting quite imperturbably in a Burmese house, with nothing to lighten the darkness except a few oil lamps, apparently completely unconcerned that his command of the Army in Burma appeared unlikely to last for more than a few days'.[14]

Alexander, Hutton, their staffs, 7th Armoured Brigade, 17th Indian Division, and the Rangoon garrison were surrounded, and apparently unable to escape. The Japanese 33rd Division were ahead of them and moving around their western flank. The 122nd Regiment of 55th Division were racing south much farther east, heading for Rangoon. The situation appeared desperate. Main's friend Philip Gwyn took him aside and told him resignedly "either we burst out like a cork in a bottle, or we go into the bag. In that event, I am putting on my boots and walking; I won't let the Japs capture me."[15]

Overnight, preparations were made for a set piece assault with all of the available firepower the escaping column could muster. The Essex Yeomanry had managed to get through the throng of vehicles jammed up through Taukkyan to join the 25 pounders of the Rangoon garrison. After B Squadron's efforts the previous day, A Squadron was selected for the attack. Two battalions of infantry from 63rd Brigade had marched through the night to attack the roadblock from east and west, with A Squadron timing their advance so they would arrive at the same time as the infantry. C Squadron, who had passed the area before the roadblock was built, would attack from the north.

The lack of jungle training became evident as the morning went on. One of the battalions of infantry was bombed and did not arrive at the roadblock, and the other was eight hours late, by which time the column was already well on the way to Prome. This was because the Japanese were gone. In a remarkable event, reflecting badly on Japanese leadership that stifled initiative, the cork was removed from the bottle for the retreating army, so they burst through. The roadblock had been a simple flank guard by the 214th Regiment, whilst the rest of 33rd Division crossed the road above them and swung south to attack Rangoon. As Lieutenant-General Sakurai's men approached Rangoon, expecting the British, Indian and Gurkha troops to make a stand, they found the city practically empty. Sakurai had let almost the entire army in Burma* and its command structure, including Alexander and Hutton, out of the bag. An aggressive commander, Sakurai had driven on for his key objective, Rangoon, without taking the opportunity that presented itself. At the very least, the size and strength of the force attacking the 214th Regiment's roadblock should have been a hint that this was not some small sub-unit escaping encirclement, but the bulk of an exhausted and desperate army. Sakurai's orders were for

---

* 1st Burma Division were well to the east retreating up the Sittang Valley towards Toungoo.

Rangoon, so that is where he went, following his orders to the letter.

As the column escaped north, 7th Armoured Brigade was tasked with patrolling the road whilst escorting them to safety. One of the patrols of the 7th Hussars covered 120 miles moving up and down their ten-mile section. The crews found this work to be a great strain, the constant passing and overtaking of vehicles as the drivers worked their way up and down the gears constantly. This was a difficult thing to have to keep doing in a Stuart, where the gear stick is awkwardly found under the driver's right arm. This was all worthwhile for the mutual morale boost, the sight of tanks for weary troops and civilians trudging north brought cheers as they passed.

Over the next ten days 7th Armoured Brigade shepherded the column towards Prome. Most of the road was covered by the jungle, and there were some attacks by snipers and aircraft. The loss of Rangoon made administration difficult. There was no overland supply line to India, and without Rangoon nothing could arrive by sea. Petrol and lubricants were refined in the Yenangyaung oilfields in central Burma and brought south. There were no heavy repair facilities available at all now, and so the B echelon workshops had to do their best to maintain the tanks. Stores continued to be dumped on the likely routes to India too, in case of further withdrawals. The Japanese now gained the logistical advantage of having Rangoon and took full advantage. After the successful campaigns in Malaya, they brought in reinforcements like the 18th Division, bringing with them vehicles which had been abandoned there by the retreating British to speed up their own advance.

There was now a short lull in the campaign. Incredible distances had been covered since the initial Japanese invasion from Thailand into south-eastern Burma. Both sides needed rest, maintenance for their equipment, and to allow reinforcements to arrive. Slim landed in Burma on 19th March, finally making Burcorps a reality. Alexander could now concentrate on the administration of the army, and relations with the now arriving nationalist Chinese, whilst Slim focused on the day-to-day fighting of his divisions. He decided quickly that the 7th Armoured Brigade should become his corps striking force, to hit out at Japanese advances and incursions before they could outflank his infantry. Alexander's plan for the campaign now rested on holding an 80-mile front from Prome in the Irrawaddy valley, across the Pegu Yomas mountain range, to Toungoo in the Sittang Valley. The Chinese Expeditionary Force (CEF) comprising the 5th Army* to hold the Sittang Valley defences centred around Toungoo, 6th Army in the Shan States covering an advance from Thailand, and 66th Army in reserve. 1st Burma Division, who had been holding Toungoo up to now, would move across to the Irrawaddy valley to join Burcorps once the Chinese forces were deployed.

The Japanese main effort was to be against Toungoo. The intention was to destroy the Chinese forces, stop a retreat into China, and eventually capture Mandalay. The 55th Division was given the task, along with the motorised 56th Division that had just arrived via Rangoon. The Chinese 5th Army fought a series of delaying actions in mid-March, until they withdrew into Toungoo. The Japanese assault began on the 25th March after a heavy bombardment by artillery and aircraft, followed by vicious house-to-house fighting. Both sides suffered heavy casualties.

To relieve pressure on the Chinese, 7th Armoured Brigade and 17th Indian Division were tasked with capturing Paungde then Okpo by the 30th March. The force assembled appeared formidable, however, most of the infantry battalions were at half strength by now, and they were short on artillery with only eight guns available. Morale was surprisingly high though. Many of the troops were looking forward to an offensive action after

---

*A CEF army was equivalent to a division in the British or Indian Army.

weeks of retreat, and many felt the Japanese were scared of the tanks.

As some of the infantry made preliminary patrols forward, a battalion of Japanese infantry was discovered attempting an outflanking movement and were assaulting Padigon from the east. Major Llewellen-Palmer's A Squadron was immediately sent to support, with the order 'Padigon flat-out' with Evans's troop in the lead racing at their full speed of 36mph.[16] As they approached, the lead tank failed to hear a radio warning that the enemy were further north of Padigon than expected, and so the squadron was to halt. Evans tried to get their attention racing after them and blowing his siren. The rear two tanks in the troop halted, but Sergeant Walton's tank and the one behind careered on. Evans followed, when they came to a small wood, when suddenly they were hit by an artillery round and small arms fire. The three tanks raced through the Japanese position still with hatches open and regrouped on the other side. They were ordered by radio to get back, and proceeded to race back the way they came. At the same time, HQ squadron was engaging another Japanese position in a copse to the east of the main road, that was cleared with the help of infantry and artillery. Around this time the first signals came through saying the Japanese had crossed the Irrawaddy to the west and were outflanking from there as well. Little progress was being made even when C Squadron went round Padigon and found Paungde was also well defended. With the threat developing in their rear, and the lack of progress, operations to capture Paungde and Okpo were cancelled.

With the offensive called off, the tanks, infantry and artillery had to return to Prome. To avoid the Japanese roadblocks already encountered and more they were building behind them, they moved west and then north to the town of Shwedaung on the way back to Prome. B Squadron with the Essex Yeomanry and two companies of the 1st Gloucesters were the spearhead, with C Squadron as rearguard. Forcing their way through multiple roadblocks in Shwedaung itself starting at 6:15pm they fought by moonlight into the night. There was fierce fighting, illuminated by tracer fire and flames from the burning trees, houses and wrecked vehicles.

'We put on speed to about 25mph and charged down the road being shot at all the way and hit several times' recalled Lieutenant Palmer.

'We were also showered by petrol bombs which helped light our way. In the next three miles or so we hit at least four more blocks. My tank was hit by an AT shell which brought down a shower of bits and pieces in the turret. I was for a time blinded by blood from a cut on my head, but Watson drove on magnificently and somehow managed to keep us on the road. Suddenly things went quiet and we appeared to be through'.[17]

The fighting around Padigon meant the Essex Yeomanry had to husband their rounds, making each roadblock tougher as they found them, with a dwindling supply of shells limiting any preparatory bombardment. In the darkness some blocks were only found when the lead tank hit them, some were manned with infantry and artillery, others were not. After Lieutenant Patteson's tank was overturned, he was captured and cruelly tied to the front of one of the roadblocks. Luckily, he survived an artillery stonk before he managed to free himself, and in the confusion slipped away, making it to Brigade HQ that evening. By now it was 2am, so Brigadier Anstice decided to pull as much of the force into as tight a leaguer as possible and move off at daylight. Another cold and jittery night was spent unsure of exactly what was lurking in the dark.

The intensity of the last few weeks, and especially the previous day meant the routine for passing roadblocks was entrenched. The Essex Yeomanry opened their fire at 6:45am on the 30th March, and the infantry began to clear the woods either side of the road. Once these appeared clear, the column began to move, B Squadron in the lead, C Squadron bringing up the rear behind the transport vehicles. At 7am, B Squadron moved and quickly cleared the first block, losing one tank in the process. The heavy fighting in the woods died down, and so the decision was made to rush the transport vehicles through. This was made partly because patrols to the south had reported a Japanese column moving up behind them, but also because reconnaissance planes had been seen overhead, it was only a matter of time before bombers would follow.

As the transport moved up, with B Squadron ahead, and A Squadron mixed with them, they realised the area was not as well cleared as hoped. Mortars, machine guns and Molotovs destroyed a number of the transport vehicles, and more tanks were knocked out. Each wreck created another blockage that needed avoiding or shoving out of the way. The tanks fired on the move trying to destroy any targets as they passed, and successfully kept the enemy at enough of a distance that allowed the column to keep moving. More smaller log roadblocks were also encountered that the tanks could drive straight into and shift them. More and more vehicles were burning and making blocks that caused the head and the rear of the column to separate. This did, however, mean B Squadron, plus Brigade HQ got through to the far side of the blocks, and met Indian infantry moving south from Prome, originally intended to follow up the assault on Paungde. These two infantry battalions attacked Shwedaung from the north to try and help clear the way.

C Squadron and the infantry who first cleared the woods either side of the main road in the morning were now fighting a running battle with the Japanese column following them up the road. Japanese bombers had also joined the fray and started to cause mayhem, dropping bombs on the column. By late afternoon the situation was getting out of hand. C Squadron was getting dangerously close to the transport they were supposed to be screening. The Japanese had reoccupied the roadblock ahead, with A Squadron trying to clear it, but the air attacks meant the infantry dispersed further into the jungle by the roads. As A Squadron pushed through the Japanese fought back ferociously, knocking out four of their tanks before they made it to safety. C Squadron, the Essex Yeomanry and the harassed transport vehicles made some progress behind them but could not keep up. The roadblock was snapped shut behind A Squadron and the transport that was closest to them.

As evening approached C Squadron's commander Major Congreve spoke to the infantry commanders. They would abandon their transport and make their escape through the night on foot in a wide arc around the Japanese position, which was held in depth, but not width. The Essex Yeomanry would fire a final barrage of their remaining ammunition, before another charge, this time through some thinner trees, over a steam, and between some houses, rather than directly through the now dangerously blazing roadblock. Every time a vehicle slowed down or stopped a Japanese soldier would try to rush it with a Molotov as their comrades kept up rifle and machine gun fire. Two of the Essex Yeomanry's guns were abandoned when their tractors were knocked out, the other six were brought out successfully, one dragged upside down by a tank. The gunners took significant casualties in individual acts of bravery saving their guns, and even engaging enemy positions as infantry.

This final desperate charge did get the rest of the column through. The vehicles made it to Prome late that evening, with the infantry arriving through the night. Unfortunately, the whole operation only partly distracted Japanese attention from Toungoo but it did not divert any troops. The operation against Paungde and Okpo was an attempt to regain the initiative in the Irrawaddy valley but had failed. Just as Burcorps advanced on the road south towards their objective, the Japanese began their own offensive advancing either side of them, catching the 7th Hussars at the head in a trap. Thankfully the firepower of the tanks, and poor Japanese AT capability meant they could fight their way out along with their supporting infantry and artillery. It was a very close-run thing though. These units had lost more men and abandoned even more equipment. 10 tanks had been lost, along with the two 25 pounders, 200 soft-skinned transport vehicles, and 400 infantry casualties. Almost all of this was irreplaceable. The 7th Hussars were down to just 38 tanks. After the hopes that were built up by taking offensive action, morale had ended up taking another severe hit. The units involved in the near miss paused to lick their wounds.

Prome was now under direct threat, and the Chinese were retreating from Toungoo. The Japanese 56th Division, originally intended to reinforce the Malayan Campaign but now in Burma, was beginning the process of pushing the Chinese 6th and 66th armies northeast through the Shan States towards the Chinese border. The 55th Division and the recently arrived from Singapore 18th Division were pushing the Chinese 5th Army north towards Mandalay. Prome was to be abandoned to protect the oilfields at Yenangyaung and avoid opening another flank for Japanese encirclement. The Japanese 33rd Division launched their attack on Prome on the 1st April, but Burcorps was already gone, withdrawing 50 miles north to Taungdwingyi. Delaying actions were fought until they found themselves on the central dry belt of Burma, far more tankable country than the jungles and paddies of southern Burma. This area is mostly flat, with rolling hills, scrub, and the occasional shallow *chaung*. The drawback was the dry belt also meant huge plumes of dust were thrown up by vehicles.

1st Burma Division had now made its way by rail from the Sittang Valley and arrived at Taungdwingyi at the end of March, before moving east to take the section of the line up to Minhla. Once the withdrawal from Prome was complete the new defensive line now ran from Minhla on the western bank of the Irrawaddy River to Taungdwingyi. 7th Armoured Brigade was in the area around Thadodan, near Kokkogwa, in the centre of the new line with the 48th Brigade of 17th Indian Division. Reconnaissance patrols went as far as 15 miles south, and plans were made to act aggressively the moment a Japanese attack approached. When they did on the 11th April, 2RTR reinforced 48th Brigade, before counterattacking the Japanese incursions. There was fierce fighting, including the action involving Lance Corporal Umeo Tokita described earlier. Eventually, however, Japanese pressure told, and by the 14th April 1st Burma Division to the west was forced back, and the Japanese 214th Regiment advanced into the gap. By the 15th April they were 12 miles south of the Yenangyaung oilfields. On their way through the gap, they laid a roadblock north of Kokkogwa that 2RTR cleared. 2RTR was reassigned to 1st Burma Division at this stage to provide support, whilst the 7th Hussars remained with 48th Brigade of 17th Indian Division, who were to continue holding the area, despite incursions north of them.

Slim wanted to withdraw westwards to the Magwe area and attack the Japanese from the rear. 'There were many risks about this scheme' Slim recalled 'but the 17th Indian Division was still full of fight and quite pleased with itself over the Kokkogwa encounter'.[18] His request was refused; Alexander was conscious this could look like they were abandoning the Chinese to the east by leaving a gap between the two nations' armies that the Japanese could exploit. The compromise was for 2RTR and the 7th Hussars to make aggressive sweeps against Japanese columns moving north between them, but the former was still having to fight rearguard actions as 1st Burma Division withdrew. With the Chinese also retreating on the left in the Sittang Valley, 17th Indian Division was becoming increasingly exposed.

On the 16th April, the day after Slim ordered the Yenangyaung oilfield facilities destroyed, the decision was made to withdraw the 1st Burma Division with 2RTR north of the oilfields and across the Pin Chaung. 17th Indian Division with the 7th Hussars remained in the Taungdwingyi area. In April, still the dry season, the Pin Chaung was a wide, east-west river, and a mostly dry tributary of the Irrawaddy. Whilst making this move, they had to pass through the now burning oilfields that left a thick black pall of smoke over the whole area, and the pungent smell of burning oil. 2RTR was escorting 150 lorries of 1st Burma Division, with the rest of the division further south of Yenangyaung. At around 11:40pm, as half the leading squadron passed a particular point two miles north of the Pin Chaung, a mortar round hit one of the tanks, breaking one of the tracks. This was followed by a burst of machine gun fire that set a staff car ablaze. This lit the area up, making it impossible to rush the rest of the column through. The lesson of the Shwedaung roadblocks was that lorries would be too easy for short range attack with Molotov cocktails at night, and Burcorps could not afford to lose more vehicles.

The Japanese 214th Regiment had advanced during the same night and taken both Yenangyaung by surprise and sent its 3rd Battalion north of the Pin Chaung to lay the ambush. The 2nd Battalion also built a roadblock between the Pin Chaung and Yenangyaung. With the town itself reinforced by the 1st Battalion brought in by river, 1st Burma Division's retreat was cut off. The BFF, part of the 1st Burma Division, tried to clear the roadblock north of Pin Chaung in the night. The rest of the division fought its way north, and by the evening set up a perimeter camp east of Yenangyaung at the village of Twingon. At the same time the Japanese 215th Regiment also arrived by river.

The situation was critical. Like at Taukkyan and Shwedaung, another disaster appeared to be at hand. 1st Burma Division, its weakened infantry, and vulnerable administration units, was now split into three groups. There was a very real risk that each group would be defeated in turn by two very confident Japanese regiments, who had chased Burcorps all the way up the

Irrawaddy valley. 7th Armoured Brigade HQ, half of B Squadron of 2RTR and a battalion of infantry were north of the Japanese roadblock above the Pin Chaung. The other half of B Squadron and C Squadron was with the BFF and some lorries between the roadblock and Pin Chaung. Lastly, the rest of 1st Burma Division and A Squadron, 2RTR was surrounded at Twingon, south of the Pin Chaung.

Under these circumstances, Alexander was able to obtain the services of the Chinese 38th Division under the American-accented English-speaking General Sun Li-Jen. They were part of the 66th Army that had been in reserve near Mandalay. The division had a good reputation for being brave and tough soldiers, although they were essentially an infantry-only outfit. Slim was in negotiations with General Sun, and to win his trust he decided to assign some artillery and tanks with the specific phrase 'under command of', rather than 'in support of' his division.[19] 'The long-suffering Brigadier Anstice, commanding 7th Armoured Brigade, threw me the look of a wounded sambhur* … [but] he and Sun got on famously'.[20]

Meanwhile, a breakout attempt was made by the C Squadron of 2RTR group in the central encirclement south of the Pin Chaung. At 8am artillery opened fire, briefly including 3.7-inch anti-aircraft guns in a direct fire role from what was basically point-blank range. The half of B Squadron to the north with a battalion of infantry attacked from the north, whilst C Squadron and the rest of B Squadron, and the transport vehicles, attacked from the south. Some of these tanks carried wounded on the engine decks behind the turret. The Japanese opened fire from a ridge to the east, and the transport panicked; many of the drivers now abandoned them. The tanks led the remains to safety. By the afternoon, the first Chinese units were arriving. There were now only two groups; B and C Squadron 2RTR had reunited, with what remained of their charges, north of the Pin Chaung.

---

* Sambhur or sambar is a deer native to southern Asia.

A Squadron and 1st Burma Division were still in their encirclement near Twingon.

The following morning, 18th April, the 38th Division with C Squadron would cross the Pin Chaung and try to extricate 1st Burma Division. After the Chinese failed to get into position on time, the attack began late. They did, however, fight well under the support provided by Slim, and managed to clear the area up to the north bank of the *chaung* but could not get across. The tanks risked getting bogged in the soft sand in the dried riverbed, so the attack was called off in the afternoon. There were heavy casualties in the Chinese infantry, especially amongst officers, who were expected to lead from the front. The disappointed, tired, and increasingly desperate Major-General Bruce Scott commanding 1st Burma Division asked Slim if his trapped troops could destroy their tanks and vehicles and make their way out in small groups in the cover of night.

The exhaustion amongst the British, Indian, Gurkha, and Burmese troops on either side of the Pin Chaung meant a lot rested on the Chinese troops to force their way through. This was not a relaxing prospect. As Slim put it 'time meant nothing to them [Chinese troops]. No plan based on accurate timing had a hope of success. Whether it was attacking the enemy or coming to dinner, eight o'clock might mean four, or just as likely, twelve'.[21] When Scott made his request, Slim was sitting in the back of one of 7th Armoured Brigade's radio lorries – the one link between the trapped men, and their only hope. April is the hottest month of the year; and many soldiers were suffering from heat exhaustion. In the back of this sweaty lorry, Slim could see the young radio operator's nervous face, waiting to hear his answer. Slim denied Bruce: they should hold their position until rescued.

"All right, we'll hang on and we'll do our best in the morning, but, for God's sake, Bill, make those Chinese attack".[22]

13th Indian Infantry Brigade in the Twingon perimeter led the attempted break out to the north, whilst the Chinese 38th Division attacked across the Pin Chaung to meet them. B Squadron of 2RTR was given the task, but again the Chinese delayed their own advance until 2pm. B Squadron decided to make their attack with A Company of the West Yorks anyway, and the Essex Yeomanry providing support. They crossed the *chaung* and cleared the southern edge before fighting off an infantry counterattack. C Squadron and the West Yorks were then wrongly diverted to reinforce Kyaukpadaung 30 miles north, which was thought to be threatened – it was not. B Squadron was therefore left on their own on the wrong side of the *chaung*.

During the last three days, the A Squadron tanks near Twingon had been helping 1st Burma Division fight off Japanese attacks on the perimeter, foreshadowing the Battle of the Admin Box in 1944. Japanese infantry closed to within yards of the tanks at times, and the commanders occasionally reverted to using their revolvers. They had supported a number of units in the perimeter at times in various positions. One of their most important contributions, however, was finding a diversion that appeared passable to wheeled vehicles around the Japanese roadblocks and across the Pin Chaung further east.

A Squadron led the breakout at 2pm, taking the transport elements first, to be followed by the perimeter units last. The tank at the head of the column was hit by mortar fire and brewed up, followed by some wheeled vehicles after they got bogged in the ground. 1st Burma Division abandoned the wheeled vehicles and made their way out on foot. They had to leave their artillery behind too, but not before spiking them. They had lost 1,000 casualties taking another heavy hit to morale as they trudged across the Pin Chaung. As they did so, they finally heard the Chinese attack go in at 3pm, linking up with B Squadron on the southern side, before driving into

Yenangyaung and withdrawing the following day as the Japanese counterattacked. They did manage to release some prisoners from Japanese hands in the process though. The Chinese assault with 2RTR, while late, did allow 1st Burma Division the breathing space for their fighting troops to break contact and completely escape their encirclement. They had held the Japanese back so they could not properly interfere.

C Squadron, 2RTR, was historically placed under General Sun: the first time British troops were under Chinese command. This was done so 38th Division could cover the withdrawal of the battered 1st Burma Division as its retreat north continued towards the transport hub of Meiktila. They performed patrols and acted as rearguard until the 26th April when, in a touching moment, the impoverished Chinese troops had whipped round to give one rupee to each of the 85 men in the squadron.

Throughout the fighting in the shadow of the burning oilfields at Yenangyaung, the 7th Hussars and 17th Indian Division were generally left unmolested at Taungwingyi. Poor intelligence and a lack of available infantry after the 17th Indian Division's mauling earlier in the retreat meant an opportunity to strike the Japanese 33rd Division in the rear could not be taken up. Chinese resistance in the Sittang Valley and Shan States was collapsing, however, allowing the Japanese advance to pick up speed. They soon threatened Meiktila and the communications of Burcorps retreating up the Irrawaddy valley. By the 22nd April the 7th Hussars and 17th Indian Division had been pulled back. 7th Armoured Brigade was together again just north of Meiktila. With the loss of Rangoon, the Yenangyaung oilfields, and the rapidly deteriorating situation on the eastern flank, it was clear that Burma could not be held.

The retreat had to be brought to a successful conclusion by saving the troops in Burma. In the final week of April the 7th

Hussars fought a series of delaying actions from Meiktila to Mandalay, counterattacking Japanese advances to give enough time for bridges to be blown, before retreating themselves on the 30th. On the 26th April Lieutenant Toshiro Matsumura of 112th Regiment, 55th Division, was advancing north in a column of lorries. 'Suddenly several British tanks came from our front right'.[23] It was A Squadron, 7th Hussars. 'As we were jumping off the lorries the tank guns started firing'.[24] Matsamura and men up and down the column scrambled for cover in a roadside ditch. A lorry carrying fuel erupted as petrol drums were ignited by tracer. 'As we had no anti-tank weapons, we could do nothing to combat the tanks…I was afraid if the tanks came forward, crossed the road, and encircled us, my platoon would all be killed. We were in an immense plain and there was no shelter nearby'.[25] Fear gripped Matsumura while he looked on impotently as the tanks methodically shelled the now abandoned lorries along the road, before moving off and attacking the rest of the column further south. The 7th Armoured Brigade war diary estimated 150 Japanese dead, 12 lorries and one artillery piece destroyed. At moments like this, as much of Burcorps was exhausted, at breaking point, and gathering at Mandalay to cross over the only bridge at Ava, delaying actions like this were crucial. The lack of effective AT weapons amongst Japanese infantry in particular allowed tanks to buy enough time for Burcorps to get away safely, and to avoid another Sittang Bridge disaster. Burcorps successfully retreated across the Irrawaddy via the Ava Bridge south of Mandalay, which was blown shortly after.

To the west, the Japanese 33rd Division had raced north from Yenangyaung to Monywa on the Chindwin River, hoping to block the retreat over the last major obstacle before India. To the east, the 6th and 66th Chinese armies were chased north and east into China, whilst the men of Burcorps and Chinese 5th Army contemplated their final moves. The Chinese 5th Army decided to head north by train to China. The loss of Monywa, however, meant Alexander had to change his plans, and head for the Shwegyin-Kalewa crossing of the Chindwin before making their way into northeast India. 7th Armoured Brigade moved to nearby Ye-U overnight 1/2nd May.

The final withdrawal arrangements were being made, whilst the Japanese considered whether to strike north to Kalewa overland or along the Chindwin River. The terrain changed as they approached the Chindwin Valley, where jungle began to encroach on the roads again. 7th Armoured Brigade helped ferry troops who had attempted to recapture Monywa back to Ye-U, before Burcorps moved west again towards Kalewa. One tank of B Squadron, commanded by Alan Barber, was given the task of racing ahead and seeing whether it was possible to find a route to get the tanks back to Imphal.

When Barber reached Shwegyin, the eastern side of the crossing, a special raft had to be made to get his tank across the river. The Royal Engineers found some pontoons and 'in three days, the raft was ready to be tested'.[26] After six hours testing, fixing, then loading the tank, they got going. Just as they reached the shore at Kalewa, however, the raft began to split. 'We were unceremoniously dropped in the water and sunk, but traction on the riverbed was good so we finally emerged and climbed up the riverbank'.[27] It had been a near miss. But Barber had to continue his mission, the rafts for rescuing the rest of the tanks was a worry for the sappers[*].

There was another near miss further down the road to Imphal. Barber had to persuade some sappers to reinforce a weak bridge that was only just wide enough for his Stuart. The bridge creaked as they inched across, and barely survived the 13-ton ordeal. The gorges in the area were incredibly steep, and the tank kept overheating as it climbed. They would wait a few hours and go again until the next overheating episode. What was clear

---

[*] Royal Engineer rank equivalent to private in the British Army, and a nickname for members of that corps.

was that evacuating the tanks along with the rest of Burcorps, refugees, and other vehicles would be at best an ordeal, or at worst, impossible. By the end of May they reached Imphal. 'The next step was quite clear: to wireless back to HQ and tell them that there was no way out'.[28] By the time they made this call, the situation had changed again.

Barber's tank's war was not over, however. At some stage it was claimed by HQ of 7th Light Cavalry and re-crossed the Chindwin in December 1944. Named 'Curse of Scotland' it returned to Burma during the 1945 reconquest as part of the 254th Indian Tank Brigade. Alan Barber, who emigrated to New South Wales, Australia, after the war, described it as a 'Burmarang'.[29]

As Burcorps retreated towards Shwegyin, the Royal Engineers, local tea plantation labourers and even elephants had improved the road significantly to allow such a large force to pass through this isolated rural area. With few passing places, the road became increasingly congested by the mixture of wheeled vehicles, refugees and soldiers on foot, animal transport, and tanks, as Burcorps converged on the tiny village. Many vehicles were on their last legs and were abandoned. Tragically, there were more and more dead refugees lying at the roadsides, exhausted from the march, and having caught diseases like malaria, typhus, and cholera from the weeks of unsanitary conditions, and lack of clean water in the hottest part of the year. Evacuation of refugees and the wounded began first before the fighting formations were brought out, mostly at night because of air attacks in the day. By the 7th May it was clear the lack of suitable rafts meant progress was slow for vehicles, about 24 per night. It became obvious that the tanks would have to be abandoned.

The Japanese 33rd Division smelled blood. There was still a chance they could destroy Burcorps before it crossed the Chindwin and make it safely to India. Perhaps hoping to claim the glory, Sakurai personally commanded the thrust up the Chindwin to Shwegyin, with his divisional HQ, 213th Regiment, and some artillery, with some of the force on boats, the rest on foot. They managed to advance undetected until they reached Shwegyin from the south on the evening of the 9th May, before attacking the outposts on cliffs overlooking the river basin being used for embarkation on the morning of the 10th. They set up snipers, machine guns, mountain guns, and mortars and fired on the evacuation.

A mixed force of tanks from the 7th Hussars, 2RTR, and the Gurkhas cleared the approach roads and cliffs of snipers and obvious targets, but some slipped away. What firepower could be brought up was used, 40mm Bofors anti-aircraft guns, 25 pounders, and mortars firing off their last rounds before embarking in the ferries themselves. By nightfall, the force withdrew, it being clear that this crossing point was no longer useable. Burcorps would move a few miles north to Kaing, opposite Kalewa for a short crossing but with fewer embarkation facilities. This sealed the fate of 7th Armoured Brigade's tanks. They would have to be left behind. Slim gave the order: Burcorps would destroy all remaining vehicles east of the Chindwin.

Just north of Shwegyin was a scene of utter desolation as the final destruction of Burcorps' vehicles took place. One squadron lined up its tanks nose to tail and fed a chain of petrol soaked rags between them before setting them ablaze. Others had their oil drained and ran the engines until they seized up, wiring was ripped out, radios and optics smashed, guns disassembled, the parts scattered and buried, and sledgehammers used to dent and bend gun barrels. Running the engines with no oil took longer than the men expected, another sign of the reliability of the tanks. They did not want to die. The men were understandably disappointed, even depressed by the need to destroy their Stuarts. The little tanks had brought them so far, endured so much, and saved numerous infantry units, even the army HQ at

Taukkyan, from destruction. They had reliably provided the army in Burma with the firepower from an almost impregnable platform for nearly a thousand miles as they retreated from the city of Rangoon to the tiny village of Kaing, on the banks of the Chindwin, and in sight of the safety of India. Slim reflected on the tanks left behind: 'True, they were worn out and, in any case, obsolete, but even they would be hard to replace in India, and they held such sentimental place in our esteem for what we owed to them and their crews that it was like abandoning old and trusted friends to leave them behind'.[30]

The men laid out their personal kit, decided on what cherished items they could carry, what was expendable was thrown into the fires of the tanks. The men took their kit and personal weapons, then began to trudge up the steep hills to the crossing to Kalewa. The Japanese did not follow up, or try to interfere, themselves exhausted. By nightfall on the 11th May, the evacuation across the Chindwin was complete, and the final march to Imphal began. They were just in time; the monsoon would break on the 18th May. The men soon became foot sore, as tank men they were not used to marching long distances. Transport was eventually organised, including the drivers from their own B echelon who had evacuated earlier, and now supplemented the transport companies sent forward to pick them up along the route. They bounced the final 45 miles to Imphal over roads on hillsides that would become battlefields in the spring and summer of 1944. 7th Armoured Brigade would not fight in these battles. They were soon sent back to the Middle East.

Wavell, and Alexander both agreed on the value of 7th Armoured Brigade. Wavell reported 'from their arrival in Burma in the third week of February till the end of the campaign, [they] formed the mainstay of the Burma Army and kept up a high standard of morale and efficiency'.[31]

Alexander summed it up best: "Without the 7th Armoured Brigade we should not have got the army out of Burma".[32]

5
Laying the Foundations

James Howard Williams set up his camp at Moreh, India, just a couple of miles over the border from Tamu, Burma. It was November 1942, the monsoon had not long ended, and preparations were being made for the Indian Army to return to Burma at some point in the future. Tamu was one of the places where refugees from the retreat earlier that year had abandoned their vehicles, many of them civilian cars. Williams had seen some of them discarded himself when he walked out of Burma earlier that year. What he saw now came as a shock. Many starving or diseased refugees at the end of the retreat, and the end of their endurance, had used the vehicles for shelter. 'Grisly figures, unbelievably emaciated, with rags still clinging to them here and there. Some sat rigid in the seats, some were tumbled into shapeless heaps, some were bent, some bowed, some sat behind steering-wheels, gazing through the windscreens from empty eye-sockets'.[1] The gruesome reminder of the human cost for mostly Indian civilian refugees who fled Burma from the Japanese were cremated in the vehicles.

Williams had not had to abandon any vehicles during the retreat. He had brought a precious piece of equipment that didn't need roads but would be valuable in getting new ones made for a return to Burma. Williams was a 44-year-old First World War veteran, having fought with the Devonshire Regiment in the Middle East, then the Camel Corps. After the war he moved to Burma and became a teak forester, where he learned how to use elephants as part of the lumbering process. Inevitably, Williams was nicknamed Elephant Bill.

Williams was in Tamu with his elephants to help improve the road. A sapper officer had come to see him asking for help dragging some logs for a bridge. Williams went with the officer and saw the overcomplicated designs for his new bridge. The plan would not do. Williams drew a new plan, made some calculations, and said he could have it ready in fifteen days.

"What class will it be, and what width?"

"First class" replied Williams, "and twelve foot wide".[2]

First class wasn't the reply the officer was after. The class reflected the tons a bridge could carry, not the quality. After some back and forth, the officer drove away to check if Williams's plan was acceptable to his superiors. Williams did not wait, he had harnesses made for twenty-five elephants to work at once. Before they began building, formal permission came through to build two twelve-feet wide bridges, to ensure two directions for travel, each capable of holding twenty tons. In thirteen days, his elephants had finished.

Whilst Williams fought constantly over the exact role of his elephants – were they pack animals or sappers? – they would prove their worth. Over the following years, they would be one part of a wider story of engineering feats that provided the logistical arteries for the reconquest of Burma.

But that was still a long way down the road.

The war in Burma was primarily a war of logistics. The sheer geographical challenge posed by the country is one of the most important aspects of the war in Burma. The country is massive and varied. Littoral jungle hills in Arakan, steep-sided jungle valleys in the Chin Hills that divide India and Burma, numerous rivers, both large and small. All of this had to be conquered if supplies were going to make it to the front. Probably the most famous aspect of the logistical work was aerial resupply, and rightly so. This took time, and political wrangling, to be set up, and without it the defensive then offensive campaigns from 1944 to 1945 would not have been possible. What is so often left out of that story, though, is the fact the airfields that handled those supplies were fed primarily by road in some way, and the really heavy equipment had to be taken forward by road. Most obviously, tanks.

So, in 1942 and into 1943, the roads would need to be improved, or built from scratch, alongside railways and pipelines. This didn't just mean Burma either, but also the north-eastern states of India, Bengal, Manipur, and Assam. Bengal contained the major port of Calcutta[*], and Manipur and Assam bordered Burma, and were in effect part of the front line. 1942 saw huge roadbuilding throughout the area. The Assam trunk road was only metalled for 59 of its 500 miles, without a single bridge capable of carrying more than 4 tons. By 1943 it was able to take heavy traffic for its whole length, using more than one million tons of stone. The key part of this road was the 340 mile stretch up the Brahmaputra Valley that fed Dimapur, a tiny village selected to be the supply base for the campaign. Through 1942 it was hacked out of the jungle and grew to be 58 square miles and was connected by rail as well as road. The next series of roads had a key vulnerability that will be seen later: they ran parallel to what amounted to a front line in the Chin Hills to the east. From the rail- and road-head at Dimapur, a 134-mile single-track road then went forward to the village of Kohima that involved a 4,000-foot climb into the mountains. The road continued to drop down to 2,500 feet above sea level at Imphal. Here was the final large logistical hub before the front. The height changes were significant: the roads were built with winding switchbacks that were so tight drivers frequently could not see the edge as they turned. Accidents down the hillsides were common, especially in the early days of the expansion of the Indian Army, where driver training had been rushed. These

---

[*] Now Kolkata

accidents alongside breakdowns could cause significant delays on the narrow roads.

In a hot office in Delhi, David Atkins awaited his fate. A 23-year-old captain in the Royal Engineers who enjoyed life in the city but had found staff work was not necessarily his natural role. This is not because he was a fighting soldier, gung-ho, or anything like that. This was a man who probably should not put 'attention to detail' on an application. One mistake was not entirely his fault. He decided to move all of the atta, the flour used in chapatis, from eastern to western India because it would make it easier to ship on to Indian troops in the Middle East. When the war against Japan began, the sudden shift of emphasis meant the atta was in the wrong place. His other mistake was simply mathematical. A badly placed decimal point during the army's expansion meant, instead of ordering two million bottles of rum, he ordered twenty million. Nobby Knowles of The Buffs remembered the economy that came out of Atkins's mistake. 'A case of a dozen bottles would buy half a dozen tins of herring in tomato sauce, six to eight would buy a Jeep'.[3] Henslow also remembered: 'in those days we had rum galore. It was part of the rations, a sort of waterproofing agent issued liberally to help us survive the monsoon'[4].

Atkins was therefore posted to an operational unit. 'I bore him [the CO] no grudge for deciding I must go' Atkins remembered 'at the age of twenty-three I never really related the orders which went out from our small office to what was actually happening around India and further afield – I could not visualise their full effect'.[5] He was happy in the army administration in India, so was quite reluctant to go. His ability to speak Urdu, the common language of the Indian Army, unfortunately made him ideal for an operational role. Fewer officers were arriving in India having learned Urdu, and so Wavell had halted all promotions above captain for those who had not learned it. Atkins's sacking from his staff role meant he ended up being promoted and sent forward to raise and command 309th General Purposes Transport (GPT) Company. With that Atkins said his goodbyes on the 9th April 1942 and made his way to Jhansi.

After training the men on the north Indian plains, many of whom had never seen a road vehicle before then, they moved forward to Dimapur in the summer of 1942 – the height of the monsoon. The lack of hill training was a problem, as was the weakening effect of malaria on drivers, which grew to epidemic proportions. At one stage in late 1942, Atkins was the only man malaria-free in his company of 400 men. The roads were washed away multiple times during the monsoon, the surface broken, crumbling, and sinking. Thick mud was a constant problem. The poor roads meant it was easy for a wheel to dip into potholes, or over the edges of the surface, risking overturning the lorry, or worse, falling off the road entirely. When lorries went over the hillsides the drivers could often walk away unhurt if they gripped the steering wheel for dear life. One man who did not hold on went head-first through the windscreen, and the broken glass cut his throat – the only man killed in Atkins's unit whilst driving. This was despite 5% of his lorries going over the side. A greater risk was being crushed if the lorry turned over on the road. On one occasion, investigating a 30-lorry jam, Atkins saw one of his men under an overturned lorry. 'He lay quiet and still and uncomplaining, but fully conscious. No legs, arms or ribs were broken … I sent him up to the hospital at Kohima. When I called later in the day, he had died of a broken back'.[6] The road being a single track meant the convoy waiting in Kohima to come the opposite way was also delayed.

'Elephant Bill' Williams and his elephants often helped shift lorries that had stuck in the thick mud. During the monsoon of 1943 near Witok, south of Tamu, 'all along the road came urgent requests for help, and the elephants were pulling the army lorries out of the mud like champagne corks out of a bottle'.[7]

Sometimes lorries were lost or damaged when the drivers started their engines and tried to help the elephants: 'they found themselves and the lorry being taken for a fifty-yard stampede into the jungle, ending up with the lorry hitting a tree or overturning'.[8]

The planning and building of roads required significant cooperation between different groups to make sure supplies continued to flow to the front whilst the work was carried out. Nothing could be wasted because of the shortages in the Indian Army, so only roads that were definitely needed were built and maintained and had to be planned very carefully to avoid further wastage. The forward area roads in particular required manpower as it was so difficult to get heavy equipment forward, not that there were many bulldozers available. The roads were built and maintained whilst they were in use, meaning the workers had to have their supplies carried on the same road, on top of those going to soldiers in the forward areas. Perched along the roads these labour battalions were often from the tea plantations or Naga tribesmen, first brought in during the retreat earlier that year. Hourly they replaced 'corduroy' and repaired sections of road as best they could. Corduroy roads were made of logs laid lengthways, with logs then laid along the road-edge to hold them in place. They sank easily. 'It is slow work' noted John Henslow, 'felling, trimming and moving trunks down to the road and requires the felling of some 7000 trees for a mile of road'.[9] The lack of building materials for hard-surface roads led to the invention of 'bithess' – jute sacks coated in bitumen laid as a road surface. The materials were easily available in India, and repairing a section was quick and easy. For now, the roads would be made and maintained primarily by manual labour, with the brave drivers taking their lorries over these dangerous roads to get supplies forward. Eventually, these roads would need to carry tanks on their transporters.

The shortage of equipment was a pervasive problem in the Indian Army dating back to the lack of investment in the 1930s, and the demands of the war in North Africa. Culturally the Indian Army was distinct by both bottom-up learning, and adaptability. This was a by-product of the need for flexibility from junior leaders on lonely outposts on the Northwest Frontier. Young subalterns could find themselves in very difficult circumstances on their own. Training emphasised initiative, and experience only confirmed this. The senior officers running the Indian Army in the Second World War had been those young subalterns in the mountains of north-western India, allowing the culture to survive the expansion of the army.

This culture combined to help alleviate the problems of shortages. This problem was not just because Burma was a low priority, although that was one of the biggest issues, but also one of bureaucracy in the early part of the war. The Indian Supply Department would receive an order and assign it to industry in the country. If the item could not be built in India, and for the heaviest equipment this was almost always the case, it would have to come from Britain, the Empire, or the USA. With the convoy system, Burma's low priority compared to other theatres, and the closure of the Mediterranean Sea, orders in 1942 could take fifteen months to arrive. Malcolm Connolly was a twenty-year-old trooper in the 26th Hussars, a unit newly raised in India in June 1941. In December 1942 he was assigned to the RAC Dock Ferrying Party in Bombay and could see the variety of supplies and equipment arriving. 'Unfortunately, hardly any of it was being supplied to the regiments based in India; the subcontinent was being used as the supply base for the Middle East. Stores came from all parts, America, the United Kingdom, Australia, and New Zealand, serviced and reloaded to be transported ... to the Eighth Army'.[10] Connolly noted the type of equipment that did end up with the Indian Army: 'The tanks arriving were mostly Shermans, Lees, Grants, and Stuarts. Very few Shermans stayed in India but most of the outdated Lees and

Grants were left and were sent to equip the Royal and Indian Armoured Corps'.[11] Connolly was disappointed they were not getting the newest toys. He would, however, soon be grateful to have the versatile Lee/Grants.

The standardised designs of US vehicles that started to flow into India was extremely helpful. They were reliable, not least due to the USA's huge automotive industry having built up a level of expertise that Japan could not match. In 1937 the USA built 4.8 million vehicles, Japan 26,000. No wonder the Stuarts of 7th Armoured Brigade, and the Lee/Grants and Shermans to follow were able to just keep going. Atkins's GPT company had received older 3-ton Ford lorries hastily built under license in Canada, and found they were inadequate compared to the USA built Chevrolets most other units used. The Fords had 'poor engines and bad fuel systems. They were not nearly as easy to drive as the long-bonneted Chevrolets'.[12] The steep switchback roads on much of the Line of Communication (LoC) meant the major problem with the Fords was the position of the front wheels directly under the cab. 'They were real pigs. The weight was half on the front wheels and so the steering was very heavy indeed'.[13]

The majority of equipment did come from US factories though. In June 1943 there were 1,400 British-made lorries waiting for spare parts and trained mechanics. The arrival of US lorries meant the British ones were simply abandoned. The USA standardised components on the design of lorries and tanks that allowed for interchangeable parts. This increased the speed at which vehicles could be repaired and limited the amount of space required by carrying fewer parts. Consequently, tanks, their maintenance echelon, and LoC supply vehicles could all be back in action fast if there were problems. With shortages in such an unforgiving country as Burma this was crucial.

The other major shortage in the early part of the Burma Campaign was with trained drivers, mechanics, and instructors.

Henslow had a frightening journey to a new unit, the 59th Independent Field Company, that illustrates the early training of Indian Army drivers. His new company was building the road between Palel and Tamu, southeast of Imphal. Henslow felt he was lucky he made the journey at night when he could not see the precipitous drop from the earth track. 'The driver negotiated all bends with a wild abandon and no thought that a vehicle could be coming from the opposite way round the bends … later the driver confessed to me that he had done a crash course in conversion from bullock cart driver to MT* driver'.[14] The principles were not completely different: 'the accelerator was equivalent to your toe up the bullock's backside, the brake was the rope you had through its nose. Steering was the only thing you had to learn because at bullock pace the animal normally did this for you'.[15] This is not to say that the Indian Army struggled for drivers. After the initial rush to train recruits quickly, and methods were refined, the problems were resolved.

Roads were not the only bulk supply system, and shortages were a problem here too. Locomotives, rolling stock, and river fleets were diverted to the Middle East at the beginning of the war. When Japan invaded Malaya and then Burma, all of this had to be replaced. Locomotives in particular had to come from Britain, the river fleets rebuilt. Railways were improved or extended, especially the single-track metre-gauge railway used by the tea planters in Assam. Pipelines were built to serve new airfields that were also being built, especially for the 'Hump' airlift – the USA's solution to the loss of the Burma Road.

The scale of the operation to lay the foundations for reconquest of Burma cannot be overstated. North-eastern India was modernising slowly, it was never expected to become the logistical base of a long-term campaign to retake Burma. In these early days of the war immediately after the retreat, lessons were learned, and new methods developed using what was available. There was a whole new logistical system that would eventually get armour to the front, and keep it there in working order against all the odds.

---
*Motor Transport

Arakan: Lessons Learned 101

Cox's Bazaar

Sinzweya (Admin Box)

Razabil Buthidaung

Mayu Peninsula

Donbaik

AKYAB ISLAND

First Arakan 1943 →

Second Arakan & Battle of the Admin Box 1944 →

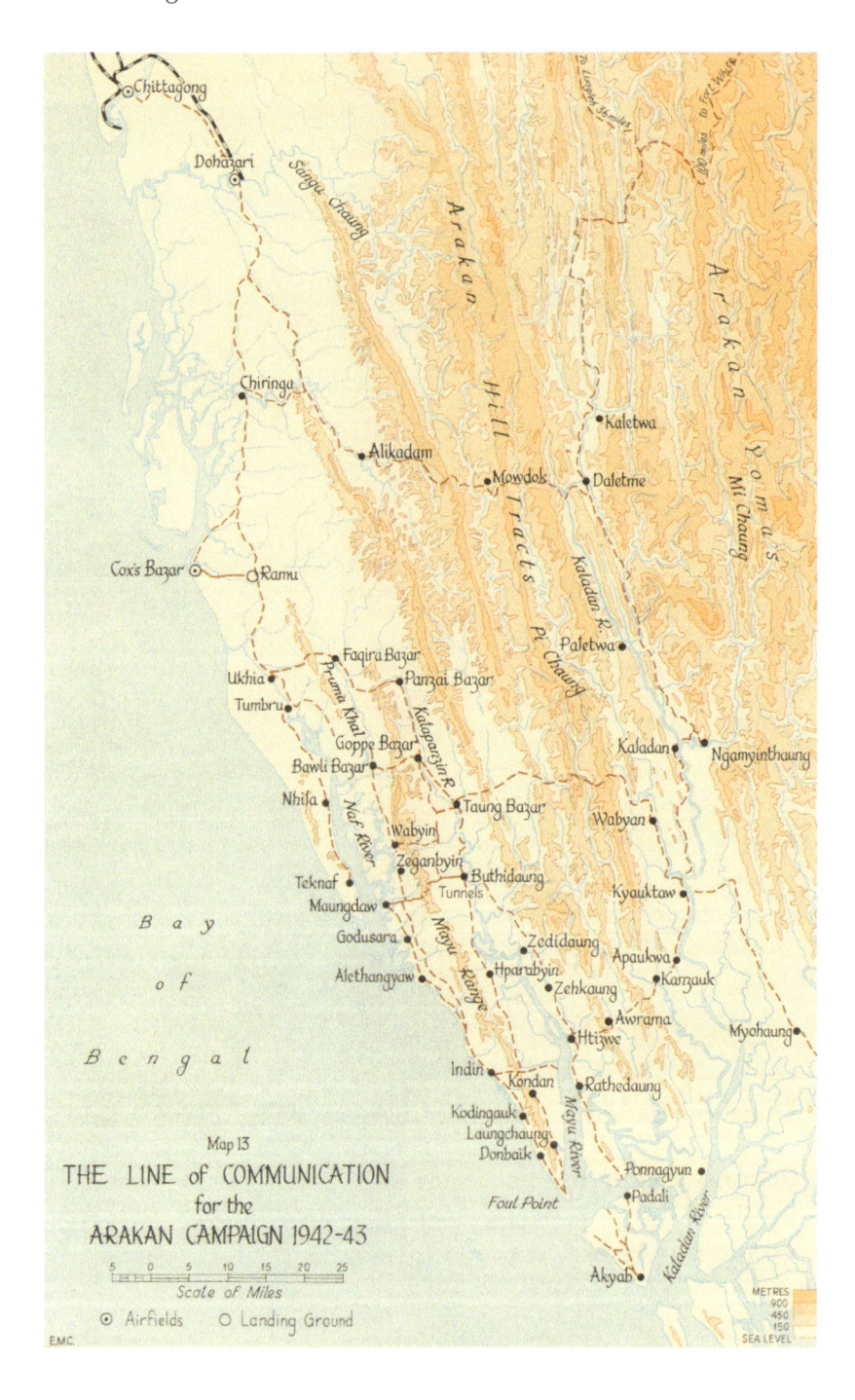

Map 13
THE LINE of COMMUNICATION
for the
ARAKAN CAMPAIGN 1942-43

6
Arakan: Lessons Learned

The Arakan operations had one specific goal at their heart. Opposite the bottom of the Mayu Peninsula is Akyab Island, with its airfield and small port. Control of the island meant the possibility of bombing Rangoon, 330 miles away. Later in the war, its value would be as a supply hub for aerial resupply missions during the latter stages of the 1945 reconquest. In 1943, however, the lack of shipping for the obvious solution, an amphibious operation, meant the only way was to fight down the Mayu Peninsula, and hop across the Mayu estuary.

The Mayu Peninsula stretches for 90 miles down the Arakan coast, with a steep line of 2,000 foot tall thickly jungled mountains, the Mayu Range, dividing the western coastal side, with the eastern Mayu River side. The coastal side is narrower than the river side, at its widest it is only two miles. The land was either mangrove swamp or rice paddy with the earth bunds that so troubled 7th Armoured Brigade. Streaming down the mountains were *chaungs* into the sea, each one a natural barrier to an advancing army. Their proximity to the sea meant they were also tidal. Almost all of the roads were fair weather, and in monsoon they were swamped. Consequently, communication with Arakan in peacetime was usually by sea.

The Arakan was in many respects, a terrible place for the Eastern Army* to return to offensive operations. Originally the plan was to have one thrust on central Burma to Mandalay, as well as amphibious landings down the Arakan. A lack of manpower soon put paid to that. Instead, the hope was a limited operation against a weakly held Mayu Peninsula that would end

---
*The name given for forces in eastern India and Burma from April 1942.

with the capture of Akyab Island; a tonic for the morale issues hanging over the army since the retreat. The problem was many of the issues Hutton had experienced in 1942 had not gone away. The troops assigned to the task were the two understrength, under-equipped, and untrained 14th and 28th Indian Infantry Divisions in XV Corps. They had been raised with the intention of fighting in the Middle East, and what training and equipment they had was therefore wrong for jungle operations. Slim, as the corps commander in this corps sized offensive, suggested using one division to advance overland, the other to make short-range amphibious landings in the Japanese rear.

Inauspiciously, the new army commander, Lieutenant-General Noel Irwin, came in and immediately stamped his authority. For the coming offensive he placed himself in charge of the operation, leaving his corps commander, Slim, to train troops in India. He disliked Slim partly because he had sacked a friend of his in 1940, but also due to the snobbery some British Army officers showed towards Indian Army officers. Decorated in the First World War, Irwin was a fighting soldier, and a strict adherent to the chain of command that bordered on sycophancy. He was a difficult man to be subordinated to, aggressive, vain, and incapable of considering other peoples' views. Therefore, when he needed to adapt, he struggled, as it would suggest that he had got something wrong. He ignored Slim's original plan and decided on a straightforward overland advance and built a supply road as they went. Building this road would end up slowing the offensive and allowed the Japanese to reinforce their positions in Arakan, and especially the Mayu Peninsular. The key position they reinforced on the coastal side was a small village on a tidal *chaung* called Donbaik.

Just a single company of the Japanese 213th Regiment occupied the position at Donbaik, where they had built a complex of seven bunkers overlooking the *chaung* north of the village. The *chaung* itself was like a natural tank obstacle, nine feet deep and steep sided. Japanese bunkers were about five feet deep, supported and roofed by logs, with earth packed tightly around the sides. The roof was covered with another layer of about five feet of earth, and then the whole bunker was heavily camouflaged. If built on hills, some of which were in the jungle to the east of the *chaung*, they could be located on reverse slopes to make it harder to spot and for artillery to target them. The complexes were built in sight of each other to provide support and were capable of withstanding their own artillery and mortars being fired on them. They were incredibly sturdy, and manned by well-motivated soldiers who would fight fanatically.

Irwin, and the 14th Indian Division's commander Major-General Lloyd tasked to take the Mayu Peninsula, approached the battle as though it was a First World War operation. Thoroughly planned artillery bombardments followed closely by an infantry assault. The bunkers could withstand the artillery, and so the infantry assaults throughout the fighting from January to March were repulsed with heavy casualties. Irwin put Lloyd under considerable pressure to clear the peninsula quickly, despite his own lack of haste in the initial advance into Arakan in December before many of these defences were built. This pressure explains the repeated attacks. They did not vary their tactics either despite the failure to break through, assuming simply increasing the numbers of men in the advance and increasing firepower would make the difference. Crucially, they failed to deal with the two jungle-clad hills overlooking the *chaung*, North and South Knob, which contained bunkers and some artillery. After the first attacks failed on the 8th and 9th January, Irwin ordered Slim to send one troop of tanks forward to take part in an attack. Before they arrived, there was another failed attack on the 18th and 19th January. The tenacity of the massively outnumbered Japanese soldiers at Donbaik added to the myth from 1942 of "supermen" – morale plummeted.

Slim protested they needed an entire tank regiment, not a single troop, but was overruled on logistical grounds. In 1942 Slim circulated a memo that included: 'Tanks can be used in any country except swamp. In close country they must always have infantry *with* them to defend and reconnoitre for them… Whenever possible penny-packeting must be avoided. The more you use, the fewer you lose'.[1] Clearly Irwin hadn't got that memo.

Captain Da Costa commanded the detachment of two troops of C Squadron, 146th Regiment RAC, that arrived about nine miles north of Donbaik to help 14th Indian Division break through. Da Costa and the two troop leaders, Lieutenants Carey and Thornton, had arrived so late on the 31st January that their long walk to the front, in sticky heat, was completed mostly in darkness. The tanks were to destroy the bunkers they were assured were in the south bank of the *chaung*. Starting from the eastern end of the position, below the hills that were due to be cleared just before the attack by the 2/1st Punjab, then turn right along the *chaung* towards the sea and destroy Japanese bunkers one-by-one. A battalion of infantry from the 17th Dogras would then advance beyond the *chaung* with the tanks in a second phase. There was no chance for anything more than this quick look in darkness before the men went back to the tank harbour, arriving about 11pm.

The next morning, the tanks moved off at 10am, Lieutenant Thornton's troop of three Valentine infantry tanks, followed by Carey's troop, with Da Costa in a general support role. There was no sign of the Dogras, who it turned out were struggling in the jungle near the North Knob and were never able to join the attack. The tanks went in around 11am, and almost immediately things went wrong. The ground was far softer than expected, especially at the edge of the *chaung*. Thornton and his troop all fell victim to the soft ground on the bank and nosed into the *chaung* and were not seen again. The fourth tank, under Corporal Wedburn managed to avoid the same fate. They started firing their 2 pounder gun and machine guns into Japanese positions, but after the second round the main gun jammed. The range was so close the Japanese managed to shoot away Wedburn's radio aerial and damaged the smoke discharger. The tank quickly filled with smoke and obscured it and Thornton's troop from the other tanks. 'I spotted the troop commander going down the *nullah** as we turned to follow, I felt tank give a lift at the back. The engine was losing power and I smelt burning inside the engine'.[2] Trooper Cooke was driving the sixth tank, commanded by Carey, and saw Wedburn's tank get hit. 'Tank in front reversed back…when I felt what I thought was a landmine on offside of tank, but tank went on OK…After advancing a short distance I felt a bump and what sounded like broken glass'.[3] Cooke and Carey's tank had been hit by a 37mm AT gun. Sergeant Seago had seen 'two flashes from extreme right flank and fired at them. I was hit on the turret and went off'.[4] The shot jammed the turret ring, wounding Carey, and killing the gunner Trooper Ronald Bird.

The surviving five tanks moved down the *chaung* to escape the murderous fire: artillery, mortars, AT guns, and machine guns. They returned fire as best they could, but they struggled to identify targets, and watch for the unstable ground that had brought so much trouble for Thornton's troop. A number of guns had jammed in the troop, both 2pdrs and machine guns. Carey tried to organise a follow up attack, but 'had to be ordered back to Advanced Dressing Station, could barely talk'.[5] Some of the men thought they could hear the distinct sound of the Valentine's Besa machine guns firing from the *chaung*, perhaps one of Thornton's tanks was desperately fighting off Japanese attack. A follow up attack was organised under Da Costa around 5pm with support of the 1/7th Rajput but made virtually no

---

*Various Indian languages version of *chaung*

progress and pulled back under mortar and artillery fire. The attack had been nothing short of a disaster.

The after-action report described the three tanks and nine men of Thornton's troop as missing, plus four damaged, one working but in need of a new wireless. Only one tank was in full working order. In 1945, Carey managed to go back to Donbaik with the Grave Registration Unit. The three Valentines were still there, virtually intact. The second tank had fallen on top of Thornton's tank as they had slipped into the *chaung* with the third nearby. There were human remains near the tanks but only five were identifiable. All nine men from the troop were killed inside their tanks or as they bailed out.

Without proper reconnaissance and close infantry support the tanks could never hope to identify and clear the bunkers on their own. The officers on the ground were not sufficiently trained in cooperation tactics to consider that the plan did not constitute close support, with the Dogras attacking the hills first and then linking up with the tanks. This was not the fault of the tank men, or the Dogras, who attacked bravely in the kind of actions not entirely dissimilar to the Western Front in 1916. The system had failed them: they had not been provided with the knowledge to work together in tandem. The tanks and infantry essentially fought two separate actions independently on the 1st February, and both failed. The rushed reconnaissance meant the tanks did not know the ground they were operating on and did not fully understand the threat ahead of them. This led to Thornton's troop being lost falling stranded into the *chaung*, and others having to reverse off the soft sandy ground. Furthermore, Japanese AT guns were just good enough to immobilise in one way or another most of the tanks. The second in command of 1/15th Punjab Regiment, 14th Indian Division, Major John Prendergast noted 'Tanks were used in too small numbers…they can be picked off one by one. A large number of tanks keeps the anti-tank gunner looking several ways at once and by the time he has in his confusion ranged on one, another tank supporting it may see his flash and engage his weapon in a second, so that more tanks suffer less casualties'.[6]

The Valentines were not well suited to the theatre either, despite their strong armour. The 2 pounder gun lacked flexibility, only firing armour-piercing (AP), but not high-explosive (HE) shot. The crew was too small at three, and so the commander and gunner were overworked. Fighting in a tank in the Burma Campaign was horrifically complicated. Threats constantly emerged from anywhere from very close range with fanatical determination. Tank commanders in particular had it tough, often engaging enemy infantry with personal weapons, whilst helping to navigate and spot and engage targets. This was exacerbated in this particular battle as the tanks ran past Japanese positions at a right-angle, exposing their weaker side, with the commander and gunner engaging what targets they could see to their left. This left the driver, in a position lower down in the hull, to ensure they did not fall into obstacles. There were certainly lessons to be learned from the experience.

The offensive in Arakan stumbled into stalemate after further attacks up to March 1943. Irwin and even Wavell continued to blame their men for lacking determination, despite Irwin's operational limitations. He even tried to line up Slim as a scapegoat. As those machinations took place, and further attacks failed, Japanese reinforcements managed to advance through jungle considered impassable – a lesson not learned from 1942. They crossed the Mayu river on the night of 24th March, threatening to cut off 14th Indian Division at Donbaik. Another retreat to escape encirclement began, with the division's 47th Indian Infantry Brigade being cut off and effectively destroyed. Another long and disorderly retreat followed until May as XV Corps fell back on Cox's Bazaar, just over the border in India. The monsoon dissuaded the Japanese following up any further.

Irwin's attempts to blame Slim and sack him in the aftermath backfired. Irwin was sacked instead and replaced by Lieutenant-General George Giffard as commander of Eastern Army. Wavell was also kicked upstairs shortly after to become Viceroy of India, to be replaced in his role of Commander-in-Chief India by General Claude Auchinleck. In August, Southeast Asia Command (SEAC) was created with Vice-Admiral Lord Louis Mountbatten as its commander. He created 11th Army Group and promoted Giffard to command, allowing him to bring Slim into the army command. To finalise the break from past failings, they renamed it Fourteenth Army.

The fighting in Arakan in early 1943 acted as a catalyst for the Indian Army, especially after the failures at Donbaik. Slim and other senior officers had to lobby on behalf of the tank units to ensure their use was not written off. The impact of 7th Armoured Brigade when saving Burcorps outweighed this one disaster in Arakan. The Japanese 'superman' myth appeared entrenched in an army low on morale, the solution to poor morale in this case was training. The expansion of the Indian Army from 1938, and especially since 1940, had been rushed. Corners were cut, leading to soldiers arriving in Malaya, then Burma, undertrained. The training had focused solely on the Middle East, and equipment reflected this, mostly in regard to their wheeled logistical tail. When they faced a Japanese army that was better trained, and better led, morale suffered as each defeat stacked onto the last. There was a dire need to develop proper jungle training methods and the ability to cooperate with other arms effectively. Tank firepower had shown its value, cooperation had been the problem.

Thankfully, the Indian Army had a long tradition for lesson-learning. A very professional army, the culture imbued a sense of relentless introspection, that dovetailed with the make-do attitude discussed earlier. Brigadier Francis Tuker was Director of Military Training in 1940, who advocated for all-arms cooperation with whatever equipment the Indian Army was given. As far as Tuker was concerned, it was all well and good complaining that the Indian Army was the lowest priority for Britain, but that would not change the situation. Get on with it and make the best of what you do have. The problem was the rapid expansion of the Indian Army struggled to scale this up in the early days, and Tuker went on to command in the Middle East and Italy. His input would have been invaluable.

After the 1942 retreat, reports and debriefs on operations were generated haphazardly: they needed to be written, centrally approved, collated, and translated into realistic changes in training. The sheer pace of expansion limited the effectiveness of this process. As units submitted their reports on 1942, the administration simply could not handle the task, meaning there were no army-wide changes until the system of expansion was refined and had peaked. This did not take place until after the failures in Arakan, when GHQ India finally formalised the system of reporting and endorsed new training methods.

A key part of the lesson-learning ethos in the Indian Army was the production of training materials by individual formations. The British Army was far more centralised in this regard, specifically forbidding such a practice. Training pamphlets were created centrally and passed down. The Indian Army was historically spread over vast geographical areas, so individual units needed to be more self-sufficient, creating training materials was therefore completely normal. This allowed for bottom-up learning to take place, where the units could create training methods, and pass them up to share their ideas. These were frequently disseminated across the entire army. Even at a lower level, those with first-hand experience wrote pamphlets and sent them to their reinforcement depots to inform new recruits of new ideas before arriving at their unit. Robin Schlaefli had joined the army in the ranks but was later commissioned into the Indian Army and noted Indian soldiers' professionalism.

'I never failed to be amazed at the different attitude of the Indian to the learning process. Off duty...we [British soldiers] tended to put our feet up or play some sport...Not so in the Indian Army...men would be seen squatting on their haunches, books in their hands, eyes half closed, muttering to themselves...I discovered that the sacred volumes were actually Army Weapon Training Drill Manuals. These were being painstakingly learnt from cover to cover, word for word, by heart'.[7]

This does not necessarily mean learning a manual by heart translated into effective soldiering, although it surely cannot hurt, but it does reflect the culture of lesson-learning.

Research was carried out based on the experience of the Australian successes on the Kokoda Trail and at Milne Bay. One finding was that the Stuart's 37mm gun struggled to destroy Japanese bunkers encountered there, and that a larger gun would be needed. That would mean medium tanks. GHQ Indian collected, analysed, synthesised, and disseminated the most important lessons across thousands of miles, and multiple commands. Australian officers came to India between July and October 1943 and toured training bases sharing their experiences. British officers were seconded to Australian units and came back to India as instructors.

One problem was cooperation between the infantry and tanks. One of the main reasons for failure in Arakan, like the retreat in 1942, was the low quality of training in general, and especially of casualty replacements. Donbaik had been a low point for armoured cooperation, considering the efforts of 7th Armoured Brigade and the improvised nature of tank-infantry cooperation during the retreat. Training could be rudimentary for tank units in India. Gordon Heynes was posted to C Squadron, of the newly raised 25th Dragoons, in June 1943. In the early days there were no tanks, and they did a lot of drill and marching instead until 'news came through that we were going to receive our tanks, so the Squadron got down to training, using lorries as tanks we went out on manoeuvres'.[8] The shortages were still a problem.

Things did improve though. In July 1943, Slim appointed Lieutenant-Colonel 'Atte' Persse to train the 25th Dragoons for deployment in Arakan. He did so by 'making himself a nuisance to all and sundry until he got what he wanted'.[9] The 5th Indian Infantry Division rotated their three brigades on exercises in Bihar Province, an area similar to Arakan, with jungle covered hills, muddy roads, and few villages. They practised attacking a hill with air support and tanks. In Ranchi, John Leyin, also of the 25th Dragoons, noted the increasing intensity of training as 1943 wore on. They practised with the 37mm and 75mm guns of their new Lee tanks, and took them over a variety of terrains, practised establishing wireless communications, and formation driving. Malcolm Connolly now of the 3rd Carabiniers, also equipped with Lees, practised hill climbing in December 1943, looking ahead to the second attempt in cracking Arakan. They took their tanks up a 3:1 incline on a jungle covered hill up to 3,000 feet.

'I quickly discovered that to keep control I would have to stand up just to keep my foot on the accelerator pedal…[you had] to pull out the hand throttle to its fullest extent to ensure the engine would keep going even if the driver was to fall off his seat, this experience was nerve-wracking but one that before the end of the conflict we would become very accustomed to'.[10]

The training was getting more realistic, frequent, and the units involved equipped more practically for the frontline. The training was based on the specific lessons of 1942-43, jungle craft, cooperation with infantry, and bunker busting. Once the men were used to cooperation, and to jungle fighting in general, morale improved. Soon, battlefield results would improve dramatically too.

The final problem was how to destroy Japanese bunkers like those encountered at Donbaik. As was painfully clear, these were the key to pushing the Japanese back now that they were, for the time being, on the defensive. No.10 Operational Research Section arrived in India and set up a system of trials through November and December 1943. They constructed a bunker system near Delhi and tested infantry weapons, tanks, and artillery against them, using different ammunition and fuses. This was also done by the Armoured Fighting Vehicle School at Ahmednagar, and by the artillery at Deolali. The testing would continue into 1944 after the initial methods devised were tested in the Arakan in early 1944 and following the experience at Imphal and Kohima. Arthur Freer, also of 3rd Carabiniers, remembered practising with the 2/5th Gurkhas in December 1943:

'The procedure would be started by the infantry speaking on the tank intercom system from the newly fitted rear box, advising the tank commander when his men were ready at the sheltered side of the tank. The 75mm gunner would be ordered to fire three individual rounds of HE, followed by one round of AP – and then cease firing. Fire cover could then continue from the much higher mounted 37mm and co-ax Browning'.[11]

Infantry would then assault the bunker and clear it. This all sounded great on paper. These methods would, however, need to be tested in combat conditions.

A train of flatbeds wound its way across India to Calcutta, with large awkward shapes towered on top covered with tarpaulins. The men on the train wore a mixture of side caps and bush hats, and badges showing they were Royal Electrical and Mechanical Engineers (REME). These were the men and machines of the 25th Dragoons being moved forward under the tightest security for the new offensive in the Arakan. Their black berets swapped as too much of a giveaway to spies reporting to the Japanese. They were going into action in Burma for the first time, they waterproofed their Lee tanks, loaded onto American LCTs[*], and made their way lazily down the Hoogly river and into the Bay of Bengal. They were dropped off ten miles south of Cox's Bazaar at Elephant Point. They had timed their arrival perfectly; it was late evening, and there was a full moon, in a cloudless sky. 'Overhead were two of our bombers to hide the noise of our tanks' engines' remembered Gordon Heynes. 'When we reached the shore, we turned right and drove along for about 3 miles keeping to the edge of the sea so that the tide, which was coming in, would obliterate our tracks'.[12] They parked the tanks in the tree line to keep them invisible from the air.

Heynes was an older soldier when called up, 39 by January 1944, and was made part of the rear echelon for C Squadron, driving a lorry. When they received their orders, he was disappointed not to be posted to a tank crew. He told his squadron leader, Major Horne, about wanting to be in a tank. 'An hour afterwards the squadron leader came in and said "Heynes, you are going to be my gunner"'.[13] Heynes was to operate the 37mm gun in the turret of the Lee, rather than the 75mm in the hull sponson, but he had made it into a tank.

The 25th Dragoons had been moved in such secrecy to ensure that their deployment in Arakan would be a total surprise to the Japanese. The wider offensive for 1944 would involve Slim's XV Corps clearing Arakan to take Akyab Island, whilst US trained Chinese troops pushed south from Northern Burma. There would also be a second Chindit operation, and IV Corps would make a limited advance into Burma from Imphal. Unlike Arakan in 1943, this time whole divisions would advance down the river valleys towards Foul Point and Akyab Island. First the 5th Indian Infantry Division, with the 25th Dragoons attached,

---

[*] Landing Craft Tank.

would capture Razabil on the western side of the Mayu Range. The 25th Dragoons would then cross the mountains and support 7th Indian Division in their assault on Buthidaung on the eastern side of the range. This also allowed corps artillery and 224 Group RAF to be used to support each attack in turn for maximum impact.

This was a nervous time for many, even those with experience of combat. Clive Branson, another older soldier at 37, wrote letters home to his wife Noreen throughout his time in Burma. He was an artist, poet, writer, and communist, who helped recruit for the International Brigade, and later fought with them in the Spanish Civil War. He joined the RAC when he was called up and sent to India. On 16th January, he wrote 'in the main I worry about whether I shall command my tank as a communist ought. I only hope I shall do the job efficiently'.[14]

The village of Razabil in the foothills of the Mayu Range, east of Maungdaw, with the centre of the Japanese position built on and around a feature overlooking it codenamed 'Tortoise'. The whole complex was built over a series of hills and called 'Razabil Fortress'. Beyond this fortress were two old railway tunnels that gave quick access to the eastern side of the Mayu Range at Buthidaung. The bunker positions built on top of the Razabil ridgeline consisted of multiple strongpoints with interlocking fields of fire. They had them on both the forward and reverse slopes, with tunnels connecting them, well built, and well hidden in the thick undergrowth. Much like Donbaik, the infantry advance had been halted. It was time to unleash the 25th Dragoons.

John Leyin had also been posted to C Squadron and took part in a reconnaissance on Razabil. He was with a number of tank commanders in an observation post trying to locate the bunkers that would need to be destroyed. 'It was all very quiet and peaceful and the dismounted tank crews were engaged in pleasant conversation in a most relaxed atmosphere'.[15]

Unknown to Leyin, the Japanese were watching. Suddenly, shells were whining down, followed by six or seven explosions around them. The men dived for cover wherever they could find it, in ditches, under tanks, anywhere. Leyin found himself half under a lorry. 'With pounding hearts, we waited for the next salvo ... and with nerve-racking [sic] expectancy, still waited. But that salvo never came'.[16] There were no casualties, and none of the tanks were damaged, but as the men got back to their feet, they laughed nervously about their baptism of fire.

The attack on Razabil Fortress (Operation Jonathan) was to go in on the 26th January 1944 with the 4/7th Rajput, 161st Infantry Brigade. They were facing the Japanese 143rd Regiment of 55th Division. Branson in B Squadron, 25th Dragoons, saw the aerial bombardment that began the assault at 10am from distance. He described what he saw in a letter he wrote later that day: 'The bombers are just coming over - we climbed up on our tanks to have a grandstand view of 12 Liberators and dozens of Vengeance dive-bombers exterminating Jap positions at Razabil crossroads. Now that the bombers have gone there is a real barrage of small stuff. This may be the solution of the Burma problem'.[17] Branson's delight at the show belied the reality, he did not realise that the operation was not running smoothly.

The tanks and infantry were one thousand yards back from the objective to allow for the aerial bombardment. The air attack consisted of Vultee Vengence dive-bombers marking the target, followed by sixteen B-24 Liberator heavy bombers, twelve B-25 Mitchell medium bombers and another wave of Vengeances from 3rd Tactical Air Force (TAF). As they were moving into position, however, the dust kicked up by the tanks led to tragedy. One bomber mistook the dust for that coming off the previous bombers' attacks and was therefore the target. Heynes was in one of the tanks in the dust. 'We had three 2,000 pounders dropped across our track. There were terrific explosions and our tank rocked like a ship in a gale. The lid on the turret was open and as I looked up the air was black with earth and we heard shrapnel hitting the side of the tank'.[18] Three tanks were disabled, two tank commanders and four other ranks were wounded, and 22-year-old Trooper John Swinburn was killed.

The attack had to continue, and the tanks of the 25th Dragoons were soon too busy to think of the friendly fire incident. Japanese artillery responded 'the shells started falling near but no direct hit. Our 75mm guns opened up on positions where the guns were likely to be…I sat in the turret, with my eyes glued to the periscope, the landscape was spread before me with the ridge…pitted with bomb craters'.[19] The different troops moved to positions around the fortress and engaged various targets on the features. Some progress had been made, but the Japanese troops still managed to hold on to a number of key bunkers. Some of the main problems were that the Japanese would withdraw to the reverse side of the hills during any bombardment, then rush to reoccupy the forward position once the fire had lifted. They would then use their machine guns and roll grenades down the hillside onto the attacking infantry. For the following few days further attacks were tried, and the other squadrons joined the fray, with few decisive results. The tanks continued to engage some bunkers, or otherwise provide general covering fire, but could not create a breakthrough for the infantry to completely clear the position. '[We had to] machine [sic] the patches of jungle. This was kept up most of the afternoon and then the infantry moved forward but then found that the Japs were still there so had to retreat'.[20] This was part of the problem; Heynes was not given a real target, just a patch of jungle. By the 30th January the tanks were withdrawn to refit and rearm. The tanks were hardly damaged, and all returned, mostly requiring only basic repairs. The 25th Dragoons made their preparations to cross the Mayu Range at the Ngakyedauk Pass*, a road recently cut through the mountains for the purpose

---

* Nicknamed the Okey-doke Pass by British troops.

further north and provide support for 7th Indian Division's operations against Buthidaung and beyond.

Always looking to learn, Major Hugh Ley, the second in command of the 25th Dragoons, was at the forefront of the new methods for engaging the bunkers. They managed to continue to refine the system they had been training since the previous autumn even in theatre. The Razabil Fortress operation had shown that if they found Japanese bunkers they could cause considerable damage – a big if. On a number of the features the tanks were able to directly engage and destroy targets. Major Howell of Operational Research submitted his report on Razabil operations and stated 'tanks firing from the west on likely features had scored direct hits and knocked out some five or six bunkers, their roof timbers being scattered in all directions'.[21] The use of delayed action fuses on HE rounds had proven useful in destroying bunkers. If they could not identify targets, they provided enough cover to get infantry fifty yards from the bunkers. Unfortunately, this was still too far for infantry to attack sustainably uphill, with fire coming from in front and from other similar positions nearby. Communication by flags, radio, smoke, and tracer fire were all trialled with mixed results. The phones recently put on the back of the tanks were difficult for infantry to use because any men breaking cover towards a tank became a target for Japanese fire. The system clearly still needed work, but there had been good signs.

The urgency for refining the bunker busting methods became apparent by the failure of artillery and aerial bombardment. They could not complete the whole job, not least because of the fanaticism of Japanese resistance, and the strength of their bunkers. The fact was they did not reduce the will or ability to resist amongst Japanese soldiers. They were simply too inaccurate for a target so small, and even so only the heaviest artillery rounds and aerial bombs could destroy them with a direct hit anyway. Howell's report noted that if artillery was to provide the firepower to take these positions 'calculation shows that short of using huge tonnages of valuable ammunition the chances of success are very small'.[22] Bringing up that amount of ordinance to the artillery in particular would increase the pressure on an already strained logistical system. The combined bombardments also meant there was a gap of between fifteen and thirty minutes before the infantry were onto their objectives, who had to be held back to avoid friendly fire – and John Swinburn's fate showed even these distances were not truly safe. These supporting arms were then silent during the final assault, when the Japanese could reoccupy positions, or dust themselves down, and prepare to halt the infantry when it approached. The assaults were usually stopped around ten yards from their objective because of the enemy fire from the objective, and from other bunkers nearby. These would also need to be engaged in future assaults.

Out of this though, a system was developed, built on the accuracy of the tanks' 75mm guns. After reconnaissance of a target to try and locate as many bunkers as possible, artillery and aerial bombardment would now aim to clear vegetation in the area rather than supress the occupants. This would make the bunkers easier to spot before the artillery moved their fire to supress other bunkers on nearby features. Ley then drilled the 25th Dragoons in a method that would be shared across the entire Indian Army and would save innumerable lives. If needed, the tanks would clear any more vegetation with HE, then switch to AP to soften the earth around a bunker's loophole – a trick Ley had trialled on Razabil. They would switch back to HE with delayed action fuses, and using the Lee's 75mm gun's superb accuracy, fire directly through the loophole into the bunker, and hopefully blow it apart and kill the occupants. The 75mm's HE always burst forward because it was a direct fire weapon, whereas artillery HE dropped down with a wider spread in all directions when it exploded. This meant the infantry could confidently close to within ten yards of the bunker and give a prearranged signal. The tanks would switch back to AP and machine gun fire and continue firing to keep any survivor's heads down, only ceasing their fire as the infantry made the final assault with grenades, sub-machine guns, bayonets, and kukris.

For the same job artillery and AT guns would need to be manhandled into final positions, that tanks could simply drive to, and were far more vulnerable to defensive fire from the Japanese bunkers. Furthermore, as Howell's report maintained, bunker positions "do NOT constitute suitable targets for "softening". Instead, it is suggested that the preliminary bombardment by available air, artillery, and mortars be devoted solely to a systematic programme of... clearance of jungle hill crests to reveal positions...[and] areas from crossfire can be brought upon infantry'.[23]

Tanks were the ideal machine for the job, and the Lee/Grant tank in particular. With its large crew, multiple machine guns, and 37mm in the turret, it could provide protection from infantry tank hunters whilst the sponson mounted 75mm could engage in bunker busting. Howell's general conclusions confirmed his feelings unequivocally: 'There is, indeed, no other weapon whose deployment is likely to have such a decisive effect on the whole course of the war against JAPAN as a medium tank with a 75mm gun'.[24] In less than a year, the tank had gone from being a failure at Donbaik, to the most important weapon in the theatre.

Progress was steady, and momentum was slowly building for Slim. The next phase of Fourteenth Army and their Allies' operations was to continue the offensives across northern and central Burma, and Arakan. His opponents, Lieutenant-Generals Shōzō Sakurai of 28th Army and Renya Mutaguchi of 15th Army, had other ideas.

122 Forgotten Armour

(Left) 1. John Henslow shortly after the war in Bangkok, Thailand. The frustrated hero of the Irrawaddy Crossing, he bravely fought through the administrative jungle in Calcutta to get engine frames made for Bailey bridge tank rafts.

(Right) 2. Val ffrench Blake with two tiger cubs he adopted in India before the war. He was frustrated by slow modernisation, but served with distinction in North Africa until wounded.

3. Vickers Mk II Light Tank. The tanks the General Staff were given. Vickers were pressured to keep costs down; light tanks were cheap to produce, and attractive to foreign buyers. The Treasury and Vickers therefore prioritised these tanks over the desires of the General Staff.

Forgotten Armour 123

4. Vickers Mk II Medium Tank. The type of tank the General Staff wanted.

5. Carden Loyd Tankettes. Showed potential in the 1935 Mohmand Uprising but were completely outdated when they faced the Japanese in Malaya in 1941-2.

124 Forgotten Armour

6. *Tochi Scouts on piquet duty in the mountains of the Northwest Frontier. These mountains were the main theatre of operations for the Indian Army in the Interwar period, tanks showed some potential but poor technological investment slowed their development.*

7. *Miles Smeeton and his beloved wife Beryl. Miles commanded Probyn's Horse with great distinction and bravery through the reconquest of Burma. With Beryl, he had an entire lifetime of adventures both before and after the war.*

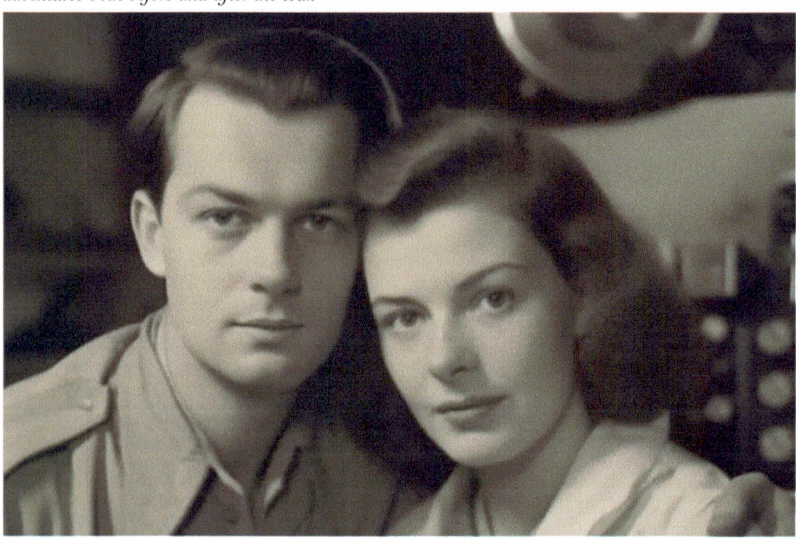

Forgotten Armour 125

8. An M3 Stuart of the 7th (Queen's Own) Hussars, 7th Armoured Brigade. These Stuarts would be the saviour of the retreating Burcorps. There were some emotional scenes when these saviours had to be destroyed on the banks of the Chindwin River.

9. An M3 Stuart from C Squadron, 2RTR, and its crew talking to Chinese soldiers of 38th Division at Chauk, in one of the oilfields north of the Yenangyaung. There was fierce fighting in intense heat at Yenangyaung, but the tanks of 2RTR brought the remnants of 1st Burma Division out of encirclement

126   Forgotten Armour

10. The first elephant bridge built for Fourteenth Army at Lokechao Creek. Elephants played an important role in maintaining supply roads, clearing trees, and building bridges.

11. Supply convoy on the Tiddim Track 1944, similar to those David Atkins and his GPT company used to run between Dimapur and Imphal.

Forgotten Armour 127

(Top left) 12. David Atkins shortly after his promotion to Major in 1942;
(Top right) 13. Clive Branson wrote to his wife throughout his time in India, and the fighting at Razabil, although never managed to write about his time at the Admin Box;
(Left) 14. Gordon Heynes, who fought through the Admin Box until wounded by a bomb dropped by a Zero;
(Bottom left) 15. John Leyin, who moved into a tank after the reshuffle that followed Cpl Howden's tank brewing up;
(Bottom right) 16. Tom Grounds, who saw Cpl Howden's tank get hit by a mortar bomb, and subsequent flash fire, during the Admin Box.

128 Forgotten Armour

17. *Reconnaissance photo of Razabil Fortress looking east towards the Mayu Range from Maungdaw. The 25th Dragoons would test new bunker busting methods, a major breakthrough in the war against Japan.*

18. *Australian photo of a Japanese bunker on Papua New Guinea. After 1942, this was the greatest tactical problem that had to be overcome, and the tank would provide the answer.*

Forgotten Armour 129

19. The Battle of the Admin Box in summary: a C-47 Dakota (and some vultures) fly over to drop supplies, with a line of 25th Dragoons tanks lined up in front of Ammunition Hill.

20. Map of the Admin Box in the 25th Dragoons' war diary. Note the 37mm AT gun on the lower slopes of Point 315 to the east, and the left-hand bend below it where Clive Branson would lose his life. The bend was nicknamed Tattenham Corner after the left-hander at Epsom Downs.

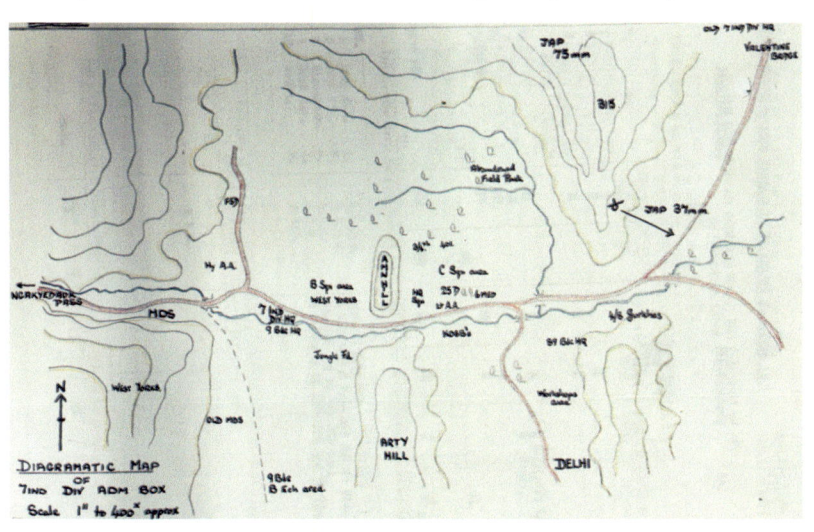

Part III

Tanks could emerge from concealed positions "like savage rabbits from their holes" to make immediate counterattacks.

Lieutenant-General Sir Ivor Maxse,
in conversation with JFC Fuller, 1918

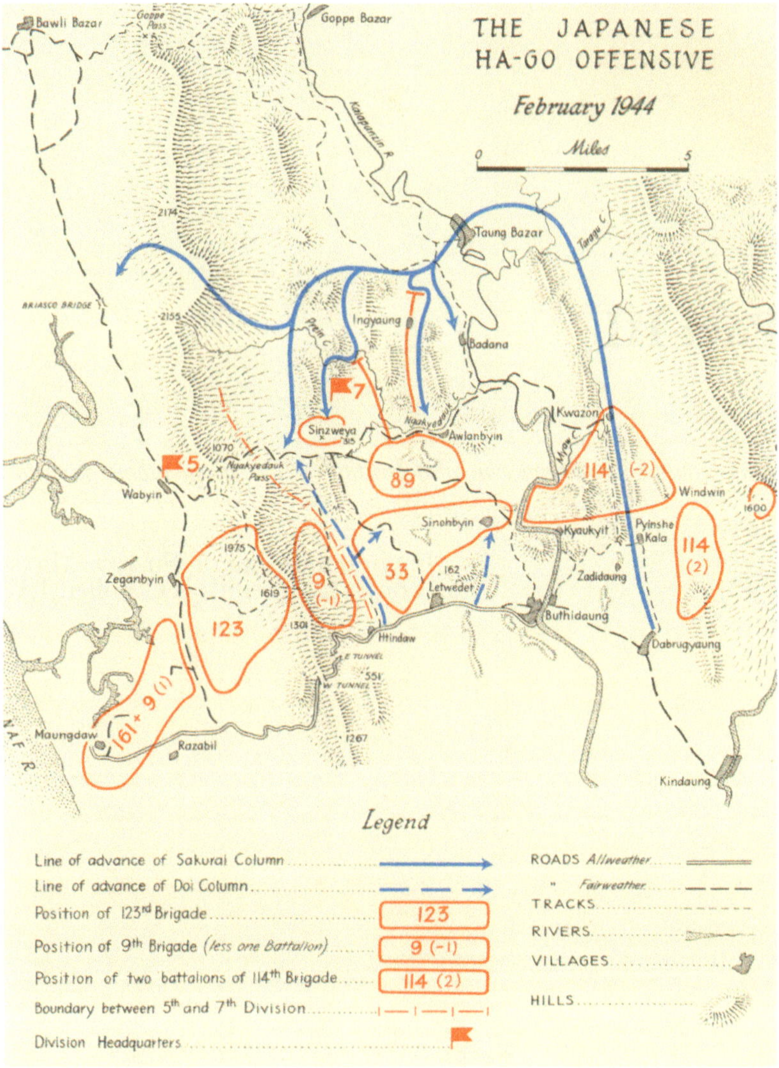
THE JAPANESE HA-GO OFFENSIVE
February 1944
Miles
0
5
Bawli Bazar
Goppe Bazar
Taung Bazar
Ingyaung
Badana
Kwazon
Awlanbyin
Sinzweya
Wabyin
Windwin
Sinohbyin
Kyaukyit
Pyinshe Kala
Zadidaung
Zeganbyin
Letwedet
Buthidaung
Htindaw
Dabrugyaung
Maungdaw
Razabil
Kindaung
123
9 (-1)
33
89
114 (-2)
114 (2)
161 + 9 (1)
7
5
Legend
Line of advance of Sakurai Column
Line of advance of Doi Column
Position of 123rd Brigade
Position of 9th Brigade (less one Battalion)
Position of two battalions of 114th Brigade
Boundary between 5th and 7th Division
Division Headquarters
ROADS Allweather
" Fairweather
TRACKS
RIVERS
VILLAGES
HILLS

7
'I felt no sorrow' - The Battle of the Admin Box

The night of 5-6th February 1944 had passed eerily, rustling jungle and rifle shots occasionally cut through the dark, some distant, some close-by. The day before had seen frantic preparations for the impending attack and some new strong points were dug in with Bren guns. Another Bren was placed on the hill to the left of the position facing the open ground to the front, ready to fire into the flank of any assault. A blocking position had been placed in the rear in case of attack from there too. The position was fully manned, and the sentries were alert. The hours ticked by slowly with the expectation of attack at any moment. By 5:30am there was waist-high mist, but no sign of an attack, the men hoped the Japanese were not coming.

 Major-General Frank Messervy was developing a habit of having his divisional headquarters overrun. A tall 51-year-old Etonian, former cavalryman in the First World War, and polo player, he had already served in East and North Africa in this war. When he commanded 7th Armoured Division at the Battle of Gazala in 1942 his HQ was overrun, and he was captured. He managed to persuade the Germans he was a simple batman* and slipped away. Gazala was a disaster, and he was sacked, following criticism that, among other things, his HQ was too far forward: his capture meant he was missing in the crucial hours of the battle. In March 1943 he became Director of Armoured Fighting Vehicles in Delhi. He had been instrumental, alongside Slim and others, in winning the argument to get medium tanks

---

*An officer's personal servant

into Burma following Australian experiences against bunkers with Stuarts.

Tucked up in bed on the night of 5/6th February, Messervy was awakened by shouting from somewhere in the camp. 'I jumped out of bed and walked about in pyjamas for an hour or so, trying to find out what was going on. The whole camp was aroused but there was confusion all around us.'[1] Men were running between positions, with extra ammunition being carried to the Bren guns. Many of these HQ men did not normally have to worry about attacks, now they were getting into position for one that seemed imminent.

One of the men coordinating the defence was Lieutenant-Colonel Hobson, in charge of the signallers. Two days earlier Messervy had sent the HQ Defence battalion, 1/11th Sikh, across a *chaung* to the east to attack a Japanese incursion there. This left the signallers and engineers to defend the HQ. He heard shouts coming from the jeep park, about 300 yards away, and received a phone call from the signals office to say there were 'a number of strange figures there and he [the caller] thought they were Japanese'.[2] There was a sudden cheer from the Japanese troops, Messervy likened it to 'when you hear Arsenal score a goal at home', before they rushed through the mist at the signals office on the right of the position.

The Bren guns on the hill overlooking the open ground in front of the whole position started firing. Some Japanese troops fell, their attack wavering just short of the signallers' trenches, and then withdrew. At this stage it was discovered the telephone cables between positions had been cut. Messervy calmly returned to his tent and dressed* before issuing his last wireless

---

* There is a story that Messervy spent the whole action and then escaped in his pyjamas and bush hat. Tom Grounds persuasively argues in Some Letters From Burma, that those who witnessed his emergence from the jungle the next day, like Philip Gabriel and John Leyin of B Squadron, 25th Dragoons, did not mention it. Grounds and Leyin both suggest that someone witnessing this would surely have remembered the incongruity of the man being in pyjamas. Similarly, Captain Smith of 89th Brigade also saw him and described

orders: 89th Brigade should fall back, and reported that his HQ was under attack.

Meanwhile, the Japanese had infiltrated between the main HQ, and the signals area, splitting the defence in two. The signallers held on for now, but it became clear to Messervy that they were surrounded, and they should escape through the jungle in small groups and head for the divisional administration area about two and a half miles away at the village of Sinzweya. He sent runners to the outlying positions, but none returned. Hobson did not get the message and thought relief was at hand when he heard C Squadron, 25th Dragoons passing by. Gordon Heynes and his tanks had been told Messervy's HQ was occupied '[the] old HQ was a smouldering ruin…we did some shelling and machine gunning into the jungle where the Japs were'.[3] Hobson recalled the impact of their fire: 'an intense and terrifying concentration of all the firepower they could muster. This was much worse than anything the Japanese had produced, and it was a relief when they were seen to disappear in the direction of the Divisional Admin area'.[4] There were no casualties from this friendly fire, so Hobson and his men slipped away after the Japanese really did occupy the hill overlooking the position.

Messervy and his group of around thirty, of whom five or six were wounded, comprised of senior staff officers. Captain Smith of 89th Brigade described their arrival with his unit at around 8am on the 7th February. 'They fell or sat down among us while we hurried to help them. There was an urgency, a nervousness about them… many were no longer young, the shock and unreality could be seen on their faces'.[5] Smith and his men patched them up, and helped Messervy to the road where reinforcements were making their way to the admin area.

---

him in his uniform – he did not recognise Messervy but did see his rank insignia to realise who it was. The 25th Dragoons war diary describes Messervy's arrival but makes no mention of pyjamas either.

John Leyin was driving a lorry in the midst of a column of B and C Squadron, 25th Dragoons, passing over the Ngakyedauk Pass. 'To my astonishment, and no doubt the astonishment of everyone else present, out from the jungle skirting the track, appeared a worried looking General Messervy'.[6] Messervy climbed the B Squadron tank in front of Leyin when 'his bush hat blew off his head and bounced along the ground directly in front of my vehicle. Since such things did not usually happen to generals, I found this a little amusing'.[7] Messervy was directed to the squadron leader, and then was taken to the administration area to get back in contact with his brigades and Corps HQ.

The Japanese plans for 1944 were essentially to invade India on the central front at Imphal and foment an anti-British uprising. This would take place under Lieutenant-General Renya Mutaguchi of 15th Army under the codename *U-Go* at the beginning of March. Mutaguchi had advocated for an invasion of India since he arrived in Burma, despite the huge logistical challenge it would mean even for Japanese light infantry armies. To aid in this Lieutenant-General Shōzō Sakurai's 28th Army was to launch a diversionary operation in Arakan in early February, Operation *Ha-Go*. The expectation for both operations was that British and Indian units would be surrounded, and they would fight bloody retreats that would cripple them. They would leave behind stores and equipment the Japanese could use, as they had done from 1942 into 1943. Fourteenth Army would have to send reinforcements from the central front around Imphal to support XV Corps in Arakan by mid-February, leaving Imphal vulnerable to the coming attack in March. This failed to account for the way Fourteenth Army was now led, and how it intended to fight.

There were two fundamental changes: the men of Fourteenth Army were better prepared for jungle conditions, and they no longer considered Japanese troops on their lines of communication as a reason to withdraw. Under Slim's leadership, there was improved training for all troops, improving capability in aerial logistics, and a consequent improvement in morale. The Fourteenth Army was quite different to the British and Indian armies the Japanese had faced since December 1941. Slim believed that if units held on to key positions with enough supplies in a defensive box, the Japanese would be forced to attack them when the unit did not withdraw, as it would have done previously to preserve its line of supply. This would deny the enemy of the supplies in the box, which in the 1942 retreat frequently aided the Japanese advance. The idea of defensive boxes was adopted from the North African desert to create all-round areas of defence, with the added dimension of large-scale aerial resupply. The Chindit operations had also proven the principle behind these boxes, and that aerial resupply, was possible. The Japanese would then break the momentum of their own advance to destroy these boxes against their massed firepower before being attacked by reserve units coming to relieve the encircled one. Aerial resupply had been done on a small scale by the Indian Army in the 1920s on the NWF, and as mentioned on a greater scale during the Chindit operations now there were enough transport aircraft and crews available. The whole plan relied on controlling the air space over the battlefield, and in the middle of January a number of air battles with newly arrived Spitfires supplementing the existing Hurricanes, took air superiority. The Japanese would continue sorties, and shoot down some transports, but they were never able to cut off the aerial supply route throughout the battle.

On the 3rd February, XV Corps' new commander, Lieutenant-General Philip Christison was making final preparations for Messervy's 7th Indian Division to press on down the eastern side of the Mayu Range. The 25th Dragoons were about to make their way across the nearly complete Ngakyedauk Pass to join them. The pass had been open to lorries for a while, but it was still being upgraded for tanks and other very heavy loads. Whilst Razabil was not yet captured, 5th Indian Division's position there seemed secure enough, especially with the recently captured port of Maungdaw. The 7th Indian Division, east of the Mayu Range, had its brigades dispersed in the jungle-clad hills south of the administration area, readying to advance. This admin area was protected by two batteries of the 24th Anti-Aircraft/Anti-Tank Regiment and was basically a maintenance area for the rear echelons: brigade transports, brigade and divisional workshops, supply units, an ordnance park, and a main dressing station (MDS).

The first Japanese movements were detected by patrols of the 114th Infantry Brigade in the early hours of the 4th February. These were the men of the main Japanese column: Sakurai Force. Major-General Tokutaro Sakurai (no relation to 28th Army commander Shōzō Sakurai) was leading a mixed column of infantry and engineers in the gaps between 7th Indian Division's brigades in the jungle. They were to capture Taung Bazaar northeast of 7th Indian Division and destroy it from behind, i.e. the north, before crossing the Mayu Range and doing the same to 5th Indian Division. Another infantry column under Colonel Doi would also infiltrate through the jungle and cut the Ngakyedauk Pass, moving off on the 5th February because of their shorter journey compared to Sakurai Force.

The detection of these movements led to the first firefights, and triggered moves to reinforce the position. Messervy ordered 89th Infantry Brigade north towards Taung Bazaar and called for the tanks of the 25th Dragoons to cross the Ngakyedauk Pass as soon as possible – Christison obliged, and by 4pm B Squadron was on the two-and-a-half-hour journey over the pass, followed by the rest of the fighting elements and regimental HQ overnight. The rear echelons and the reserve tanks remained on the western side of the pass*. By the evening of the 5th, Slim gave

---

* These reserve tanks were manned by rear echelon troops and helped 5th Indian Division break through the Ngakyedauk Pass whilst the main battle took place.

XV Corps control of 26th Indian Infantry Division, so Christison immediately ordered it to Arakan ready to reinforce the area as the size of the Japanese attack became apparent. Messervy's HQ was overrun at 5:30am on the 6th and in his absence, Christison sent Brigadier Geoffrey Evans to control the defensive 'Admin Box' being set up around the 7th Indian Division administration area at Sinzweya. Christison also sent the last reinforcements into the Admin Box: 2nd Battalion West Yorkshire Regiment moved there from 9th Infantry Brigade to the south, with two artillery batteries of the 25th Mountain Regiment. That night, the pass was cut by Doi's column. The Admin Box was on its own.

The Admin Box was a rough square of disused paddy fields. Around a mile north-south and three-quarters of a mile east-west, with a small *chaung* along the north of the box, and the Ngakyedauk chaung running alongside a track near the southern edge. This *chaung* was between six and ten feet deep, mostly dry at this time of year bar a tiny stream, up to 40 feet wide, with a rocky bed. The centre of the box was divided by two jungle covered hills – the smaller one north of the Ngakyedauk chaung and track was 150 feet tall, 200 yards long, and thin. This was nicknamed Ammunition Hill because of the stores dumped on its western side. To the south, over the Ngakyedauk chaung and track, was Artillery Hill, a larger feature that dominated the box. Immediately west of Artillery Hill, the Ngakyedauk chaung splits, the main branch continues west and follows the track that becomes the Ngakyedauk Pass, the other flows south. To the east there was a gap in the hills where the track exited the box, this gap was called the eastern gate. The whole area was surrounded by further hills that would become the main defensive positions for the infantry.

Brigadier Geoffrey Evans had only been in the area for a couple of days after taking command of 9th Infantry Brigade when he was reassigned to command the Admin Box. His first phone call was to set up a meeting that afternoon with Major Hugh Ley, bunker busting pioneer, second in command of the 25th Dragoons, and a former member of Evans's staff. He wanted to make sure the tanks were in the box, knowing how important their firepower could be in the coming fight. 'I ordered him to bring them into the Box and keep them in the open paddy so that they could have a good view of anybody who tried to rush them'.[8] Knowing that Evans could be difficult, Ley became the obvious liaison officer for 25th Dragoons. They shared a slit trench throughout the battle and used Ley's tank as an armoured run about.

B and C Squadrons were the first tanks to set up inside the box late on the 6th February, after helping drag some medium guns and other vehicles through the mud for most of the afternoon and early evening. B Squadron made a screen of tanks north of the track to the west of Ammunition Hill, and in front of the 7th Indian Division HQ that was just south of the track. C Squadron did the same on the east side of the hill, with the 25th Dragoons' Regimental HQ behind. A Squadron would join C Squadron on the 7th February after delivering supplies to 33rd Infantry Brigade to the south and bringing their wounded back to the Main Dressing Station (MDS) in the box. The crews had a difficult first night. It was already dark by the time they were settled, having dug trenches in a U-shape around the front and side of the tanks so they could reverse them out in the mornings. John Leyin described how these trenches 'were to be manned by the tank crews every night to meet a Japanese onslaught…each night the Browning machine-guns, mounted in the turrets of the tanks, were removed and, as part of the defence fortifications, mounted on the trench walls'.[9]

The tanks of B and C Squadron were therefore guarding the open paddy in front and either side of Ammunition Hill. The north and eastern sectors were not held by infantry, the firepower of the tanks was to deny the enemy the approach over the open paddy. The problem was infiltration at night. To help with this B Squadron was partly supported by the 2nd West Yorks on C Company Hill to their left, whilst C Squadron had the 25th Dragoons' attached infantry support, the 3/4th Bombay Grenadiers. B Squadron's position was in a slight L-shape with the shorter edge on the western side of the box near the Bofors Anti-Aircraft (AA) guns on the other side of a small *chaung*.

Gordon Heynes and his crew had prepared their tank for action, performed normal maintenance, and dug in. They became conscious of the administrative nature of the troops occupying nearby positions, and the Japanese threat – how well would the admin-types fight? 'Trenches were dug on the bank of the stream, and these were manned by HQ staff, cooks, lorry drivers and batmen. Japs occupied the tops of all the ridges, so we were looked down on us from all sides'.[10] The Japanese were not quite looking down on them on that first night, but Heynes speaks for the likely feelings of many men in the Admin Box. John Leyin noted 'the wave of fear that swept over me, as I am sure was the experience of all of us, cannot be described. And it was with much apprehension that, towards dusk, I made my way to the tank line-up…I took up my position in the trench'.[11]

Certainly, the situation was still very confused with exact Japanese locations still unknown, but soon they would occupy positions in the hills with a full view of the Admin Box. Nervousness was an obvious problem in the early days of the battle. Tired men frantically getting themselves to the safety of the box during the first day, then digging, digging, digging. Once inside, they were dragging or carrying ammunition boxes into the positions on the hills around the box, moving vehicles around delivering supplies, then getting them out of the way of any fighting, and setting up telephone links to various HQs. As darkness settled in the rounds of sentry duty began for exhausted, worried troops with itchy trigger fingers. 'We found ourselves in a position which in all our training we had been told to avoid', Heynes noted, 'tanks were so vulnerable after dark unless they had a line of defence between them and the enemy'.[12] The Japanese were adept at silent night-time infiltration, and the worry was without a proper defensive line in front, and relying on firepower alone, Heynes and the 25th Dragoons' tanks could be put out of action with a single grenade through an open hatch.

To guard against this, each tank put two men on sentry duty, one in the trench dug around the tank, the other up in the turret of the Lee. The large, seven-man crew made the responsibility less onerous on the crew by sharing the burden. The 37mm was then loaded with canister shot that fired thousands of ball-bearings like a shotgun for short-range defence. Heynes was just starting his turn on sentry duty when some of the tanks to his right started firing into the dark. Almost as a reflex, he began firing too until he realised he didn't have any targets and stopped. 'I stood up and the sight of all these tanks belching out sheets of flame and the stream of tracer pouring into the jungle opposite was awe inspiring.'[13] The night dragged on, and Heynes took a couple more turns on duty. Tom Grounds, also of B Squadron recalled the Burmese night 'it was all too easy to 'see' all sorts of figures moving silently amongst the bushes and tall grass – only a light breeze was enough to activate the illusion'.[14] The first night passed by with lots of rifle and machine gun fire by the tense soldiers across the box, but no Japanese attack came. They were not quite as close and were still moving through the hills ready to make their first move. In light of their encirclement Evans gave orders to conserve ammunition and to fire only at visible targets – there was no guarantee when they would be resupplied.

The general plan for the defence of the Admin Box was for the infantry to hold positions as best they could, and if they lost a particular feature around the box, the tanks and infantry would counterattack. During the day the Japanese defended any gains from hastily dug bunkers and fired long range artillery from well-constructed camouflaged bunkers into the box. They left their offensive actions mostly to the night, where the defenders, and especially the tanks' advantages were limited. This pattern asserted itself from the first full day – 7th February, the day the Ngakyedauk Pass was cut.

At the eastern side of the box was a hill, Point 315, that Evans wanted the 4/8th Gurkhas to occupy as part of the perimeter, but the Japanese got there first, and pushed the Gurkhas back into the box. Their immediate counterattack failed, between this and the initial attack they had lost around 30 men. C Squadron with D Company of the West Yorks were called up to help take the position. Firing from the flat paddy in the box, they fired into the jungle, and the West Yorks were able to help get the Gurkhas onto the hill, who were dug in by dark, and the tanks went back to their defensive position. On the west side of the box B Squadron did not sally out but supported some firing on Japanese positions. Heynes watched the 5.5-inch howitzers of the 6th Medium Regiment, some targets were only 400 yards away and shrapnel fell amongst their position. The 25th Dragoons had their first fatality of the battle that day when a shell landed near Lance-Corporal Walter Heesom killing him and wounding two others.

The night of 7th February became infamous in the Battle of the Admin Box, and for the war against Japan in general. The MDS was built on the side of a jungle-clad hill in the southwest of the box, on top of which were A Company of the West Yorks, and just below was the track running west to the Ngakyedauk Pass. Most of the wards and the operating theatre were dug in by extending parts of the dry *chaung* nearby, but a few administrative buildings were in tents on the surface. The walking wounded had been taken out the previous day, leaving just the stretcher cases and the medical staff inside.

The Japanese rushed the position after infiltrating between the units of the West Yorks, using the cover of darkness and the thick jungle. John Leyin spent his nights in B Squadron trenches just a couple of hundred yards away: 'the screams of the patients, doctors and medical staff as they were shot and bayonetted, and the blood-curdling yells of the attacking Japs through the night, was for us all a nightmarish experience, but an experience we had to silently endure'.[15] There was nothing they could do. The standing order at night was to stay in your trench and shoot at anything that moved. The Japanese questioned some of the survivors in the MDS, then used them to pack up medical supplies and were taken off. Many of these were later shot or bayonetted as well, although some miraculously survived being shot and kicked into a *chaung*.

After a day of the tanks helping infantry consolidate gains by pushing Japanese positions further away on the 8th February, the 9th saw the counterattack on the MDS. The MDS had to be recaptured because it was so close to the Divisional HQ, and behind one of the West Yorks positions. The Japanese had camouflaged their machine guns with stretchers and other medical equipment, and even used dead and wounded British and Indian soldiers as part of the defences. A troop of B Squadron fired into the positions, inevitably leading to some British and Indian prisoners receiving further wounds. The West Yorks made their way forward and indicated enemy machine guns to the tanks. The work took most of the day, but they killed 50 Japanese soldiers, including an officer who was carrying the entire plan for *Ha-Go* that was passed back eventually to XV Corps HQ. 31 patients and four medical officers had been murdered.

Supplies were becoming a worry after a couple of days cut off. The Admin Box was also getting congested, so it was decided to send A Squadron to help 33rd Brigade in their separate box further south, hoping to alleviate both problems, and give some firepower to the other brigade. Fighter cover from Spitfires and Hurricanes was becoming more and more noticeable, part of the aerial resupply operation that started on the 8th February. 'It was a cheering sight to see two Dakotas overhead circling round and started dropping supplies,' recalled Heynes, 'blue sky, green jungle, and red, blue, yellow, and white parachutes floating down'.[16] The men had to be careful though, sometimes parachutes did not open. Heynes' 75mm gunner jumped off the tank to pick something up when out of nowhere a bag of sugar landed on the tank. 'Had he not jumped down his neck would have broken. The bag burst and there was sugar everywhere, we gathered it up and after that had a lovely, sweet tea'.[17] Not even a comrade's near-death experience could take away the delight of extra sugar for a British soldier's tea.

As the tanks and infantry got used to working together, target indication improved. This was often the biggest problem as the tanks were usually at the edge of the box, or on a track in the clear, firing into jungle and up hills. The artillery and tank fire cleared much of the vegetation as planned, but targets were still small and well camouflaged. B Squadron, working closely with the West Yorks were having success with radio communication from the infantry back to someone on the telephone fitted to the back of the tanks. The tank commanders were also having luck spotting on their own. Heynes' tank commander, the squadron leader Major Horne, was scanning for targets through his binoculars.

"Heynes, I can see some Japs" he said, and directed the tank onto his target.[18] There were some men under a tree. 'I fired nine rounds as quickly as my loader could reload, and then he ordered me to stop'.[19] As the dust cleared Horne scanned the area again and saw some of the bodies on the ground. '"Heynes, you killed a lot of Japs then". I felt pleased, at last I knew that some of my shooting had had an effect. I felt no sorrow, this was war'.[20]

The routine was fully established by now. Major Anthony Brett-James, a 5th Indian Division signals officer in 9th Brigade had ended up in the Admin Box and described how 'the tanks were on call to any quarter of the box to drive off the Japanese with their guns and mobility'.[21] Second Lieutenant Satoru Inazawa of 112th Regiment had advanced in Sakurai column 'our positions were shelled by tanks every day for fourteen days until 20th February, a terrible experience. One man kept watch on the enemy and others hid low in their holes. We did not fire unless the enemy came over the blast hole'.[22] The tanks were not just effective in driving the Japanese away from gains at the edges of the box but were vital at night too. The Japanese understood that as long as the tanks were there, they could not clear the box, could not get across the Mayu Range and destroy 5th Indian Division as well, or march on India. To deal with this, they brought up some AT guns. The problem was the Japanese had not improved their technology. The 37mm and newer Type 1 47mm AT tank guns that were used in 1942 had struggled to disable or destroy 7th Armoured Brigade's Stuarts and were still in use in 1944. The Lee tanks were virtually impervious to their fire, Leyin remembered seeing tanks return from their assaults. 'The whole of its lower front expanse of armour pock-marked with neatly drilled out conical shaped holes, of about two inches deep, where it had been hit repeatedly with Japanese 47mm armour-piercing shells'.[23] Suicide attempts were made with mines strapped to Japanese soldiers who would fling themselves onto or under the Lees, but these were easily mown down by nearby tanks, or the supporting infantry.

More refinements to the bunker busting infantry support techniques took place, such as infantry use of Very lights* to signal the switch between HE and AP rounds, and even a pole with a flag to point out targets. Attempts were made to move up the Ngakyedauk Pass as well, and the close nature of the terrain meant that infantry cooperation was vital. As B Squadron were

---

* Flare pistols/guns. Sometimes spelt Verey.

closest, they moved about two and a half miles up the road to the foot of the pass, but the infantry of the 2nd West Yorks could go no further against Japanese positions. It became normal to have infantry with radios with the tanks. On Heynes' tank they went looking for snipers 'we moved off along a track with the infantry major kneeling behind the turret through some thick undergrowth'.[24] They were scanning the trees when the major pointed forwards. Heynes, looking through his machine gun's eyepiece could see him clearly once directed over the intercom; his tank commander, Major Horne said he could fire when ready. 'One short burst was enough, and his body crashed to the ground'.[25]

The Japanese were making gains though. On the night of the 11th February, they captured Artillery Hill, the dominating feature at the southern end of the box. Brigadier Geoffrey Evans knew it had to be taken back: 'they had a perfect view of Headquarters, and Ammunition Hill; they could cover by fire the track which ran from the Western to the Eastern Gate for most of its length'.[26] They could also dominate the harbour areas of the 25th Dragoons on both sides of Ammunition Hill. The Japanese had made numerous attempts to destroy the ammunition dump; twice it had caught fire with shells exploding for hours through the night and causing casualties. Having a Japanese artillery observation post on the hill just a few hundred yards away was intolerable.

After a failed infantry attack, the tanks were called up to help clear the hill. The operation was one of the largest ones in the battle, with a large concentration of all the artillery and nearby mortars. C Squadron provided two troops, and joined the bombardment, plastering the hill, helping to clear the vegetation with their HE. The barrage was so great that the 5th Indian Division on the other side of the Mayu Range heard it. The artillery and mortar fire stopped so A Company of the West

Yorks could advance up the hill. When they closed on the hastily built, and now exposed, Japanese bunkers they fired a Very light, and the tanks switched to AP, and kept up the fire as the infantry got into position. John Leyin was not in the attack but watched it from his location in the B Squadron harbour. 'It was an extremely strange experience to know that less than 200 yards away there were Japanese and British troops fighting for their lives in close combat... all we could see was the effect of the eruptions on the jungle covering the hill as the high-explosive shells exploded one after the other'.[27] The tanks halted their fire and the West Yorks swept over the bunkers with grenades and bayonets, finally clearing the position by 5:25pm. Japanese infiltrations were repeated over the following days, and it took a further three days of tank and infantry fighting before the whole hill was captured.

To allow rest and maintenance not every troop of tanks in a squadron would go out on 'duffies' the nickname given for operations to clear Japanese incursions on the box. For these men, the biggest problem during the day was artillery, mortars, and snipers. On the 9th February, a big Japanese gun, a 105mm nicknamed 'Big Willie' and a 75mm called 'Little Willie' made themselves known to the defenders. They were well concealed, and would come out of a jungle hide, fire a round or two, then hide again from the direction of the Buthidaung tunnel.

Whilst the attack on Artillery Hill was taking place, Tom Grounds's troop in B Squadron were firing on enemy positions to the northeast of the box with the help of artillery observation officers. Corporal Howden was at the head of a triangular formation towards the target, troop leader, Lieutenant Eric Miles, rear right, and Grounds at the rear left. Rounds were crashing into the hillside in front of them, when there was a sudden flash on Howden's tank, followed by a billow of yellow smoke from the large crew hatch above the 75mm gun. A Welsh voice shouted over the intercom, Taffy Poole:

"Howden's hit. By God, *he's hit*" but there was no movement from the tank.[28] John Monger, the troop leader's driver got out and had a look. Monger was able to pull out Howden, and the badly burned, but living, Ray Evans and Corporal Peake. The 75mm loader Wally Mowle was killed immediately along with the gunner John Stainbank. Gordon Barnes, the driver, and Frank Myers, the wireless operator, were both badly burned as well, in complete shock, and died a couple of days later. Monger was awarded the Military Medal for pulling the crew out. He had no idea whether anyone was alive, and the tank could have exploded at any moment. He later joked to John Leyin that he only went because one of them owed him money. But what had happened? This was the first time a Lee had gone up like this. The Japanese guns could not penetrate the front armour and struggled with the side armour. The top armour, however, was very thin: it was probably hit by a mortar. Mowle had laid out the cordite charges for the shoot, which caused the flash. Flame had ripped suddenly through the hull of the tank and up through the turret enveloping the crew, and out through the hatches, rather than going off in a concentrated explosion, explaining the yellow smoke from flaming cordite.

The tank was towed back to their defensive positions west of Ammunition Hill. Grounds and some of the others in the troop helped get the dead out of the tank. 'I shall not forget the burned and wizened, half crushed head of the loader. In shocked silence they were passed through the side hatch and lowered to the ground'.[29] For some men this was too much, and a reshuffle took place in Miles's troop. John Leyin, who had been working delivering supplies in a lorry between the tank harbours, was swapped with the 37mm loader in Miles's tank. This was also a co-driver position, so Leyin might be called to take over the driver's seat if they were killed or wounded. 'I welcomed the transfer, for being a member of a tank crew instead of being on my own, now with some armour wrapped around me for protection, made me feel more secure'.[30]

On the 13th February C Squadron were providing fire support to the West Yorks, again with an officer with a radio. Not everyone needed to be in the tank for the longer-range shoots, so Heynes and others were milling about outside. Suddenly eight Zeros swooped over the position. They were machine gunning and bombing the tanks, Heynes and the nearby crews dived for cover, some in the tanks, some in trenches. Horne and Heynes dived under their Lee, while the infantry officer crouched at the rear. 'We had just got under when there was a terrific explosion. It seemed as if the whole of my body had been hit, and then, for an instant, which seemed to be much longer, there was complete silence and I thought I was dead. Then sound came back, I suppose it was the air rushing back into the vacuum created by the explosion'.[31] Smoke and flame was everywhere as Heynes squirmed out from under the tank. The lorries nearby were on fire, and he could hear the screams of the Indian drivers. One tank was rolling forward and the kit bags were on fire, when it stopped at the edge of the paddy where there was a slope. Heynes jumped onto the tank and used the fire extinguisher to put out the flames with two others. Someone pulled him off the tank. Heynes struggled trying to release himself from his comrade's grip and look for Horne, but he was taken away to the first aid post. Heynes' beret had been blown away, and his denims cut to pieces by shrapnel. He was bleeding and in shock. Horne was found with a shrapnel wound in his throat, but alive, although four Indian drivers and the infantry officer were killed. A bomb from one of the Zeros had landed behind the tank. Whilst not critically wounded, Heynes had been peppered with shrapnel, he spent the rest of the battle as a stretcher case in the MDS, where he spent his 40th birthday. Once the siege was lifted, he was evacuated back to a hospital in India.

After over a week of fighting the box was becoming a shambles. The vegetation surrounding it was almost bare, the open paddy was torn up by the tanks' tracks, leaving a layer of dust over everything. Burnt out vehicles littered the area and flies from Japanese bodies in particular were everywhere. Tiredness was becoming a problem too, not least due to Japanese night attacks or smaller scale infiltrations, called jitter parties, or jitter raids. John Leyin remembered 'sleep, or rather lack of it, was still a problem…if you stopped moving, nature immediately took over and made you instantly nod off... tiredness, through lack of sleep as a consequence of the unrelenting barrage of attacks, became a factor that increasingly affected our responses and actions'.[32]

The fighting was not over yet, and Leyin was now in action in his new tank for the rest of the battle. He discovered the armour of a tank had disadvantages. He could not see what was going on for one, he only had a tiny visor out of the side of the tank and relied on the orders coming from the commander over the intercom to orient himself. The heat was intense 'sweat running down my bare torso into an already sweat sodden waistband of my shorts, and with the smell of expended cordite'.[33] He had to be careful of the recoil of the 37mm gun he loaded, the rate of fire demanded of them meant he had near misses with his head only just moving out of the way of the breach as it flew backwards. 'The difference between being in actual combat and taking part in training exercises was vast'.[34]

By the 19th February there were signs the battle was being won. Japanese troops were seen moving in large numbers west to east over the Kalapanzin River to the east of the box. They were retreating, and those who remained were starving because the plan was predicated on British and Indian troops panicking and fleeing, leaving behind supplies for the Japanese. They were also under pressure from relieving forces, especially 26th Indian Division to the north. More patrols were sent south to harry the Japanese and continue clearing the area. The Ngakyedauk Pass was slowly being cleared from both ends too. The Japanese were still putting in attacks around the box each night so other units could get away. The tanks and infantry continued to sortie out and clear any gains they made.

On the 23rd February, the 2nd Battalion, King's Own Scottish Borderers, supported in the previous days by C Squadron, had pushed up the Ngakyedauk Pass and made contact with 5th Indian Division troops. They cleared the surrounding features to open the track, and by 24th the wounded at MDS, including Heynes, were evacuated and convoys and relief troops arrived. The siege was over.

There were still dangers though, and the 25th Dragoons were still fighting. The Japanese AT guns near the east of the box that had pockmarked the tanks were finally pinpointed on the southeast side of the ridge leading to Point 315. It overlooked a slight left-hand bend on the track through the Admin Box, nicknamed Tattenham Corner, the famous left hander at Epson Downs*. To pass it safely to support infantry on the other side of the hill they would speed up to race past as fast as possible. On 25th February, Leyin's troop was racing across when they heard a bang behind them. Sergeant Clive Branson, who saw the bombing on Razabil, had been directing his driver from his open turret hatch. The AT gun had aimed for the hatch and hit Branson. Leyin saw the body, in the shade by the tank after the crew had lifted him out. The AP shell had 'taken the whole of the back of the sergeant's head completely away, leaving a pulpy red mash, a sight so terrible that it numbed the senses'.[35]

The operations in Arakan had to go on, and the 25th Dragoons, with Grounds and Leyin, continued to be involved despite their efforts in the Admin Box. The 7th and 5th Indian Division were pulled into reserve, with 36th British Infantry Division and 26th Indian Infantry Division taking over. The 81st West African Division continued their advance down the Kaladan River. The 25th Dragoons moved south to their original objective at the end of January, to clear the Buthidaung area and the rest of the Mayu Peninsula. Japanese resistance was now weaker, but still fanatical. Miles Smeeton, the cavalry officer whose training at Quetta Staff College had focused on a repeat of the First World War, was with them in preparation for his own command of Probyn's Horse, in 255th Indian Tank Brigade. He

---
*The same place where Suffragette Emily Davison was killed.

saw his first tank action, and the now perfected tank assaults, to clear the road to Buthidaung. Vengeance dive bombers, followed by artillery, struck the hill some Indian infantry were assaulting, and the tanks opened up as the infantry closed in. The Sikh soldiers 'slipped and scrambled up the slope under the roofing trajectory of the shells…the bursts of the HE shells had stopped as the first Sikhs neared the crest, and now the tracer bullets from the tank machine guns were drawing short lines above their heads, until the firing stopped altogether, and we could see the men running along the top of the ridge and flinging grenades down the far slope'.[36] Fighting continued in the hills further south until the monsoon in May halted operations, although events on the central front were to change the complexion of the Burma campaign for good.

The Arakan campaign in early 1944 had not achieved its original objectives. The Mayu Peninsula had not been cleared, and Akyab Island with its vital airfield remained in Japanese hands. The operations there had, however, been a success. The Japanese suffered 3,106 killed and 2,229 wounded in the Battle of the Admin Box alone, whilst the British had 3,506 casualties. The battle had been won by the three-dimensional nature of the defence, compared to a two-dimensional attack. The immense firepower that the box could generate was only possible because of the ability to supply the tanks and artillery from the air – the vital third dimension. In the three main weeks of the battle in February, and the month or so after, the Japanese 55th Division lost nearly half its strength. Their failure to force the retreat or destroy 5th and 7th Indian Divisions, and 55th Division's own effective destruction in such a short period, allowed Slim to deploy reinforcements from Arakan to the Imphal and Kohima battles, rather than the other way around.

At the tactical level, the tank was the decisive factor in the Battle of the Admin Box. The Japanese thought they faced an entire brigade of tanks which could operate anywhere in the box impervious to most of what the Japanese could throw at them.

What damage was done to the tanks was often freak, one-in-a-million shots; like the mortar round on the 75mm loader's hatch setting off cordite charges in Corporal Howden's tank, or the bomb dropped by a Zero on Heynes' tank. The few AT guns the Japanese had could not penetrate the armour, and suicide attacks failed to get close enough to them to cause a single loss. At night, the tanks' firepower held the Japanese infiltrations at bay, before they spent the day driving the Japanese from newly captured positions. They used the bunker busting methods they tested at Razabil, then perfected them in the Admin Box, particularly regarding communication between the infantry and the tanks. The highly accurate 75mm guns, with their flexibility in both ammunition type and fuses, worked successfully with infantry to clear the hurriedly constructed bunkers that the Japanese built when they got onto a position. They put the West Yorks back on their hills astride the entrance to the Ngakyedauk Pass, got the Gurkhas onto Point 315, and again with the West Yorks, cleared the vital Artillery Hill.

The overall success in Arakan was exactly what the morale of the British and Commonwealth troops needed. The myth of the Japanese 'superman' was broken over the barrel of the Lee's 75mm cannon, and the grit and determination of the infantry that fought alongside them. This was not the last test of tanks and infantry in defence, as events on the central front were about to show. Before Arakan, officers like Slim and Messervy had fought tooth and nail to keep tanks in the theatre. The 25th Dragoons had repaid their faith. Going forward, tanks would become the backbone of everything that happened in Burma, and especially into 1945. A report made in March 1944, looking back at both the Razabil operation, and the Admin Box made this new direction clear. 'We must fight on ground suited to our tactics…[tanks] are a decisive weapon. Where it is possible to do so the whole op should be designed to get tanks to the target. The 7 Div Box could not have been held without them'.[37]

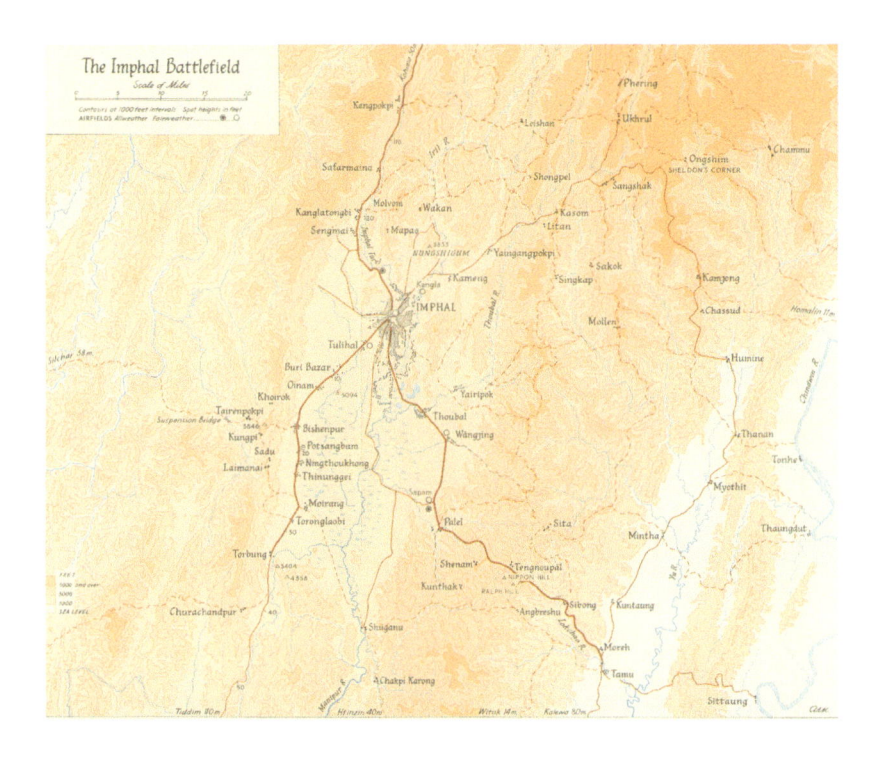

On Mountains and Plains: The Battle of Imphal   155

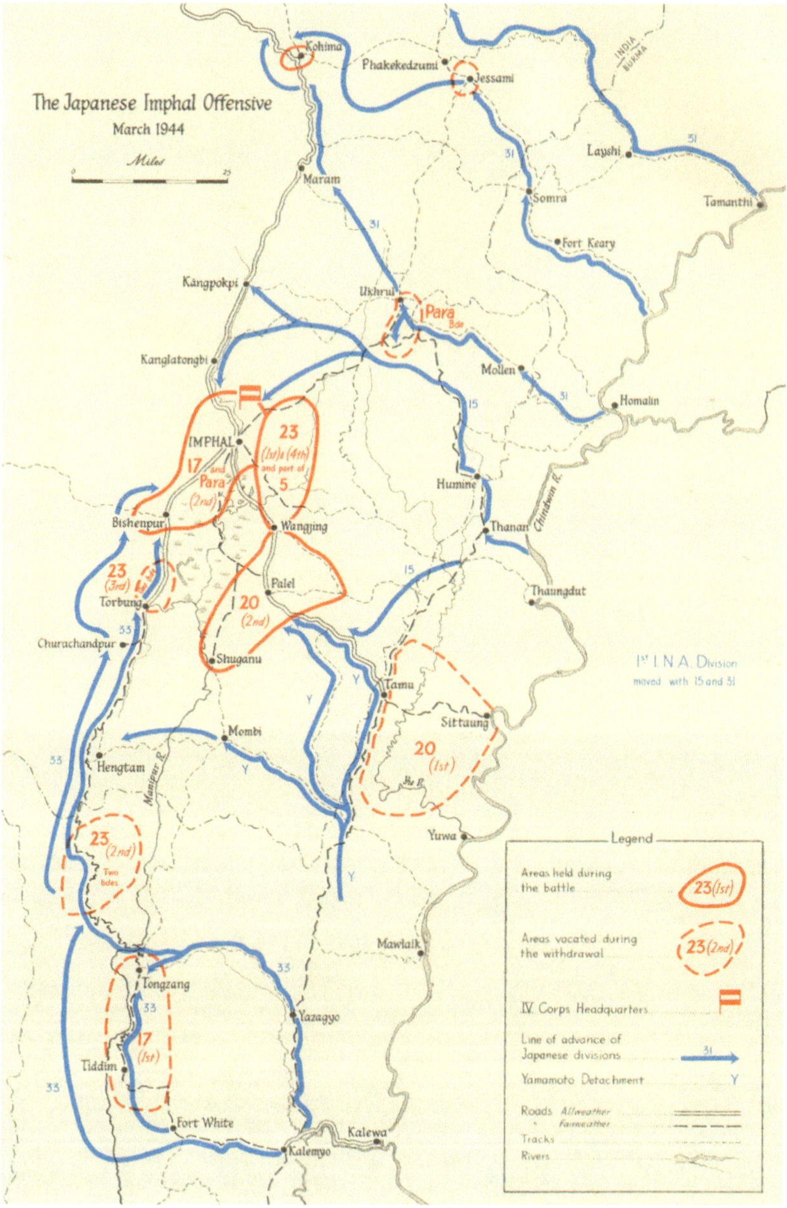

The Japanese Imphal Offensive
March 1944
Miles
0
25
INDIA
BURMA
Kohima
Phakekedzumi
Jessami
Layshi
Tamanthi
Maram
Somra
Fort Keary
Kangpokpi
Ukhrul
Para
Bde
Kanglatongbi
Mollen
Homalin
IMPHAL
17 and Para (2nd)
23 (1st) & (4th) and part of 5
Humine
Bishenpur
Wangjing
Thanan
Chindwin R.
23 (3rd)
Palel
Thaungdut
Torbung
20 (2nd)
Churachandpur
Shuganu
1st I.N.A. Division
moved with 15 and 31
Tamu
Sittaung
Mombi
20 (1st)
Hengtam
Manipur R.
Yuwa
23 (2nd)
Two bdes
Mawlaik
Tongzang
17 (1st)
Yazagyo
Tiddim
Fort White
Kalewa
Kalemyo
31
15
33
Y
Legend
Areas held during the battle
23(1st)
Areas vacated during the withdrawal
23(2nd)
IV Corps Headquarters
Line of advance of Japanese divisions
Yamamoto Detachment
Roads Allweather
Fairweather
Tracks
Rivers

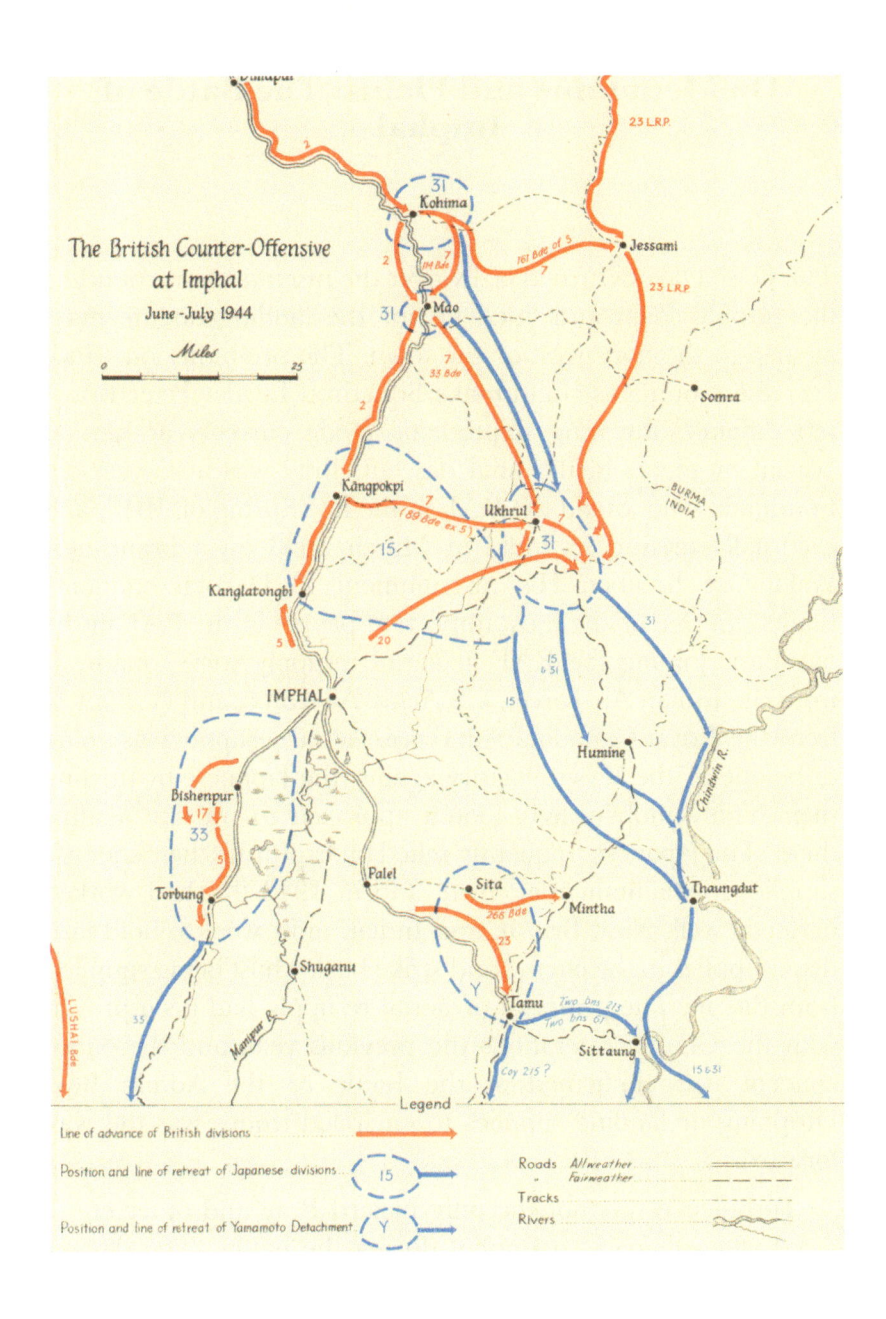

On Mountains and Plains: The Battle of Imphal 157

8
On Mountains and Plains: The Battle of Imphal

The C-47 Dakota turned lazily over the mountains surrounding the Imphal Plain and lined up for the landing on the main airstrip to the northwest of the town. The pre-monsoon winds over the mountains could make Squadron Leader Peter Bray's job difficult, throwing unpredictable air currents at him at crucial moments in the final descent. Bray was a 25-year-old Londoner, who joined the RAF in the late Spring of 1940, and eventually arrived in India in March 1943 on a brand-new Wellington bomber. His reassignment to Dakotas suddenly made him one of the most important people in the RAF in the Far East. Joining the RAF in aerial resupply were squadrons from the Indian Air Force[*], US Army Air Force, and even a few from the Royal Canadian Air Force. Aerial resupply was going to be one of the keys to victory against the Japanese by turning their highly mobile, light-footed approach to warfare against them. The Japanese frequently relied on capturing their enemy's supplies to maintain their own, and in 1942 this had worked perfectly well. Now, British, and Indian units were to hold fast, deny supplies to the enemy and strike back whilst being supplied from the air. The principle of aerial resupply had been proven with the Chindit operations the previous year, and the entire concept was confirmed at the Battle of the Admin Box. Dropping or landing supplies to encircled troops was the way forward.

Turbulence was not the only hazard Bray and other crews faced when flying into Imphal during the battle. 'The danger

---
[*] King George VI added the prefix 'Royal' in March 1945, in recognition of their role in the war.

being from ground fire, and the shelling of course… over the plain, the dust clouds meant you couldn't see much more than a mile in front of you. Early on, you had to keep a good lookout for Jap sneak fighters coming at you out of the murk'.[1] Beginning in November 1943 with the introduction of Spitfires to the skies of Burma and continuing with American long-range fighters like the P-38 Lightning and P-51 Mustang, air superiority was won by 1944. The Spitfires alone accounted for 49 Japanese aircraft destroyed in the first months of their arrival. The long-range fighters meant the Japanese air force, part of their army's organisation, took even heavier casualties. The lack of early warning systems meant the American fighters destroyed over 100 Japanese aircraft on the ground at airfields on the central Shwebo Plain, and a further 76 in the air. The Japanese withdrew their fighters from central Burma to Rangoon in the south, 600 miles from Imphal. Direct air support from fighter-bombers and dive-bombers, and aerial resupply was therefore completely feasible.

Bray brought his plane into Imphal on over twenty sorties in April and May of 1944 during the siege phase at Imphal. 'The Japs were so close to the landing strips that you could see them looking up at you with their machine guns spraying bullets. You had to hold your nerve'.[2] John Hart was one of the men stripped to the waste unloading supplies in Imphal, 'it was bloomin' hot work – in the middle of the day it was over 100 degrees in the shade. We unloaded all the supply stuff for the Imphal squadrons – ammo, petrol, and spares'.[3] This was the lifeblood of the men on the Imphal Plain.

There are some incredible statistics for aerial resupply during the battle. There were supposed to be 300 sorties per day, although this was only managed twice during the siege. There were 155,000 men to feed in IV Corps, and 11,000 animals – meaning 250 tonnes of food per day. All but the heaviest loads could be dropped by parachute, including engines, but also live mules, goats, and chickens. Most of the supplies were delivered by landing at the airstrips and hurriedly unloading them before they took off again. Men like Peter Bray delivered 6,518 tonnes of rations, 423 tonnes of sugar, 919 tonnes of food grain, 5,000 live chickens, 27,500 eggs, 5.25m vitamin tablets, 1,303 tonnes of animal grain, 12,000 bags of mail and 43.5m cigarettes. Crucially, there was 3.8m litres of fuel and lubricants, along with ammunition, for, among others, the 254th Indian Tank Brigade. The men of this brigade were an emergency service across the entire Imphal Plain. They became indispensable; hence the supreme effort to keep their tanks running and firing.

The Japanese wanted what became the Battle of the Admin Box, Operation *Ha-Go*, to be a distraction for Fourteenth Army. Slim was supposed to send reinforcements from the central front, who were pushing south and eastwards through the mountains towards the Chindwin River from Imphal. Thus weakened, the Japanese would sweep in, invade India, and foment an Indian nationalist uprising. Operation *Ha-Go* signally failed because it was defeated using the units in place and local reserves: its failure opened the possibility for 5th and 7th Indian Infantry Divisions to be flown to Imphal between 18th and 27th March. The attempt to weaken the central front actually allowed Slim to strengthen it.

The forward base for the British operations on the central front advancing towards the Chindwin was the capital of Manipur state, Imphal. The city is at the northern end of a flat valley that was known at the time as the Imphal Plain, 45 miles long and 25 miles wide, surrounded by mountains in the border region of India, with Burma to the east. This was the perfect place for Fourteenth Army's IV Corps to launch an invasion into Burma, or for Japan to advance into India. During the 1942 retreat Imphal was practically undefended, only the Japanese decision to stay on the east bank on the Chindwin saved it as

Burcorps trudged to safety and 7th Armoured Brigade's Stuarts were left smouldering. By early 1944, it was a vast forward logistical hub, with airstrips and supply dumps, and with newly restored or upgraded road links to the rear. The crucial road was to Kohima, 85 miles to the north, and on to Dimapur, another 30 miles away. Dimapur was the railhead from India, and where the supplies for the front arrived in bulk, before being taken along the roads in lorry convoys to Imphal, via Kohima. The kind of work done by men such as David Atkins in the GPT Companies, risking their lives on the narrow, twisting, mountain tracks up to Kohima, then back down to Imphal.

Imphal had therefore become the main hub for Fourteenth Army's plans for 1944, with both the Army HQ and IV Corps HQs in the area. The advances out from Imphal were along the tracks that already existed but with engineers improving them as they went with an eye on the future reconquest of Burma. The well-trained but inexperienced 20th Indian Infantry Division were 68 miles away on the south-easterly Tamu-Palel road heading directly towards the Chindwin, while 17th Indian Division, the main survivor of the retreat in 1942, were 151 miles south in Tiddim. The 49th Indian Infantry Brigade was near Ukhrul to the north, with the resting 23rd Indian Infantry Division, and 254th Indian Tank Brigade in reserve at Imphal itself.

The Japanese offensive, Operation *U-Go*, was to be carried out by Lieutenant-General Renya Mutaguchi's 15th Army. He had been a divisional commander in Malaya and Singapore; consequently, he underestimated the men of Fourteenth Army and their transformation in training, equipment, morale, and subsequent fighting ability. He hoped to win a victory that would make him a hero. This made him a difficult man to get on with, domineering and arrogant, he planned a battle that had such fine logistical margins that he would have to rely on his subordinate commanders in a way in which he was temperamentally unsuited. He did not like or trust his divisional commanders, and the feeling was mutual. To succeed, the battle required close coordination in a lightning strike across difficult terrain, over two simultaneous battles at Imphal and Kohima. Instead, Mutaguchi allowed the battles to descend into an attritional struggle that suited the Indian Army's reinforced IV Corps where its superior firepower and logistical strength could defeat badly supplied and uncoordinated Japanese thrusts in detail.

Mutaguchi's plan called for a fast-moving operation that would effectively surround and overwhelm IV Corps, which should have been weakened by sending reinforcements to Arakan. Lieutenant-General Motoso Yanagida's 33rd Division would make a conventional attack from the south in mid-March, and a week later Lieutenant-General Masafumi Yamauchi's understrength 15th Division would attack from the north where IV Corps' defences were weaker. The 31st Division would also move with the 15th Division but turn north towards Kohima at the same time. The 33rd Division's advance was essentially a strong supporting feint to draw reserves from Imphal to the south, so 15th Division could take the city by mid-April, or before the Emperor's birthday on the 29th March. Certainly, it would have to be before the monsoon in May, when it would be impossible to maintain them in the mountains around Imphal. To allow swift movement in this mountainous terrain, Japanese troops were to operate on very tight logistics, carrying only twenty days of food, and relying on the capture of Imphal to feed them. Whilst the timing between the Battle of the Admin Box and the coming Operation *U-Go* was tight, Mutaguchi could have identified how his colleagues' battle was lost on a logistical level because 7th Indian Division stayed in place and was resupplied by air. He was expecting a different outcome from a potentially similar situation with a similar plan. The Japanese experience of British and Indian forces on the defensive up to the end of 1943 from Malaya to Burma was that they retreated

On Mountains and Plains: The Battle of Imphal   163

under pressure to preserve supply lines, leaving behind stores they could not transport. But the trend of Allied operations from 1943, the Chindits and Admin Box specifically, was of aerial supply and could have been spotted. The fact it was not is a poor reflection on Japanese leadership who, at the very least, should have had a backup logistical plan in case they failed to capture the supplies at Imphal. The result would be Japanese soldiers dying of starvation in the aftermath because of their leadership's arrogance.

The build-up of Japanese forces on the east bank of the Chindwin did not go unnoticed. Presuming correctly that the Japanese would attempt to capture Imphal, Slim and IV Corps' commander Lieutenant-General Geoffrey Scoones made plans to draw the Japanese into an area of their own choosing. They would fight using their key advantages: logistics and firepower. They would use the Imphal Plain's flat terrain as a way to ensure supplies and reinforcements could be moved to the troops on the mountains at the periphery quickly to the areas most in need. Conversely, Japanese troops would operate at the maximum distance from their own logistical bases, over the Chindwin and through possibly the most difficult terrain to transport supplies. The 17th and 20th Indian Divisions would withdraw towards Imphal and then destroy the Japanese there. These fighting withdrawals would need to be timed perfectly, too early and the enemy would advance to Imphal without loss or interference and be able to concentrate their attacks, holding the initiative. Too late and the two divisions risked being cut off without support, in difficult terrain, and be defeated in detail.

The gap in the plan was to the north. Slim and Scoones assumed the road would be cut by perhaps a single Japanese regiment. When they first detected Japanese advances in these areas, they swapped the 49th Brigade with the newly arrived 50th Indian Parachute Brigade. At Sangshak between the 22nd and 26th March, this single brigade held up columns of both the

Japanese 31st Division's advance on Kohima, and the 15th Division's advance on Imphal. The delay was crucial, Mutaguchi's plan relied on a strict timetable due to supplies and the threat of the monsoon in May. This bought much needed time to improve defences in Imphal, and for SEAC's commander Vice-Admiral Louis Mountbatten to arrange extra Dakota aircraft for aerial resupply throughout the battle. This also allowed the fly-in of 5th Indian Division from Arakan – 9th and 123rd Brigades to Imphal, 161st to Dimapur to support the relief of Kohima.

At the end of January, the 254th Indian Tank Brigade were in the process of concentrating at Imphal. The 3rd Carabiniers with Lees, 7th Light Cavalry with Stuarts, and C Squadron of the 150th Regiment, Royal Armoured Corps, were already there, with the rest of 150th RAC still in India. C Squadron of 150th RAC were flown into the perimeter once the battle began and took over the 3rd Carabiniers' reserve tanks. The 3rd Carabiniers were on the Manipur road north of Imphal, at milestone (MS) 108 near the village of Kanglatongbi. They were commanded by now Lieutenant-Colonel Ralph Younger, who had been second in command of the 7th Hussars during the retreat in 1942. They were training with 37th Indian Infantry Brigade of 23rd Indian Division and conducting tests on 75mm ammunition and fuses for assaults on bunker positions. This continued into February and included preparations to move into the Kabaw Valley with 23rd Indian Division if the Japanese crossed the Chindwin. As the threat from the Japanese forces began to develop in early March, plans were made to split the regiment ready to support different units in the area. A Squadron of the 3rd Carabiniers were secretly sent into the Kabaw Valley at the end of February to support 20th Indian Division*. On 14th March, however, the Japanese 33rd Division

---

* The 3rd Carabiniers war diary comments 'none of Elephant Williams bridges showed any sign of distress at all!'

arrived behind the 17th Indian Division at Tiddim. These two divisions were old foes, having faced each other at the Sittang Bridge disaster in 1942. Scoones order came too late, and now 17th Indian Division had to form a column and begin a fighting withdrawal, only now they were having to break out of encirclement – exactly what Scoones wanted to avoid. As Mutaguchi hoped, Scoones sent reinforcements from the reserve 23rd Indian Division to attack the Japanese from the north and help 17th Indian Division. Imphal and IV Corps HQ was now left vulnerable.

With these reinforcements went A Squadron of 7th Light Cavalry. This would be the first time that Indian tank crews with British officers as troop commanders, would go into action. Lieutenant JS Morgan's 1 Troop was sent off to break through to 17th Indian Division with support from a Gurkha battalion. One of his men was a wireless operator Sowar[*] Jot Ram. As they moved south near MS99 on the 18th March, they had to fight through a roadblock of logs across the track, with a ditch on the far side. For much of the length of the Tiddim Road, the track was dug into the side of the hill, with a drop to one side, and a slope on the other. There were flat sections, and in most places, there were trees on both sides. When they reached the block Ram got the order:

"Close down, action front, Mike One Baker to watch flanks and rear".[4]

Ram heard gunfire, followed by a loud thud on the tank. Ram was confused, the sudden overwhelming nature of combat from inside a tank was more than anything training could prepare him for. The view through his periscope in the front of the tank's hull was narrow, he could see very little. 'There is a flash in front of my eyes. I cannot see, even in front. It must be the Japs coming, I open fire with the lap gun. There is smoke in the tank. I get a

---

[*] Sowar is the cavalry equivalent of a sepoy in the Indian Army, or a private in the British Army.

kick in the back of the head; my ears are scorched with shameful abuse on the intercom'.[5] Ram had opened fire without identifying a target, firing blind in panic. An injured officer from the Gurkhas approached the lead tank and started talking to Morgan. Suddenly, twenty Japanese attacked the troop of three tanks from the right rear, but they were all killed by infantry fire and the tanks' machine guns and canister shot. Morgan ordered the troop forward.

Just as they approach the roadblock more Japanese troops rushed Morgan's tank, throwing bombs. Ram opened fire '[I] see my tracer go into them. This time I am not kicked. Everyone is firing. The Japs fall in heaps on the ground'.[6] It was beginning to get dark, and the ditch beyond the log roadblock was too big, crossing it risked ditching a tank. There was no way round with a deep *chaung* to one side of the road, and a steep slope on the other. Morgan decided to pull back for the night. Ram's tank got briefly stuck as they manoeuvred, but they managed to move out. When they reached their harbour, they dismounted and had a tense night with gunfire and flares through the night.

The next morning was foggy, and as they started to mount up to move again there were sudden *crumps* as mortars fired into their position. Then a shower of grenades landed. Ram was on the deck of his tank when the Japanese infantry charged them. 'I fire my ack-ack Browning[*] until it stops…there are more Japs. Gurkhas charge with the bayonet and shoot at the same time…then things are quiet…is anyone alive? I can see the Jemadar Sahib[†] staggering about. He is hurt with blood streaming from his neck and shoulder. I can see the Sahib's gunner, lying half out of his turret. He must have been looking over the top'.[7] The Gurkhas had charged into the jungle after the

---

[*] The .30 calibre Browning machine gun fitted to the outside of the Stuart's turret, ostensibly for anti-aircraft defense (hence 'ack-ack' – AA – anti air)
[†] Jemadar is the VCO rank equivalent to lieutenant. Sahib is a respectful term similar to 'Mister', often used by Indian soldiers when referring to superior officers.

Japanese infantry but not returned, the clearing around the tanks was empty.

Morgan gave orders to destroy the important equipment inside his damaged tank and to abandon it. His crew scrambled into Ram's tiny Stuart – six of them including the wounded Jemadar. As they moved off there was more firing, then three bangs and the tank filled with smoke. All the guns started firing, and someone started shooting with a tommy gun out of a pistol port.

"Pull the main fire extinguisher" shouted Morgan, "Look out! Here they come, gunner! Fire!"[8] More Japanese rushed the tank; one man had a pole charge – a long pole with a mine attached to the end. Ram and the cramped crew opened fire, and some Japanese soldiers fell. But no one hit the man carrying the pole charge. There was another bang, but miraculously, no one was hurt. The pole charge had been used to break the tracks, immobilising the little Stuart. For some reason the Japanese did not attack again, perhaps regrouping themselves, or they assumed the pole charge finished the job. On the radio, Risaldar[*] Bharat Singh's tank that got away made contact – reinforcements were on the way. 'Hours pass. Nothing happens. It is terribly hot and stifling, all huddled up in this tank'.[9]

Later, a Gurkha approached. The wounded Jemadar looking through a pistol port was not convinced.

"He is dressed like a Gurkha, but I don't like the look of him. Shall I shoot?"[10] After a pause, Morgan replied, ignoring the experienced Jemadar's caution:

"He is holding a message. He must be alright. Here goes!"[11] Morgan opened the turret flap. 'Then it all happens, shades of Rama, may I never experience the like again! Explosions-smoke-shouting'.[12]

---

[*] Risaldar is the VCO rank equivalent to captain in Indian cavalry units.

"Abandon tank and fight like hell!" someone shouted. Ram got a foot in the back, another on his head, as five people scrambled to escape. He started to choke on the smoke 'I must surely die. Then I try to get out of the driver's hatch. I cannot move. I am caught. I hold my breath. Then I take another breath full of smoke. My ears sing and I shake. This is the end. I give one more heave. Something gives and I struggle out and fall in front of the tank. There is smoke all around, and shots and explosions and shouting'.[13] Ram rolled into a culvert, as he ran, he had felt a sting on his face. It was his lanyard on his uniform whipping him – it had caught on something when he tried to escape the tank and had now broken. He also saw the bodies of the other five men who bailed out of the tank, they had been shot as they climbed out. The lanyard that had delayed Ram's exit meant the Japanese took their eye off the tank for just a moment, thinking it was now empty. When he eventually broke the lanyard with his final heave, they were not prepared, giving him the chance to get away. After a few moments, Ram decided to make a run for it. He leapt out of the culvert and rolled down the hillside, followed by shouting and a few rifle shots. When he hit the bottom he lay still, dazed for a few moments. A couple of days later he stumbled into A Squadron's harbour, having sneaked through the jungle to escape. Apart from Risaldar Singh's crew, Ram was the only survivor from 1 Troop.

The roadblock was cleared by a stronger combined attack on the 22nd March, but further casualties were sustained from a Japanese 75mm gun firing AP shot, and more fanatic infantry attacks with firebombs. Bunker busting methods were used on Japanese positions as they cleared roadblocks in both directions, not unlike 7th Armoured Brigade two years earlier. By the 29th March contact was made with 17th Indian Division, and by the following day it had passed through.

Confused fighting took place all along the Tiddim Road, as opposing units occupied various hilltops. Hurribombers, the tanks and artillery concentrations were able to support the infantry and get 17th Indian Division out, all the while causing heavy casualties and further delays to Japanese plans. A Squadron of 7th Cavalry formed the rearguard, and by the 5th April 17th Indian Division was in the Imphal perimeter. They would soon take up positions holding Bishenpur*, a village on the plain between Loktak Lake and the mountains to the west, the perfect defensive position.

To the southeast of Imphal, on the Tamu-Palel road, the 20th Indian Division found themselves in a similar position. There was no defined frontline in this area, more a front-line area, and the Chin Hills were roughly it. 20th Indian Division had been patrolling and probing the Japanese presence through the hills and on and up to the Chindwin. The road was important because it was the most direct route to or from Burma. The road also had three airfields along its route, one of which was all-weather, along with a supply dump at Moreh. This was part of the infrastructure being built up for the planned limited invasion into Burma for that year, that the Japanese invasion would stop. Along this route was Yamamoto Force, made of the majority of the 33rd Division's 213th Infantry Regiment, two more battalions of infantry from 15th Division, some heavy field artillery, and the 14th Tank Regiment. This column contained the greatest firepower of all of those advancing on Imphal.

The first skirmishes with Yamamoto Force took place on the 14th March. Two days later, Scoones gave his order for the 20th Indian Division's withdrawal, timing the move better than he did for the 17th Indian Division. The planned fighting withdrawal began, with support from A Squadron, 3rd Carabiniers, who had been sent into the Kabaw Valley at the end of February as planned earlier. During the withdrawal to Imphal they helped escort infantry, much like the retreat in 1942.

---
* Now Bishnupur

On the 20th March A Squadron's HQ and 7 Troops with infantry from 9/14th Punjab and some 1st Battalion, Northamptonshire Regiment, universal carriers were sent to help a group of cut-off infantry from the 20th Indian Division, under Major Pettit. They were on a track five miles north of Witok at Nanmunta chaung, with Major Pettit's HQ troop bringing up the rear of the column, when he heard over the radio the lead tanks had met an ambush. He raced his troop to the front of the column, while using the radio to order the infantry to dismount and use the jungle to flank the ambush. As he reached the front of the column, the nature of the ambush became apparent. Lieutenant Millar's 7 Troop had broken into a clearing and were engaging a line of well-camouflaged Japanese Type-95 tanks. The Japanese rarely handled their tanks well, often using them as mobile pillboxes. The position they were in was apparently well chosen, with the tanks on one side of the road and infantry on the other. At the opening of the ambush, the Lee tanks were attacked in their relatively vulnerable sides – thickest armour is always on the front of a tank. The sponson-mounted 75mm gun could not reach their target, but once the whole tank was turned, the strongest armour was facing the enemy. The Type-95's main gun was a virtually obsolete 37mm AT gun that was no match for the Lee's armour. Only one of their rounds managed to cause any damage, an AP round hitting the fuel tank of the last Lee in 7 Troop and setting it on fire. One man was killed, the rest of the crew were wounded, but safely rescued. The Lee tanks turned their tanks round for their 75mm guns to return fire, turning their back on the enemy infantry, and trusting the Punjabis and Northants to clear them.

Trooper Costain was a 37mm gunner in his Lee, the secondary gun up in the turret, and sat next to the commander. He was busy engaging the Type-95s when his commander, Squadron Sergeant-Major Whiting, collapsed into the turret next to him. The enemy infantry behind had shot him in the head. Costain now tried to juggle his own gunnery with commanding the tank and helped destroy one of the Type-95s. He was having to climb up to the turret hatch to survey the situation, issue orders to the crew, then climb down to engage targets, until the wireless operator, Lance Corporal Cantor, moved up to take over the gun.

The Punjab and Northants infantry were now behind the Japanese, who began to melt away. The weight of fire the Lee tanks, with two guns capable of penetrating Type-95 armour, and the well-trained infantry were taking their toll, when another sudden change in the battle took place. A mixture of panic and poor Japanese armour tactics became apparent. The Type-95s now tried to disengage by emerging out of the jungle towards the Lee tanks and heading for the road away and in front of them. Now presenting clear targets they were picked off, and soon five of the seven tanks were smouldering wrecks in the clearing, one was abandoned slightly damaged, and one tank charged off slightly damaged. The column continued on to the cut-off infantry, rescuing their wounded, before returning to the main 20th Indian Division area. They also towed the abandoned Type-95 back to Imphal.

This was the only time Japanese armour engaged a similar number of British or Indian tanks in the battle. For the whole of the war, they would avoid contact with armour whenever they could, and continued to use them as infantry support or in this passive mobile pillbox role. Had they reversed into the jungle, the tanks may have got away to fight another day. By remaining stationary up to the end of the fight they lost all initiative once the first shots were fired against tanks that could penetrate their frontal armour, when their own guns could not do the same. This problem was especially acute once the Lees turned on them – a menacing sight to the young Japanese crews. The Lee's 75mm sponson configuration meant they would *always* present their frontal armour, and so the nature of the ambush meant it was doomed to failure from the moment the Japanese camouflaged those Type-95s at the side of the clearing.

The general retreat towards Imphal continued. 20th Indian Division was able to get to its planned position in front of the eastern gate to the Imphal Plain, keeping the three airfields protected. The main position was the Shenam Saddle, a collection of mountains that dominated the area. These hills would see fierce fighting throughout the battle, but there would be no breakthrough; the airfields would remain in use throughout the battle, keeping the men fed and equipped. The Japanese would be poorly supplied and eventually starved without the riches at Palel and Imphal.

The strength of the northern thrust surprised Scoones and Slim. Using a single regiment to cut the main supply route to Dimapur, via Kohima, was obvious. But launching a divisional attack from the most mountainous area and with the least developed roads was less obvious. There were three main directions the Japanese 15th Division now approached from: the Imphal-Kohima road, the Iril river valley, and the Ukhrul road. The incredible delaying action at Sangshak on the Ukhrul road – the first obstacle the Japanese faced – had brought time for the 5th Indian Infantry Division to be flown in. There was also time for the largest supply dump on the Imphal Plain, just north of Kanglatongbi on the Imphal-Kohima road, to be moved into a new defensive area in the village called Lion Box. Numerous boxes were formed across the entire Imphal Plain like this, self-sufficient, and ready for all round defence. The 3rd Carabiniers were split into their squadrons, A was already in the south with 20th Indian Division, with C going to Lion Box. B and HQ squadrons were based in a box at Sawumbung with 123rd Indian Infantry Brigade, 5th Indian Division, at the junction of the Iril Valley and the Ukhrul road. This latter box guarded the fair-weather airfield at Kangla, as well as two routes into Imphal.

Malcolm Connolly's tank was sent into Lion Box on 6th April, where there had already been fierce fighting. Connolly had helped unload Lend-Lease tanks for the Middle East and was one of many who trained for hill climbing in his Lee. 'On entering Lion Box, the signs of war were everywhere. Huts were burning and big Jap guns were firing from the tops of mountains that bordered the valley'.[14] Almost immediately, Connolly's troop of tanks were called into action. 'The ferocity of them [the Japanese] just cannot be described. They had few means of destroying our tanks but came so close to us that we could not depress our guns low enough…our infantry were hard pressed to stop them climbing upon the tanks'.[15] They saw off this small patrol, and pulled back, and rested a moment in the tanks whilst the officers and NCOs worked out what to do next.

Connolly watched some infantry of the 2nd West Yorks, who had fought at the Admin Box, and were digging slit trenches in front of his tank. There was the crump of artillery firing in the distance, followed by an explosion well behind the tank. But the experienced infantry knew the noise better than Connolly and his crew. '[They] all leapt up and ran as fast as their legs could carry them…another shell landed in the half-finished slit trench…within seconds we were to learn our first lesson: that big guns…bracket onto a target'.[16] There was a third explosion, this time hitting the tank on the 75mm sponson. 'Someone shouted through the intercom "move, move, reverse, reverse!" So, I immediately engaged reverse gear and pulled back just in time as another 105mm shell landed exactly where the tank had been standing'.[17] The damage wasn't too bad, they were able to drive back and get a damaged track repaired with the squadron's Light Aid Detachment (LAD). As they did so at the side of the road a few miles back from Lion Box, hundreds of admin troops now came past. Lion Box was being evacuated.

Connolly's tank returned, and the squadron searched the box for survivors. The Japanese had raided the box the night before and got into some of the buildings whilst soldiers were asleep, bayonetting them through mosquito nets. They destroyed some of the stores that could not be lifted before the RAF bombed the box at 4pm. 'The day had been long and hard, and we had had nothing to eat since early breakfast…the heat within the tanks was almost unbearable. What with the stench of cordite from the guns and the crackle of the wireless constantly in your ears and the incessant orders being given over the intercom my head felt as if it was blown up to twice its size'.[18] The plan now was to stay at a new box – Oyster Box – with C Squadron patrolling forward to keep as much of the road to Kanglatongbi open as possible, and deny Lion Box to the Japanese in daylight.

On the 24th April, Connolly's 5 Troop, 2nd West Yorks, and A Company of the 1/10th Gurkhas patrolled to Lion Box, as they had done many times before. After weeks of fighting, the former supply depot had the heavy smell of death hanging over it, bodies were everywhere. As Connolly's tank approached the crew saw the now familiar sight: 'at the entrance of this terrible place lay the body of an Indian soldier which had been quickly pushed to the side of the road to stop the tanks running over it. Slowly it had split open and flies in enormous amounts were devouring the putrefying flesh, but the stench was horrific'.[19] The body was the danger sign, that they were now entering the combat area. Without a word being said, crews always closed down their hatches at the sight of the body and prepared for action.

As so often happened, everything seemed fine, until it wasn't. 5 Troop had been sent round to the east side of the box to engage troops in a *nullah*, which was completed with a minimum of fuss. They then entered the box and moved on to a roadblock that needed clearing. Almost as soon as the tanks reached the clearing in front of the roadblock, they were engaged by 75mm artillery. The troop sergeant immediately lost a track. 'The armour of my vehicle was being struck by 47mm* projectiles as if someone was outside with a sledgehammer'.[20] The flash of the guns could be seen in some scrub near the foot of the valley side about 150 yards to the northeast. Connolly's tank fired three rounds of 75mm, when, an AP round ripped a hole in the tank and embedded itself in the breech, jamming the gun.

The firing had barely lasted more than a few moments, but to Connolly in the driver's seat, impotently watching the gun flashes ahead, it felt as though the commander had frozen. They were sitting there doing nothing, when they should be manoeuvring, especially now their main gun was damaged. He looked over his right shoulder to see the the 75mm loader had received a full blast of shrapnel wounds in his chest and that our 75mm would certainly never be of use again. Still no word of command came from my commander and the sound of projectiles hitting the tank could still be heard'.[21] Connolly turned his body all the way round to see the bottom of the turret. The 37mm gunner was on the floor with a massive head wound, with the commander and gunner leaning over him.

"For Christ's sake get us out of here" Connolly shouted over the intercom.

"Charlie Seven, Charlie Seven, my crew is knocked out. I am coming out. Driver reverse".[22]

Thankfully, the guns had been striking the front and side of the tank, the engine compartment was undamaged. They managed to get out, under cover of the other tanks, and the infantry trying to engage the enemy guns. When they got back to the harbour, they found they had been struck twelve times by AP shot, five had penetrated. One had disabled the 75mm, another had gone through the 37mm gunsight, striking the gunner in the head, with the projectile settling in the wall of the

---

*The reports at the time suggest these were actually 75mm artillery, there were no Japanese AT gun units in the force attacking on the Imphal/Kohima road. Both the Type 38 and Type 90 75mm gun could fire AP shot.

turret behind. The losses to tanks were already becoming a concern. The LAD cannibalised a 75mm gun for Connolly's tank from another that had its engine compartment wrecked. Nothing could be wasted, with the road to Kohima and Dimapur cut, they would not get any new tanks. Only spare parts could be flown in.

The fighting around Lion Box and the hills overlooking the road was fierce, with C Squadron assisting infantry patrols forward up the road. The Japanese would advance no further. Whilst the fighting around Lion Box had been going on, another threat developed a few miles to the east in the Iril Valley sector.

In the middle of the Iril Valley lies the Nunshigum massif. Shaped a little like an inverted Y, it consists of a series of peaks and saddles, and is about 7,000 yards long. One peak on the lower left spur was nicknamed the Pyramid, then the tallest peak nearly 1,000 feet above the valley floor called the Southern Bump, and another slightly lower peak called the Northern Bump. The ridgeline was a knife-edge, with almost a 45-degree slope on either side. On 6th April, when Connolly had first entered Lion Box, the Japanese 51st Regiment attacked the 3/9th Jat Battalion, 9th Indian Infantry Brigade, 5th Indian Division, and captured it. There were fierce counterattacks over the following days, with the feature changing hands multiple times, and a posthumous Victoria Cross for Jemadar Abdul Hafiz. By the 11th April, however, the Japanese 3rd Battalion, 51st Regiment, held the ridge, and were busy installing their customary camouflaged bunkers amongst the scrub-like bushes and dry grass on the two Bumps.

Nunshigum lay only five miles from Imphal, whilst overlooking both Imphal Main and Kangla Airfields. The entire command structure from IV Corps down was in view, as were many of the supply dumps. If the Japanese could hold onto Nunshigum and bring up field artillery, the whole plain would be under threat. The airfields would be rendered unusable, starving the defenders of food, medical supplies, and ammunition. They had to take it back.

On the morning of 12th April, Major-General Harold Briggs held a meeting at his 5th Indian Division HQ. Brigadier Evans was there, having commanded the defence of the Admin Box he was now commander of the 123rd Brigade of 5th Indian Division. He was joined by 254th Indian Tank Brigade's commander Brigadier Reginal Scoones*, and 3rd Carabiniers' CO Lieutenant-Colonel Ralph Younger. Scoones and Younger immediately said they could get tanks up there. Evans recalled they were 'quite certain they could…but to the uninitiated it looked impossible'.[23] To help them, two squadrons of Vultee Vengeance dive-bombers, and one of Hurribombers were laid on by 221 Group RAF, along with 5th Indian Division's entire artillery support in the valleys either side of Nunshigum. 6 and 7 Troops of B Squadron, 3rd Carabiniers, would sit in these valleys with the artillery as well to provide extra fire support. B Company of 1st Dogras, 5 Troop and half of HQ Troop would climb up the southwestern spur, take the Pyramid, then rendezvous with A Company 1/17th Dogras and 4 Troop below the Southern Bump (1,000ft) after climbing the south-eastern spur. From there they would advance up the knife edge ridgeline and clear the rest of the feature.

The morning of the 13th April was cloudless, by 8am the sun was already high. The heat and humidity that built before the monsoon season was going to make being in a tank all day even more uncomfortable than normal. Corporal Arthur Freer, a 22-year-old Yorkshireman, was the wireless operator in the squadron leader's tank: Major Edward 'Dizzy' Sanford. Freer looked up to Sanford: tank fighting in Burma was usually a small unit affair, since arriving they were taught to expect them to be parcelled off as squadrons for specific jobs. This meant the

---

*IV Corps' GOC Lt Gen Geoffrey Scoones's brother.

regimental commander, Ralph Younger, could feel superfluous beyond administration sometimes, handing his squadrons over to infantry commanders wherever the need was greatest. This put great pressure on men like Sanford. The infantry battalion or brigade commanders coordinating attacks outranked the squadron leaders, leading them to be used in the wrong manner, like splitting up squadrons. Too often they heard the refrain "oh, just one tank will make all the difference" as though that would bring the reluctant tank commanders onside.

The attack on Nunshigum was different. This was thought through by the tank commanders as much as anyone else. The nature of the feature meant two-and-a-half troops, eight tanks, was all they would send though; it was going to be tight up on the ridgeline. The operation was supposed to begin at 10am, so Freer and the other seven crews were in the tanks at 9am, when they heard of the delay. By 9:30am they advanced across the paddy fields, Freer could see the infantry walking next to the tank through his little left-facing porthole. At 10am the Vengeance dive-bombers swooped across the two Bumps, and for half an hour each plane took their turn. Explosions threw spurts of mud into the air on the crest, most of the bombs appeared to hit the target area. At 10:30am, the guns and tanks in the valleys either side of Nunshigum opened with three minutes of rapid fire, followed by normal fire up to 10:50am. The scrub and dry grass covering the hill was slowly being shot away, exposing the dusty, muddy, knife-edge ridge. Lastly, for ten minutes from 11am the Hurribombers flew in on bombing and then strafing runs.

Whilst this was going on, 5 Troop's three tanks moved forward, followed by Freer and Sanford's tank, and the FOO tank bringing up the rear. This FOO squeezed in behind the driver, and was otherwise a normal Lee, in this case commanded by Squadron Sergeant-Major William Craddock. The infantry continued to follow in the wake and to the sides of the tanks. They were making their way up the western spur of the inverted Y, whilst 4 Troop went up the eastern spur. The route was not straight, so as the front of 5 Troop moved up, Freer could see the regiment's Royal Engineer officer, Lieutenant Ryman, walking backwards out front. He kept turning his head to check he wasn't about to fall whilst giving hand signals to the driver to stop them falling over the edge. The climb was steep, about 1:2, so the drivers could not see the ground as they went forward. They were barely making one mile an hour, going up in first gear, the engines straining. All the while the two Bumps were being pounded first by the Vengeances and Hurribombers, then by the artillery.

After an hour or so they reached the Pyramid, both tank troops and the infantry companies arrived around the same time – 11:15am. Rifle shots rang out and the infantry scattered, jumping into the brush on the hillside or behind the tanks, Ryman followed. Now the tanks and infantry were close to the Southern Bump, the artillery and tank fire had stopped, the Japanese in their bunkers on the peaks, and slit trenches on each side of the ridgeline had opened fire. It was a tentative fire as they were still a little far away on the Pyramid from the Japanese position on the Southern Bump. High-pitched *dings* rang out as bullets peppered the tanks. In shelter behind the tanks, Sanford, the tank troop commanders, and Dogra officers had a short conversation to finalise the actual assault.

5 Troop would take the lead, followed by Sanford's tank, then 4 Troop, with the FOO at the tail. The knife-edge ridge meant they would advance in single file; less than ideal as it limited the amount of firepower that could be used. Looking up at the first peak, the tanks fired a few rounds at the Southern Bump before the column advanced, with the infantry in the scrub to the side. So far, the operation was going well, if slowly due to the difficulty moving the tanks safely. There had only been one casualty in the Dogras so far, and they were now climbing over the Southern Bump. Japanese had been seen running along the saddle from the Southern Bump to the Northern Bump and other positions hidden in the scrub to each side of the ridgeline. At 12:15 they moved forward to nearly 20 yards from the Northern Bump, then ran into the heaviest resistance so far.

Freer heard the crash of the guns firing up front, whilst he kept his eye on the periscope and his hand on the .30 Browning. 'We fired a few rounds and we saw them run away, we *thought*. When we got nearer, some of them ran out of the bunkers and up to the sides of the tanks'.[24] They stormed in with pole charges, Freer opened fire, but the Lee's bow machine gun only elevated and depressed, there was no traverse. He could spray up the side of the tank to deter the Japanese, hitting anyone who crossed the line of bullets he fired, but little else. The noise was incredible: 'the sides of the tank rattling with bits of metal hitting it at high speed, and the noise of our guns going off'. Through his periscope he could see the tank commanders in every tank ahead had their head and shoulders out of the turret hatches. They were desperately firing pistols, tommy guns, and throwing grenades, but most importantly, making sure the tanks did not slide over the edge. 'Heavy fighting was taking place on all sides. The Japs were in some cases within 10 yards of the tanks, which were 10 to 15 yards in front of the infantry'.[25] The heavy fire was making them hang back.

Lieutenant-Colonel Ralph Younger was at 123rd Brigade's HQ listening to his men in real time. He was relaying what he heard to Brigadiers Scoones and Evans. Soon, his ears were filled with chaotic chatter, and the news he was dreading. Evans remembered 'First one tank would come up: "Commander killed." Then another: "Commander wounded"'.[26] In one tank, a crewman took over and was also killed. Then, Younger turned and looked up at Evans.

"Good Lord! Sanford's been wounded!"[27]

Back on Nunshigum, Freer heard a thump behind him. He looked round into the bottom of the turret; his eyes were normally at the same level as the turret crews' ankles. Instead, he saw the crumpled heap of Sanford. He called up to the 37mm gunner 'Sherley' Holmes.

"Holmes, what's happened?" A matter of fact reply came back: "Dizzy's been hit in the head."

"How badly is he hurt?"

"It's gone into his head, he won't survive," said Holmes, concentrating on working the gun.

"Is he in pain?"

"Maybe, I don't know, he just said something as he fell."[28]

Freer passed back two morphine tubes, and Holmes injected him. He had been shot under the chin, and the bullet had passed out of the top of his helmet. In the moments when this was happening driver Paddy Ryan, a London Bus driver, had been rolling forward the whole time. All three of the lead troop's tank commanders had been killed or wounded along with Sanford, in the heavy fighting just south of the Northern Bump. Only 4 Troop's commanders and Squadron Sergeant-Major Craddock remained. Similarly, the infantry had lost all of their officers too.

There was much confusion, as each tank privately dealt with their commander being killed inside the tank, all of them by rifle fire.

Freer's tank was now ahead of the rest, having overtaken the others on the wide section in front of the Northern Bump. The turret lid had been closed to avoid grenades coming in, whilst Ryan was spotting targets from the driver's position. All of the guns fired, and they went over one of the bunkers, to the far side, before realising the others were not following. 4 Troop commander, Lieutenant Fitzherbert was commanded over the radio by Younger to take command. They agreed the first order was for 5 Troop to head back down the mountain. 'I was glad of that order' reflected Freer.[29] They reported the position of the Japanese bunkers as they returned back over them, and carefully passed 4 Troop. The Japanese position on the Northern Bump was larger than anticipated – three bunkers, one about 10 yards behind the reverse slope, with two at each side firing up at the crest, plus the usual slit trenches in the scrub to each side of the ridgeline.

The attack was in the balance. The tanks and infantry were able to hold on, keep the swarming Japanese infantry at bay, but the final bunker complex had to be cleared. Despite what had happened to 5 Troop, the 4 Troop commanders remained out of their turrets, and at 12:45pm, resumed the attack on the bunkers. Inevitably, the radio calls resumed reporting the death or wounding of tank commanders, Fitzherbert was one of them. Evans reflected: 'one by one these fearless officers and non-commissioned officers fell back into their tanks either dead or mortally wounded. In all, five out of the six tank commanders died in the space of a few minutes'.[30] Looking through binoculars from the HQ, Evans and Younger now saw one of the tanks roll over the side. Luckily the tank stopped on a flat ledge around 100 feet from the peak, rather than falling 1,000 feet to the valley floor. The men were shaken, but unwounded, and the tank had only broken a track, it was recovered a few days later. Things were going from bad to worse.

At times like these, either the whole plan could fall apart, or leaders can grip the situation. The last tank commander left was the Squadron Sergeant-Major; Craddock had been at the rear with the FOO so far, and now pulled the tanks back to regroup near the Southern Bump. He dismounted and spoke to the ranking Dogra, Subedar Ranbir Singh, all of their officers were dead and wounded too. The tanks were to get within 15 yards of the three bunkers on the Northern Bump, and provide normal bunker busting covering fire, while A and B companies of the Dogras then charged. The Japanese position was so strong, however, that the Dogras were stopped on the crest of the Bump just five or ten yards short of the reverse slope bunker and withdrew again. Craddock and Singh had another conversation and came up with a new plan. Craddock sent one tank up the steep slope to sit just over the crest, dropping the nose down just enough to allow them to fire point blank at the reverse slope bunker. Craddock and the other tanks went round each side of the Bump and fired at the other bunkers, and the middle one from the sides. With the Dogras now filtering between the tanks and over the crest they made it to the bunkers and finished them off with grenades, sub-machine guns and bayonets. They finally cleared the area by 2pm. Immediately Singh got his men building wire defences, digging new defensive positions, and clearing Japanese bodies. 47 Japanese dead were counted on the Northern Bump, and 277 in total on the hill since the fighting began on the 9th April.

The operation to clear Nunshigum had been a costly success for the 3rd Carabiniers. For IV Corps it was a crucial one. Nunshigum was the closest the Japanese got to Imphal, only 5 miles away, where the airfields and the supply dumps they so desperately needed to reach were located. The Battle of Imphal relied on those airfields, without them, and the administrative units based in and around the city, the bulk of the forces would have been starved of the food and ammunition they needed. If the city had been captured, the different units fighting at the fringes of the Imphal Plain would be separated from each other too, allowing the Japanese to defeat them in detail. It was bloody on Nunshigum, but vital.

Once Freer made it to the bottom, he felt a 'tremendous surge of relief, and then we had the anxiety of the Major's body in the bottom of the turret. And thinking about how to get that out, and a certain amount of 'mess' to clear up'.[31] As the crew removed Sanford's body, they had a real fright. When Sanford was shot, he was about to throw a grenade, which had dropped into the tank, before his body fell on top. Ryan spotted it, the handle was gone: it should have exploded. Without thinking clearly, he started to undo the baseplate of the grenade in the tank with all the ammunition until Freer stopped him, and they took it out onto the paddy. There they found the fuse had burned out but not ignited the charge, it was a dud. They had more than one lucky escape up on Nunshigum.

That night Younger came to see them, he was happy. Whilst he had lost a lot of important men in one day, he was experienced: he had fought in the desert and in the 1942 retreat. He was not unused to losses. They had got their tanks up a 1,000-foot mountain and cleared it, an incredible feat. Freer was not so sure about the sacrifice: 'he looked upon that as one of the risks of war, *I didn't*...we were all shocked, they were all old friends, officers were respected'.[32] The small unit actions of tank fighting in Burma meant the loss of so many experienced commanders was hard on the less experienced troops like Freer. Younger said:

"I must congratulate you on your tremendous effort, you are all excused guard duties for tonight."[33] This was nice, a whole night without being disturbed for guard duty. They had other concerns though, aside from Sanford's remains in the turret, they had to clean the outside of the tanks, oil the guns and replenish the ammunition. 'The tank tracks were clogged with Japanese uniforms and bones and bits of meat we'd to clean up…I wrote in my diary 'this is my first taste of action. And I do not like it".[34]

The situation on the Imphal Plain was reasonably settled by the end of April. The shock of the initial Japanese invasion was over. The 15th Division had been stopped to the north at Kanglatongbi, Nunshigum, and the Ukhrul road. Yamamoto Force were very much stuck in the complex of hills at the Shenam Saddle, and 33rd Division was being held at Bishenpur between Loktak Lake and the western mountains. In an attempt to outflank Bishenpur, the Japanese had gone into the mountains building their own road as they went, to attack Bishenpur from the Silchar Track area to the west. 17th Indian Division sent 32nd Brigade to contest the area, with support from a detachment of 150th RAC from the tracks.

Slim and Scoones now organised their divisions to drive the Japanese back. In the north, the reinforced 5th Indian Division was to push up the Imphal-Kohima road through Kanglatongbi, whilst 20th Indian Division would move up the Iril Valley to cut off Japanese 15th Division's line of communication. This would also break the siege by reopening the road to Kohima and eventually Dimapur, from where XXXIII Corps were pushing south. 20th Indian Division was replaced on the Shenam Saddle by the 23rd Indian Division, who were ordered to hold position for the moment. The most dangerous area was Bishenpur, where 17th Indian Division continued to hold, but were under pressure because of the Japanese flanking movements in the mountains on the Silchar Track, and due to their casualties in the opening phase of the battle.

Towards the end of April, A Squadron of the 3rd Carabiniers had shifted from the Shenam Saddle area supporting the 20th

Indian Division and were now supporting 17th Indian Division at Bishenpur. The fighting would be very different to what they had experienced so far. Bishenpur and the surrounding villages lay on flat paddy sandwiched between Loktak Lake and the mountains over the Silchar Track, an area only a few miles wide. The villages themselves consisted of clusters of buildings, interspersed with fruit trees, and surrounded by clumps of bamboo. There were small embankments and fishponds that created channels of advance within the villages, making perfect defensive positions. The wooden huts were slightly raised in case of flooding, the gap underneath frequently turned into bunkers by the Japanese. Most villages had a small stream running through them from the mountains to the lake. With the pre-monsoon rains beginning slightly early at the end of April, the area was liable to flood in the coming weeks and months. The men of the 3rd Carabiniers met a weapon they had not yet faced, the Japanese 47mm AT gun*. They would also find some British 2-pounder AT guns pressed into service by the Japanese. The 47mm had been used in small numbers since 1942, and at close range it could penetrate the front of the Lee tanks and was reasonably effective against its side armour. The more open terrain would allow them to be used effectively for the first time in the battle.

To push the Japanese back, two troops from A Squadron and 1/4th Gurkhas would advance south from Bishenpur, through Potsangbam and attack the village of Ningthoukhong. The normal way to deal with AT guns was with either infantry or artillery, and on open ground the latter was best. When the attack met AT gunfire, their FOO ordered down artillery. This cleared the first obstacle, but soon the FOO tank was hit. One of the tank troops' attacks began to stall around 200 yards west of Ningthoukhong, when a 2-pounder knocked out two more tanks before it was destroyed. The other troop advancing round

---

* For reference, a 2 pounder AT gun is approximately 37mm, and a 6 pounder is 57mm.

the east side of the village also came under AT gunfire, destroying two of them. With only two tanks on the west side, and one on the east side, the attack was called off, and they returned to Bishenpur. The Japanese took the opportunity to push forwards and capture Potsangbam, just a couple of miles south from Bishenpur. This area was the main threat to Imphal at this point, 33rd Division had been battered, but it was far from defeated. There was little standing in the way of Imphal after Bishenpur, so this became Mutaguchi's main effort, even moving his HQ to the area in the middle of May.

As the fighting continued in the mountains west of Bishenpur, the units in the village improved their defences and licked their wounds. The 17th Indian Division's commander, Major-General 'Punch' Cowan contemplated his next move. He decided to send his 48th Brigade east around the Loktak Lake, behind Japanese lines, and set up a roadblock on the Tiddim Road just south of Torbung. This was well in the rear of Japanese forces operating around Bishenpur and would effectively cut them off. They would have to respond. When they did so, the 63rd Brigade would advance from Bishenpur and crush the Japanese 33rd Division between them.

The plan was ready to be executed from the 8th May, beginning with an attack on Potsangbam*. The attack would begin in the early morning to allow some cover over the open ground during darkness, followed by artillery concentrations. After losing a few tanks in the area at the end of April, A Squadron was given the chance to go again alongside the 9/14th Punjab who were dug in closer to the village. Lieutenant Shepherd, commanding one of the tank troops taking part wrote a report after the action. Shepherd's tanks went forward with two Valentine bridge-laying tanks and a platoon of Indian Engineers riding on the back. To approach Potsangbam from the west they would have to cross five *nullahs*†, three of which

---
* Nicknamed 'pots and pans', and today called Potshangbam.
† Same as a *chaung* in Burma, a stream, often dry except for during monsoon

were on the final approach to the village, and a ditch. Things went wrong at 5:30am, Shepherd's tank rolled over crossing the first *nullah* on the approach to Potsangbam and trapped six Indian sappers under the engine deck. After crossing the second *nullah* Shepherd continued on foot to check the third *nullah* and found a crossing around 6am. Rejoining another crew, Shepherd formed his tanks and moved towards the village. Shells began to fall amongst them, 75mm and possibly a 105mm. One of the tanks was hit by the shelling, killing the driver, and another overturned crossing one of the Valentine bridges. These did sterling work, often under fire, but were quite narrow for the American built Lees and later Shermans.

The problem was marrying up with the infantry. They were dug into the last *nullah* before Potsangbam and had been pinned down my Japanese machine-gun fire. After some confusion, Shepherd took his tanks to the slightly wooded northwest corner of the village. All the while shooting up the huts with machine guns and 37mm fire. 'Through the periscope I was watching the MG fire spraying the wood, when about 10 yards from me I saw three flashes and through the smoke the outline of an anti-tank gun. The co-ax* was almost on, so I put him on, and saw spots of daylight appearing all over the gun shield'.[35] The co-ax machine gun was fired by the 37mm gunner, so the latter gun remained silent. 'I got very excited and loaded and fired the 37mm myself three times…1 AP and 2 HE, then I collected my wits, put the 75mm gun on and gave the A/T gun 2 75 HE, which completely wrecked it'.[36] Shepherd looked behind through a rear-facing periscope and noticed another troop had joined them, and was firing at the village. He pulled his tank back a little and then heard a voice over the infantry phone on the back. Using their directions he destroyed a machine gun that was holding up the infantry. After destroying it, and shooting

---

season. I have chosen to use *nullah* when discussing them in India.
*Coaxial - the .30 Browning machine gun mounted alongside the 37mm gun in the turret.

some Japanese troops trying to withdraw, the Punjabis moved up to the ditch at the edge of the village. The tanks could not get across, and now Shepherd found he had run over a mine that had blown a track, they hadn't even noticed. Another tank in the other troop was hit by an unidentified 47mm AT gun, and the troop leader had his track blown by a mine as well. Shelling continued around them from the hills to the west: the attack was clearly stalling. Even after gaining the ditch, too many tanks were getting stuck or were damaged, and the infantry could only move when the tanks cleared machine gun positions in the village. Another shell landed on the front of Shepherd's tank, a large piece of shrapnel bent the bow-mounted machine gun's barrel, concussing the gunner. Ammunition was running short in a number of the tanks too, so the squadron leader decided to call it off. The Stuarts of 7th Cavalry moved up to give some covering fire, as the tanks withdrew. Shepherd's crew destroyed the vital equipment, bailed out, and evacuated back the way they had come on foot.

The attack failed for two reasons according to Shepherd. There was the failure to work closely with the infantry who 'had been fighting almost all the day before…it had not been possible to have a close liaison between inf and tks, which is so necessary prior to an attack'.[37] They had also not had the opportunity to reconnoitre the route, crossing the number of obstacles meant the sun was well up by the time they were in position, when they should have been opening the attack in the half-light to allow infantry to get to the village under some cover. Shepherd missed out another reason though, the Japanese had actually made an effective anti-tank defence here, using mines on the ground in front of their guns. Orders were given that in any action going forward, AT guns needed to be identified and dealt first, reversing the normal doctrine of destroying machine guns to allow the infantry forward.

The casualties in both tanks and men meant A Squadron was given a rest. B Squadron was brought down to continue the attack on Potsangbam on the 10th May alongside two battalions of Gurkhas. The Japanese brought up further reinforcements to the village in the intervening days too, and increased heavy mortar fire caused further casualties amongst the infantry. B Squadron's first attempt also stalled, needing help from bridge-layers, and having trouble navigating around the bomb craters from an RAF attack. They spent the 11th May doing some shooting on the village, and even stayed with the infantry overnight to keep their tentative hold on the northwest corner. They formed a circle of tanks, and persuaded whatever infantry they could find to dig in between the tanks. Without mosquito protection, and leaning awkwardly in different corners of their tanks, the men caught what sleep they could. B Squadron would have another go on the 12th after another bombing raid.

Corporal Arthur Freer, 5 Troop, was one of the men who had stayed in Potsangbam overnight. 'When dawn came, after standing-to inside the tanks, we all dismounted, stretched our weary limbs and made some attempt to wash'.[38] The Vengeances and Hurribombers bombed the southern end of the village for twenty minutes only a few hundred yards from the tanks. There were even more craters now, and one tank bogged down after sliding into one. The flat terrain made it safer in one regard for the tank commanders, unlike at Nunshigum they did not need to navigate for the drivers, and so remained inside the tank turrets and relied on periscopes.

The main Japanese position was in the southeast corner, and so the attack was now split into two. 4 and 7 Troops would hook to the west with the 1/3rd Gurkhas, and 5 and 6 Troops on the eastern axis with 1/10th Gurkhas. The attack went in, and soon the tanks in both groups were engaging bunkers, but the infantry started suffering casualties, and they began to fall behind the tanks. Snipers were a problem, any movement on the tank attracted their fire, and artillery and mortar fire were being called down onto them. This meant the infantry could not try and use the phone at the back of the tank to coordinate. 5 and 6 Troops crossed a Valentine bridge on the west side of the village and turned left to head towards the main stronghold. Freer, being the wireless operator, heard the movements and orders for any operations they took part in. 'Despite being heavily shelled, 4 Troop turned to the left and came up against strong Japanese bunkers which they engaged at very close range. One Jap ran up to Sergeant Shuker's tank from behind it and stuck a magnetic mine on the rear'.[39] The mine exploded but, as the men of the 25th Dragoons had learned at the Admin Box, they were not strong enough to breach even the thinner armour on the side and rear. The tools and stowage were blown away, and Shuker reported a small fuel leak, but no other damage. He was still ordered out of the fight as a precaution. The shelling also damaged another tank in 7 Troop and the crew bailed out.

The tanks withdrew to Bishenpur for the night, being too vulnerable for a second night harboured within Potsangbam, especially now they had kicked up a hornet's nest. Despite their casualties in the heavy fighting, the Gurkhas fought through the night, and had cleared most of the village. The West Yorks were added to the attack, and B Squadron was back in the northern half of Potsangbam to clear the final area by late morning. At 2pm, their attack went in, and bunker busting resumed. Freer saw at close hand the outcome 'bunkers were quickly destroyed and flattened. Odd rifles, steel helmets and Jap bodies were mixed up with the timber and mud which had once been a stronghold. The procedure now seemed to have become commonplace'.[40] The infantry mopped up the final remaining Japanese, some acting aggressively trying to take an enemy with them, others had clearly killed themselves with grenades in their foxholes or bunkers. By the following day, and after Freer and the other men in B Squadron spent another difficult night sleeping in their tanks, the last remnants of resistance was cleared.

By now, 48th Brigade had set up their roadblock near Torbung, and fought valiantly to hold it, but the advance through Potsangbam had not materialised as hoped. The fighting there was attritional and bloody, not a rapid breakthrough. The 48th Brigade ended up fighting north up to Potsangbam, which they reached on the 24th May. Whilst Cowan's tactical plan had failed, for 63rd Brigade to advance to 48th Brigade crushing any resistance in between, his strategic goal of inflicting heavy casualties on 33rd Division was a success. They had also completely disrupted the 33rd Division's attempts to advance on the Tiddim Road to Imphal in this direction. The Japanese troops in the mountains to the west on the Silchar Track continued to fight hard but had also been disrupted by 32nd Brigade receiving only limited supplies since 48th Brigade's roadblock. The 214th Regiment managed to get a battalion into the mule compound in Bishenpur, and another battalion captured a hill overlooking 17th Indian Division's HQ six miles to the north. The 3rd Carabiniers and a battalion of Baluchis cleared the hill on the 28th May. The fighting in Bishenpur and near 17th Indian Division's HQ practically wiped out the 214th Regiment, losing 360 of their 380 men who made the assaults. The threat from the south had been broken.

In all directions the advantage had well and truly swung to Fourteenth Army. The Japanese 15th and 33rd Divisions had taken huge casualties, and the momentum of their advance had petered out. The attrition through April and May was terminal, especially as the Japanese had only brought with them supplies for twenty days since the beginning of March. They had been using mule trains through the mountains, but this was simply not enough. The monsoon was in full swing, and the low-lying areas began to see rising water levels, and boggier ground. The rivers began to deepen, and they raged as the water came down from the mountains. Disease became more of a problem for the men of both sides.

The fighting could not stop though whilst the Japanese urged their men on in the mountains over the western Silchar Track and launched a final attempt to breakthrough from the south through Ningthoukhong with tanks. They all failed. The eastern Shenam Saddle, northern Iril Valley, and north-eastern Ukhrul road sectors still held and saw the first advances to try and cut off 15th Division. The most significant fighting in June, however, took place on the Imphal-Kohima road to the north. The Japanese were still only a few miles from Imphal Main Airfield, and the city itself, posing a threat despite their casualties. The mountains between the road and the Iril Valley were proving too difficult to clear, and the logistical situation in the Imphal Plain was becoming a worry now the monsoon weather had decreased the rate of aerial resupply. Estimates suggested there would be a shortfall of 15,000 tons. The priority therefore became reopening the road to Kohima by 15th June. The 2nd British Infantry Division had ended that siege on 20th April, cleared the area, and were now pushing south to relieve Imphal.

C Squadron of the 3rd Carabiniers and the 7th Cavalry would be unleashed with the infantry of 5th Indian Division from attritional patrolling in and around Lion Box, and actually move to clear the road and meet 2nd Division. In the first week of June 123rd Brigade had moved up the hills to the east of the Imphal-Kohima road. The exhausted and hungry Japanese troops of 15th Division grimly held on for every inch. At the village of Modbung, there was a line of hills to the east, with peaks connected by saddles, from south to north George, Harry, Isaac, James, Dot, Dash, Pip, Squeak, and Wilfred. There were more of these features further north too. Unsurprisingly, it was proving difficult to clear these ridges of Japanese troops, although their proximity to the Imphal-Kohima road meant they could not be left to starve. They could have been isolated where they now stood, but this would have meant fewer British and Indian troops clearing the road to Kohima. If the Japanese troops were left in place they could raid the Imphal Plain, and disrupt operations on the road. Leaving them was not an option. The laborious task of getting the tanks up the hills therefore had to continue. By the evening of 6th June 1944, C Squadron were atop George, which had already been cleared by the 2nd Suffolks. Captain Morgan, C Squadron's second-in-command, led the four tanks with his HQ tank, and 5 Troop. After struggling to get to Harry, Morgan called for a D8 bulldozer to go and tow the tanks up. One managed the climb by 3am the next morning, and the four tanks were on top of Harry by 6:30am. After a long night, the attack went forward at 9:30am.

The going was not easy, it had been raining heavily for much of the last few days, with tanks slipping frequently on the ridgeline. As one tank reached the top, it climbed over a neutralised bunker, but slipped back. They kept trying and managed to destroy more bunkers from the position they had gained, but the recoil of the gun and the way the tank rocked back meant it slid back 50 yards into dead ground, throwing a track in the process. Morgan called in more sappers. They worked out they could build a log track up the peak in the dead ground where the tank had slipped into. As soon as the engineers began their work, however, the Japanese opened fire with light mortars or rifle grenades, wounding three sappers. They called off their work until nightfall when they completed the track.

The tanks were showing their wear and tear, the tank chosen to lead the assault was the HQ tank because it had the best engine. The tanks in an HQ Troop normally carried the squadron commander, or the FOO, so to lead an attack was unusual. After months of intense fighting, the strain on the engines, gear boxes and difficulties with spare parts meant they were beginning to struggle. The tank was handed over to one of the regular fighting crews, commanded by Lieutenant Cole, who got the tank successfully onto the ridge. The sappers track had worked. As Cole turned to head along the rest of the ridgeline, the tank was hit twice by *Tateki* M2 hollow charge AT rifle grenades*, one of which penetrated the armour. The tank caught fire and Cole ordered the crew to bail out. They were silhouetted against the skyline at the top of the ridge in full view of multiple bunkers just a few yards away. Japanese light machine guns opened fire. Only three men made it back to Harry. One man was found shot on the ground, the other three shot and burned on the hull of the tank, including Cole. The infantry moved up as close as they could, and a Hurribomber strike went in at 5pm, but the attack was over for that day.

The next day they were able to make progress. The D8 was used again to pull them up, before the Suffolks and the tanks cleared the bunkers. Over the next two days they captured the other hills over Modbung and took the village, again utilising log tracks and D8s to get them where they needed to go. At the same time the Japanese roadblock on the Imphal/Kohima road was cleared by the West Yorks and a troop of C Squadron. Japanese resistance was beginning to slip away on some of the hills to concentrate on others. The tanks in the hills pressed on, linking up with other infantry units who had assaulted other hills from the road. The weather was atrocious when these operations began, but by mid-June it was becoming almost impossible. Brigadier Evans, commanding the 123rd Brigade fighting with C Squadron, noted how 'the rain teemed down almost incessantly, so that although a few tanks were laboriously winched up the hills, attacks had to be called off because neither men nor mules could stand on the slippery slopes'.[41] On the 15th June, the tanks in the hills were called down, and returned to their old harbour at Oyster Box. The tanks on the road did help the infantry in the hills by firing from the road, although this was no more than harassing fire.

---
* The *Tateki* M2 anti-tank rifle grenade was an ingenious hollow-charge weapon - one of the few German weapons to be used by the Japanese

The concerns about supplies were becoming more and more acute as the estimated deadline for reopening the road passed, so a final push on the road was made. This included a wide outflanking march in the hills west of the road by the 1/17th Dogras, whilst the West Yorks and part of C Squadron destroyed roadblocks in the valley. The whole country leant itself to defence, especially during the monsoon. The Japanese held on for as long as they could, fighting savagely. The difficulty for the men of 5th Indian Division breaking out of the Imphal Plain is reflected by their progress; from 3rd-22nd June they cleared seven miles up the road. 2nd Division cleared 65 miles travelling south from Kohima. On 22nd June the 1/17th Dogras met the spearhead of 2nd Division on the road, followed shortly by 7 Troop, 3rd Carabiniers. Another siege was broken.

The 3rd Carabiniers were withdrawn to Oyster Box on 23rd June to rest and refit after a long three months fighting in the mountains and villages on and around the Imphal Plain. In early July, Mutaguchi eventually admitted defeat after trying to order his divisions to attack Palel on the south-eastern corner of the Imphal Plain. His battered divisions were simply too weak to even attempt an assault. His order was given on the 16th July, by which time Ukhrul in the north had already fallen. To give time for the Japanese troops to cross the Chindwin, Mutaguchi ordered Yamamoto Force to hold on to their Shenam Saddle positions, under the increasing pressure of the newly arrived XXXIII Corps. IV Corps was able to reinforce Bishenpur and Silchar Track areas in the south to begin their advance to recapture Tiddim. Slim's decision to drive on at this stage through the height of the monsoon was significant. Instead of holding position and consolidating the Imphal Plain, he pursued the critically weakened 15th Army back to where they had started. Slim was able to cross the Chindwin later in the year with the minimum of fuss, rather than fighting in the mountains they had so tenaciously held themselves against a reinforced enemy.

The Japanese were well and truly defeated, the worst land defeat they would suffer in the Second World War. At Imphal and Kohima, estimates suggest 30,000 Japanese and their allies were killed, with a further 23,000 wounded. Staggeringly, the death rate in the combat units was 81%. These include the huge numbers who died of starvation and disease that were found on the routes back to the Chindwin. They left behind all of their heavy equipment. In comparison, Fourteenth Army lost 16,000 casualties, 12,000 of whom at Imphal.

A Japanese 15th Division signals intercept from 3rd June suggested a complete fixation with tanks after the fighting around Lion Box. They stated that "tanks must be defeated at all costs…complete preparation, both mental and material is absolutely essential when dealing with tanks."[42] The details of the signal showed how basic their methods were, highlighting the inability to really target tanks with AT guns from the front, and advising close quarter fighting with grenades and Molotov cocktails. If an AT gun opened fire too soon, it was liable to be destroyed because it could not damage the enemy tanks. In a reflection of the quality of Indian Army support services, the Japanese ordered abandoned tanks to be attacked and destroyed immediately because they were so often rescued and put back into service. The inability for the Japanese war economy to give their soldiers truly effective AT weapons, or for their leadership to develop a common doctrine for AT defence, is underlined by this signal's rudimentary solutions.

The 254th Indian Tank Brigade, and especially the 3rd Carabiniers, had been one of the most important aspects of the battle. As had happened when 7th Armoured Brigade arrived in 1942, they provided direct firepower against Japanese positions. Tanks proved more economical than artillery because of their ability to get so close to their target to accurately destroy a bunker in just a handful of rounds. They broke roadblocks, rescued surrounded infantry, and gave general fire support from the roads. Most importantly, they were able to perfect the bunker busting methods developed over the second half of 1943 that were tested and refined in Arakan in early 1944 to recapture the mountains and villages that the Japanese captured. The ability for information to be shared between corps so quickly is testament to the quality and professionalism of the Indian Army. Tanks, and the 3rd Carabiniers in particular, were sent to the key battlegrounds at crucial moments. The 7th Cavalry to Tiddim, the 150th RAC to the Silchar Track, the 3rd Carabiniers to Bishenpur, Shenam Saddle (briefly), the Imphal-Kohima road, and most importantly, Nunshigum. Many of these places had caused significant casualties to infantry units, or they had changed hands multiple times. These issues were often overcome when the tanks arrived, and infantry's immediately reduced casualty rates. The battle had shown that through skill, determination, and if needed with support from the Royal and Indian Engineers, tanks could get anywhere. And once a tank was there, it was always decisive.

KOHIMA RIDGE

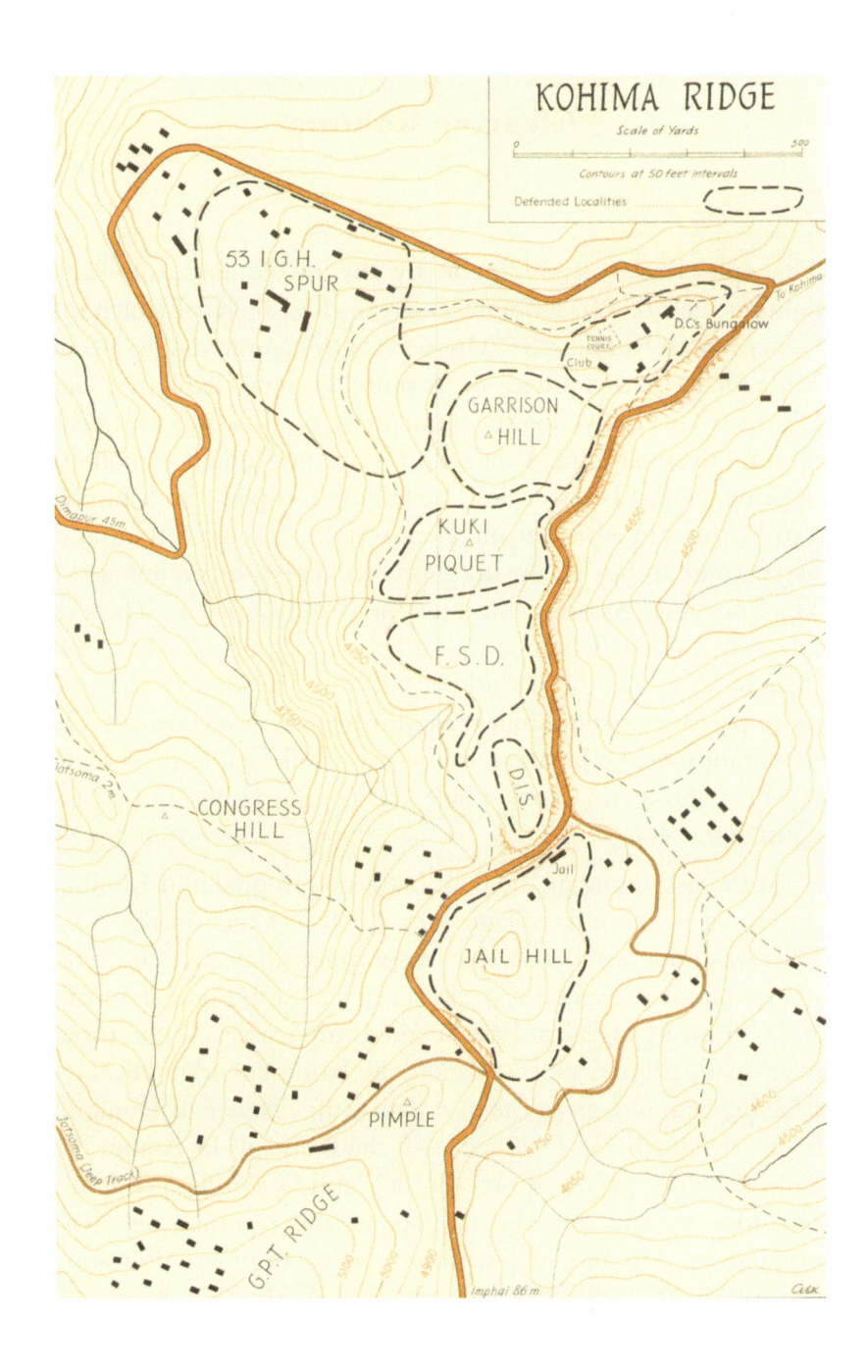

Scale of Yards
0 — 500
Contours at 50 feet intervals
Defended Localities

- 53 I.G.H. SPUR
- D.C.'s Bungalow
- Tennis Court
- Club
- GARRISON HILL
- KUKI PIQUET
- F.S.D.
- D.I.S.
- Jail
- CONGRESS HILL
- JAIL HILL
- PIMPLE
- G.P.T. RIDGE
- Dimapur 45 m.
- Jotsoma 2 m.
- Jotsoma Jeep Track
- To Kohima
- Imphal 86 m.

9
Clearing Kohima

The epic 16-day stand made by the mixed force of 1,500 fighting men of the Kohima Garrison had halted Lieutenant-General Sato Kotoku's 31st Division. Sato's commanding officer, Mutaguchi, had wanted to capture Imphal, Kohima, and Dimapur for his own logistical purposes, on the way to his drive up the Brahmaputra Valley and start an Indian nationalist uprising against British rule. The failure to capture both Imphal and Kohima in April meant there were now tens of thousands of Japanese troops occupying positions across the mountains of Manipur and Assam with little logistical support. The 31st Division, in much higher mountains and much further from their bases across the Chindwin 120 miles away, were in a far more precarious state than those further south at Imphal. The desperation of the Japanese soldiers was reflected in the ferocity of the fighting that took place during the siege, and in the fighting to follow.

At the beginning of the twin battles of Imphal and Kohima, the threat to the little village over 4,000 feet high in the Naga Hills was underestimated. The assumption that anything more than a Japanese regiment could reach such inhospitable terrain so far from its logistical base seemed impossible. As the threat developed, Slim decided to hold at Kohima, originally as a delaying action to give time to organise the defence of Dimapur, before striking back. The success of the Battle of the Admin Box allowed Slim to transport the 5th and 7th Indian Infantry Divisions by air from the Arakan to the central front. Two brigades of 5th Indian Division went to Imphal. After some confusion, 161st Brigade of 5th Indian Division eventually rushed into Kohima itself to provide most of the infantry for the siege just before the first Japanese assaults. The brigade HQ and artillery formed a defensive box at the nearby village of Jotsoma to the west to provide artillery support to the garrison.

Kohima itself is spread over a series of wooded hills that the infantry now occupied. The defensive positions were roughly centred on the hill where the District Commissioner's (DC) bungalow and tennis court were, called Garrison Hill*. These hills overlooked the winding road from Dimapur to Imphal as it passed through Kohima. Sato's men, with one column being delayed at Sangshak near Imphal, and another at Jessami nearer Kohima, captured some of the hills to the east and south of the village, cutting the road to Imphal on the night of the 5th April. They finished surrounding the garrison the following day. Launching fanatical attacks, the Japanese clawed their way onto the different positions, tightening the noose until Garrison Hill was the last position, only a few hundred yards across. The tennis court at the DC's Bungalow famously became no-man's land on that side of the ridge, the defenders fighting hard and inflicting horrendous casualties on the unimaginative Japanese assaults. The garrison held on despite their own casualties in some of the most vicious fighting of the war anywhere, in horrific conditions, waiting for their relief to arrive.

Reinforcements were soon arranged: the 2nd British Infantry Division, who were training and acclimatising in India before deployment. 7th Indian Division was also to be airlifted after the 5th Indian Division lift, from Arakan. They would gather at Dimapur to fight south and relieve the siege. 2nd Division arrived at the vast supply base first, and found the personnel there were in a state of panic, expecting an attack at any moment. The piecemeal arrival of 149th Regiment, Royal Armoured Corps (RAC), in early April helped relieve the tension before the tanks made their move south over the following week. The reinforcements faced their first Japanese positions at Zubza,

---
*Some accounts refer to this as Summerhouse Hill

whilst fighting through the mountains. They met up with troops of 161st Brigade on 16th April, although they continued working forward to take over from the garrison completely.

When the men of the 2nd Division got through and took over the trenches of Garrison Hill on 20th April, they could see the ferocity of the siege before them. The corpses and smell of decay was atrocious, the trees were stripped bare, with parachutes hanging in the few remaining branches, and discarded equipment was everywhere. Japanese snipers and artillery harassed the relief, but it had been planned carefully enough to avoid too much of the movement happening in view of the Japanese. The defenders of the siege made their way down the gullies by Indian General Hospital (IGH) spur to lorries waiting on the Kohima-Dimapur road to the north, where the relief had come from. Standing guard over the lorries, ready to escort the brave defenders of Kohima to a well-deserved rest, were Grant tanks* of Lieutenant Lochhead's 2 Troop, A Squadron, 149th RAC.

The armoured story at Kohima therefore begins halfway through the battle itself. When the 2nd Division infantry took over the Garrison Hill positions, they were attacked by Sato's men immediately, and would be constantly, usually at night. They came in waves, just as they had before, but were now facing fresher troops. The Japanese were having to start all over again but with fewer troops who were more exhausted. Sato decided to go onto the defensive to force the British troops to have to go onto the attack and into the open, where they would be killed by Japanese soldiers in bunkers. This is why the tanks would become so important. After providing mobile artillery against outposts from the roads in the valleys from Zubza to Kohima,

---

*The difference between the Lees of 25th Dragoons and 3rd Carabiniers, and the Grants of the 149th and 150th RAC was the Grant's British designed cast turret, which rounds inward at the base. The Lee turret is vertical down to where it meets the hull. The Grant's turret had a rear bulge to contain the radio, meaning the crew could be reduced from seven in the Lee, to six in the Grant. The 37mm loader often took on the radio operator's role.

they were to take on the more difficult task of helping the infantry clear the Japanese bunkers on positions they now occupied with intention of holding them to the last. The first operations began on 22nd April with A Squadron and would centre on the area around the DC's Bungalow. B Squadron was still on its way to the front by train. Two troops moved up, with Lieutenant Lochhead's 2 Troop destroying three bunkers after driving through their own artillery fire, before one of the tanks was slightly damaged by a 37mm AT gun firing at long range. They could not get up the hill properly though, it was too slippery because the monsoon rains had come early, in April rather May. The next few days involved keeping the road open and setting up a secure harbour at the Royal Engineer's dump nearby, with whom they started to discuss how to get up to the DC's Bungalow and the tennis court. This was the area of immediate concern because it directly overlooked the road to Imphal, which curved round the whole complex. The tank men's coordination with the Royal Engineers and infantry was going to be very important in the coming weeks if there was to be any hope of removing the tenacious Japanese soldiers in their bunker complexes.

Sitting just below Garrison Hill, to the northeast, the area around the DC's Bungalow consisted of four terraces. The terrace nearest Garrison Hill-proper was the highest point with a clubhouse, then the tennis court, the bungalow itself, and then a garden that itself overlooked the road. Each drop was between ten and forty feet, and each was very steep if not near vertical. This meant, that, unless you were at the edge looking down, you could not see what was on the terrace below, and anyone who tried to look down was liable to be shot at immediately. This meant the exact position of Japanese defences was unclear. The middle two, the tennis court and the bungalow, were the heart of the Japanese position, and they had built strong mutually supporting bunkers throughout, with crawl trenches between many of them, and plenty of camouflage as usual. Most of the vegetation and buildings were gone by now, reduced to rubble, although the chimney of the DC's Bungalow stood. There were skeletal trees, sheets of corrugated iron, sandbags, discarded equipment and other detritus. To try and clear the Japanese bunkers attempts were made to get tanks onto the terraces from the end of April. The rains made the going very slippery, and even with a ramp built by the Royal Engineers and winches, the attempts made on 29th April and 4th May ended with half a dozen tanks destroyed or damaged, and a number of killed and wounded crew. Although during the second of these operations they did manage to get some tanks through to the troops fighting for Naga Village to the northeast, giving 5th Brigade the benefit of their firepower.

B Squadron, under Major Ezra Rhodes, finally arrived in the area at the end of April and were soon in action. Most of A Squadron of 149th RAC had been in constant action for two weeks, engaging Japanese positions on the route down from Dimapur, and now in the hills around Kohima. The failures to get a tank onto the DC's Bungalow area, and the need to rest A Squadron, meant a change of direction. B Squadron with infantry from 2nd Durham Light Infantry (DLI) would attack the hills south of Garrison Hill, opening up a new route onto the clubhouse terrace.

The attempt to get a tank to the DC's Bungalow on the 4th May was done during a bigger operation to get to these hills. The following days saw atrocious monsoon rain, making the job of getting the tanks up the hills even more difficult. From Garrison Hill working south they were named Kuki Piquet, Field Supply Depot (FSD), and Detail Issue (DIS). The southern end of FSD and DIS were the objective for that day, clearing these hills, then Kuki Piquet the following day. After damaging four tanks to mines on the road, by the evening of 5th May, Rhodes had got a scratched-together troop of three tanks onto the top of FSD. After destroying some bunkers through the day, they harboured for the night with the infantry, having failed to get on to Kuki Piquet. This setback meant 6th Brigade decided to evacuate FSD for now and get a tank up onto Garrison Hill. After trying to move round the western side of Kuki Piquet, Rhodes tried the eastern side, where he had more success.

They rounded the bend on the track and were now around behind Kuki Piquet where Japanese troops thought they were safe. The tank took the Japanese infantry completely by surprise and Rhodes's crew opened fire. The Japanese soldiers jumped to the floor, and started crawling for their bunkers and trenches, although some stayed in place. Rhodes pressed on, but the track towards Garrison Hill began to narrow, with the rising hill to their left, and a steep drop to their right. The wet mud on the right started to give, and the tank slithered off the muddy track: 'there, trouble started' reported Rhodes afterwards, 'every effort was made to put the tank right again, but owing to the trees, state of the ground and steepness of the slope, it proved impossible'.[1] The tank had broken a track on the way down, a common occurrence when tanks slid sideways.

Japanese infantry now started to stalk the tank like a fly in a spider's web. Infantry crept forwards through the trees towards the 28-ton monster that had fallen right into their position. Rhodes called up another tank nearby to provide some help; Sergeant Brearley began making his way round Kuki Piquet to Rhodes's stranded tank. The slide down the hillside had slightly thrown the crew's normal procedures. Not quite realising the danger they were in; Rhodes had not closed his turret hatch. Suddenly, a grenade dropped into the turret, wounding Rhodes on the head. The following explosion and head wound dazed Rhodes for a moment, but miraculously, no one was seriously hurt. Moments later, he came round, another grenade dropped in through the hatch. Incredibly, this one also failed to cause any damage or wounds. Rhodes now reached up and closed the hatch taking a moment to orient himself, but the Japanese continued to snipe at the pistol ports and driver's hatch. He realised they might be able to reverse back up the hill to the track they had slipped from. Rhodes gave the order, and the driver, Lance Corporal Henderson, put the tank in gear, and opened the throttle. Immediately it was clear this was a bad idea.

"Can't hold her" Henderson shouted.[2] The tank started to slide again, and they fell further down the slope before the front smashed against a tree, the rear slewing round before it came to rest.* 'There were two courses left, one to stay and fight to the end, two to make a run for it'.[3] By now Brearley's tank had moved round the hill and was able to provide some covering fire, keeping Japanese infantry at bay, and giving Rhodes and his crew time to destroy the vital equipment. They made their escape, springing from the hatches. A light machine gun opened up on them but failed to make any hits, although one man heard a bullet whistle by his ear. They made their way southeast in bounds along the road to the RE ramp built from the road up to Garrison Hill, where they made it into the 2nd battalion, the Dorsetshire Regiment's lines.

'An exciting party' Rhodes wrote in his after-action report, 'one tank lost, the crew saved, one slight head wound'.[4] The incident confirmed that tanks needed to work closely with infantry, or at least with other tanks. They had been called up on their own and nearly paid the price. 'The crew behaved magnificently…there was no 'flap' on detanking, otherwise the party would never have got away'.[5] The operations had failed to clear FSD and Kuki Piquet, although they held a toehold on the former, but the 1st Royal Welch Fusiliers had taken significant casualties trying to take the latter. While the hills in the wider area were slowly getting cleared, the road was still blocked by the

---

*The tank is still there with the inscription 'after the battle the 2nd Division requested that the tank remain in the exact position from which it had to be abandoned as a memorial to the heroism and sacrifice of all those who fought in the battle'.

DC's Bungalow complex. This meant they would need to find another way to get a tank onto the tennis court.

The tennis court had seen some of the most intense fighting of the entire battle, if not the whole campaign in Burma. The once pristine tennis court had become no-man's-land on the northeast side of the perimeter, and held by 2nd Dorsets, with their HQ to the rear of the clubhouse terrace, directly above the tennis court. They had been tasked with retaking the DC's Bungalow sector, but had faced severe attacks from the Japanese, and constantly exchanged grenades over the tiny area. Shortly after occupying the position, 2nd Dorsets had attacked from the west side of the area and tried to hook behind the tennis court towards the DC's Bungalow. They had failed to clear it, but A Company did establish a small position in the northeast corner of the hill directly over the road, on the lowest garden terrace. The Japanese were desperate to hold the area to keep dominating the road winding around the hill. Even with the rest of Kohima cleared, if the DC's Bungalow complex was still under Japanese control, Imphal would remain cut off.

Sergeant Charles Gerard Waterhouse was a sinewy, moustachioed, tank commander in Major Ezra Rhodes's B Squadron, 149th RAC. 'Gerry', as he was known, had left school at 14, and through his teacher got a job at the Columbia Pictures Distribution Office in Leeds. He had a difficult day on the 11th May supporting an attack and bunker busting on FSD. His troop commander Lieutenant Peter Wood had got stuck, so Waterhouse's tank went to tow him out. As the vehicle and Wood approached each other, the tank ran over a mine, immobilising the tank and fatally wounding Wood. Both tanks were abandoned.

The following afternoon Waterhouse was called back to 6th Brigade's HQ, where the commander Brigadier Shapland held a briefing. He was told to take his crew and a new tank and get it onto the tennis court and clear the whole sector down to the

DC's Bungalow itself with 2nd Dorsets. They had already taken heavy casualties trying to take the tennis court, with its multiple bunkers sighted to support one another, and crawl trenches connecting them. Sappers had been working away for a number of days, despite the wet ground and the steep gradient, making a track up to Garrison Hill from IGH Spur to the northwest. Luckily 'the Kohima area is very good bulldozing country: there seems to be no hard rock', a bulldozing sapper's paradise.[6] From there, Waterhouse was to take his tank onto the clubhouse terrace, hide the tank behind a small rise called The Pimple*, and next morning get onto the tennis court.

Waterhouse left the briefing in no doubt that his tank was to be the final piece of the puzzle. He returned to his crew and climbed into their tank. Brigadier Shapland approached Waterhouse's wiry driver, Trooper Sydney Bull.

"Keep going whatever happens and ignore what you will run over".[7]

Bull was not entirely happy with this exchange, finding the idea of running over anyone as distasteful. Bull carefully drove Waterhouse and their tank up the recently completed slippery track arriving at 2nd Dorsets' HQ near the clubhouse that evening, 12th May. They camouflaged the tank, and the crew made their preparations for the next day's operation, while Waterhouse liaised with the infantry. The second-in-command of the Dorsets was Major Geoffrey White, and he recalled how 'nearly every man who could get away from their post came to look at this monster which was to help us annihilate the stubborn defenders of the bungalow the next morning'.[8] To provide some local fire support a Sikh-manned 3.7-inch mountain gun from 10th Field Regiment was dragged up to fire over open sights, in addition to the infantry's mortars. Longer distance fire would be too inaccurate after the initial bombardment. Waterhouse was

---

*Confusingly, there is a second, larger and more famous, hill to the south of Kohima that was called The Pimple during the battle.

introduced to Lieutenant Lintorn 'Snagger' Highett of C Company, 2nd Dorsets, who would ride behind the driver Sydney Bull. Highett would act as a guide, having fought on the tennis court when his company took a turn in the line there and had been there on night patrols, so he knew the locations of most of the bunkers. None of the Dorset's companies were in a particularly fit state after the last couple of weeks fighting. C Company had not long been pulled out for a rest, B Company could barely field a strong platoon, and A Company was occupying the garden terrace on the northeast corner of the DC's Bungalow area. Captain Clive Chettle's D Company was chosen because they were the freshest troops available. Geoffrey White explained the infantry plan: 'we based our hopes on getting a hold on the northeast corner of the tennis court, from where the infantry under the supporting fire of the Lee* tank would clear the position under the club bank, whilst a further platoon working on the right…would clear the water tank and long tin shed area…a third platoon…would exploit to the bungalow terrace'.[9] White's description misses some important details that help picture how the attack was to proceed. The platoon attacking the water tank and long tin shed would move around the east side of The Pimple and destroy the three Japanese machine guns. This would allow them to attack the tennis court from the south-eastern flank. At the same time, Waterhouse and another platoon of D Company would attack the tennis court directly from the southwest of The Pimple. The two platoons, plus the platoon in reserve, and Waterhouse's tank, would then continue together to assault the DC's Bungalow.

Waterhouse, White, and Highett went on a reconnaissance of the route to the tennis court before last light, carefully making their way to the observation post on The Pimple. They identified a likely place to drop the tank, before going back to check everything was set. The attack was due to start at 9am, 13th May,

---
*Non-armoured corps troops almost invariably called all Lee/Grants Lees, even if they were not.

but there was a delay of an hour. Bull drove Waterhouse and the rest of the crew along a winding track from the Dorset's HQ to the start line. An artillery bombardment began, hammering the far edge of the tennis court and the DC's Bungalow area. By 10am the guns stopped.

At 9.55am, Bull put the tank in gear and moved forward slowly. They made it to the drop point Waterhouse, White, and Highett had identified, and paused. Highett remembered 'the longest part of our action appeared to be whilst we were at the top of the vertical drop onto the tennis court…it was probably just a few minutes as we could not be stationary for too long because of the threat of the Japanese anti-tank gun'.[10] Bull balanced the tank on the edge, making the final call whether to try it.

"'Old on!" shouted Bull.[11] He lurched the tank forward and the tank dropped down the ten-foot near-vertical terrace. Outside the tank was the sound of crunching logs as the tank dropped onto one of the Japanese bunkers, crushing and burying the occupants. The men felt a bump as they landed, but no one inside heard a thing. They could hear little else apart from the roar of the engine, gunfire, and radio static in their ears interspersed with orders and information being exchanged on the intercom. The signal for Chettle's D Company to begin their assault was the first 75mm round being fired into the Japanese bunkers. The flanking fire from the water tank and long tin shed was the biggest threat to the infantry in the opening stage of the attack. 2nd Dorsets had also laid a smokescreen with their 2-inch mortars behind the tennis court to separate it from the DC's Bungalow and hide the tank attack. The 3.7-inch gun fired 48 rounds from just 100 yards on the cluster of small buildings at the end of the long tin shed at the same time.

Highett's knowledge of the Japanese position came into its own. Instructing Bull to turn right as the tank loomed onto the tennis court area. The tank rattled and dinged as rifle and machine gun fire now uselessly peppered the armour. Desperate Japanese troops tried and failed to blind the tank by aiming at the periscopes. The 75mm gun swivelled menacingly in its sponson onto the water tank, the Japanese had reinforced it with sandbags. *Bang!* The first 75mm round barked out of the barrel, sandbags and chunks of metal flew up and out from the water tank. They shifted attack onto the long tin shed. 'My 75-gunner dealt with this position so effectively that the Nips started to leave in a hell of a hurry without even arms or equipment' reported Waterhouse afterwards.[12] Infantry machine guns opened up and most of the Japanese infantry fell as they ran.

That first shot into the water tank signalled the beginning of the infantry attack. Sections of infantry charged into some trenches on the western side of the tennis court, and after a delay as they repositioned to better take on the bunkers, they began using their pole charges. They could be quite dangerous to the user, consisting of an eight-foot bamboo pole using a gun cotton charge and a short time-fuse. The risk of the Japanese pushing the charge out the way it came meant the user had to pull the fuse, wait about five seconds then shove it into a bunker's aperture. Sergeant Cook of 2nd Dorsets closed upon the water tank as they followed up Waterhouse's assault. He was fairly close and started to prepare a pole charge. He pulled the fuse, waited, then turned and thrust it against the remains of the water tanks. The charge exploded, but Cook had forgotten to close his eyes as debris and dirt flew into his face when the charge went off. He was temporarily blinded, and was evacuated, but recovered later.

The time was now 10.40am, the water tank and long tin shed area was being mopped up by the platoon on the right. The platoon on the left flank, attacking the tennis court directly, was pinned down by machine gun fire from some servant's quarters near the edge of the terrace. Waterhouse turned his tank to the left 'we next paid our attention to a series of crawl trenches and

MG posts all around the tennis court and had a hell of a party for the next twenty minutes or so'.[13] The infantry made their move under cover of Waterhouse's tank; by this time Highett was using the bow machine gun himself. 'A section under Corporal Cook* then went forward and occupied the area of servant's quarters and bamboo clump, covered to within approximately five yards by tank Browning MG fire'.[14]

From the observation post on The Pimple, Colonel Jock McNaught CO of 2nd Dorsets, Geoffrey White, Richard Sharpe from the BBC, and Lieutenant Norman Havers, 2nd Dorsets intelligence officer, were watching the proceedings. They only saw fleeting moments of the action through the smoke drifting across their view from the explosions, gunfire, and dust that was thrown up throughout the action. Havers remembered seeing one of the platoon commanders, Sergeant Given, approach the tank that was still firing at some positions: 'we watched him use the telephone carried at the rear of the tank to speak to its commander inside'.[15] He told Waterhouse that all of the Japanese positions had been destroyed.

Waterhouse ordered Bull to get the tank to the top of the terrace overlooking the DC's Bungalow. They started hammering the remains of the building with everything they had. At 11:10am the infantry had got into positions above the bungalow to make their final assault. The tank switched to AP shot, allowing the infantry to move in. 31-year-old Corporal Alfred Siggins single-handedly attacked a Japanese bunker with a pole charge. As he emerged from cover and moved forward, he was shot and killed, the only fatality in the entire operation.

"The Japanese are getting out" someone shouted from the observation post on The Pimple, remembered Havers.[16] 'We moved to where we could look out eastwards over the Imphal road, and there the Japanese were running from the battle. Not in any controlled groups, but in ones and twos. They had had

---

* Not to be confused with the now temporarily blinded Sergeant Cook.

enough'.[17] Next to Havers, Sergeant Marlow opened fire until his rifle became too hot to hold as the trickle of Japanese troops retreating quickly turned into a flood once the tank turned on the DC's Bungalow. They were escaping to the east, dropping down onto the road, then on to Treasury Hill 800-yards to the northeast. A mortar and artillery concentration was called down on the line of retreat, and anyone in view opened up with rifles and Bren guns, causing heavy casualties.

By 11:15am, just over an hour since Bull had dropped his tank onto the Japanese bunker, the 2nd Dorsets had control of the entire the DC's Bungalow complex. Waterhouse and his crew pulled back to their maintenance area to the west on the Dimapur road. Chettle directed his men consolidating the position, bringing up barbed wire, ammunition, and reserve platoons to bolster the position in case of counterattack. Thuds and bangs of grenades and pole charges continued until early evening as the maze of Japanese bunkers and trenches were checked. Some still had living occupants who were quickly shot. Too many Japanese soldiers tried to take someone with them with a grenade or bayonet in these situations, so the Dorsets took no chances.

The 4th Royal West Kents had grimly held on at the tennis court for sixteen days through April, and the 2nd Dorsets had tried to wrest control of it for another twenty-three days after that. Hundreds of lives had been lost from both sides, and more wounded. Many of the bodies lay around, decaying, and black with flies, along with personal equipment, empty boxes of ammunition and other supplies, and broken or abandoned weapons. General debris, corrugated iron sheets, logs, splinters, and loose earth lay fresh over everything. A few white lines could still be made out on the tennis court, along with some silver cutlery around the bungalow, little reminders of the once idyllic little hill station. Despite the tiny area and numbers of men involved, in a war spanning the globe and millions of people, the holding, then clearing of the tennis court is surely one of the grimmest, most heroic, and impressive feat of arms ever undertaken.

There had been over five weeks of fighting on the tennis court, finally it was over. From A Company's first attack on the night of 26-27th April to the 12th May, the Dorsets lost 75 men, virtually all of whom around the DC's Bungalow. After all those casualties, 2nd Dorsets' assault on the 13th suffered just one fatality, Alfred Siggins, and four wounded. Once again, the Japanese had no answer to a tank when it was brought up, and once Waterhouse and his crew started to methodically neutralise the bunkers for the infantry, the survivors ran. The catalyst for victory around the DC's Bungalow was undoubtedly Waterhouse's Grant tank. Although, this was not just his victory, nor was it just the West Kents', Dorsets' or RAC's victory. This was also about the Royal Artillery's firepower and the Royal Engineers effort, building ramps and towing tanks, often under fire. For 39 days the battle for the tennis court had raged as an infantry and artillery fight, and in just eighty minutes with one tank, it was permanently in 2nd Division's hands.

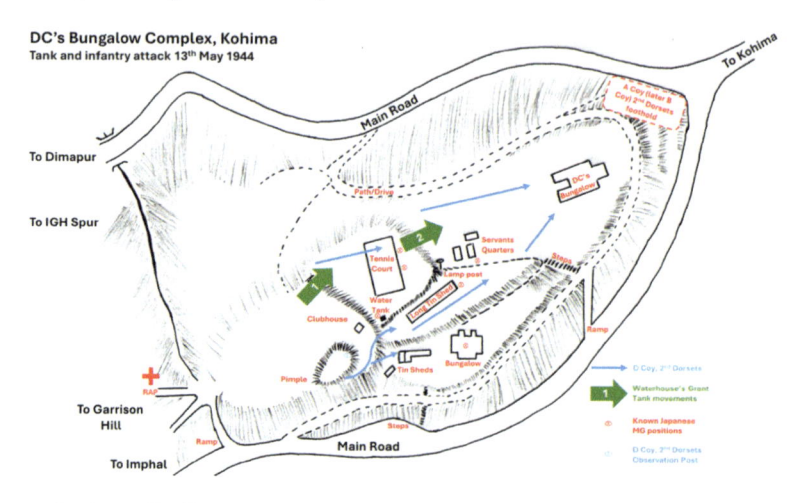

DC's Bungalow Complex, Kohima
Tank and infantry attack 13th May 1944

Sydney Bull spent the rest of his life remembering 'with a wry smile' his drop onto the tennis court, 'what could be termed "his finest hour'".[18] The Japanese held a number of very difficult positions overlooking the road nearby, however, and the battle would continue as it had done since 2nd, and 7th Indian Divisions, and 161st Brigade arrived to clear them. The acute threat to traffic on the Imphal-Kohima road had now been cleared. Soon the road would be fully opened, and the fight would continue south to relieve Imphal. As Waterhouse himself remarked in his after-action report: 'altogether quite a useful shoot'.[19]

The hills southeast of the tennis court battle were next. Some tanks had got through to the 4th and 33rd Brigades fighting here on the 4th May and had been supporting the infantry inching their way up the hills clearing Japanese bunkers one by one. The steepness of some of these slopes meant the tanks could not elevate their guns enough, and again the Royal Engineers solved the problem. John Henslow, for example, who had come up with the 33rd Brigade, 7th Indian Division, was one sapper put to work building upward-angled tank platforms with ammunition boxes filled with earth. This was in preparation for an attack on the reverse of Jail Hill in the middle of May, where the artillery could not supress the bunkers, but the same platforms were built in multiple valleys in the hills around Kohima. Building these platforms was a frightful proposition as they were often built in no-man's land below Japanese positions, so they were made at night. When preparing for one of these excursions, he asked an infantry sergeant what he should do to avoid being mistaken for a Japanese soldier on a jitter raid. Henslow was six foot four. The sergeant looked him up and down.

"No one is going to mistake you for a Jap sir, but if you whistle God Save the King in tune, we'll not open fire on you".[20] Henslow and his Indian sappers worked away, freezing when flares were fired and taking cover during sporadic shelling. They finished the job without a hitch, and they made their way back. The night had been nerve-wracking but successful. As they approached the infantry position, Henslow's nervousness meant he had a very dry mouth, and struggled to whistle as arranged. In desperation he called out.

"It's the sappers returning through your lines. Hold your fire".[21] There was no reply, nor was there the crack of rifle or Bren fire. He kept crawling ahead of his men.

"Well done, sir" whispered a voice from the dark "I'm glad you spoke when you did. I was about to give the order to open fire".[22] At first light the tanks trundled round Jail Hill and took up their positions on the platforms, and provided vital fire support against the bunkers as they were cleared. Similar operations would happen to the north at Naga Hill and south at the Aradura Spur. Before May was over there were some bloody assaults, repulsed by Japanese soldiers at the extreme end of their endurance.

Sato exhorted his men to fight to the death, although privately he recognised it was nearly the end. On 25th May he messaged Mutaguchi, who was meddling in the battle around Potsangbam south of Imphal, with an indirect appeal to withdraw because of the lack of supplies. Mutaguchi told him to hold on for ten more days. Incredibly, they did manage to hold on a little longer as the worst of the continuing monsoon struck. The exhausted 2nd Division were at their lowest ebb as they failed in repeated attempts to clear Aradura Spur. In the north, Naga Hill was cleared by 33rd Brigade on the 1st June, once again by getting tanks into a key position across a valley on sandbag platforms to fire at the bunkers. In the aftermath, Japanese troops were seen pulling back, the first sign that Sato's starving 31st Division was collapsing.

There were some unseemly exchanges between Sato and Mutaguchi towards the end of May. Sato informed his superior Mutaguchi that the failure to send supplies to 31st Division left Sato with no choice but to retreat. Sato perhaps did not realise that Mutaguchi's divisions at Imphal were suffering similar problems, although less acutely due to the shorter distances back to their supply bases. Mutaguchi did not understand just how close to collapse 31st Division was at Kohima either. He threatened Sato with a court martial if he retreated. Sato's response: 'Do as you please. I will bring you down with me'.[23] The radios were shut down, and Sato began his fighting withdrawal.

After 33rd Brigade's success clearing the northern-most Japanese-held hills, 7th Indian Division now swung southeast to outflank Aradura Spur during Sato and Mutaguchi's bad tempered exchange. This was in support of 2nd Division who had failed in a number of attempts to clear the position to continue opening the road south to relieve Imphal. There was growing criticism that Grover had not pushed his 2nd Division hard enough in the battle, and he would ultimately lose his job. As the Aradura Spur was cleared on 4th June, Sato's withdrawal began. 2nd and 7th Indian Divisions could now get beyond the hills 31st Division had held for months, driving down the road to Imphal. Japanese positions were now, therefore, improvised rearguards, rather than the well-laid bunker complexes built on Kohima ridge and the surrounding hills.

Now that the chase was on, 2nd Division would advance down the actual Imphal-Kohima road, with the tanks in support, and 7th Indian Division would advance in the hills to the east using mule and jeep transport. Fittingly, the advance really got going on the 6th June 1944, the same day as the Normandy landings in northwest Europe. A Squadron took part in a shoot that turned out to be against now empty bunkers, before some 45th Cavalry Stuarts advanced a couple of miles before finding their first blown bridge. Sappers quickly built a replacement that was open the next day, and the tanks harboured between MS54 and MS55. This was to become the routine; sappers sweeping for mines and repairing bridges, with small Japanese rearguards effecting weak ambushes.

On the morning of 8th June, the sappers lifted some stolen British mines before the column set out. Sergeant Gerry Waterhouse was leading his troop in B Squadron when they came across another blown bridge just beyond MS58. As the sappers moved forward, they came under fire and Waterhouse's troop provided cover, silencing a 37mm AT gun almost immediately after it opened fire. The small ambush was soon cleared, and the sappers made their repairs. Waterhouse's troop continued at the head of the column, although his tank was third in the line, with infantry now on the alert and moving on foot to the sides of the road. About halfway between MS59 and MS60 the lead tank was hit by a well-hidden Japanese 75mm gun, so Waterhouse nosed his tank forward to try and find it. As they creeped forward straining eyes to identify anything that might give away a gun hidden in the scrub, there was a heavy metallic thud. A 37mm AT gun had fired an AP shell that had lodged into the Grant's 75mm sponson and jammed it in place. Waterhouse's tank needed to pull back, so his troop corporal's tank moved up to take his place. This tank was then hit three times in quick succession from a 75mm gun. The gunner and loader both shouted and fell backwards. One of the three hits had hit their sponson and sent tiny shards of flaking metal from the interior wall of the tank[*] into the two men manning the 75mm. Another had caused the 37mm gun barrel to bulge. The Japanese guns appeared to be deliberately targeting the tanks' guns, and the damage suggested a range of around 100 yards. Still, no one had actually spotted any flashes, so the column pulled back and halted for the night. The next day they tried again, and a new troop took over whilst Waterhouse's troop were rested. This time the flash was spotted, the gun destroyed, and the column moved on.

What the 2nd Division's column had discovered was the first line of ambush points near Viswema. This was a small village of

---

[*] Called 'splash' at the time.

wooden *bashas** just to the east of the road near MS60 where Sato had decided to make something of a stand. The delaying tactics in the few days before had allowed what remained of 31st Division to build some bunkers and lay a more significant ambush. The advance came up against a stone roadblock this time, which the sappers de-mined and the Grants then blew out of the way with 75mm HE fire. No sooner had the column moved on than another 37mm AT gun opened up, this time from just 30 yards away. The leading tank's turret ring was jammed, the next tank had its drive sprocket† damaged, although it managed to destroy the gun and kill the crew. The infantry moving up to support either side of the road and patrols into the hills were also coming up against stiffer opposition, so it was decided to halt and make more formal plans. Over the next few days artillery was brought up, further infantry patrols worked out the lay of the land and gathered intelligence on the Japanese defences and captured local features overlooking Viswema to the north. Tanks supported these patrols with shoots from the roads, sometimes simple harassing fire, other times in more direct support destroying bunkers, including at the edge of Viswema village itself.

The main attack was to take place on 14th June. One part of the operation (Michael) was a complete success. After a short but heavy artillery concentration, with supplementary tank fire, the 7th Battalion, Worcestershire Regiment quickly overwhelmed the starving and desperate Japanese defenders, all forty of whom were killed. The second operation (George) that took place simultaneously was an A Squadron-led column with sappers and infantry on foot, in carriers, and on armoured cars, who were to race ahead and repair a bridge so the column could move forward quickly once Viswema was cleared. Everywhere there were clear signs of sudden withdrawal, such as abandoned

---

* Huts
† The spiked wheel that drives the tracks at the front of the tank.

equipment, until the column reached the bridge where the sappers got to work.

By 5am on 15th June the column could cross the repaired bridge and get moving again. In another sign of Sato's 31st Division's collapse, ambushing tactics became increasingly desperate. There were fewer guns waiting in ambush, replaced with suicide tactics, snipers, and tank-hunting parties. Near MS62 a magnetic mine was thrown onto the rear deck of A Squadron tank 'Awake', destroying the engine, although the crew was unhurt, and the guns and other equipment were all salvageable. None of this held up the inexorable advance to Imphal, with tanks offering fire support against the few remaining Japanese bunkers on some high ground above the road.

Another 75mm gun ambushed the column on 19th June near MS80, doing no damage, and was abandoned before it was destroyed, another sure sign of Japanese collapse. There was virtually no opposition now, more and more equipment was found abandoned, and increasing numbers of emaciated Japanese soldiers were found dead at the roadsides. By the 22nd June 2nd Division had advanced about 65 miles since 1st June, forty-nine of which were since continuing on from Viswema on the 15th June. At MS109 they met a patrol of 1/17th Dogras, 5th Indian Division, on the road at 10.30am of 22nd June, finally joining hands with the defenders of Imphal. Shortly after, 149th RAC joined the 3rd Carabiniers at Oyster Box in the Imphal perimeter to rest and maintain their vehicles before they would both continue the chase to the Chindwin River.

Kohima had been another disaster for the Japanese 15th Army. 31st Division lost 6,000 men, although the original garrison during the siege phase, and the XXXIII Corps troops who cleared it after paid dearly with 4,000 casualties. The British, Indian, and Gurkha casualties could have suffered far more.

There is no escaping the fact that the tennis court was a place of bleak, bloody, stalemate for over a month, until Waterhouse and his crew cleared it with 2nd Dorsets in just eighty minutes, and 5 casualties – only one of whom was killed. Similarly, the other hills, FSD, DIS, Jail Hill, Naga Hill and more were cleared after tank support was put into the right places to snipe Japanese bunkers from close range, or from the roads and hillsides nearby.

The need for cooperation with other arms was further underlined. The loss of Ezra Rhodes's tank between Kuki Piquet and Garrison Hill was because the troop had been sent along an unreconnoitred track on their own. Their escape was frankly a miracle, being in the middle of Japanese territory. The Japanese would not have been able to stalk it and throw their grenades into the turret if infantry was nearby, and the tank could then have been recovered. The tennis court was a near-perfect example of a well-planned and executed tank-infantry assault. Cooperation with the Royal Engineers had been vital, without whom no tank would have been in position to support the infantry and clear these areas. Mine clearance, tank recovery, ramp and platform building, and later bridge building when the tanks spearheaded the drive to relieve Imphal, was the foundation to success 4,000 feet up in Assam.

The continued absence of effective anti-tank weapons and doctrine undermined the Japanese ability to succeed in the battle. The few available AT guns, or artillery pieces capable of firing AP projectiles, that were manhandled into the area were simply unable to inflict real damage. Too many times a Grant tank was damaged but recovered to be put back into action later on, limiting the attrition of this key piece of allied equipment. Some were lost of course, but the vast majority were recycled back into service, and many more were never effectively damaged at all. With the Japanese on the defensive, and the stripped vegetation due to the weeks of fighting, even fanatical tactics were rarely attempted, let alone successful.

The battles in the first half of 1944 had proven that the tank was now the decisive weapon in the war against Japan in Burma. The simultaneous battles of Imphal and Kohima were the biggest single land defeat for the Imperial Japanese Army in the war to date. This is not to disparage in any way the work of other arms at all. Armour was the crucial extra ingredient: as a 7th Indian Division report at the end of May argued: 'the trump card is the tk appearing on the objective and destroying bunkers at pt blank range'.[24] They saved innumerable Allied lives clearing stubborn positions that were a defender's dream by soldiers fanatical in their desire to hold on and sell their lives dear. Wherever there was a stalemate, a tank usually broke it. Tanks had played a decisive role in stopping the Japanese invasion of India from the diversion at the Admin Box, to the main thrusts at Imphal and Kohima. Next, they would spearhead the reconquest of Burma.

Forgotten Armour 223

21. At the Battle of Imphal Lee tanks showed of their mountain climbing skills, most significantly at Nunshigum with the 3rd Carabiniers.

(Left) 22. Arthur Freer, 3rd Carabiniers, who took part in the entire Imphal battle, including the intense fighting on Nunshigum. (Special thanks to the Welburn/Freer Photo Collection).

(Right) 23. RSM William Craddock, the last surviving tank commander on Nunshigum, who took control of the deteriorating situation and saw the operation through to the end. This was the closest the Japanese got to Imphal before the 3rd Carabiniers and 1st Dogras pushed them back.

224   Forgotten Armour

24. Japanese 47mm AT gun near Bishenpur, possibly the one fired on by Lt Shepherd on 8th May 1944, when he could see daylight through the bullet holes as his machine gun hit its target. Japanese AT guns had greatest success on targets they could hit from close range in the sides or rear.

25. Lee tanks making their way across the Imphal Plain.

26. The Grant tank abandoned by Major Ezra Rhodes, 149th RAC, left in its final resting place below Kuki Piquet as a memorial to 2nd Division.

27. Sgt Gerry Waterhouse giving the V for victory sign from his tank at Kohima, probably after clearing the Tennis Court.

28. *View from the Tennis Court terrace (which is out of shot to the left) possibly from the Long Tin Shed. To the left are the tin huts behind the tennis court. The remains of the chimney from the DC's Bungalow are visible just beyond the tin huts.*

29. *Waterhouse's tank in the area near the DC's Bungalow during or just after clearing the Tennis Court.*

Forgotten Armour 227

30. *A Diamond T tank transporter carrying a Grant ARV makes its way along the road to Tamu, January 1945. Almost all of these roads were hacked out of the mountainsides for the campaign.*

31. *Tank maintenance had to be brought further forward to make sure they could stay in action as much as possible. Here a Sherman from 255th Indian Tank Brigade has its engine and radiator repaired on the road, late March 1945.*

228   Forgotten Armour

32. Combined operations in the coastal chaungs, mangrove swamps and islands off the Arakan coast in 1945 almost proved too much for tanks. They did manage to play a crucial role in holding Hill 170 at Kangaw.

33. A Lee tank crossing the Irrawaddy in 1945 on sections of bailey bridge fixed to pontoons. Either outboard motors for which John Henslow had to find frames for in India, or they were towed by DUKW amphibious lorries.

Forgotten Armour 229

(Left) 34. John Prendergast in India in the 1930s. Prendergast managed to get tank support to help his men assault Mandalay Hill. (Right) 35. John Masters, who survived being 'Pete' Rees's Chief of Staff on the road to Mandalay.

36. Looking down from Mandalay Hill over Fort Dufferin under aerial bombardment. The tanks struggled in the street fighting around the fort, the last Japanese stronghold in the city made famous in Britain by Rudyard Kipling.

37. Much of the fighting in central Burma took place near the great Buddhist pagodas found across Burma. Here tanks of 3rd Carabiniers approach Mandalay from the south.

38. Japanese AT weapons were never really capable of posing a serious threat to the American designed tanks in use by the British and Indian tank regiments. Here a hollow charge weapon has damaged the gun mantlet, but barely damaged the armoured turret underneath.

Forgotten Armour   231

39. Sherman tanks of Probyn's Horse near Kaing, on the Thunder Run to Meiktila. The armoured column of 3,000 vehicles made one of the most audacious operations of the Second World War, striking hard and fast, surviving solely on aerial resupply. It deserves a greater place in our collective memory of the war.

40. An image depicting the classic sweep operation undertaken in defence of Meiktila, with the tanks out front. All-arms columns moved across the plain to the outlying towns and villages destroying Japanese concentrations before they could mount a significant attack on the city.

41. A Stuart tank, probably of 7th Light Cavalry, on the race to Rangoon. The advance was so rapid that at times the tanks overtook Japanese troops retreating. They were not rapid enough, and the capital of Burma was captured by combined amphibious and parachute landings.

Part IV

"Cry 'Havoc!' and let slip the dogs of war!"

Marc Antony
in William Shakespeare's *Julius Caesar*

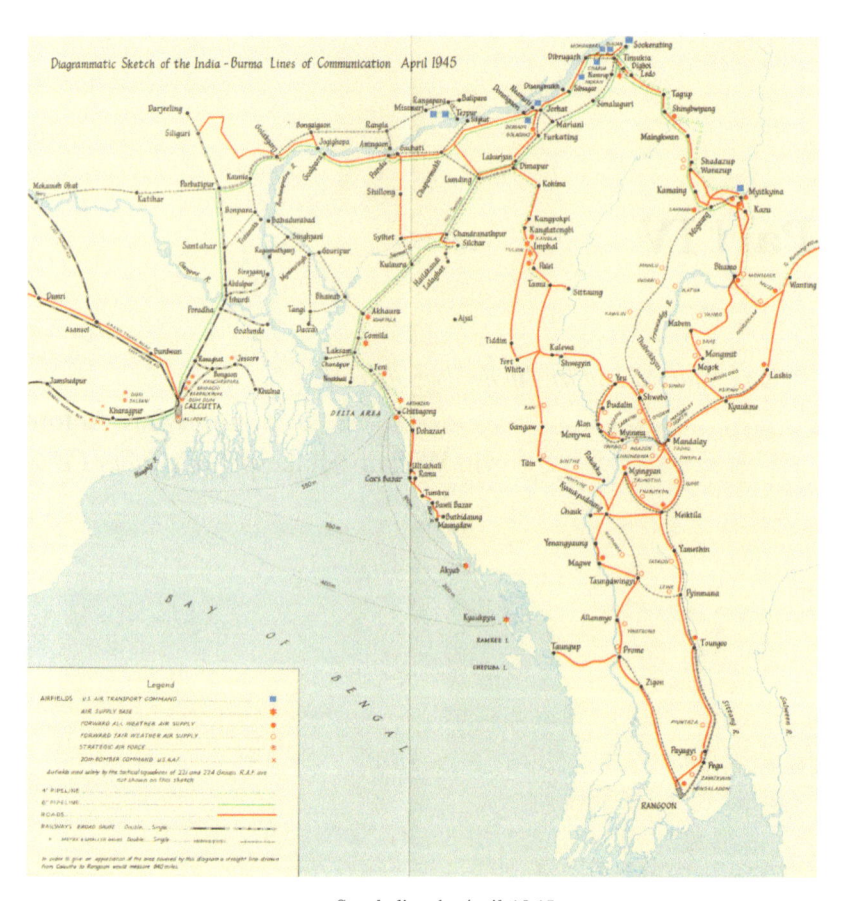

Supply lines by April 1945

10
Capital Investment: Engineering and Logistics

Malcolm Connolly's Lee tank was straining its way along the mountain roads south of Imphal on the Tiddim Road. Following the Battle of Imphal, six Lee tanks of the 3rd Carabiniers had been selected to go with the 5th Indian Infantry Division during the monsoon down this road to provide their now customary fire support. The tanks were long overdue proper maintenance, and probably needed replacing. The road was cut into the side of the mountains, occasionally crossing ravines and small rivers that passed lazily through the jungles that coated the entire landscape. Connolly's troop, part of C Squadron, 3rd Carabiniers was doing its bit alongside 5th Indian Division slowly clearing the road in preparation for a crossing of the Chindwin River. Since the Japanese 15th Army's collapse at Imphal and Kohima in July 1944, XXXIII Corps had been unleashed, pushing the now air-supplied 5th Indian Division down this road to capture the town of Tiddim – where 17th Indian Division had nearly been destroyed at the beginning of the Battle of Imphal. From there, they would turn east and capture the Chindwin crossing point at Kalewa – where 7th Armoured Brigade had abandoned their Stuart tanks in 1942. At the same time 11th East African Division were heading southeast towards Tamu and the crossing at Sittaung.

The opportunity that now presented itself before Slim and Fourteenth Army could not be wasted. The Japanese had taken incredible casualties in Operation *U-Go*; this was the time to strike back whilst the enemy was weak and get back into Burma. Whilst Slim's immediate superior, General Sir George Giffard, did not agree with Slim, Giffard's boss did. Vice-Admiral Lord Louis Mountbatten, Supreme Allied Commander SEAC, met with Slim on 2nd July 1944. Slim persuaded Mountbatten they could reconquer Burma without any reinforcements from outside of SEAC, and they should start as soon as the monsoon cleared at the end of October. Mountbatten ignored Giffard's and London's reservations, and over the summer managed to gain enough leeway for Slim. They had been told they should recapture Burma at the earliest opportunity so long as it would not jeopardise the airlift to China. Slim therefore made plans that would involve an advance by American equipped and led Chinese troops from the north, as well as the main thrust by Fourteenth Army. By default this matched the strategic goal.

So, the 3rd Carabiniers' tanks would trundle on, their tired engines wheezing their way up and down the hillside roads. They were approaching the tallest mountain in the area, the 8,900-foot Kennedy Peak: almost twice as high as the surrounding mountains. To make the climb Connolly's tank would need a new engine block. They stopped at a convenient place on the roadside, with the engine deck parked underneath a sturdy tree. Connolly and his crew then 'rigged up a block and tackle, removed the engine plates and disconnected the prop-shaft and fuel lines'.[1] The next day a new engine block was parachuted to them on the hillside. The crew lifted the old engine out, lowered in the new one, and reconnected all the lines and components. 'The only task we were incapable of doing was timing the new engine and so we had to wait for the squadron's sergeant-fitter to arrive and to bring the special tool required'.[2] The tank was out of the line for less than 24 hours, had its entire engine replaced without specialist mechanics, and could have been fixed even quicker if the timing belt tool had been readily available. The next day, Connolly's refreshed tank engine managed to get their 28-ton beast to the top of Kennedy Peak. The operation turned out to be an anti-climax; the Japanese had abandoned it the night before. For Connolly it was worth it, looking at the view across the mountains from his tank: 'it was completely exhilarating to watch the supply aircraft flying through the valley at a height much lower than that which our tanks were now sitting'.[3]

The 5th Indian Division advance, and Connolly's experience below Kennedy Peak, illustrate a number of the advances in engineering and logistics that had taken place since the relatively large-scale use of tanks in the theatre began from January 1944. Various innovations had been made that would support operations going forward into 1945, across the Chindwin, then the Irrawaddy, before launching Fourteenth Army at Rangoon. From 1943 the Indian Electrical and Mechanical Engineers (IEME) expanded significantly as the Indian Army was mechanised. By April 1944 there were 150,000 vehicles of over 100 types, including 1,800 tanks. IEME's ranks swelled to 2,000 British officers, 4,000 British other ranks, and 120,000 Indian other ranks. They worked alongside British REME units too, and as Connolly's tank attests, the American designed equipment was both reliable and easy to maintain.

During the key battles of 1944, replacing damaged or destroyed tanks was almost impossible, therefore keeping the tanks in fighting condition was imperative. Their risky use up the mountainsides at both Kohima and Imphal, in siege conditions, meant the maintenance system had to be overhauled in a way that would become standard for the rest of the campaign. The manner in which tank units were penny-packeted by squadron, troops, and even single tanks, meant that brigade level repair was impossible, so it was decentralised. In April 1944, for example, the 3rd Carabiniers had tanks operating in nine different locations in the Imphal perimeter in ten different detachments. REME and IEME units improvised new ways of working to keep the tanks fighting at the front as much as possible and made huge efforts to recover those that were damaged. This was usually done with the help of the Royal Engineers and Indian Engineers using the same D4 and D8 bulldozers that were used for bridging, roadbuilding, and towing vehicles up the mountains. They became so important for recovery, ramp, and bridge building that it became the norm to keep bulldozers close behind the armoured spearhead.

The brigade level was the third echelon in the organisation of a tank brigade, where the heaviest equipment to effect major repairs was found in the Light Aid Detachment (LAD). The dispersed nature of the fighting meant tank maintenance was decentralised during Imphal and Kohima. During the reconquest of Burma to follow in 1945, the lines of communication would be far more tenuous, and so the decentralised maintenance system was formalised. The LAD and their workshops would go forward to the 2nd echelon, where they would be expected to reach a tank harbour within an hour of being called up to make repairs. A further development was the Advanced Workshop Detachment (AWD), who would go forward with the fighting elements, the first echelon, able to change engines, weld damage, and make other reasonably heavy repairs. These new methods brought maintenance closer to the front lines, reducing the time a tank was away from the front line down to just one day in the AWD, and two days in the LAD. Consequently, tanks remained effective at the front far beyond their maintenance schedules suggested was possible. The system of maintenance was flexible, innovative, and effective, ensuring that the armoured formations provided crucial close fire support, whilst covering huge distances at pace, with as little wastage as possible.

That was so long as the spare parts could get to them. During the multitude of battles from February to July 1944, spares had been flown out and either landed in Dakotas or dropped by parachute. In August 1944, Mountbatten even made enquiries into the possibility of flying the new Sherman tanks into forward areas disassembled in Dakotas. The official report said: 'the proposition was turned down after investigation had revealed that the weight and size of the stripped-down hull was too great for a single aircraft, and that the ground staff and equipment necessary for reassembly at the forward landing point was too large'.[4] There was a reason no one had tried before.

The initial plan to reconquer Burma was by an overland route, named Operation Capital, intended to take advantage of the momentum following Imphal and Kohima. This was not everyone's first choice. Both London, and Slim's immediate superior, Giffard, preferred an amphibious route. These amphibious plans had first been mooted immediately after the retreat in 1942 and were later named Operation Dracula. This was to involve parachute drops and seaborne landings near Rangoon, which would then advance north to meet Fourteenth Army and the US-led Chinese troops, both of whom would have embarked on limited offensives. The Japanese Army would be cut off from resupply through Rangoon and then crushed in central Burma. This was entirely contingent on receiving more aircraft, landing craft, and other naval assets currently in Europe. In the aftermath of Imphal and Kohima though, those assets were still not yet available, and Slim was pressing for the offensive whilst his troops were hounding 15th Army towards the Chindwin. As mentioned, Mountbatten persuaded Giffard and London that the overland route in December 1944 gave the best hope of success, and he did this by submitting two plans. One was Operation Dracula, which would never be accepted because it needed landing craft they could not have. The other was Slim's Operation Capital. London preferred Dracula, but agreed Capital could go ahead, with Dracula following as soon as practical at a later date, preferably before the monsoon.

 Operation Capital would entail the crossing of the Chindwin, where XXXIII Corps and IV Corps would clear the Shwebo Plain to the Irrawaddy River. This was perfect for the Indian Army's new modern way of fighting. Newly mechanised divisions making rapier-swift thrusts and using superior firepower to destroy the infantry-based Japanese armies where these advantages could be brought to bear. At the same time the US-led Chinese forces would advance from Lashio and eventually meet with Fourteenth Army at Maymyo to the east of Mandalay. Some tentative plans were also made to push on to Rangoon, what would later become part of Operation Extended Capital. To help Slim focus on Operation Capital, Giffard took over responsibility of XV Corps in Arakan and the line of communication in Assam and Manipur. Shwebo's strategic value lay in its suitability for the construction of airfields that could be used to supply the forward units when they advanced towards Rangoon. Supplying these airfields would be difficult as they would be around 400 miles from Dimapur. Fourteenth Army was also facing the battered, but not destroyed Japanese Burma Area Army, who were being reinforced. Logistical limitations meant Slim's five divisions and two tank brigades would be outnumbered by the ten Japanese divisions in Burma.

To get the tanks and heavy supplies forward for Operation Capital from Imphal meant restarting the roadbuilding that was interrupted by the Battle of Imphal. Immediately after the battle the engineers worked hard to keep IV Corps moving. They were able to keep contact with the retreating Japanese, harrying them out of Manipur through the monsoon, before they were relieved by XXXIII Corps. For the reconquest, there were two potential supply routes available, but only enough engineering resources to build one: either the Tiddim Road 5th Indian Division was clearing, or the Tamu Road 11th East African Division were advancing along. The latter was chosen because it was shorter and avoided some of the engineering challenges posed by the Tiddim route. The 11th East Africans would advance south down the Kabaw Valley towards Kalewa, and the engineers would build the road as they went. This would be the main supply route, excluding air, for the initial advance into Burma, and would be the main route entirely once supply airfields were built in the central plain. Therefore, the road would be made all-weather, and two-way. At the beginning of October 1944, despite the Kabaw Valley still being a sea of mud, the engineers began their work repairing washed away bridges and building miles of corduroy roads. Five miles per day was considered outstanding whilst trailing behind the advance of the 11th East Africans, who were clearing the last embers of Japanese resistance. As October continued, the ground dried out and became dustier. This was a different challenge, but not insurmountable. The engineers were able to catch up, and their progress was then defined by the speed of the East Africans' advance.

One of those building the roads was Bill Williams – Elephant Bill, whose work on the road to Tamu had been interrupted by the Battle of Imphal. On 5th April 1944 he had been ordered to take forty-five of his best elephants and some refugees, first to the north of the Imphal Plain, and then west to a tea plantation deeper in the mountains. By October he and his elephants were back in the Kabaw Valley behind 11th East African Division. The Royal Engineers' Bailey bridges were prioritised for the Chindwin crossing, so the elephants played a vital role bridging the smaller rivers and ravines in the area. There were four routes to the Chindwin radiating from Tamu, the priority being the one to Kalewa. Across the four routes though, the elephants built 270 log bridges, suitable for all vehicles including tanks and their transporters. They worked with the forestry units too, bringing in the tree trunks needed to make wooden assault craft and barges for the river crossings to come, and for Bailey bridge decking.

The elephants had well and truly become part of the army. They helped clear trees for airfields to be built working alongside bulldozers, even under fire. On the advance to the crossing point at Kalewa, the town of Kalemyo needed to be taken. To get a squadron of tanks around the south of the town, Williams's elephants built a bridge over the Nayanzayah river. The fighting nearby did not deter the elephants, nor did the sound of aircraft. Throughout the day, Williams saw that 'Dakotas were circling two to three hundred feet above and airdropping in a dropping-zone, not half a mile from where the animals were working. Three Dakotas were shot down by enemy fighters that day…they [the elephants] took no notice whatsoever'.[5] The bridge was finished as required that evening, and the elephants were taken to the dropping zone. When they had the chance, they slipped away from their handlers* and ate the salt that had been spilled by bags that had been split open when they hit the ground.

John Henslow was also building roads and bridges down the Kabaw Valley, after his escapades in no-man's land at Kohima. He witnessed the shocking defeat of the Japanese, and the effect of the monsoon climate, as he did so: 'I shall never forget the sight of clean, white skeletons, still with their steel helmets on their head, a pile of bullets and buckles in their lap and their rifle and grenades by their sides. Maggots had consumed their flesh, and white ants…had eaten their clothes, their leather and webbing equipment'.[6]

To speed up the process of road building, the roads were first cut and brought up to the basic standard for lorries, before being upgraded to all-weather heavy loading. Henslow found this frustrating. 'If you start with a road trace for 15cwt trucks you cannot just upgrade it for transporters by widening it…where you could get round a feature in a 15cwt truck the requirements for a tank transporter would demand a different route to avoid sharp bends which it could not negotiate, but these were problems our superiors did not seem to appreciate'.[7] Speed was the determining factor, however, to make sure that supplies continued to flow over the roads in the short term, even as they were being prepared for heavier loads that would follow in the

---

* Called 'oozies'.

long term. This would have an impact later on, when tanks were laboriously unloaded to make these bends then reloaded to continue, or worse, to tow the transporter themselves, adding unnecessary wear and tear.

For the men driving these roads to Tamu, like Major David Atkins, life had improved considerably. The job was still difficult, but there were new systems and vehicles that made bringing up supplies that bit easier. New drivers had intense mountain training in India, where weak performers were rejected, before they were sent to the front. The drivers worked in teams: 'up this road day and night roared a steam of great 10-ton diesels each with two Madrassi drivers in the cab. On the hill sections the spare driver helped turn the wheel. We were astonished by their skill. Their accident rate was lower than that of British and American drivers'.[8]

Despite his professional objections to the method of road building, Henslow pressed on blasting and bulldozing the new roads to the Chindwin, which they reached in mid-December. Many of the new roads were made of bithess, the waterproof bitumen-soaked hessian strips, laid overlapping each other to create a new road surface. The process was expensive, but fast to put together, easy to repair if damaged, and used materials easily found in India. Bithess also weighed only 5% of the equivalent amount of stone that would have been used, making it easier to transport in bulk. The road from Imphal to Kalewa was to be the main overland supply route for 1945: 76 miles long, with 145 bridges, and had to handle a minimum of 350 tons per day. The roadbuilding would continue behind the advance in Burma, even when they came to the metalled roads on parts of the central plain. Henslow reflected on how his colleagues felt: 'such was the pride of the sappers that they were prepared to move mountains rather than say it cannot be done. So, in the end we moved mountains'.[9]

At the end of Williams's and Henslow's roads, the forward units prepared to make the crossing of the Chindwin. Some crossing points had been established at Sittaung and Mawlaik, but the prize was Kalewa, the most direct route into central Burma. The 11th East African Division had crossed here on the night of the 3/4th December 1944 and secured a beachhead eight miles deep holding the area in front of the line from Kalewa around a sharp meander to Shwegyin. They were still chasing the remnants of the Japanese 33rd Division, although intelligence had revealed that the 49th Division had arrived in Rangoon from Manchuria. Advanced parties from 2nd British Infantry Division and 3rd Carabiniers, both XXXIII Corps, had crossed just after the East Africans had secured the area. The 3rd Carabiniers were being ferried across in the exact reverse of the 7th Armoured Brigade retreat in 1942. There were other crossings taking place all along the Chindwin, with IV Corps further north, but 2nd Division was furthest south.

Morale was on the up, Arthur Freer and the 3rd Carabiniers had helped chase the Japanese out of Manipur, 'we had a holiday feeling, due to the improving weather'.[10] Kalewa was built at the confluence of the larger Chindwin, and the smaller Myittha rivers. The Chindwin is about half a mile wide on this stretch, with fast currents. The muddy river turns sharply north a few hundred yards east of Kalewa under some high cliffs on the outside of the initial bend. The river then meanders round to the south again before a straighter stretch to Shwegyin. The weather meant the sandy shores were baked hard making loading the tanks on barges easier with jetties made by the sappers. The rafts were sections of Bailey bridge laid onto four pontoons, powered either by outboard motors, or by DUKW amphibious lorries. When it came to Freer's tank they loaded onto the raft easily and the crew 'made the journey riding on the raft but sitting outside the tank and keeping it between ourselves and the eastern bank of the river'.[11] Despite the 11th East Africans establishing a beachhead, there was still the risk of

Japanese patrols infiltrating through the jungle to fire on the crossing. This method was not, however, the long-term solution to keeping Fourteenth Army going on the far side of the Chindwin. By 10th December the sappers had built a 1,153-foot Bailey bridge from Kalewa to Kaing, the longest pontoon bridge built by the Western Allies in the war. The bridge was built to take 30 tons, so the Lees that would follow could only cross one at a time.

As important as the roadbuilding was, the key part of the logistical plan for the reconquest was aerial resupply. This had worked well in the defensive battles of 1944, and it was now adapted to an offensive system. This had been done through the methodical advance out of the Imphal Plain with 5th Indian Division, for example, who had been supplied by air through the monsoon on the Tiddim Road, as had the East Africans down the Kabaw Valley from October. The advance to the Chindwin, the imminent reconquest, and the expected pace of operations on the central plain meant that Imphal could not stay the main base for the aerial resupply squadrons in the long-term. The distances the aircraft would have to make would be too great, especially by the time Fourteenth Army were looking beyond the Irrawaddy River. Airfields would be needed closer to the front as it moved further east, then south. Furthermore, air and road supply were unpredictable: the aerial resources relied on the Americans to agree, and their primary concern was always with the Hump airlift to China. The road and air routes were also liable to be slowed during the monsoon starting in May and could even be halted. The limits of the logistical lift, therefore, meant Slim would have to reconquer Burma with five divisions and two tank brigades, and one of those divisions would also need to be removed once they reached the Irrawaddy. The method of fighting that had been developed, primarily bunker busting that was now virtually perfected, consumed huge quantities of resources, especially ammunition. Airfields were captured in the Kabaw Valley, like at Tamu, and others were built from scratch. This would still not be enough for the reconquest of the whole country. To aid them, there would be an offensive in Arakan. Akyab and Ramree islands would be captured, providing airfields that could offer supply flights to Operation Capital and the budding Operation Extended Capital in central and southern Burma. Once Arakan was cleared, this would release at least one division and logistical capacity for further operations, such as Operation Dracula.

Everything was set. On 10th December, just before the 3rd Carabiniers and 2nd Division crossed the Chindwin and began their drive to Shwebo, the tank men received a visitor. 2nd Division's GOC Major-General Cameron Nicholson came to speak to the 3rd Carabiniers. "We in 2nd Div. are delighted to have to work with the Carabiniers. It is nearly 25 years ago since I last fought with the Carabiniers, and that was when we were hunting the Boche out of France in 1918, and now there is every prospect of us hunting the Jap out of Burma…wishing you all the best of luck on what may well be a great adventure."[12]

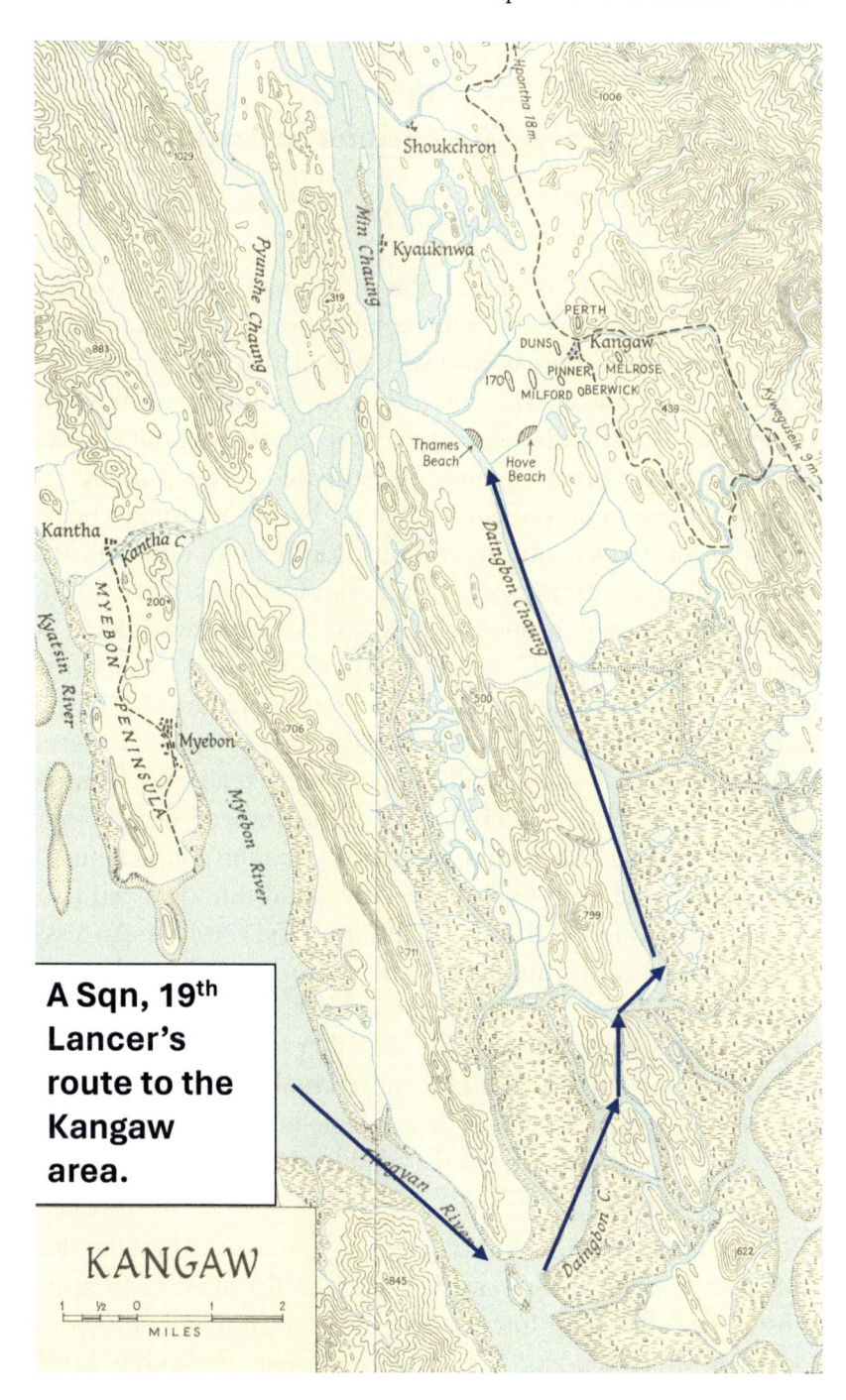

Combined Operations in Arakan   247

A Sqn, 19th Lancer's route to the Kangaw area.

KANGAW

11
Combined Operations in Arakan

Arakan in monsoon is one of the most unpleasant places that anyone could wish to fight. The region is hot all year round, with thick jungle in most areas, and with one of the wettest monsoon seasons. The place was miserable for soldiers to have to campaign. Tropical diseases were a problem throughout Burma, although they were frequently accentuated in Arakan by the humid climate. The difficulties caused by the unusually heavy monsoon of 1944 meant operations were halted, although this was common at this time of year anyway. Certainly, there was no option of fighting through like XXXIII Corps was doing in Manipur. Lieutenant-General Philip Christison's XV Corps therefore held the line against the battered Japanese 28th Army under Lieutenant-General Shōzō Sakurai. For 1945, however, Arakan remained strategically important. Akyab and Ramree islands in particular offered vital airfields over central and southern Burma that could support Operation Capital up to Mandalay by air, and Operation Dracula as an advanced base for amphibious forces. Lastly, inland from the coast the An Pass, near Kangaw, and Taungup to the south both allowed access into central Burma. As stretched as 28th Army was, Sakurai needed to try and hold firm. On the other hand, Christison had to capture the strategic islands and coastal towns primarily to ensure aerial resupply would be available for Fourteenth Army's drive south on Rangoon; what would later be called Operation Extended Capital.

A significant part of the strategy was to use a method familiar to the naval man Mountbatten. Using the Royal Navy to insert mostly brigade-sized forces onto strategic islands or coastal locations, whilst sending divisional sized forces overland to crush

28th Army. Mountbatten was able to secure enough resources for these smaller amphibious operations, at least compared to those proposed for Dracula. This was despite some initial reservations from his American Chief of Staff, General Albert Wedemeyer, who was concerned the whole plan would be a distraction from Operation Capital.

The new campaign in Arakan, the third attempt, began at the same time XXXIII Corps crossed the Chindwin, in mid-December 1944. The first campaign that failed at Donbaik became a catalyst to improve the fighting capabilities of the Eastern Army, including the development of bunker busting methods with armour. The second was checked by the Japanese Operation *Ha-Go* that culminated in the Battle of the Admin Box. The opening moves of this third try went far better than anyone imagined possible. After two years of trying to clear the Mayu Peninsula, it was now achieved in just twelve days with the capture of Foul Point at the tip on Boxing Day 1944. This had been achieved through a mixture of improved tactical ability and operational manoeuvre rather than the brute force attempted previously. Armour, artillery, and air power that worked with the infantry were key to the rapid advance.

The 19th King George V's Own Lancers, commanded by Lieutenant-Colonel Gerald Critchley, were the last Indian Army cavalry regiment to be mechanised at the end of 1940, and had not yet fired a shot in anger. They were initially given Stuart tanks but were eventually supplied with new Sherman tanks for the coming campaign. They were split by squadrons to support different divisions or brigades in the operations down the different axes of advance. B Squadron assisted 25th Indian Infantry Division down the coastal strip on the western side of the Mayu Peninsula, with C Squadron moving down the eastern side with 82nd West African Division. A Squadron was held in reserve. The 82nd West African Division were to turn east at Hitzwe then link up with the 81st West African Division, who were advancing down the roadless Kaladan Valley, at Myohaung. The 81st West Africans effectively fought behind the front lines, such as they were in Arakan, being supplied entirely by air for nine months. Their aim was to get behind Sakurai's forces occupying the Mayu Peninsular and Akyab island.

The biggest tactical innovation at this time was the Forward Tank Officer (FTO). Critchley had developed this after spending some time with the 25th Dragoons after their experience at the Admin Box, operating in much the same way as a FOO for the artillery. They would move with the infantry on foot, and direct tank fire in support of infantry operations, correcting the fall of shot as needed. For this job, the FTOs were equipped with a 38 wireless set, throat microphone, and an awkward four-foot aerial. Under fire, or from behind shallow cover, this often meant the FTO had to lie on their back holding the aerial up whilst also transmitting his fire order. C Squadron's FTO Lieutenant Bray had their first assignment, firing on some bunkers north of Buthidaung on 16th December. They destroyed the target through a mixture of tank, artillery and napalm dropped by fighter-bombers, although they soon found signs that the Japanese were pulling out of the area.

The rapidity of the advance to clear the Mayu Peninsular allowed Christison to bring the next phase forward. The original plan was for the 26th Indian Infantry Division to assault Akyab, but the relatively light casualties suffered by the 25th Indian Division in their charge to Foul Point meant Christison could keep the 26th Indian Division fresh for later operations. Instead, he would take 25th Indian Division's 74th Indian Infantry Brigade, 3 Commando Brigade, and A Squadron 19th Lancers, straight away. They loaded onto landing craft and made the short hop across the mouth of the Mayu river and landed unopposed before harbouring at the village of Kaundaga. The next day they made their way to Akyab town itself, crossing derelict tank ditches, and meeting no resistance. The Japanese had evacuated the island, the threat posed to them by 81st West African Division as it came down the Kaladan Valley was too much for Sakurai to ignore. He had started to withdraw his forces towards Taungup to try and oppose any moves into central and southern Burma. This was a sound plan as this was a narrow part of the coast, flanked by mountains to the east, where they could make a stand. To avoid this, Christison acted quickly to get troops across Sakurai's line of retreat, again using combined operations.

To do this, Christison first used 3 Commando Brigade and A Squadron, 19th Lancers, to assault the Myebon Peninsular on 12th January 1945 securing a beachhead. 74th Brigade, 25th Indian Division, still with 19th Lancers' support, pressed on to clear the area by the 17th and head east to cut off further Japanese retreats. The worry was even only a small rearguard could halt this advance long enough for a large part of 28th Army to get away. The Japanese manpower shortage in the region meant Akyab island had been abandoned, and Myebon was lightly held as a delaying tactic. Lieutenant-General Miyazaki's 54th Division would make stands at Kangaw, near the entrance to the An Pass, and Taungup, the last town before the road to Prome in the Irrawaddy valley. If these were lost, what remained of 28th Army would be trapped in Arakan, and unable to support the defence of central and southern Burma by allowing XV Corps a dramatic breakthrough behind Major-General Shihachi Katamura's* 15th Army. Kangaw was only eight miles from Myebon by the most direct route, but this was covered by Japanese artillery. To trap more Japanese troops, avoid the artillery near Myebon, and bypass potential resistance west of Kangaw, 3 Commando Brigade, would again lead a combined operation to outflank the town from the south. At the same time, 74th Brigade would attack from the Myebon Peninsula on the direct route.

---

*Katamura replaced Mutaguchi on 30th August 1944 after the failures at Imphal and Kohima.

The area was difficult enough for infantry landings, and really quite unsuitable for combined operations with tanks. This part of Arakan, where many of the rivers running down from the mountains empty into the Bay of Bengal, is a maze of coastal *chaungs* winding between mangrove swamps, mudbanks and long shallow beaches. These floodplains are flat, with the odd wooded hill, and firm paddy fields interspersed with jungle, until you reach the vast Arakan Yomas mountain range that divides the region from the Irrawaddy valley to the east. In a sign of the quality of Allied seamanship, the mostly Royal Navy flotilla for the combined operation delivered their charges with professional precision along a *chaung* that was barely 30 yards wide with overhanging mangroves. To attack Kangaw from the south, 3 Commando Brigade would sail south and enter the Daingbon Chaung, which lopped round to the east and offered a route through the maze back north to the inlets where two beachheads were to be established. This route was 27 miles, but the Daingbon Chaung had not been mined, and its circuitous route would hopefully allow for the element of surprise.

Nos.1 and 5 (Army) and 42 and 44 (Royal Marine) Commandos were loaded onto landing craft on the 21st January, along with a multitude of vehicles, and even eight 25-pounders ready to fire from the deck in support of the landing. The flotilla sailed down to the estuary and anchored for the night. No. 1 Commando had one advantage; during their time in North Africa they had managed to acquire American .30 M1 Garand rifles, a self-loading rifle giving the men a greater rate of fire. They were escorted by two Indian Navy sloops – *Narbada* and *Jumna* – with a total of 50 vessels that would weave their way single file along the Daingbon Chaung. No. 1 Commando landed first on 23rd January, and headed straight for Hill 170, capturing it without much of a fight. The other commandos came ashore and captured the other nearby hills overlooking Kangaw, Milford and Pinner, by the evening. The Japanese reacted quickly, counterattacking 44 Commando's position on

Pinner that night, and showered Hill 170 with artillery fire, both coming from the east.

The beaches were a bit of a nightmare. They were steep, and the gaps between mangrove trees were soon slippery, muddy messes. Wheeled vehicles could not get ashore, and so supplies were laboriously manhandled instead. Reconnaissance patrols towards Kangaw were beaten back fiercely, the commandos realising that this was where the Japanese stand would be made. The worry was whether they would strike back and eject 3 Commando Brigade. Reinforcements were required, so the 51st Brigade and a troop of A Squadron, 19th Lancers, reinforced the beachhead between the 26th and 27th January. The troop of 19th Lancers were brought in on Landing Craft Mechanised (LCM), which were not designed for tanks since they could only find an even trim by traversing the turrets. The difficulty trimming and handling the LCMs during offloading would cause further problems. To help the tanks grip the muddy bank, some sappers put down a wire mesh for the tanks to drive over. An argument broke out whether this was a good idea, and the sappers won.

The LCM lowered its door, and water poured in. The water then kept pouring in, before someone realised that closing the door would be a good idea. The deck was now awash with water and the LCM listing. After a short discussion, a new plan was made by the naval officer in charge: they would rush the tanks out. 'Amid much splashing we were then told to ride the tanks straight at the door, knocking it down, and from there go straight up the bank. Virsa Singh did as he was bid and literally leapt out of the LCM, which in its turn leapt back into the middle of the stream'.[1] When the tank tracks had hit the muddy beach, the tank tracks had pushed the LCM backwards away from the beach. As they brought their tank up the bank, the sapper's wire mesh entangled itself in the tracks and bogeys of the Sherman, taking half an hour to remove. There was more shouting amongst the LCM crew and the rest of the 19th Lancers' tank crewmen, and eventually the rest of the tanks were unloaded using a similar method. Two infantry battalions from 54th Brigade also arrived as reinforcements.

The troop of Shermans made their way to Hill 170, harbouring at the northern end, where they were targeted by a 75mm firing from one of the hills to the east. There was little they could do but shield their tanks on the west side of the hill. Lieutenant Sam Fitze took part in some shoots on the hills around Kangaw still occupied by Japanese troops: Fingers, Perth, and Duns on the 29th and 30th January. By now, though, something was brewing. A composite force, Matsu Detachment consisting of three infantry battalions and one artillery battalion, was now brought south from fighting the 82nd West African Division, to clear the blockage on 28th Army's line of retreat.

On the 31st January, Matsu Detachment began their attack. Hill 170 was significant because it was the main defensive position protecting the beachhead, and also dominated the road 28th Army intended to retreat down. Both sides needed it desperately. The 19th Lancer's harbour was on the line of part of Matsu Detachment's attack. Whilst Lieutenant George Knowland of No. 1 Commando was firing Bren guns and 2-inch mortars from the hip in his famous Victoria Cross action, slightly to the north, the 19th Lancers played their part in holding Hill 170.

At around 5:45am heavy shellfire landed in the tank harbour, lasting about half an hour. Then, the attack came in. Confused fighting broke out almost immediately, the Japanese infantry had infiltrated around Hill 170 and were attacking from the west – the rear of their position. The Japanese were in the perimeter. Two of the British officers emerged from their dugout and were driven back in a shower of grenades. The first return-fire was from 'Bing' Wilson, who came out from his trench directly in front of a Japanese officer, and quickly shot him with his Sten gun, but was soon followed by more fanatical men charging, so he too pulled back. 'Grenades were whizzing through the air from both sides…after overrunning our forward position, [they] planted some large type of explosive onto the truck. There was a terrific green flash and a tremendous bang which drove most people back to their trenches'.[2] All was confusion. Men were everywhere fighting their own private battles, two men from underneath the D8 bulldozer. A suicide attack by Japanese engineers with pole charges made for the tanks. Some were shot down, but one group fought hand to hand with a Sherman crew who were scrambling onto their tank. One of the Japanese engineers climbed onto the tank and detonated his charge, killing himself, the tank crew, and nearby comrades. Lieutenant-Colonel Ken Trevor, CO No. 1 Commando, could see the tank harbour from his position on Hill 170 during the attack, and saw the tank explode: 'Flames shot up at the foot of the hill as the tanks caught fire[*]. Ten men attacked the mortar position, but we managed to repulse them. There were no Jap survivors'.[3]

The initial shock soon died down, and the 19th Lancers found the Japanese attack was as much a diversion as anything else, as they realised some had managed to position themselves on the northern slope of Hill 170 looking down onto them. 'Bing' Wilson led some Bombay Grenadier infantry on a counterattack into the jungle on the hill. In the meantime, Major Bill Sample got the tanks into action: Fitze's and Jemadar Piara Singh's. They soon fired onto the hillside in support of the Bombay Grenadiers and reinforcing Commandos who were clearing them. In the fighting that followed, one of the tanks threw a track, but by the end of the day, the area was successfully consolidated, and two new tanks were brought up.

By the 2nd February, over 2,500 Japanese had died in their last-ditch attempt to capture Hill 170 and crush 3 Commando and 51st Infantry brigades. This broke the Japanese 54th Division as they tried to retreat from Hill 170 and Kangaw. 74th Brigade

---
[*] Only one tank caught fire

advancing from the Myebon Peninsula had met the 82nd West African Division, almost closing the noose. Those that got away regrouped at the An Pass, south of Kangaw, and would need to be dealt with. Christison highlighted the impact tanks could have even in such small numbers: 'I feel this battle might well have been lost on Hill 170 had it not been for the morale raising presence of the tanks'.[4]

Whilst the Myebon, Kangaw, and Hill 170 battles were taking place, there had also been landings on Ramree and Cheduba islands to allow for future aerial resupply efforts into central and southern Burma. The island was quite difficult for vehicles, there were virtually no roads, and like so many of the flat areas of Burma, covered in rice paddies with earth bunds separating them, and vast mangrove swamps. There were also low scrub covered hills, and steep-sided *chaungs* criss-crossing the area. In a sign of the material dominance of the Allies coming to bear, Ramree island was subjected to a significant bombardment. On the 21st January the battleship *Queen Elizabeth*, cruiser *Phoebe*, and some destroyers and sloops, hammered the northern shore of Ramree island near the town of Kyaukpyu. There were also air strikes and bomb runs by P-47 Thunderbolts, B-25 Mitchells, and B-24 Liberators to soften up any resistance. 71st Brigade, 26th Indian Division, landed first, followed by 4th Brigade the following day.

In the initial stages mines and blown bridges were the main obstacle as the Japanese 2nd Battalion, 121st Regiment, 54th Division, withdrew south. This small force garrisoning the island was completely independent and had attached artillery and engineer detachments. Their main defensive position was on the Yanbauk Chaung, which held despite the naval and aerial bombardment that was called down onto it. On the 31st January, as the fight on Hill 170 began, 71st Brigade flanked to the northeast, then south to Ramree town, leaving 4th Brigade to hold the Japanese in place on the *chaung* – if the enemy withdrew, they could follow up.

The tank men selected to support the operation had a score to settle. After an anti-climactic landing at the beginning of the operation, these tanks had reimbarked and were to outflank the Yanbauk Chaung as well. The size of the mangrove swamps on the north of the island had proven too difficult, but the 28-ton Lee tanks would fare better further south, beyond the worst of the swamps. They landed on the eastern side of the island, near the town of Sane on the 31st January to link up with the 71st Brigade. From here to Ramree town there were no swamps, just paddy and low jungle covered hills. As they made their way to shore, the Lee tanks pushing determinedly up the beach, the 146th RAC were out to avenge their comrades killed in the Donbaik disaster almost two years to the day earlier. They arrived at the outskirts of Sane just before dark. They were to continue on for two more days to get behind the 121st Regiment on the Yanbauk Chaung, on a route where the bulldozer became their biggest asset. The tracks they found were far too narrow for tanks to pass, so trees had to be shoved, battered, blasted, and even ripped out with towing chains to clear a route.

They passed by the village of Yebadin on the main road to Ramree. To the south of the village the road passed through a gap in the jungle-clad hills, where 146th RAC assisted the 1/8th Garhwal Rifles and the 1st Lincolnshire Regiment take the hills overlooking the road over the course of the 4-5th February. These attacks used what were often known as 'oil' bombs, better known today as napalm, to clear vegetation for the infantry assault and the identification of bunkers. The flames burned through the night, and Japanese patrols were very active against both the Garhwalis and Lincolns. The following morning the Japanese had retreated again, the night patrols were an attempt to deter too swift a follow up the next day, giving time for an orderly withdrawal. The next couple of days were spent pushing south to Ramree, again with the sappers and a bulldozer clearing obstacles, mines, small-scale ambushes, and even a captured 25-pounder, until they reached a righthand bend in the road, underneath a wooded hill.

The obstacle they found highlights the Japanese troops' great skill in a fighting withdrawal. The had placed mines just before the apex of the corner which stopped the tanks engaging bunkers on the other side but were still in view of the ambushing troops who could fire on any sappers trying to clear the mines. The jungle was thick either side of the road, so outflanking the position with tanks was impossible. The Lees engaged what bunkers could be identified, especially on the nearby hill, along with naval and artillery fire, but it was the Lincoln's who had to head into the jungle either side of the roadblock and engage. The Lincoln's started to take casualties, even losing A Company commander, Major Cheer. It was getting dark, and the position was clearly the last line before Ramree, so the battalion commander Lieutenant-Colonel Sinker called off the attack, 'the Japs were making their last stand and were obviously going to die in the positions they held'.[5] The next day, 9th February, the Lincoln's infiltrated further in the jungle and captured a hill behind the main Japanese line, and finally they could clear it. They were soon into Ramree itself, surprisingly undamaged, on 9th February. The Japanese defence of Ramree was broken, and many died trying to cross the mangrove swamps to the east coast to get across to the mainland, which was patrolled by the Royal Navy. All but 20 of 1,000 men in the garrison died, mostly of disease, dehydration, starvation and from their wounds, or in mopping up operations carried out primarily by the infantry[*].

---

[*] There is a myth of a massacre by crocodiles in these swamps. This probably grew from some Japanese bodies being devoured by scavengers and possibly crocodiles. Certainly the 1st Lincoln's History in 1949 makes no mention of crocodiles at all when it describes their mopping up operations in the swamps. At the very least, zoological consensus is that the island would never have been able to sustain the number of crocodiles the myth suggests were needed to kill hundreds of Japanese troops.

Sakurai made no concerted effort to reinforce the island, failing to realise its importance for aerial resupply and the Allies' overall strategy, or that Rangoon was now in bomber range. Furthermore, 146th RAC had played their part and finally exacted their revenge.

Including the unopposed capture of the neighbouring island of Cheduba, Christison had completed his main objective: taking the islands so they could be used as supply airfields. He continued to pursue the Japanese 28th Army, to make sure it could not interfere with Fourteenth's Army's operation now developing in central Burma. He kept up the relentless pace of combined operations, getting his troops behind the Japanese and interfering with their withdrawals. To a degree, Christison was able to use the sea in the same way they Japanese had used the jungle in 1942, hooking in behind unmolested from unexpected directions.

The 19th Lancers, after supporting operations around the An Pass, and 146th RAC both made further landings supporting infantry in March and April at Letpan and fought south towards Taungup, the last town before the road into southern Burma. Their support mostly consisted of shoots onto Japanese positions on the hills and mountains from the roads, often getting forward to flanking positions. On 15th March the Lees of A Squadron, 146th RAC saw five Type-95s who turned and ran before they could engage, three were destroyed by PIATs* brought up by the Frontier Force Regiment, the other two were abandoned with the crews fleeing into the jungle.

At the end of April, Japanese resistance had shattered, Taungup was captured, and survivors were fleeing into the Arakan Yomas mountains just as the monsoon broke. The

---
* Projector Infantry Anti-Tank – a spring-loaded shaped-charge weapon. At short range against the weak armour of Japanese tanks it was deadly. Its spring loading system meant it did not give away its position either, making it perfect in a jungle ambush.

crucial phase had ended with the capture of Ramree, but the fighting had remained bitter, even if its result against an increasingly desperate enemy appeared inevitable. Christison's combined operations were far beyond anything the 28th Army could cope with after its defeat in 1944. Once Christison had the resources for such operations, the sheer length of complicated coastline with his inlets and *chaung*s that allowed for rapid insertion, Sakurai could not effectively hold XV Corps. Tanks were used in small numbers, often single squadrons were landed for a task, then split into troops, before fighting intense struggles such as at Hill 170. They provided significant morale boosts as much as physical support to troops fighting in the Arakan, and the opposite to Japanese troops, as resistance so often crumbled when tanks appeared in unexpected places. The Arakan campaign in general also kept two divisions away from the central Burma front just as Operation Capital began and was virtually destroyed as Fourteenth Army closed on Rangoon. That thrust was kept supplied and supported from the air by the airfields at Akyab and Ramree before XV Corps provided the coups-de-grâce in Operation Dracula.

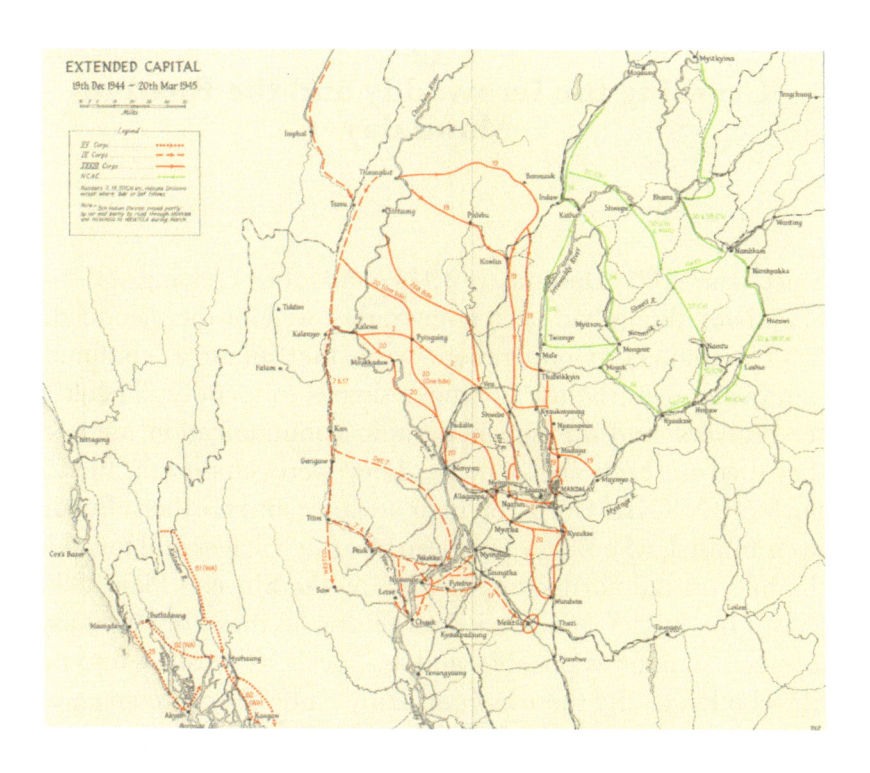

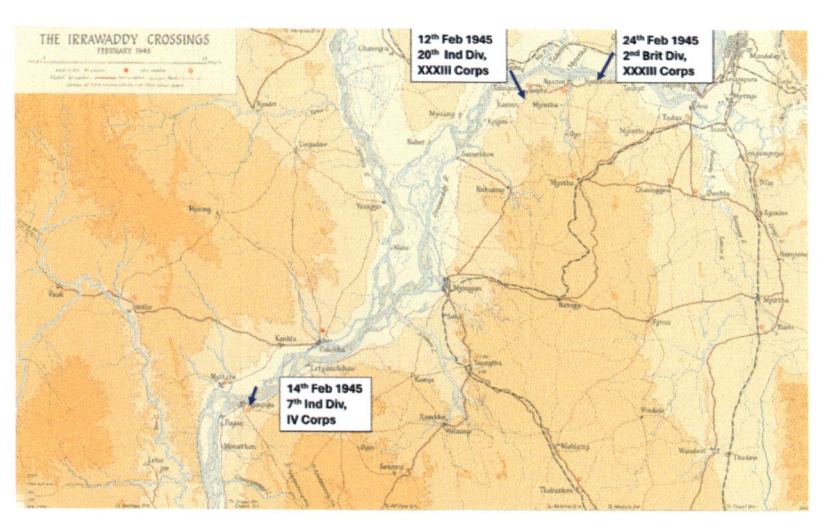

Crossing the Irrawaddy and the Road to Mandalay 261

12
Crossing the Irrawaddy and the Road to Mandalay

Since the 10th December 1944 and the crossing of the Chindwin, things had been going rather well for the men of the 3rd Carabiniers. Cooperation with the infantry continued improving, with the use of smoke signals to identify difficult to see bunkers, and through new radio communication methods that sped up each engagement. They were supporting the 2nd Division, XXXIII Corps, on their advance into northern Burma from Imphal, where they had been clearing villages and towns in the hills on the north-western edge of the Shwebo Plain. Slim knew Operation Capital relied on getting 'as many divisions and as much armour as possible, and as quickly as possible, into the Shwebo Plain, and there fight an army battle'.[1] Across the entire country, there were ten Japanese infantry divisions, one tank regiment, two independent mixed brigades, 100,000 line of communications troops, two Indian National Army (INA) divisions of 6,000 men each, and the ten battalions of the Burma National Army. Although many of the divisions were understrength or of questionable combat value, replacement troops were coming in, and all Japanese troops, even those in administrative jobs, were liable to be as stubborn as any other Japanese soldier in defence.

Yet it was soon obvious that resistance was not what Slim expected. The assumption was that Fourteenth Army, operating along tenuous lines of supply over the mountains from Dimapur to Imphal, then more mountains to the Chindwin crossing points, would be seen as vulnerable. Slim was expecting the Japanese to counterattack, and he would use his superior firepower to destroy them. Their commander General Heitaro

Kimura was not playing ball. Arthur Freer's tank in B Squadron, 3rd Carabiniers, had been fighting through since Imphal. Major-General Nicholson, GOC 2nd Division, sent another letter to B Squadron on the 30th December explaining 'my admiration…during the last nine days. That we have covered 80 miles and broken through at least four enemy positions in this time has been largely due to the action of the tanks…by doing so you have already saved many infantry casualties'.[2] Many positions had been weakly held, however, and in some cases the Japanese ran before the infantry could close in and destroy them in their bunkers. The fact was Japanese resistance was slight. 15th Army's commander, Katamura, planned to delay the advance and preserve the fighting strength of his troops in Burma, whilst buying time to receive more replacements for those killed in the defeats of 1944. Slim would not get his army battle on the Shwebo Plain, the decisive engagement that would destroy the Japanese.

Running down the centre of the Shwebo Plain, splitting it in two, is the Mu river. North of Ye-U there was an irrigation weir that Slim worried could be destroyed by the Japanese to flood the plain, slowing his advance. On 31st December, the rapidity of the 3rd Carabinier's advance allowed them to capture it undamaged: XXXIII Corps now had a genuine foothold in the Shwebo Plain that was soon to be expanded. Kimura pulled his two armies in central Burma back across the Irrawaddy, whilst to the north, 33rd Army was pushed south and east by US and Chinese troops, meeting XXXIII Corps at Indaw. The Irrawaddy is the most formidable river in Burma, wide, with shifting sands. This was just another major obstacle that Slim's already stretched logistical system would have to contend with, to support another major operation over a difficult geographical feature against an enemy concentrating in one area.

To engineer himself an advantage, Slim looked at how he could catch Kimura off guard, and identified the town of

Meiktila, 70 miles south of Mandalay, as his target. Meiktila is a town on and between the banks of two lakes where both the main road and railway from Rangoon to Mandalay passed through with two airfields nearby. The Irrawaddy Plain, the flat area east of the river, was the ideal place for logistical and administrative bases, and so Meiktila had become a hub for all Japanese forces in northern and central Burma. If this could be captured, then the bulk of Japanese forces on the shores of the Irrawaddy would be cut off. If Mandalay could be captured too, and with mountains to the east, practically all of Japanese 15th Army could be trapped and destroyed, before driving south to capture Rangoon before the monsoon struck. The flat land would allow Slim to use his armour and air power to its maximum advantage too. This was Operation Extended Capital, devised in mid-December in great secrecy.

For this to work, Kimura would need to continue to believe the strike would take place at Mandalay, where the current movement of IV and XXXIII Corps suggested it would. Operation Extended Capital, however, would see the Mandalay thrust become a feint to draw in as much of Katamura's 15th Army before IV Corps crossed the Irrawaddy later. IV Corps would secretly switch their direction of advance south and cross the great river near Pakokku and then capture Meiktila. This would draw a desperate response from Kimura, who would need to recapture the logistics hub, giving Slim the opportunity to destroy 15th Army between his two corps. In early January XXXIII Corps was on the banks of the Irrawaddy, waiting for the order to go.

The final piece of the puzzle was the provision of transport aircraft for the continuation of the reconquest of Burma. Operation Capital was going far better, with advances moving at greater pace, than anyone had expected. Making sure there were enough aircraft for Operation Extended Capital was vital. On 1st January 1945, Mountbatten informed the Chiefs of Staff that planning for exploitation south of the plain to Rangoon was taking place, and he would need four months' notice if the US transport planes were to be withdrawn. Considering the success of Operation Capital, the situation in China, and after some negotiations between the USA and British Chiefs of Staff, an agreement was made, giving Slim the lift he needed. Operation Extended Capital was on.

The speed at which Fourteenth Army had cleared the Shwebo Plain had taken everyone by surprise. On the 14th and 15th January, the 19th Indian Division had rushed units across the narrower sections of the Irrawaddy about 50 miles north of Mandalay at Thabeikkyin and Kyaukmyaung and were holding them against fierce counterattacks. The rest of XXXIII Corps and the administrative tail were constructing airfields on the plain, redeploying RAF units, building up supply stocks, and bringing up bridging and rafting equipment. Slim's plan was for further landings on 12/13th February by 20th Indian Division at Myinmu southwest of Mandalay, followed by the 2nd Division at Ngazun on 24/25th, ten miles east. This was after a 90-degree bend in the Irrawaddy just south of Mandalay, where the crossing was north-south, rather than west-east where 19th Indian Division had crossed. The build-up of forces here was difficult because all priority was for IV Corps making their secret moves south, but everything was eventually gathered in time for Slim's planned timetable.

The timing of 2nd Division's crossing was crucial, it would take place shortly after IV Corps' planned crossing for its assault on Meiktila, which itself was only 36 hours after 20th Indian Division's at Myinmu. Slim was 'anxious, therefore, to push 2nd Division across the Irrawaddy, still nearer to Mandalay, just as Kimura must begin to realise the threat to Meiktila, and thus make him hesitate to detach troops from the Mandalay front'.[3] The 20th Indian Division got their first battalions over with only a few navigational mishaps and met some patrols as they rushed their brigades across and extended their beachhead. Their position was consolidated when the 4/10th Gurkhas with two squadrons of Stuart tanks from 7th Light Cavalry took the town of Talingon. This including their HQ tank 'Curse of Scotland', the only tank rescued from 7th Armoured Brigade in 1942, back for revenge. Fighting raged over the town until the 25th February when the Japanese 16th Regiment were exhausted. Some Japanese tanks were destroyed by Hurribombers who had found them by shooting up suspicious heaps of foliage in fields.

To the east with 2nd Division the final preparations were made once 20th Indian Division's bridging and rafting assets were sent upriver. Harry Hopton was one of the men assigned to help with the crossing. He was in the 387th Company (Amphibian), Royal Army Service Corps, in 2nd Division, and drove the US-made DUKW amphibious lorry – based on a six-wheel-drive GMC 2½ ton truck. They had been used to ferry infantry and to drive the barges of Bailey bridge sections carrying heavy equipment like tanks. He had fought as part of the infantry during the Battle of Kohima on the Aradura Spur and was not unused to operating under gunfire. Whilst crossing the Chindwin his company's DUKWs had covered 32,000 miles on the river ferrying men, equipment, and supplies from Kalewa to Shwegyin. He was to take the follow up waves of the 5th Brigade after the initial crossing was made in assault boats.

The 2nd Dorsets were in the follow up waves, behind the 7th Worcestershire Regiment and 1st Queens Own Cameron Highlanders who were landing at two beaches near Ngazun. Major Geoffrey White, who had commanded the clearing of the tennis court at Kohima, noted 'there was nearly a full moon, which in Burma means a very bright night...no one was prepared to wait a few days extra to allow the moon to go down'.[4] To help the Worcesters save their energy for the crossing and the battle to come, White got the Dorsets to carry the assault boats the 600 yards to the riverbank. The Irrawaddy is nearly a mile wide at the crossing point, fast-flowing at four knots with sandy islands and narrow channels constantly shifting, a navigator's nightmare. Hopton and the 387th Company's commander, Captain Hugh Clark, waited for the signal to move once the first wave had landed.

Surprise felt lost almost immediately when the operation began at 10pm. Apart from the moonlight, the assault boat's engines were very noisy, especially if the rope start took a few attempts. The Worcesters crossing went wrong almost immediately, getting caught in the difficult flow of the river and coming under mortar and machine gun fire, before pulling back to the north shore. The Camerons did not fare quite so badly, but still came under fire. They got one company onto the cliff edge overlooking part of the beach, a precarious foothold at best, and sent the assault boats back but they came under fire again, some sinking, others drifting downriver with their dead and wounded operators. Clark was ordered to get his DUKWs moving to ferry more infantry to the Cameron's beachhead, and Hopton got to work under heavy machine gun fire. The metal clanged in the dark around him, as the DUKW was hit, and the men helped hammer wooden pegs into holes lower in the hull, bringing in water. Some got stuck on the unpredictable sands and Clark went up and down the river getting them out to keep the infantry reinforcements moving, including White and the 2nd Dorsets.

At 6am the next day, the Camerons and Dorsets were holding on. 6 Troop, of A Squadron, 3rd Carabiniers, was ordered forward to provide further supporting fire, opening up at 10am. 'There were LMGs on the opposite bank, but although every effort was made to locate them, they were not pinpointed and therefore the Camerons received a few casualties…by the end of D+1 the whole of the Camerons and most of the Dorsets had established themselves on the south bank of the Irrawaddy'.[5] The next day, A Squadron's commander, 24-year-old Captain

Hubert Cornaby was sent over the river to see how they could get the tanks into the Cameron's beachhead. 4 Troop would cross on pontoons, towed by the DUKWs, and then fire from an island in the river, whilst 5th Brigade fought east along the river towards Ngazun itself. Artillery hit the village first, replaced by fire from the tanks at 2:05pm just as the infantry reached the village, which was cleared in short order. 4 Troop stayed on the island, while Cornaby and the rest of A Squadron crossed the river and were reassigned to support the 6th Infantry Brigade from the 27th February.

For the next couple of days, Cornaby's A Squadron, 3rd Carabiniers, helped the infantry clear some villages near the bridgehead, before heading south to claim some high ground. They left at 7:45am on 2nd March and were joined by the 2nd Durham Light Infantry before heading for the villages of Tamabin and Lewingon. The soil was very light and easy to dig into, in a tomato growing area where the Durhams were able to supplement their rations simply by reaching out of their trenches to grab the ripe fruit before they moved off. The days were swelteringly hot, and inside the tanks the men were stripped down to their waists and sweating profusely as always. After shooting up a dozen Japanese troops they saw, they moved on to Lewingon.

As they passed the village, 4 Troop set the town ablaze with tracer fire. The rest of the squadron were engaging some Japanese to their front in some thick scrub, when two Japanese soldiers broke cover and climbed the rear of Cornaby's Lee tank. One of them was later identified as the commander of the Japanese 5th Medium Artillery Regiment, the other an unidentified other rank. Cornaby was directing his tank's fire from his open turret hatch, unaware of the Japanese officer, who had reached the turret from the engine deck. 'They were not noticed by anyone until the officer was in the act of plunging his sword into Captain Cornaby'.[6] There was a clatter of Browning machine gun fire, and bullets pinged off the rear of the Lee. The Japanese other rank tumbled to the ground killed, but the officer was apparently unhurt and started climbing into the turret, and immediately killed the 37mm gunner. The 37mm loader, Trooper Vernon Jenkins, saw what was happening, and was now in a fight for his life in the tiny confines of a Lee tank's turret with the rest of the crew oblivious to his desperate struggle. He awkwardly pulled his pistol from his belt holster, and fired wildly across the 37mm gun's loading mechanism, wounding the Japanese officer. The Japanese officer, fighting with all of the fanatical spirit expected of *Bushido**, continued to fight hand to hand with Jenkins. Luckily for Jenkins, whose pistol was now empty, there was clearly no space for the Japanese officer to swing his samurai sword. Jenkins managed to reach into the gunner's belt and pull out their pistol, firing three rounds that finally killed the Japanese officer. The three bodies were now lying in the floor of the turret and might jam the mechanism if they moved it too much. The tank reported their predicament, and under cover of the rest of the troop, they withdrew. The rest of the squadron cleared the nearby villages, and destroyed a 47mm AT gun, although two tanks were burned out in the process.

Throughout the action, Japanese troops had tried to climb other tanks, each Lee shot intruders off of the tank in front, or those nearby. The Japanese were displaying for the 3rd Carabiniers their continuing inability to face tanks on anything close to equal terms. Their desperation had led to a medium artillery regiment officer joining the infantry in a suicide attack armed with his sword against a troop of tanks. Jenkins was awarded the Military Medal for saving his crew in the desperate struggle, possibly the most intimate fighting any tank man faced in the war. He was also presented with the officer's sword. The 3rd Carabiniers lost three tanks and twelve casualties during the

---
* The code by which Japanese soldiers, and especially officers, were expected to fight, just as their samurai forbears had done.

attack. The report in the war diary concluded: 'This was an extremely unpleasant day and during the whole of it the squadron fought and behaved exceptionally well, and the loss of the men, who were killed, was a great blow to the squadron'.[7] As unpleasant as it had been, the area had been successfully consolidated, and far greater casualties had been inflicted on the Japanese. The following days saw the beachhead secured, and whole of 2nd Division were across, ready to capture Mandalay. On the 5th March 20th and 2nd divisions began the advance to the ancient capital in earnest.

"Where are you going Jack?" the general asked the thin Lieutenant-Colonel waiting for a plane in Calcutta. The Lieutenant-Colonel had recently been a Chindit in Operation Thursday and was still recovering his strength after the ordeal when he was reassigned to 19th Indian Infantry Division.

"G-1 of 19 Div, sir." Came the reply. The general paused a moment.

"Hmm. You'll be back in a month. Shall I reserve a room for you at the Bengal Club?"[8] John 'Jack' Masters paused a moment, then asked what the general was implying. Masters was about to become the Chief of Staff to Major-General Thomas 'Pete' Rees, commanding 19th Indian Infantry Division – the Dagger Division due to its shoulder flash. Rees had sacked thirteen G-1s that year, and even eight years earlier when Masters had first met Rees on the Northwest Frontier, he had a reputation for 'being a ruthless fire-eater. Apparently, he had not changed'.[9] After flying out of Calcutta, he was at the recently finished Kalewa airfield waiting for a flight to the front. There Masters met XXXIII Corps' commander, Lieutenant-General Stopford, who continued to add to Rees's formidable reputation. "Your general's a superb soldier, but…Pete sometimes seems to think 19th Indian Division must win the war single handed'.[10]

Rees was certainly one of the real characters of the war. A short, stocky man, who wore a distinctive red scarf, a bush hat with a red band, and had a nose like Julius Caesar. British troops referred to him as their 'Pocket Napoleon'. As two of history's finest generals, these features were possibly not unhelpful in building a certain aura. Slim's assessment: 'What he lacked in inches he made up by the miles he advanced. Whether he was hallooing on his troops from the roadside or leading them in his jeep, he was an inspiring divisional commander. The only criticism I made was to point out to him that the best huntsmen did not invariably ride ahead of their hounds'.[11] Masters clearly had his work cut out.

Rees had been controversially sacked before the Gazala fiasco in the Western Desert in 1942, ostensibly for lacking resolve. He had warned his corps commander that his 10th Indian Division was not ready to face a full-scale German assault and was later proved correct. Rees had to throw off any hint of an irresolute reputation, and so his pre-existing aggression that Masters was aware of in the 1930s on the NWF, increased. He had driven 19th Indian Division rapidly across the Shwebo Plain, made the first link with the forces coming south from China, and crossed the Irrawaddy first in mid-January 1945. Despite Slim's plan for 2nd Division to capture Mandalay, Rees had other ideas, he wanted to capture the city himself.

As the 20th Indian Division positioned itself to protect the flank of 2nd Division, and as they prepared to advance on Mandalay from the southwest to cut off any potential retreat, Rees's 19th Indian Division made its own arrangements to capture the city. The entire Mandalay operation was intended to draw Japanese troops from the Meiktila area, and then destroy them between XXXIII and IV Corps. Originally, 19th Indian Division had been part of IV Corps, but its rapid advance across the Shwebo Plain, and the development of Operation Extended Capital, Rees's division had been transferred to XXXIII Corps.

This helped in the deception plan to make the Japanese think *both* IV and XXXIII Corps were attacking Mandalay. Rees advance on the city was to follow a similar pattern. He would advance south down the ten-mile strip of flat plain between the Irrawaddy and the mountains to the east. He would split his force, one a feint by 64th Brigade with a contingent of armour down the most obvious route from his Irrawaddy bridgehead along the only metalled road on the left (eastern) flank. At the same time, the main advance with the rest of the division would go down a cart track on the mud flats nearer the Irrawaddy on the right (western) flank. If either route met stiff resistance, they were close enough for him to switch his main effort and made sure his artillery was placed in such a way to support both advances. Most importantly, the Japanese had to believe the feint was the main effort so his actual main force could get to the city more easily and cut off any Japanese force that opposed the feint.

Mandalay was forty miles from the bridgehead, and as always with Rees, pace was key. They were to set off at 8pm on 5th March, led by Stiletto Force, a composite force of C Squadron, 7th Light Cavalry in Stuarts, the 1/15th Punjab Regiment in lorries and Stuarts with the turrets removed, a battery of field artillery, a machine gun company, AT artillery and some Indian Engineers. This was followed by the rest of the division, with 98th Brigade up front, and 62nd Brigade in reserve, and the Lee tanks of 150th RAC split by squadrons to each. Robin Schlaefli, one of the officers in the division's machine gun battalion, 11th Sikhs, saw them off. 'As many as possible had been encouraged to clamber on any vehicle with a spare hand or foothold. Nearly every tank looked as overloaded as a Bombay bus…oblivious of the heat and dust, urged on by General Pete himself, in evidence as always in the forefront of the operations'.[12]

The advance began well, and after three days they were at Madaya, halfway to Mandalay. On the right flank, there was a delay trying to get the tanks over a *chaung*. Rees ordered the engineers to sink three lorries into it, then blasted the sapper officer for not thinking of the solution himself. On the feinting left flank resistance was crumbling, but the men of 64th Brigade were exhausted after three days of continuous fighting. Their commander, Brigadier John Flewett, radioed Rees, and Masters was invited to listen on another set of headphones. The exchange began with Flewett reporting his position, and saying his men would carry on at first light the next morning.

"Well done, you're doing marvels. Press on at once, keep pressing on. Over" orderedRees.

"The men are exhausted, out on their feet" Flewett replied nervously. "We'll push on at first light." Rees carried on gently, as though he had not heard this message.

"You've done very well indeed. Keep up the pressure. Over."

Flewett repeated his problem again, his nervousness now clear through the crackle of the radio. Rees was beginning to lose patience and spoke clearly and a little harder.

"I said, keep up the pressure. *Do not harbour or stop at all.* Keep advancing all night…Over."

"Yes sir. But…I don't think we can do it. Over."

"You can do it! *Who's winning this war?* Out!" The radio went dead. Masters looked at his commander, hunched next to him and just as exhausted as anyone else.

"We've all got to be driven sometimes, Jack. He's cursing me and thinks I don't know what it's like there. But I do. I also know what it'll be like tomorrow, and next week, and the week after, if they don't conquer themselves now."[13]

Stiletto Force were onto open flat ground and making excellent progress. Major John Prendergast was the second in command of the 1/15th Punjab. Another graduate of the NWF, he had been awarded the Military Cross there in 1937, was considered a mountain warfare specialist, and had fought in the disastrous Norway campaign in 1940. There was little opposition on their track closest to the Irrawaddy, riding in their improvised Stuart carriers at 15mph: 'it was an exhilarating feeling for one accustomed to moving at Pongo-pace'.[14] In a sign that locals could feel the impending defeat of the Japanese, Burmese people began emerging from their homes throwing flowers on the vehicles. As they reached Mandalay, one of its dominating features became apparent. 'Then Mandalay Hill appeared mistily in the distance. It seemed to draw me as a magnet, as if it were my ultimate goal'.[15]

Stiletto Force harboured for the night a few miles away, not wanting to try and clear the hill so late in the day, with only their small mobile force's support weapons. The next morning, around 6:15am on 8th March, Prendergast and A and B Companies of the 1/15th Punjab made it to Obo Railway Station, on the northern outskirts of the city, and below Mandalay Hill to the east. The rest of the battalion arrived soon after. They were the first Allied troops to enter the city since the retreat in 1942. Obo Railway Station was a station in name only, it was simply an open, dusty space where a train could be loaded if it stopped on the line that ran through the centre.

Mandalay Hill rises nearly 800 feet out of the flat landscape, a mile long north-south, and over half a mile wide at its widest point. The widest point includes a hillock attached by a saddle to the rest of the hill on the north-western side, known as The Pimple*. Along the length of the ridge are a series of structures, including four Buddhist pagodas, and other buildings making up a monastery. Running from the central 'Big Pagoda' as the troops called it, were covered walkways and stairways along the ridgeline connecting buildings, and down each side to the north, south, east, and west. The whole complex dominates the city even today, as well as the famous Fort Dufferin at the

---

*Another hill named 'The Pimple'.

southwestern corner of the hill that would also need to be cleared.

As Prendergast looked up from his position west of the northern staircase, something caught his eye to his right. Streaming down the western staircase was a long line of Buddhist monks in their orange robes. 'I learnt afterwards that the Japanese had arrived back in great disarray, having failed to stop the division's thrust'.[16] They had missed a wonderful opportunity to capture it: the Japanese had just got there first. Prendergast immediately sent his two companies forwards. A Company came under heavy machine gun fire from the flat country to the east of the hill. To neutralise these guns, Prendergast found a troop of C Squadron Lee tanks, 150th RAC*, but two were hit immediately by AT guns. They were only disabled and managed to keep firing and destroy the guns, before being recovered later. One of the guns was found to be a 105mm artillery piece.

At 2:15pm B Company was sent to get onto The Pimple. To support them some Stuarts from 7th Light Cavalry and a Lee tank firing onto the feature. B Company made it up to the summit without a single casualty and cleared bunkers on the reverse slope by 4pm. They soon came under fire from the main hill. Around the same time, Stiletto Force's tactical HQ at Obo station was shelled by Japanese artillery, and one of the recovered Lees was hit and started burning. Prendergast saw this, later reflecting in both horror and with a pinch of dark humour: 'Their steel hulls were oxidised red with the heat of their blazing fuel, and ammunition exploded out through the circular turrets…This is what the armoured soldier has to face, far worse than the infantryman's lot – to be caught, claustrophobic and kebabbed'.[17] He had not seen his own CO yet, or even his brigadier. Although true to style, Rees made a brief appearance

---
* In Prendergast's excellent memoir Prender's Progress, he describes them as Sherman tanks; however, this is probably him misremembering. The 150th RAC were equipped entirely with Lee tanks in 1945.

in his jeep, asked Prendergast where he was on a map, then shot off as quickly as he had arrived. Classic Pete.

The infantry of Stiletto Force were relieved, although the tanks continued to provide support. The infantry selected to attack the next night, the 8/9th March, were the 4/4th Gurkhas. Their CO, Lieutenant-Colonel Hamish Mackay requested the job because he had been posted in Mandalay pre-war and knew the hill and its layout well. At 4:15pm he led his company to the northeast side of the hill, when they found an assault by 64th Brigade with support from 4 Troop, C Squadron, 150th RAC. This attack was actually lost having moved too far west into 98th Brigade's area. The 5/10th Baluchis assaulted the Japanese position immediately north of Mandalay Hill but got no further due to heavy Japanese machine gunfire. During the attack Sergeant Shaw's Lee was hit by a 47mm AT gun, although it did not damage the tank. Having spotted the flash Shaw's secondary 37mm gun destroyed it with HE.

The Baluchis were pulled back to allow the Gurkhas to storm the hill, using the north-easterly route Mackay had identified. 2 Troop of 150th RAC now arrived to support the attack, along with two Stuarts from C Squadron, 7th Light Cavalry. These tanks and their supporting infantry, 3/4th Bombay Grenadiers, cleared the field and far hedgerow of Japanese bunkers, giving a safe route for the Gurkhas to attack from this direction.

Mackay got his men round the eastern side of the hill, by which time it was nearly dark, and the tanks went back to their harbour a few miles north. The next morning, 9th March, the Gurkhas stormed the summit, with 2 Troop, C Squadron, 150th RAC, clearing the Japanese position north of the hill that could have disrupted the Gurkhas' attack. There was some careful artillery fire, Rees and the senior commanders wanted to avoid destroying one of the most sacred places in Burma. The 150th RAC also gave supporting fire from the roads at the base of the hill. By the kukri, bayonet, and grenades the courtyards and buildings around the Big Pagoda were cleared over the rest of the day. The rest of the hill was cleared by the 12th March, with Schlaefli's Sikh machine gunners setting up on the flat roofs of the buildings. The Japanese had dug underground bunkers and tunnels under the buildings and were emerging behind units advancing south along the ridgeline, building to building. The machine guns worked out the entrances from where the Japanese would emerge and kept them under fire until a solution was found to deal with these holdouts. 'Horrible though it was' Schlaefli remembered, 'the sappers rolled in drums of petrol, or blew holes in the concrete and poured it in. Very pistols or tracer bullets would ignite the fuel and that would be that. Imagining the underground scenes sickened me more than any other aspect of our battles'.[18] Schlaefli comforted himself by the crumps and earth-shaking vibrations under them; at least the flames were exploding ammunition. Hopefully the deaths were quick. Even so, 'some Japanese soldiers staggered out from the different escape holes, some with their clothing aflame, still firing their weapons until finally silenced by our machine guns'.[19]

Whilst the Gurkhas, and later 2nd Royal Berkshires were clearing the hill, Stiletto Force started to clear the area east of the hill, although the going for tanks was hard because the Japanese opened an irrigation gate and flooded the area. One Lee tank was damaged as they were forced to stay on the raised roads and were in clear view of some Japanese guns, but they cleared the area successfully. Similarly, the ground west of the hill criss-crossed with *chaungs* towards the marshy banks of the Irrawaddy were cleared with another armoured column. Inevitably, the Lee tanks and infantry, despite the difficult ground, were able to destroy the Japanese bunkers they encountered. These actions practically surrounded Mandalay Hill just as it was cleared, and now put troops into the edge of the city proper, below the imposing walls of Fort Dufferin.

Now that Mandalay Hill had been cleared, the city itself could be attacked. The biggest obstacle was Fort Dufferin, built in the late 1850s by King Mindon for the Burmese monarchy as a palace and seat of government. During the colonial period, when Britain took control in 1885, it became an administrative and military base. The 23-foot-high dark brick walls had earth embankments on the inside making them 30-feet wide at the base. Each wall was about a quarter of a mile long and surrounded by a 40-foot-wide moat with a bridge into a gate. This was a formidable defensive position even with the incredible change in weapons technology since it design and construction in the 1850s*.

The street fighting that was now taking place was making it difficult for the infantry and tank men. Masters saw how they fought in the 'brick and stone rubble of the burning city, among corpses of children and dead dogs and the universal sheets of corrugated iron'.[20] Prendergast was getting support from the 150th RAC, and they used their bunker busting techniques against positions built in the foundations of buildings. 'Armour-piercing shells fired at solid buildings created an impenetrable cloud of brick dust', covering the men, the masonry dust sticking to the sweat on their skin and in their clothes.[21] The armour was very vulnerable even with close infantry support; it was easy for them to be ambushed by well sighted and camouflaged AT guns firing into the flanks of the tanks from point-blank range, and several Lees were burnt out. 'Tanks are not in their element in a built-up area' thought Prendergast.[22] The intense heat also meant the air was heavy with the smell of putrefying bodies.

For four days from the 10th March, while Mandalay Hill was still being mopped up, Rees threw everything at the walls of Fort Dufferin. Tanks, 5.5-inch artillery pieces, firing at point-blank range, P-47 Thunderbolts skip-bombing the walls, bouncing the bomb off the moat, and B-24 Liberator heavy bombers hammering them, although this led to some friendly casualties. Attempts using assault boats in a small breach on the 10th and

---

* For comparison, the 1850s was the era of the Crimean War, flintlock rifled-muskets, the very beginning of the transition from smooth-bore muzzle-loading cannon to the first screw-breech rifled cannons, and the very first steamships and ironclads.

14th had ended in failure, with the 4/12th then 8/12th Frontier Force Regiment losing a third of their men even under the cover of all this firepower and a smoke screen. Most of the buildings inside had been destroyed, and smoke rose from the compound in thick clouds. The whole enterprise had the air of a siege in the Peninsular War, with forlorn hopes failing to get through the breaches. More guns were brought forward, and further breaches made until there appeared to be a breakthrough when a local government worker was found. They knew the layout of the sewers and suggested sending an assault underneath the fort and appearing behind the Japanese. On 20th March, as this was prepared, six Burmans emerged from the fort under a white flag, and a Union Jack. The Japanese defenders, barely one hundred of them from the 60th Regiment, 15th Division, had slipped out themselves, possibly through the same sewers. By 1:30pm a medium artillery regiment gunner had climbed the remains of the fort flagstaff. The next morning, the sappers blew open the main gate. 'Pete walked in, surrounded by a cheering, yelling mob, of a dozen races. Just as Pete – but not his superiors – had planned, the Dagger Division had taken Mandalay'.[23]

The mopping up actually continued through the city a little longer, although the intensity of the fight waned significantly now the two key defensive positions were captured. Most of the remaining Japanese 15th Division men slipped out of the southern suburbs across the Myitnge river and made towards the battle around Meiktila. 2nd Division entered the city from the south on the 20th March. Arthur Freer noted how the city seemed almost normal, people were going about on foot and on bicycles, even fruit and vegetable stalls were open for business. 'We felt rather like tourists – until we heard the machine guns firing inside the fort'.[24] Freer's squadron helped clear the city in the immediate vicinity but was redirected to help liberate an internment camp nearby with a show of force to the camp guards. There was a risk that 19th and 2nd Division troops might meet each other unexpectedly and risk friendly fire. By the 21st

March the 2nd British and 19th Indian Divisions had joined hands, ready for the push south, as Slim described it, the hammer against IV Corps' anvil.

The fight for Mandalay was a mixed experience for the armoured regiments. They did not play the same dramatic role they had played in other major engagements up to that point. Their greatest contribution was in the speed and mobility they provided Rees, something that was so important to him. At the same time, however, the nature of the battle once across the Irrawaddy and especially once in Mandalay, did not lend itself to tanks. The Japanese had made the right decision opening sluice gates to flood fields, which made tanks more vulnerable as it limited their routes in the area. This was on top of the natural marshes near the Irrawaddy itself, and the difficulties inherent in using tanks during street fighting. The Japanese could predict where the tanks would be, channelling them into kill zones where well-placed and well-camouflaged AT guns could attack them in their vulnerable sides from close range. The tanks would provide their customary bunker busting from the roads, not dissimilar to the fighting in much of Kohima, or the road between Kohima and Imphal. The speed Rees demanded of his subordinates, the drive to push on, meant they did not attempt more complex or methodical operations to get a tank up onto Mandalay Hill, like at the tennis court or Nunshigum. Fort Dufferin was a variable not prepared for, a highly unusual obstacle for Burma that Fourteenth Army faced, and was captured after the Japanese evacuated it, rather than by force.

Despite this, armoured warfare was already coming into its own even as XXXIII Corps started moving south to join the battle raging around Meiktila. The actions of IV Corps' 17th Indian Division and 255th Indian Tank Brigade around that vital supply hub were the greatest all-arms, manoeuvre warfare operation in the Second World War.

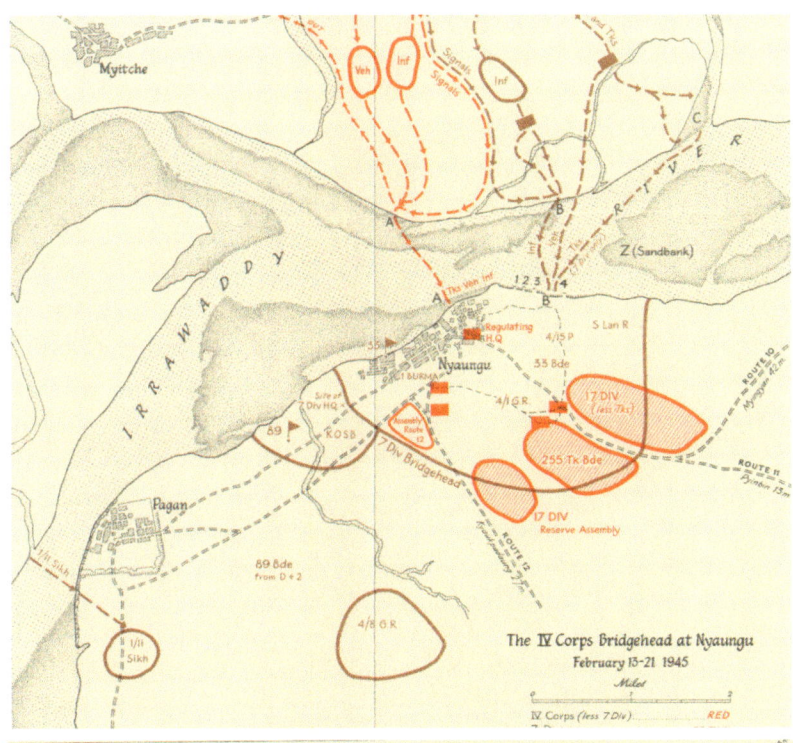

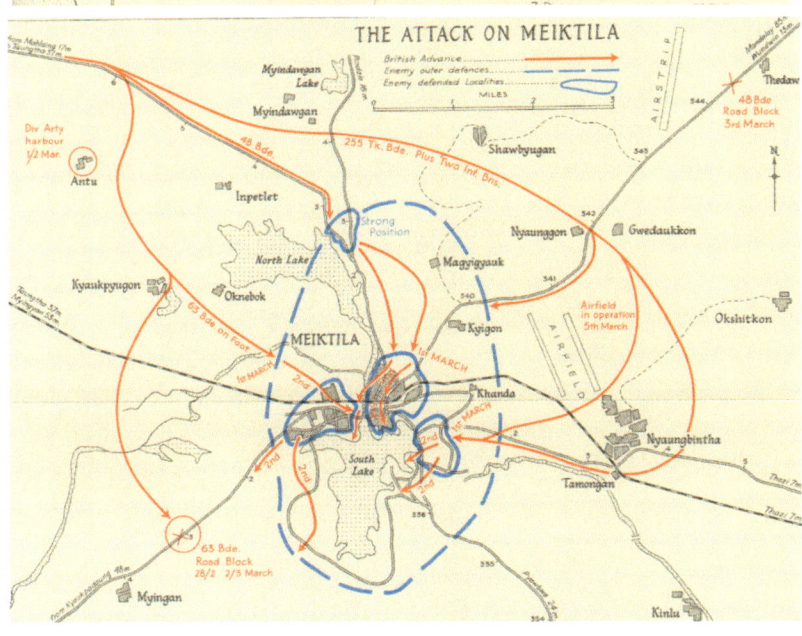

Thunder Run to Meiktila 281

The IV Corps Bridgehead at Nyaungu, February 13-21 1945

THE ATTACK ON MEIKTILA

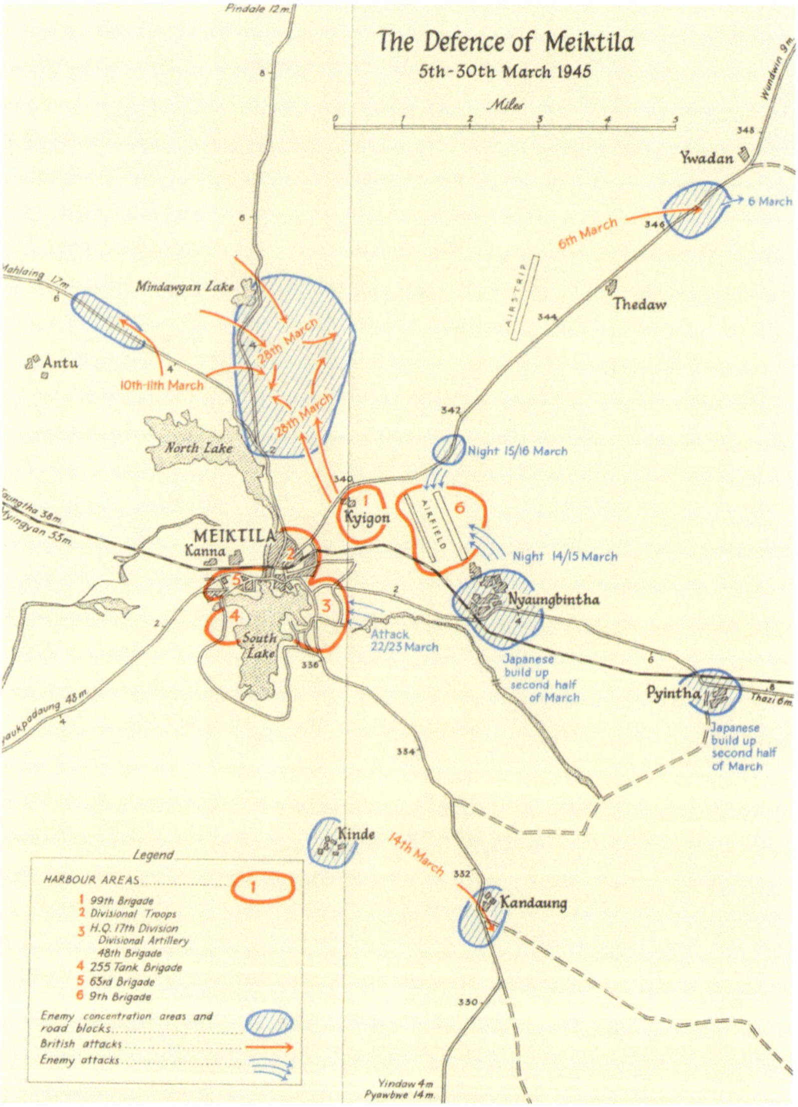
The Defence of Meiktila
5th-30th March 1945
Miles
Pindale 12m
Wundwin 9m
Ywadan
6 March
6th March
Thedaw
AIRSTRIP
Mahlaing 17m
Mindawgan Lake
Antu
10th-11th March
28th March
28th March
North Lake
Night 15/16 March
Kyigon
AIRFIELD
Night 14/15 March
MEIKTILA
Kanna
Nyaungbintha
South Lake
Attack 22/23 March
Japanese build up second half of March
Pyintha
Thazi 6m
Japanese build up second half of March
Kyaukpadaung 48m
Kinde
14th March
Kandaung
Yindaw 4m
Pyawbwe 14m
Legend
HARBOUR AREAS
1 99th Brigade
2 Divisional Troops
3 H.Q. 17th Division
Divisional Artillery
48th Brigade
4 255 Tank Brigade
5 63rd Brigade
6 9th Brigade
Enemy concentration areas and road blocks
British attacks
Enemy attacks

13
Thunder Run to Meiktila

After his attachment to the 25th Dragoons observing the fighting around Buthidaung in March 1944, Lieutenant-Colonel Miles Smeeton had returned to India to help raise the 255th Indian Tank Brigade, commanded by Brigadier Claude Pert. In August 1944 Smeeton was given command of the prestigious Probyn's Horse – the 5th King Edward VII's Own Lancers - who had been motorised in 1942 initially receiving Lee and Stuart tanks. The brigade's sabre squadrons also included the 9th Royal Deccan Horse, and 116th Regiment, RAC (Gordon Highlanders). Smeeton felt the pressure of some of the tank units who had been fighting in 1944: 'They got their tanks into places where no one would have believed that tanks could go...both the Carabiniers and 25th Dragoons...had made a reputation for themselves in Imphal and Arakan which we were going to have to live up to when we arrived'.[1] The pressure was not relieved when the officers and men of the regiment were sent to Imphal and taken around the sites of fierce tank fighting, analysing their performance. The regiment had recently been reequipped with new Sherman tanks in Secunderabad, before heading to Ranchi where they got up to speed with the new kit. They took on the lessons from 1944, including hill climbing and most importantly infantry cooperation, reflecting the constant lesson learning in the culture of the Indian Army. In preparation for the coming campaign, they practised forming defensive boxes and the importance of tank placement around the perimeter.

Pert, and his second in command, Colonel Ralph Younger, ensured they focused their training and tactics on the context of the dusty plain in central Burma they were about to fight across. Ralph Younger was an excellent choice, having fought with the

7th Hussars in the 1942 retreat, and with the 3rd Carabiniers at Imphal – he was the only senior tank officer who fought throughout the entire Burma campaign. Once the regiment reached Imphal in September 1944, ready for operations, the Japanese were already behind the Chindwin. Smeeton grew confident as they mingled with troops in the rear areas who were glowing from their victory in 1944, and with the pursuit still taking place. 'I felt that no commanding officer could be as lucky as I was, in his men and in his officers and in the time; for it was the beginning of a new campaign, we had a good tank to fight with, and of training we had had almost more than enough'.[2]

The armour of the 255th Indian Tank Brigade was at the heart of the reconquest of Burma. Operation Extended Capital was built around the 17th Indian Division and 255th Indian Tank Brigade's operation to capture the logistical centre of Meiktila, 200 miles south of Mandalay. The 17th Indian Division had been fighting the Japanese since their initial invasion in December 1941, and were now to play a central role in driving them out again. The operation was to be of overwhelming firepower, and vast scale mechanised manoeuvre warfare. Up to the end of 1944 it had been rare to put more than half squadrons into action at once, most often they were parcelled out by troops. Now they could attack in the kind of modern formations only dreamed of in 1944. If the tanks were to act as a whole brigade, however, they would need infantry support that could move with them. The sudden need to turn Operation Capital into Extended Capital meant 17th Indian Division had to be literally brought up to speed so they could act in concert with the tanks. In January 1945 they were still in Ranchi resting and refitting when they received orders to return to Burma. Ominously, they left their mules behind. In just eight days, IV Corps reshuffled their transport arrangements by taking most of 11th East African Division and 5th Indian Division's transport and reassigned it to 48th and 63rd Brigades of 17th Indian Division. 99th Brigade, 17th Indian Division, was made air transportable, and sent to Palel airfield ready to be called forward. They would be airlifted into Meiktila once the airfields had been captured.

In essence, the plan was for IV Corps to head south down the Kabaw, Myitha and Gangaw valleys, building the road as they went, then 7th Indian Infantry Division would cross the Irrawaddy at Nyaungu, creating a beachhead. 17th Indian Division (minus 99th Brigade) and 255th Indian Tank Brigade would cross the river and pass through the 7th Indian Division. Then, to use a more modern phrase, they would head out on a thunder run to Meiktila 80 miles east of Nyaungu. Speed was the most important aspect of the operation in this first stage of the assault, striking across country just after the crossings 200 miles north at Mandalay that would draw in Japanese reserves. They would capture the supply hub at Meiktila and its two airfields, then the 99th Brigade would be flown in to bolster the defence. They would then sit tight and defeat any counterattacks while **XXXIII** Corps advanced south and crushed the Japanese armies between them.

Kimura's fixation on defending Mandalay seemed to confirm that he misunderstood the plan that Slim was carrying out. Slim was not out to capture Mandalay for the sake of it, despite its value as the ancient heart of Burma, a centre of British power, and its romantic and cultural allure to Britain from, among others, Rudyard Kipling. Slim was out to destroy Kimura's Burma Area Army, and would do so using his primary advantages. So, when 17th Indian Division and 255th Indian Tank Brigade broke out, they would move swiftly and aggressively, using their superior firepower and air supremacy to force the Japanese into a battle of Slim's choosing. To keep up the momentum, they would not leave a logistical tail behind them, they would not have to maintain any road back to the Irrawaddy or have to protect supply convoys. They would survive on air drops, turning another aspect of Fourteenth

Army's defensive success of 1944 into something offensive. This would increase the pace of their advance, and simplifying the column that was moving across country. Once the battles around Meiktila and Mandalay were won, Slim would exploit the situation and strike south for Rangoon. The threat of the monsoon added another layer of pressure to the situation, with Slim supplying two corps, 200 miles apart, from a supply base on the far side of a significant mountain range and over two major rivers. Capture Rangoon, and those problems disappeared; resupply would thereafter come by sea.

The 400-mile advance to the crossing point at Nyaungu began on 22nd December 1944 under strict radio silence. Staff officers were overworked writing orders and sending them by dispatch riders up and down IV Corps and its attached formations in a column that was eventually 200 miles long. One of those attached formations was the 28th East African Brigade. They were out in the lead, followed by 7th Indian Division, who left Imphal for Tamu just over the border in Burma at the top of the Kabaw Valley. They moved in lorries to the Chindwin crossing, before moving on foot down the Myitha valley to Gangaw, where there was a Japanese rearguard destroyed by the Lushai Brigade on 10/11th January. The Lushai Brigade was a lightly equipped all-Indian infantry force formed in March 1944 at the beginning of the Battle of Imphal and had moved into the Gangaw valley ahead of IV Corps' advance. The use of the Lushai Brigade and the 28th East African Brigade suited the deception plan for IV Corps' surprise advance on Meiktila. The two brigades were independent, that is they did not belong to a specific corps, and the Lushai Brigade had been in the area for a while. 28th East Africans could conceivably be part of the independent 11th East African Division, who had been withdrawn as the advance began. Their presence did not give away the fact IV Corps was moving south. The Japanese did not suspect a thing.

One concern was that these valleys were known malaria hotspots in the monsoon. This was not such a problem in December, although the latent threat of it never fully disappeared. The ground was an issue though, turning into a powdery dust in the dry season. John Henslow in the 77th Field Company, RE, was making his way down the Kabaw Valley, and remembered how the dust 'rose in smog like clouds that enveloped everything. After a few miles of driving through it we were all coated in the stuff'.[3] Henslow was part of the spearhead building the road the tanks of 255th Indian Tank Brigade would have to drive down, even working alongside one of Elephant Bill's teams, using the elephants to clear trees. He would be followed by other engineer units with heavier machinery to upgrade the road to take the tank transporters.

During the advance beyond Gangaw in mid-January there was unusually heavy rain, and mud became a problem. The muddy roads were also cut into the sides of hills, and had frequent turns and switchbacks, making it very difficult for the long tank transporters in particular. In the twenty miles south of the town tanks were unloaded no less than seventeen times, and occasionally even towed the transporters. 'Throughout this period 590th Tank Transporter Company, RIASC*, worked extremely hard under terrible conditions. They had little opportunity and no facilities for maintenance until they completed a task which the Tk Bde described as "well-nigh impossible"'.[4] Royal Deccan Horse ended up driving 200 miles on their own tracks before they reached the Irrawaddy. All of this created a maintenance headache they could have done without, with practically every tank and support vehicle needing repairs. Part of the problem was because the spares had to be airdropped, this potentially drew attention to the corps trying to make their way south undetected. IEME units worked wonders, often through the night, to make sure the column was ready to move off each morning.

*Royal Indian Army Service Corps.

Once the head of the vast column reached the Irrawaddy Plain west of the great river, the town of Pakkoku needed to be cleared. The 7th Indian Division GOC, Major-General Geoffrey Evans, assigned his 114th Brigade to capture it. The Japanese 214th Regiment held a strong position on the high ground overlooking some crossroads at the village of Kanhla. The infantry attacked immediately on 5th February and failed with heavy casualties on both sides. Evans had a decision to make about what he did next, he needed to clear the west bank of the river quickly to ensure there was no interference with the crossing. He could call on tanks, although the presence of armoured units could risk giving the size of this operation away, and therefore the whole plan. The tanks were not supposed to be in action until they had crossed the Irrawaddy: 'The country was very different from the jungle to which we had been used to. There were no trees, visibility was good over long distances and tanks could go almost anywhere'.[5] Evans contacted Messervy at Corps HQ and was immediately given permission to use tanks earlier than planned: speed was the priority now. The Japanese would know soon enough that this was not a feint.

The 255th Indian Tank Brigade sent forward the 116th Regiment (Gordon Highlanders), RAC, taking a few days to get forward through the column. They attacked Kanhla from three directions with the 4/5th Gurkhas, and the 4/14th Punjabs attacking on their own from the south. Major Craig's C Squadron carried the Gurkhas on their tanks until they were 400 yards from the Japanese position, where the infantry spread out ready to move. At 8am the tanks opened fire on the identified bunkers, and the infantry moved forward. The left-hand troop came under mortar and field gun fire, and one tank commander was killed by a shell splinter, but the contest was unequal. Soon Japanese troops were running from bunkers and through the village behind. Snipers were the main problem, but the tanks' machine guns made short work of them. The Gurkhas lost thirty killed and wounded, but twenty-two bunkers were destroyed and around 100 Japanese soldiers were killed. The tanks were withdrawn in the afternoon, receiving a message from 114th Brigade "Well done! You seem to have had a good party!"[6] Over the following days the infantry were counterattacked before pushing on and clearing villages up to Pakkoku, until the town was taken by the 15th February.

The operation set the pattern for future operations in the open Irrawaddy Plain, with tanks playing the key part. Quick identification of bunkers was critical in these fast-moving battles and was not an easy task with well camouflaged Japanese positions. The tanks began moving forward in staggered formations so that if a bunker stayed quiet and was missed by the first line of tanks and infantry passing over them, the second line could destroy them when they opened fire from behind, or on the following infantry.

The rest of the area required for the crossing was cleared around the same time, centred on the beaches opposite Nyaungu, rather than from Pakokku which was deemed too obvious a crossing point. Messervy selected Nyaungu after balancing various different issues: speed was imperative, yet he also had a limited number of assault boats. The current was fast, there were sandbanks both above and below the water, and the river varied between three-quarters of a mile to two miles wide. Opposite Nyaungu the river is only three quarters of a mile wide, but the approach was very exposed on the western side over hundreds of yards of sandy beach. Messervy decided to make the crossing diagonally across the river, from two miles upriver. This made the crossing take longer, but it would be safer by maximising surprise. The crossing of the Rhine was made with the most modern equipment, including amphibious vehicles and landing craft. There were vast resources at their disposal with the advantages of western European road networks over mostly flat terrain. IV Corps was making their crossing hundreds of miles from their logistical base that was along a narrow newly built road winding through mountain ranges and along jungle covered river valleys. The crossing of the Irrawaddy for the master stroke that would defeat the Japanese in Burma was made with a limited number of flimsy assault boats, and improvised rafts for the longest opposed river crossing in the Second World War.

After his successful mission to India to get the frames made for the tank rafts, Henslow's unit, the 77th Field Company, RE, was assigned to the second wave of the crossing. Evans had agonised over the decision whether to go over silently and make a surprise attack or go loud from the start and plaster the other shore with everything they could muster. 'It seemed doubtful whether enough gun ammunition could be air-landed at Sinthe to allow for such a plan'.[7] Reluctantly, he opted for the silent crossing. The crossing was to be made by 33rd Brigade, although the first troops across would be the 2nd South Lancashire Regiment, detached from 114th Brigade, with the companies going over silently using paddles. They would leave at 3:45am, 14th February. Their objective was to seize the cliffs overlooking the beaches under the cover of dark. Henslow would follow in assault boats fitted with outboard motors at 5:30am, timed to arrive on the beach near Nyaungu as the sun came up, and to reinforce the first wave on the cliffs, and expand the beachhead. Reflecting their anxieties, the men got into the boats sitting in the rear seats first, with each man having to climb over the last one in, accompanied by lots of whispered swear words as they did so. No one wanted to be at the front.

To cover the noise of the engines in the second wave, observation planes were flown over the river. There was a stiff breeze, making the crossing rougher than expected, and the distance made it seem to Henslow like the boats were barely moving. It was getting lighter as they neared the landing beach, and Henslow saw something quite unexpected: 'the leading assault craft appeared to be circling in front of them. As I drew closer, I could hear the rattle of enemy machine-gun fire and see the line of white plumes of spray as the bullets swept across the water'.[8] Henslow could not get a straight answer for why the boats were circling, sitting ducks just 200 yards off the beach. He noticed some boats drifting away with holes in, and no sign of the men who should have been aboard. One company had made it ashore and prepared to fight for its life in their tiny beachhead. Miraculously, it seemed the Japanese did not notice them, and the South Lancs had a nerve-wracking five hours waiting for reinforcements to arrive. Mixed messages had caused some of the leading boats to head back to where they had come from, and the rest, with no leaders and under orders to follow the other boats, had hesitated. Having taken casualties, they paddled back to their own beaches just as the 4/15th Punjabs started their crossing. REME teams were sent to the banks to repair damaged outboard motors and boats so they could be reused.

The might of IV Corps now came to bear. Henslow noticed that the Sherman tanks of 116th RAC were now lining up on the sand dunes and began firing on the cliffs, followed by an artillery bombardment booming from out of sight. B-25 Mitchell bombers and P-47 Thunderbolts now came over and joined the demonstration of firepower. Evans, who was flying over the scene could see the action clearly: 'The guns opened up, the aircraft began to bomb and strafe and the tanks' 75s were firing hard. The far bank was covered by a pall of smoke through which only the bursting high explosive was visible'.[9] As Henslow was crossing with the Punjabs, he saw the scene from the water 'the cliffs ahead of us were erupting with exploding shells and bombs. The scream of the Thunderbolts dive-bombing the enemy position not only gave us confidence, but stimulated our morale for we felt that this time we had the power and support of an army corps behind us'.[10] After dropping off his infantry, who charged up a re-entrant between the cliffs, Henslow spent the next few days ferrying troops, artillery, and tanks into the beachhead. The rest of 7th Indian Division would be across shortly as well, and the clearing of the area could begin, including Nyaungu itself and nearby Pagan. Once the beachhead was large enough, 17th Indian Division and the bulk of 255th Indian Tank Brigade would concentrate on the far bank, and breakout for Meiktila.

The tanks of Probyn's Horse, to use a cavalry cliché, were like horses chomping at the bit waiting for the charge. The senior squadron commander, Major Bernard Lorraine-Smith of A Squadron, the only squadron commander with recent battle experience, was going over the details for the coming operations with his troop commanders. It was a warming, dry and clear morning, the men sitting about their Sherman tanks scattered under the shade of the cactus hedges, palm trees and thorny scrub. Their commander, Lieutenant-Colonel Miles Smeeton sat by his tank *Clear the Line*, named after one of the fabled stud horses from Probyn's Horse's illustrious history. He looked out across the dry landscape to the east, criss-crossed with paddy fields and small ravines, with only occasional small patches of trees. This was good tank country. 'We could see the brown cone of Mount Popa and behind us, in the trees by the riverbank were the white pagodas of Nyaungu, but we couldn't see the smooth-flowing river where the crossing was still going on'.[11] Even as the 7th Indian Division was bringing over its last units, Messervy had already decided to start sending the Meiktila strike force into the expanding bridgehead. By the 20th February 255th Indian Tank Brigade, minus 116th RAC, and 17th Indian Division, minus 99th Brigade, were concentrated in the area east of Nyaungu ready for their thunder run.

The 7th Indian Division had done a sterling job, despite the difficult beginning to the crossing. In one stroke of luck, they had crossed at the junction between the Japanese 15th and 28th Armies; always an area of weakness where the responsibilities are inevitably blurred by a simple line on a large-scale map. This had led to INA units covering the area; troops of questionable quality to say the least. Furthermore, the deception plans had been a complete success, keeping the IV Corps advance a secret, and persuading the Japanese that Mandalay was the main thrust. To Kimura, commanding the defence of Burma, everything apart from Mandalay was a diversion. A lone battalion of the 153rd Regiment had tried to counterattack 7th Indian Division's beachhead, but it was easily repulsed. Once the tanks and infantry set off for Meiktila, 7th Indian Division would have a new task to secure the bridgehead and expand it south to stop reinforcements from coming north from the Yenangyaung oilfield area. This would also double as a feint towards the strategically important resources available there, although they would halt once they captured the town of Myingyan.

The main fighting units making up the thunder run to Meiktila were 48th and 63rd Indian Infantry Brigades of 17th Indian Division, with Probyn's Horse and the Deccan Horse of 255th Indian Tank Brigade. They also took their attached artillery, engineers, and thinned down supporting services. Once they broke out of the bridgehead, the 3,000 vehicles in the column were on their own and completely reliant on aerial resupply. They would first move to Pyinbin where there was an important crossroads where the column would split. 48th Brigade and the Deccan Horse would take a direct route east to Taungtha, a town astride the main road and railway to Meiktila. Meanwhile, 63rd Brigade and Probyn's Horse would head south to Seiktein before turning northeast and meeting at Taungtha with the other half of the column. The reformed column would then strike south for the airfield at Thabutkon where 99th Brigade would be flown in, and the full force would capture Meiktila.

The Japanese defences in the area were made of a mixture of units, with different regiments from multiple divisions and from three army formations all identified. Resistance was almost always centred around villages. There were usually lots of trees in the villages for shade in the hot dry belt. The buildings were mostly bamboo and thatch huts built on thick wooden posts, under which the Japanese dug their customary bunkers to the same pattern as always, with thick earth roofs supported by logs. These huts were in little compounds made of earth banks, sometimes walls, or a cactus or thorn fence. The fields around the villages were surrounded by similar bunds with hedges on top. The Japanese often built their main defensive position in and around a large artificial community pond, called a *jheel*. Each village that was away from the river had one to serve as an alternative water source in the almost desert-like conditions. They were made from a high earth bank and topped with tamarind trees. A similar bank often surrounded the whole village, again with palm and other shady trees on or near them.

The column set off early on 21st February, meeting sporadic resistance and reaching Pyinbin by the evening. The 48th Brigade and the Deccan Horse set off on the northern route straight for Taungtha the next day, ambushing Japanese infantry in lorries heading for Nyaungu. By the 24th they were clearing a rearguard before Taungtha and preparing to assault the town. Meanwhile, 63rd Brigade and Probyn's Horse went south, where the column's reconnaissance force identified some resistance at the village of Oyin. Kimura had rushed forward two companies of the 16th Regiment, 2nd Division, who had been in reserve the day before, hastily digging in amongst the bamboo huts, the bunds, and on the banks of the *jheel*.

The attack was to go in at 11am. Smeeton sent B Squadron, under Major Stewart, in the lead, with C Squadron the main reserve. A Squadron would remain with the soft skinned vehicles of the column. The main road ran north-south along the western edge of the village, with most of the buildings stretching eastwards along a minor road. At the eastern end of the village was a *jheel* that overlooked the west-east road. Stewart reported after the action 'my plan was as follows – to go 2 up astride the road. No.1 Troop left, No.4 Troop right with sqn HQ supporting No.4 on the right. No.3 Troop I sent on to do a wide sweep on the right [west from Stewart's position] cutting the road at MS21 [south of the village] with the intention of cutting off the enemy line of retreat'.[12]

The tanks trundled forward, with the infantry of 6/7th Rajputs spreading out just behind them. As they approached the village the first sporadic shots were fired by a screen of snipers in the trees on a bund. The tanks started 'brassing up' the trees, firing their machine guns into them. A few trees gave the tell-tale shudder of its occupant losing their grip after being hit before the body fell to the ground with a thud. The infantry took cover behind an earth bank while the tanks kept moving as heavier fire from the village became apparent, red earth spitting up from the bank as it was peppered by light machine guns. Artillery from new US-made Priest self-propelled guns boomed as their 105mm howitzers opened fire, providing some cover as the tanks manoeuvred. The bank and huts were hit as they erupted under the fire, and some of the wooden huts caught fire. No.1 Troop stayed to the north side and engaged the bunkers in the bank facing them, while Stewart led 4 Troop to the right, hooking into the west side of the village and engaged about ten bunkers built into the bank of the main road facing west. This was the first action that Probyn's Horse had taken part in, and their training had been in exercise conditions. Throughout the fighting in Burma, cooperation improved the longer units worked together, and so on this occasion things did not go as well as they expected. 'Indication by the infantry was not good and it took some time to spot these bunkers'.[13] Now that bullets were flying it was much harder for an infantryman to expose himself and talk through the tank telephone, and nor does a commander want to climb out of his tank. Smeeton knew the infantry wanted his tanks 'to go on ahead and clean up the mess so that they could advance with the least danger – but they didn't always understand, in this very close fighting amongst the smoke and trees and burning huts how blind, ungainly and vulnerable the tanks themselves could feel, in spite of their power'.[14]

As the tanks and infantry got into their new positions the artillery fire lifted and bunker busting took place methodically, using the tried and tested methods laid out since early 1944. The difference now was the greater intensity of Japanese fanaticism when attacking tanks. As Stewart's 4 Troop crossed over the north-south main road and onto the west-east road into the heart of the village, visibility was reduced. Smeeton saw how 'nearly every hut was burning so that a dense pall of smoke drifted through the trees, through which, against the flickering outline of the burning huts, loomed the bulky shape of the tanks, with the flashes of their guns stabbing suddenly into the murk'.[15] The villages were dense, with the mud banks and shady trees offering lots of opportunities for suicidal attacks on the tanks. The infantry and other tanks would provide their protection as they could, but the fighting was surprisingly close. Stewart's tank hit a tree, and as they pulled back a Japanese soldier ran out from cover and jumped under the inside left of the drive sprocket. The horrible dull clang of an explosion ran up through the tank. A burst of red earth, chunks of track, limbs, and bits of the bogie assembly flew out. The tank halted and the dazed men inside took stock. The 25-year-old driver, Sowar Dayal Singh, was injured in his seat. The blast had come up through the now bent and buckled plate beneath him. He died later that day.

1 Troop to the north skirted Oyin and started opening fire on the east end of the village as well, while 4 Troop made their way through the centre. To the south 3 Troop had seen very little action but could see Japanese troops withdrawing eastwards. They got permission from Stewart, now in a new tank, to move east and engage. By 2pm B Squadron was reaching the east of the village, and clearing bunkers in the banks of the *jheel*, and

Major Arkinstall's C Squadron was called in to mop up the village behind the main assault. There were still a number of Japanese troops and bunkers that had been missed. Arkinstall watched as a Japanese soldier broke cover and started climbing Jemadar Mohammed Shaffi's tank. Shaffi had his turret hatch open, and quickly ducked inside just pulling the hatch closed in time.

"Badmash!" Somone shouted over the radio. This was the codeword for tank hunters and for those nearby to open fire on anyone climbing the tank. Risaldar Mohammed Araf traversed his turret and sprayed the Japanese soldier with Browning fire as he struggled with the hatch. As they moved forward, Shaffi's tank was attacked again, this time a Japanese soldier rushed forward with a wooden box of explosive picric acid and jumped under the front end. Araf saw the soldier leave the hedge from his own tank, and had warned Shaffi, whose driver shifted the tank into reverse. The tank backed off 'like a horse shying, and one could imagine that the crew felt the soles of their feet tingling'.[16] There was no explosion. The Japanese soldier may have been hit as he jumped under the tank, explaining his failure to detonate the improvised mine, or was waiting for the tank to come forward again. Either way, the soldier was shot again for good measure.

They continued mopping up, and helped clear the southeast corner of the village, until 3:30pm when they were relieved by Lorraine-Smith's A Squadron. They were to help clear the *jheel* but were given orders not to fire their 75mms because of the risk of hitting friendly troops and tanks on the other side of the village. C Squadron's ordeal was still not over, however. Another Japanese soldier emerged from a hedge and charged for Jemadar Feroze Khan's tank. Everything happened so quickly, the Japanese soldier holding the picric acid box like a rugby ball, he swerved between shocked Rajput infantry. Arkinstall saw him try to push the mine into the tracks 'but got entangled in the sprocket the mine going off, taking his head with it, and his body whipped around and thrown onto the top of the tank'.[17]

Back in Oyin, the *jheel* was proving a tough nut to crack, with open ground on every side that infantry would have to cross from opposing bunds and hedges. A Squadron were approaching from the southeast side, under fire from bunkers in the earth bank, and from snipers in the tamarind trees above. 4 Troop led the way slowly, shooting up suspect trees and the bunkers. The troop leader was the future Maharajah of Bundi, Bahadur Singh, and was operating with his hatch open and spotting targets; his pericopes had been shot away. After the action there were 40 bullet marks on the turret. Lorraine-Smith was also hit on the helmet by a sniper and closed down.

The action, so close to ending, was looking like it could fall apart. Light was fading now at around 5pm, and the infantry were taking casualties. The Rajput's C Company commander, 26-year-old Major George Marriott, had twice ran from cover to use the call box on the back of the tanks to indicate targets. On a third run his luck ran out when he was caught by a burst of machine gun fire and killed. The attack continued under command of Subedar Chunni Singh. The infantry now hesitated, and it was clear the tanks would have to grip the situation. They moved round to a new flank along a sunken road when they saw three Japanese soldiers crawling east to escape, followed by a white dog. Perhaps in a sign of unusual compassion in such a vicious war, Lorraine-Smith's after-action report stated the reason 'they could not be engaged as the infantry Bde soft vehicles were lined up nose to tail along the road'.[18] Despite losing another Sherman to a mine, they pushed on and up onto the banks of the *jheel* and destroyed the last bunkers left. Oyin was cleared by about 5:30pm.

After the fighting Smeeton went with the infantry and recovery vehicles to collect one of the tanks. He walked through the village just before it was dark. 'Only the tank hunters had been killed outside their foxholes. All the others were full. There they still sat. Some pockmarked and smashed with bullets, some with their clothes still smouldering from the tracer'.[19] The tanks harboured to the south of the village, in preparation for the advance to carry on the next day along the southern route to Taungtha, before heading to Meiktila. The infantry and armoured officers debriefed, and discussed how they could work together better, but also reflected that they had defeated a significant enemy position and destroyed the best part of two companies. There were at least 200 bodies, and there were many more buried in destroyed bunkers. In return, Probyn's Horse and the 6/7th Rajputs had lost 17 dead, all but two from the infantry, and 41 wounded.

The Japanese tactics were desperate in the extreme. In a good defensive position, facing an enemy intent on making fast progress, the Japanese were overwhelmed by firepower, and by tanks manoeuvring rapidly around them searching for weaknesses. The Japanese were simply not prepared for what war now entailed. There were two unused small field guns, but both were insignificant to the action, a statistic to be counted in the aftermath, and taken as a trophy. They had been captured intact with barely a mention in the war diary or after-action reports, and so were clearly badly handled. Suicide tactics that relied on the devotion of battle-hardened Japanese soldiers adhering to the ideas of *Bushido* were all well and good. But in the face of tanks and infantry that were being blooded in their first action, most suicide attackers were cut down the moment they broke cover. Smeeton reflected on the fanatical tactics. 'Their anguished look of determination and despair, pitting their puny strength against such tremendous force. This desperate form of courage was something that we knew little of and saw with amazement, admiration, and pity'.[20]

Oyin was the only strong opposition met on the way to Taungtha. On 23rd February, Probyn's Horse and 63rd Brigade continued their southern route to the town, attacking small pockets of resistance on the way. The Deccan Horse and 48th Brigade made their attack on the 24th and captured it against light and disorganised opposition from 214th Regiment, 33rd Division. Probyn's Horse and 63rd Brigade arrived at Taungtha later on the same afternoon it was taken. The tanks of 255th Indian Tank Brigade harboured for the night and prepared to charge down to Meiktila via Thabutkon Airfield. The Japanese sent over a few fighters to strafe them, destroying some B1 echelon lorries carrying what few spares, fuel, and oil they brought with them, a reminder of how important it was to capture the airfield over the next few days. Next morning 48th Brigade was left behind to collect an air drop, whilst the rest turned south and raced for Mahlaing, the last town before Thabutkon Airfield, and Meiktila.

The further from the Irrawaddy they went, the more the landscape changed, the sight of trees and hedgerows became fewer and further between. They were really into the plain, and a long way from the mountains and jungles now. The tanks could spread out more, and Smeeton recalled the effect this had on the men. 'We could look across the fields and see the tanks climbing over the low banks that made the field edges, rising up and dropping down the other side, for all the world as if this was a hunt riding across country…this spirit of the hunt was affecting us all'.[21] The weather was hot, and the ground very dry, throwing up plumes of dust like rooster tails in the wake of 3,000 vehicles, lorries, jeeps, self-propelled guns, armoured cars, and of course tanks. The Sherman's engine deck allowed ample space for an infantry section to cling on around the stowed equipment: Gurkhas, Sikhs, Rajputs, Jats, Baluchis, and the mix of men now making up British regiments, the 1st West Yorks and 9th Border Regiment. If the enemy were spotted, usually by the armoured cars screening out front, the tanks spread out, the infantry dismounted, and P-47s Thunderbolts might be radioed in from the 'cab-rank' by an airman in a Visual Control Post (VCP) jeep riding with them. The Priest self-propelled guns would lay their fire, and the tanks and infantry would advance. What Japanese resistance was encountered was locally outnumbered and outgunned, frequently being caught in the open. Compared to operations over the last three years, almost as soon as an action like this had started it was over, and the men were mounting up and were on their way again.

On 26th February, Probyn's Horse and the Deccan Horse were leapfrogging down the road to Meiktila, with the former capturing Mahlaing, and the latter hooking east across country to take Thabutkon Airfield. They had brought with them American airfield engineers, who immediately surveyed the airfield and cleared it for use by C-47 Dakotas, who landed a vital fuel delivery later that day. The next day 99th Indian Infantry Brigade began their fly-in from Imphal and was fully landed by 2nd March. In the meantime, the Daimler and Humber armoured cars of 16th Light Cavalry had been making a reconnaissance of the route to Meiktila and discovered a roadblock at MS8 near two small airfields on either side of the road. The position was built around a deep *chaung* and its heavily mined bridge. Major Lorraine-Smith's A Squadron was sent on a wide outflanking mission with one company of the Rajputs, and another of the Borderers, and set up a roadblock two miles down the road to block any withdrawal. Arkinstall's C Squadron then attacked from the north from both sides of the road and came under immediate rifle fire from a hedgerow. Some machine gun fire from the tanks soon saw them off, fleeing into the steep-sided *chaung*. This made it hard for the tanks to engage, and so Captain Riazul Karim Khan took his tank to the left and down into the *chaung*, then turned right and drove 'towards the bridge 'drumming up' the snipers' with the survivors fleeing south.[22] The other tanks had crossed the *chaung* either side of the road where they could and continued the chase. The Japanese now broke cover, the after-action report suggesting the effect tanks had on the defenders during the brief action. 'Enemy did not stay to receive tanks other than the usual determined snipers and retired rapidly giving the sqn [A Squadron] which had remained on roadblock good shooting'.[23] Around 60 Japanese soldiers were killed, most of whom whilst fleeing straight into A Squadron's roadblock, without a single loss in return. Again they captured unused artillery pieces, some of which were capable of firing AT rounds, similar to those found at Oyin. The only explanation appears to be that the Japanese did not have time to bring them into action in the rush to set up defences before the column arrived. The tanks made a new harbour on some high ground six miles from their objective, with everyone digging in for the night. Smeeton looked down from his hill overlooking Meiktila 'there, silent, and still in the evening light, was the key to the war in Burma. With two big lakes guarding its approaches and forcing the northern and western entrances onto causeways, and from which there ran irrigation ditches and escape channels that would limit the movement of tanks'.[24] The plan for 255th Indian Tank Brigade, however, was not to conform to those obvious and limiting routes into town, but to use their speed to hook around the town and attack it from the east.

This was the first sign of the organised defence of the vast supply hub at Meiktila. The problem for the Japanese was clear: they could not counter the speed of the tanks and their ability to take infantry on wide flanking movements, to destroy static Japanese defences from a direction of their own choosing. The Japanese continued to lack effective AT guns, although there were plenty of guns of all sizes available in the town in storage depots, just not enough crews. There was plenty of ammunition and aerial ordnance to turn into improvised mines too. 255th Indian Tank Brigade would soon face these suicide mines, usually a soldier in a hole in the ground ready to strike the aerial bomb with a rock when a tank came along.

The other problem was the leadership in the initial phase after Fourteenth Army crossed the Irrawaddy. On 23rd February, a week after 7th Indian Infantry Division crossed the river, Kimura held a conference with the staffs from his Burma Area Army HQ, and those of 15th, 28th, and 33rd Armies. They were focused on the crossings near Mandalay, assuming anything else would be a feint, and were considering options to counterattack over the Irrawaddy north of XXXIII Corps' crossings. They thought a raid on Meiktila was possible, but they believed the troops in the area were capable enough of dealing with that on their own, with administrative troops augmenting the defence if needed. The staggered timing of the crossings at Mandalay and at Nyaungu helped considerably, building a confused picture in Japanese eyes. When reports came in of armoured columns charging across the plain towards Taungtha, the Japanese leadership ignored them because they did not fit with their preconceptions of how the battle would develop.

The seriousness of the threat to Meiktila was only realised after Thabutkon Airfield was captured, and 99th Brigade began their airlift. The proposed counterattack in the north was cancelled, and the 18th and 49th Divisions were sent to reinforce the scratch infantry force being assembled in the town from administration troops and other units. This was to be led by Major-General Kasuya Tomekichi, normally in charge of transport for 15th and 33rd Armies. Men from the hospitals were sent out to occupy bunkers being built in the city and surrounding area, with booby traps and mines placed throughout. These reinforcements did not arrive in time. The only 'professional' infantry to reach the town before it was isolated was 1st Battalion, 168th Regiment, 49th Division, who were placed in the western sector just before 255th Indian Tank Brigade and 17th Indian Division began their assault.

Now that 17th Indian Division and 255th Indian Tank Brigade were massed just a few miles north of the town, its commander could now fight the type of battle he really wanted. Up to now, they had been fighting disparately on the two routes to Taungtha or leapfrogging along the single road down to Meiktila. Major-General David 'Punch' Cowan put into action his main plan, to isolate the town, and assault it from multiple sides. He was an aggressive commander, leading 17th Indian Division since the 1942 retreat, and through the Battle of Imphal. On 28th February he sent 63rd Brigade and the divisional artillery on foot around the west side of the town, dropping the artillery and one company of infantry off at the village of Antu. From here they would be able to offer fire support to any unit as they attacked the town and surrounding villages. The rest of 63rd Brigade moved on to set up a main base immediately west of Meiktila, and sent troops to form a roadblock on the road into town from the southwest. They sent patrols into Meiktila that evening to find this approach between the lakes to be well defended. At the same time, 48th Brigade went in from the north from the Mahlaing road and sent in patrols that also found intense resistance. The tanks were to make a surprise attack from the east, using their mobility to head rapidly across country. This was where the fiercest fighting would take place on the first day. Two reconnaissance groups went ahead of the main force, each with A Squadron each from the Deccan Horse and 16th Cavalry. One took the undefended village of Kyigon, two miles from the town, another group took Meiktila's airfield, then moved eastwards. As they headed into Meiktila itself, they met resistance at the final village of Khanda astride the railway line that ran parallel to an irrigation canal running east-west.

The main force of 255th Indian Tank Brigade now moved up and surveyed the situation. The Japanese were in an area of thick scrub dominating the railway line from the south. The reconnaissance group pulled back and hooked back east then south across the canal and moved onto Point 860, a hill on the eastern shore of the southern lake with a large pagoda dominating the area. They had to fight their way across, and there was clearly a petrol dump nearby as the Japanese tried to use burning barrels to neutralise the tanks. The main attack on the Japanese position was put in by B and C Squadrons, Probyn's Horse, with the latter squadron coming under heavy machine gun fire the moment it crossed the railway line. Their infantry, the Rajputs, went to ground after taking casualties. C Squadron, led by 23-year-old Captain Reginald Anderson's troop, pushed on another 300 yards towards the petrol dump, clearing the bunkers and hoping the infantry would follow up. Smeeton was listening on the radio and heard Anderson's calm voice:

"How Easy Baker, not much opposition here. May I go forward?"

As the tanks reached the dump there was a sudden '*wooph*' and sheets of flame towered into the air. The Japanese defenders had fired tracer into barrels at the sides of the road. 'For a short time, there was a battle scene which one would have thought overdone if produced by Hollywood'.[25] Everything became confused, mortar shells rained down on the tanks, their 75mms spat back their reply and the machine guns clattered away. To try and get a hold of the situation, Anderson opened his hatch to get a better look and to direct his guns. There was a high 'crack' of a sniper's bullet, and Anderson slumped down into his turret mortally wounded. He died two weeks later in a base hospital. Further bunkers were destroyed, but as the light began to fade, it was decided to pull back.

Smeeton was quite affected by the loss of Anderson. He had been born into the regiment; his father was a former commander. A few months earlier Smeeton had admonished the young officer for some loud laughter outside his office. If Anderson would not grow up, then Smeeton might not take him into battle. Anderson went pale and replied quietly and tight-lipped.

"You don't know how well I shall do in battle."[26] Just the day before he was shot, Smeeton had spoken to him about his conduct since they had crossed the Irrawaddy barely a week earlier. Anderson had been in action a couple of times, including at Oyin, and had done well. 'I had found out and I had told him and seen him flush with pleasure'.[27]

The next morning, 1st March, Cowan ordered a general attack on Meiktila. The position on Point 860 had been abandoned the night before as there was not enough infantry, although it was taken back that morning without much effort in a bold attack from the northeast. They turned around and began mopping up the area north of Point 860 but were halted because they were getting too close to 48th Brigade's attack going in around the same time from the other side. There were artillery and air strikes through the town in preparation. Meiktila is a large town, it is not a wooden village where most of the men had previously fought the Japanese, although there were areas like this at the fringes. Many of the buildings were brick, so the artillery and air bombardments reduced some buildings, and damaged many more, adding rubble and dust to the attackers' problems. The dry season, blazing as hot as ever, meant the men were soon bathed in sweat and covered in a fine layer of earth from riding on tanks, then brick dust from street fighting.

To the north, 48th Brigade with two squadrons of the Deccan Horse on the Mandalay road, made their way through a monastery complex into the north of the town. The attackers began to notice just how many machine guns they were facing. Amongst the stores in Meiktila was a large armoury with light and medium machine guns and plenty of ammunition, which had been distributed liberally to the cobbled together infantry force now defending. Bunker busting methods were easily adapted to fighting building to building in the outskirts, although this became riskier the further into town they advanced. They had to check every house and pagoda, anyone could lie dormant then emerge behind the advancing British, Indian, and Gurkha troops. The improvised nature of the defence was also revealed, with dummy minefields laid using a brick under a layer of earth, or aerial bombs half-buried with no detonating device, the idea being to send tanks and men into kill zones or expose engineers unnecessarily.

Despite 17th Indian Division and 255th Indian Tank Brigade operating 80 miles from the Irrawaddy effectively behind enemy lines and relying solely on aerial resupply, Slim decided now was a good time to pay Cowan a visit. Using a curious American general's B-25 Mitchell, the general, Messervy, and Slim went forward, the latter 'feeling rather like a schoolboy who had dodged his masters and was playing truant'.[28] After being brought up to speed, Slim left Cowan to his business, and went to see 48th Brigade's work, his party making its way by jeep to a recently captured pagoda on the north-eastern side of the northern lake.

Slim joined some Indian observers and their signallers calling in artillery fire crouching behind the wall of a wide terrace. 300 yards head were a platoon of Gurkhas, heads down behind hillocks and hedges avoiding the automatic fire Slim could see spurting puffs of earth above them. There was another platoon of Gurkhas firing their Bren guns from behind another position from the left flank. There was also a tank – one of B Squadron, Deccan Horse – in a dip behind the left flank Bren gunners. 'Then the tank revved up its engine to a stuttering roar, edged forward a few yards, fired a couple of shots in quick succession, and discreetly withdrew into cover again. I watched the strike of the shot'.[29] Looking through his binoculars he could see the Japanese bunker position built in three low, grassy hummocks, with tiny loopholes where flashes and puffs of smoke could be seen as they fired.

The tank grumbled again as it moved forward, firing three smoke grenades from its discharger, laying a white screen to drift in front. The Gurkhas advanced into the smoke, once clear, they were now 100 yards closer to the bunkers, and back behind cover. The crump of mortars now brought another smokescreen, and the tank had moved round again, this time firing AP shot slowly, more methodically, at the loopholes sending up spurts of earth. The Gurkhas had now got to within 30 yards. Slim and his party moved round to a cactus hedge closer to the fighting. 'The tank reappeared…advancing still shooting. Gradually it worked round the rear of the bunkers, and suddenly we were in the line of its fire with overs ricocheting and plunging straight at us'.[30] The American general, Messervy and Slim leapt to the ground. The only casualty in their group was another curious American, an airman stripped to the waste, who landed in a cactus bush, emerging covered in blood.

The tank moved again, the tank's gun firing alongside the Brens and Lee-Enfields of the infantry before the final charge. 'Suddenly three Gurkhas sprang up simultaneously and dashed forward. One fell, but the other two covered the few yards to the bunkers and thrust tommy guns through the loopholes. Behind them surged an uneven line of their comrades…bayonets glinting. They swarmed around the bunkers and for a moment all firing ceased'.[31] Some Japanese made a run for it but were soon brought down. With an air of professionalism, the Gurkhas dusted down, made a few adjustments to their kit, and they and the tank moved off, to repeat the process at the next bunker. Slim noted 'it was one of the neatest, most workmanlike bits of infantry and armoured minor tactics I had ever seen'.[32] By evening 48th Brigade advanced to about 100 yards north of the railway station, the infantry dug in, and the tanks withdrew to replenish their ammunition and make repairs.

The 63rd Brigade made their assault on the outlying villages west of Meiktila, closing up to the gap between the two lakes. A

Squadron of Probyn's Horse were sent on the long journey back around the north lake to provide their support to the 1/10th Gurkhas. They cleared the village of Kanna and reached the main road and railway without much difficulty and could see Japanese troops withdrawing towards the causeway between the lakes. One troop was split up either side of the main road into Meiktila, and advanced with a company of Gurkhas each. The left (northern) advance was held up by sniper fire from a prison and was cleared after Captain Nicolson blasted a hole through the wall, the infantry rushed in and cleared it. The right-hand tank (southern) was bunker busting in the grounds of a hospital, many of the garrison were pulled from the beds a few days before to man the defences. Tank-infantry cooperation was now becoming a well-rehearsed art: 'perfect communication was maintained throughout the action between the Sqn Comdr's 38 Set and Inf Comdr's 48 Set'.[33] The rest of the squadron helped clear the village of Magyigon, under another artillery strike, before harbouring at Kanna for the night.

The next day, 2nd March, 17th Indian Division and 255th Indian Tank Brigade made it even deeper into the town. The Japanese had reoccupied some of the positions cleared the day before and had to be removed all over again. The close nature of the fighting was making it more difficult for the tanks now they were inside the city itself. C Squadron, Deccan Horse, supporting 4/12th Frontier Force Regiment, reached the railway line at 11:30am after another methodical advance through the streets. As they pushed on one tank was knocked out by a 75mm gun firing AP, the crew bailed out safely. It was such short range that the infantry spotted the flash and immediately swamped the crew with rifle and machine gun fire. B Squadron lost a couple tanks in similar circumstances.

To the west, A Squadron, Probyn's Horse, continued their push with 63rd Brigade towards the causeway between the two lakes. They were engaged by a 75mm gun, but little damage was done. Once clear they moved south, there was no intention of crossing the causeway because it would be too dangerous to introduce more troops into the centre of Meiktila from a third direction. They attacked the nearby village of Kyaukpu on the edge of the southern lake and were attacked in thick scrub by Japanese tank hunters with suicide mines and petrol bombs, before further bunker busting took place in and around the village. The centre of resistance here were three brick buildings and some large bunkers that they fired on, silencing them in short order. As they emerged from the village and further scrub, they caught retreating Japanese troops in the open.

The final day of the battle to capture the town was completed by 48th Brigade and the Deccan Horse, whilst Probyn's Horse and 63rd Brigade mopped up the villages and other pockets on the outskirts. The Deccan Horse had moved back up to the railway line by 11am and found a crossing over the canal to the south. A Squadron prepared to squeeze the Japanese to the southeast out of the centre of town towards C Squadron moving in from the east. After a brief mortar barrage, they pushed along and the attack slowed, but never stopped. Methodically, the infantry moved from building to building, as the tanks supported with fire where they could, but it was now an infantry battle. There were more artillery pieces and AT guns firing point-blank range, although they were usually destroyed immediately – one tank was damaged this way.

There was still some mopping up in the town over the following couple of days, but to all intents and purposes, Meiktila was captured. Around 2,000 Japanese were dead, virtually the whole garrison, along with the capture of dozens of artillery and AT guns, lighter weapons, and vast quantities of ammunition and other stores. These were supplies that Kimura's army could not afford to lose. Slim's plan was built on this knowledge, however, understanding that the Japanese would have to take it back. Having caught the Japanese between his anvil and his hammer, Slim would destroy the fighting strength of Burma Area Army once and for all, on the Irrawaddy Plain around Meiktila.

The town and its outskirts now became alive with activity, with vehicles driving back and forth across town and new defensive positions being dug in. There was the occasional thud of a grenade or flurry of rifle fire as snipers and other holdouts were dealt with. Cowan's defence was to be based on his own aggressive instincts, and to use his strengths against Japanese weaknesses. He divided the town into two, with 63rd Brigade and 255th Indian Tank Brigade based in the town west of the lakes, with easy internal access across the causeway to send tank support into other areas. Divisional infantry and artillery held the centre of Meiktila, with 48th Brigade slightly south on the banks of the southern lake, covering the southern and eastern approaches. With the town's airfield now available, 99th Brigade were brought south, abandoning Thabutkon, to bolster the defence in the north at Kyigon on the Mandalay road and the airfield. This airfield was the lifeline* of the force and needed to be held, so from 15th March 9th Indian Infantry Brigade, detached from 5th Indian Division, were flown into the town to hold the airfield itself as it became the focus of Japanese attacks. Each of the positions was a defensive box with slit trenches, wire obstacles and supporting firepower behind. Really, these were positions of last resort; Cowan's plan was not to rely on these defences, but to seek and destroy his enemy. Within the boxes, all-arms columns were formed: armoured cars, tanks, self-propelled guns, VCP jeeps calling in cab-rank air support, and lorried infantry. Using superior firepower and mobility, the columns would sweep the plains in every direction as far as ten

---

*Thankfully, despite some awkward diplomacy with China in late February, Slim was able to appeal to the Combined Chiefs of Staff and keep US transport aircraft for Fourteenth Army until the monsoon, or 1st June, whichever came first.

miles away, set up overnight defensive boxes if needed, and destroy Japanese concentrations before they formed up.

The speed of Cowan's thunder run to Meiktila meant the reinforcements originally sent by Kimura, 18th and 49th Division, did not arrive in time. The only exception was 1st Battalion, 168th Regiment, 49th Division. The experienced but weakened 18th Division was still making its way south from the Mandalay direction, having been brought down from facing US and Chinese troops in the far north, whilst the unbloodied 49th Division was heading north from Rangoon. Progress was slow because the Japanese army was not properly motorised, and Allied air supremacy limited their movement to night. Movement on the plain was a considerable problem because of the dust that was thrown up, allowing fighters and bombers to home in on vehicles if they ventured out in the day.

These reinforcements would not be enough. Lieutenant-General Shihachi Katamura, commanding 15th Army, added a regiment and two further battalions (Sakuma Force) from other divisions to 18th Division, along with most of his army's heavy artillery. The artillery group was named Naganuma Force, and was quite formidable, consisting of two 150mm howitzers, nine 105mm, twenty-one 75mm, and thirteen AT guns, all supplementing the normal allocations in the infantry units. The artillery would concentrate north of the city just south of Lake Myindawgan, whilst Sakuma Force would move across to the Mahlaing road, Cowan advanced down from the northwest, cutting them off from the Irrawaddy. One regiment from Sakuma Force would move round the northern lake and attack from the west, whilst the rest of the force and 18th Division would attack from the northwest to northeast, whilst 49th attacked from the south and southeast.

Cowan's first sweep was sent out on 5th March after locals reported movement to the northeast. A screen of armoured cars moved up the road to Mandalay, with Probyn's Horse, infantry, and artillery behind. They cleared a concentration of 18th Division near Ywadan, killing around 180 Japanese and destroying and capturing some artillery. The next day five sweeps went out in all directions attacking smaller groups of Japanese probing forward. From 7th March the intensity grew as more Japanese units made it into the area, and a clearer picture formed of the attackers' intentions. As the days went on the sweeps became more violent, the Deccan Horse and Probyn's Horse both were in the thick of the fighting, catching Japanese units in the open and in the villages, losing some tanks and taking casualties. The Japanese had brought with them a new threat, the *Ta-Dan* hollow charge round which could penetrate a Sherman from fairly close range but the gun that fired it was often destroyed when it revealed its position with the first shot. The tanks caused significantly more casualties on the Japanese, however, in the hundreds most days, and continued to capture or destroy more guns on the roads and villages outside Meiktila. The tanks were beginning to need heavier maintenance after weeks of intense fighting, so an attempt was made to break out to the Irrawaddy and escort the rear echelons to Meiktila. Sakuma Force, and the artillery of Naganuma Force, dominated the road making this impossible; the attempt was abandoned after hitting these positions and guns, that had used slit trenches Probyn's Horse had dug on the 27th February. The move had caused significant casualties on the Japanese and pushed them back. The Japanese were here in greater strength than originally thought.

Smeeton, had been up in his tank *Clear the Line*, as he often was, following the action closely and sometimes taking part. The last few days trying to break through to the Irrawaddy had taken a toll, especially on the infantry operating on such open ground. Smeeton decided to give the infantry a rest and take A, B, and HQ Squadrons, on a sweep to clear the guns of Naganuma Force. If this were the Western Desert, this would have meant disaster, but the confidence the men had in their tanks against

Japanese AT capability meant Smeeton was quite excited. 'It was a thrill, not incomparable perhaps to the excitement of a cavalry charge of the old days, yet it was a cavalry charge of today, and a great thrill indeed to be able to move like this, unfettered by our responsibility to the infantry'.[34]

Smeeton's cavalry charge was to head out on the morning of 10th March. The infantry remained in their harbour, watching the tanks move out, before they 'stood on their vehicles and cheered the spectacle like a racehorse crowd'.[35] After clearing some snipers on the left flank, the main assault began. The VCP jeep called in an airstrike, fighter-bombers swooped onto the scrub-covered hill and the area behind the Japanese position, hidden from view to those on the ground. Then the artillery started up plastering the hill throwing up clouds of dry, red-brown dust. The tanks moved up two abreast in a wide move to the left and swung into the rear flank. Japanese troops panicked and left their trenches, some running between tanks that had passed them, but were soon caught by the machine guns of tanks behind. The tanks stopped to destroy two 75mm guns and fire on the fleeing infantry 'who were running so hopelessly to cross the road and gain once more the shelter of the trees, as men might run before an approaching flood or molten lava pouring down a hill'.[36] Smeeton's charge then continued on up the Mahlaing road, before he spotted a 47mm gun about 800 yards away at the edge of the village of Kyaungyagon. Smeeton saw the puff of smoke first, followed by a sharp metallic scrape above his head in the turret. The 47mm had fired first, missing him by only a few inches, it 'ploughed a groove in the armour on top of *Clear the Line's* turret' whilst his own shot landed short.[37] As he corrected the fire, another AP round jammed the gun's elevation mechanism on the front of the turret. Smeeton fired again anyway, this time getting lucky. The HE round hit a tree and exploded above the Japanese crew.

They moved on through the village, finding another AT gun that another tank had already destroyed, the barrel bent by a direct hit. They were a long way from support and called in an artillery strike on the village while they withdrew. There was one final sting in the tail, as Smeeton's tank passed a burning copse off the road 'suddenly *Clear the Line* rang like a cracked bell and flinched away'.[38] The two following tanks were hit too, but an artillery strike silenced the gun, and they continued pulling back to harbour. When Smeeton's crew inspected the tank, they found the AP shell had passed through the armoured ammunition bin, knocked off three shell fuses before landing on the floor. Smeeton kept it as a paperweight.

'This action was thoroughly enjoyed by both those who took part and by those who watched it…the action certainly had the effect of sending everyone home in the best of spirits'.[39] With no casualties sustained, Smeeton's charge had killed a large number of the enemy, destroyed two 75mm guns and three 47mm AT guns. The tanks were cheered into the harbour by infantry as they loaded into their lorries, and the tank men chattered excitedly running their own debriefs 'they might have been riders talking at the end of a point-to-point before the war' reflected Smeeton.[40]

The northwest-northeast arc was clearly the main threat to Meiktila, with defences cutting off an emergency route back to the Irrawaddy, and heavy artillery able to strike anywhere in the area. Cowan started making plans to clear the area and ordered Smeeton to complete the job after his tanks had a couple of days maintenance. From their temporary harbour on the Mandalay road in the northeast, near Paukchaung, they move in a curved arc around the north of Meiktila to the Mahlaing road to the northeast and the site of Smeeton's charge. The attack followed a similar pattern, with artillery and tanks doing the damage. The Japanese sensed the danger, and they were shelled on the move until they found the guns, including two 105mms of Naganuma

316   Forgotten Armour

Force. Smeeton was forward with C Squadron, who had swept in behind the guns when a shell landed nearby. One splinter whistled up towards Smeeton slicing through his nose. One of the men in his turret, Frank Sedman, helped him by giving him a boiled sweet, reassured him the nose was still intact, and tied a dressing to his face. Major Lorraine-Smith took overall command of the action, and saw it through, destroying more guns and killing around 30 Japanese gun crew. Smeeton was evacuated in a bad way, the strain of the last few weeks showing. One of the brigadiers[*] saw him in the dressing station and tried to lift his spirits.

"Why can't you keep that bloody great nose out of trouble?"[41] As he said this a shell landed with a crump nearby. Smeeton flinched.

"You can send for your orderly and kit. You are going to stay here for a day or two…you'll just be a bloody nuisance with the regiment. Stay here. Read a book. Relax. I'm going to have to the MO[†] keep an eye on you for a day or two."[42] An artillery officer approached Smeeton with a letter from his beloved wife Beryl. She was at Monywa volunteering for the Women's Auxiliary Service (Burma) and was there running a mobile canteen for the troops. He got permission from his commander, Brigadier Claude Pert, and was soon in a light aircraft flying from a temporary airstrip by the northern lake, still with a dressing over his nose. He spent a night with Beryl and some friends, before flying back the next day 'into battle once more'.[43]

The battle now shifted. 18th Division, Sakuma and Naganuma Forces had taken a beating in the first week since they began their attack. They were no closer to recapturing the city or destroying Cowan's garrison, which was now growing with the

---
[*] Probably 255th Indian Tank Brigade's and Smeeton's commander Claude Pert.
[†] Medical Officer

airlift of 9th Brigade, 5th Indian Division, beginning on 15th March. The Japanese could see the constant flow of transport aircraft into Meiktila Airfield. This became their new objective, take the airfield, and starve Cowan's men out.

There was renewed energy to do so; to the north Mandalay Hill had fallen on 12th March, and 19th Indian Division were now banging on the doors of Fort Dufferin. 2nd Division were closing in on the southern outskirts, and 20th Indian Division were moving to cut off the road and railway that came south to Meiktila. Kimura decided to reassign the Meiktila battle, Katamura had his hands full at Mandalay and was neglecting the real threat. He gave Meiktila to Lieutenant-General Masaki Honda commanding 33rd Army, who took over from the 18th March, and moved his HQ to Thazi, directly east from Meiktila. Kimura also ordered 28th Army to crush 7th Indian Division's bridgehead at Nyaungu to stop any further breakthrough and cut off a potential retreat for Cowan's force. Honda kept 18th Division in the north but shifted its emphasis onto the airfield. The big guns of Naganuma Force would shell the airfield to try and halt flights, and infantry would attack. 49th Division would set up to the east on the Thazi road at the village of Nyaungbintha and use its troops to attack from the south and east. The moves were made at night because of the risk of air attack in the day.

Cowan kept up the armoured sweeps across the area as usual, whilst he contended with the threat to airfields as it developed from the night of 14th March. 9th Brigade began their fly-in the next day, just as the first probing attacks by Japanese infantry were pushed off. As the planes began landing, Naganuma Force started shelling the airfield. The men in the planes thought the landing would be easy, but they could hear the gunfire over the roar of engines, see shells landing around the airfield sending up clouds of dusty earth. When the plane touched down there was a mad rush, equipment hurriedly thrown out the doors, followed by the men, who then did not know where to go. Soon they were directed off and took up positions around the airfield. The problem was that even with the addition of 9th Brigade, Cowan did not have enough men to man the entire airfield perimeter, so each night the Japanese would infiltrate and open fire in the morning. On 15th March flights were stopped by the shelling and B Squadron, Probyn's Horse was sent to clear an observation post to the north of the airfield. Overnight two battalions of the 55th Regiment infiltrated the northwest corner of the airfield, which was cleared before the next morning's sweeps could take place, establishing a pattern for the rest of the fighting around the airfield.

The other sweeps around Meiktila continued their success, inflicting more and more casualties, and capturing or destroying AT and artillery guns. Once the 9th Brigade had been landed, they took on the defence of the airfield, releasing 99th Brigade to join in the sweeps, but the main Japanese effort was undoubtedly the airfield. Once 49th Division was in position, they started making more attacks from the south, with a base around the villages of Kinde and Kandaung. The Deccan Horse took significant casualties attacking the area due to bold handling of Japanese AT and artillery guns against their tanks, notably by Colonel T Uga of the 49th Artillery Regiment personally commanding them in the open. On 23rd March Probyn's Horse were sent to clear the area with 63rd Brigade, who had moved over from the western side of Meiktila. As they approached, Captain Desmond O'Beirne-Ryan's tank was hit by a hollow-charge shell and caught fire. The crew bailed but O'Beirne-Ryan went back seeing the fire was not so bad. He managed to drive the tank back in on his own, then climbed onto Smeeton's tank. Two of his crew had already gone past wounded.

"It's Mubarak Ali, the spare driver, I never saw him. I think he's still there. I shall have to go back."

"You've done all you can" said Smeeton, "ten to one he's out, and if he isn't, he's dead. Stay right where you are." O'Beirne-Ryan looked at Smeeton, who turned forward towards the action. He then saw O'Beirne-Ryan walking in front pistol in hand towards where his tank had been hit, he had slipped off the tank when Smeeton turned away. Infantry from the Borders in reserve were shouting, imploring him not to go forward. 'He was walking to his death, but he had to make sure that he had not left a man behind'.[44] O'Beirne-Ryan was found dead from shrapnel fragments near where the forward infantry were. His death reflected the comradeship of the men, but it was all in vain. Mubarak Ali had already been evacuated to the advanced dressing station.

They failed to clear Kinde that day but went back next morning and cleared it. That evening as night began to fall, a curious incident occurred when another unit Kimura assigned to the recapture of Meiktila made their first foray. The 14th Tank Regiment, now reduced to just nine tanks[*] drove one tank onto the airfield from the south and drove the full length of the runway towards 3/2nd Punjab's defensive box at the western edge. No one opened fire until two more tanks arrived with infantry when they were attacked with PIATs. The 49th Division was by now exhausted, having lost almost half its infantry strength, and withdrew. The end was coming. Cowan sent 48th Brigade up the Mandalay road, first with Probyn's Horse, then the Deccan Horse took over a couple days later, clearing villages, more and more of which were found empty all around Meiktila. Probyn's Horse now supported the clearing of the area to the north with 63rd and 99th Brigades, with the last resistance being destroyed around the 28th March, marking the effective end of the battle. The same day, XXXIII Corps troops link up with 48th Brigade on the Mandalay road, and 5th and 7th Indian Divisions

---

[*] It is unclear exactly what they were, although most were probably Type-95 *Ha Go* tanks.

had broken out of the bridgehead at Nyaungu and opened the road to Meiktila.

Cowan had won an incredible victory using boldness and effective use of his strengths against his enemy's weaknesses. Tanks were the key. A rare prisoner reported to his interrogators "we are helpless in front of your tanks they stop 50 yards away from us where we cannot harm them and shoot our position to pieces."[45] To the Japanese Meiktila was a tank battle that they were wholly unprepared to fight, with the speed of the initial thunder run suggesting a light force. As the battle went on, they saw no perceptible reduction in the number of tanks. This was in part due to the supreme reliability and ease of maintenance of Sherman tanks, but also Japanese inability to even seriously damage them, let alone destroy them. Cowan therefore always had an advantage and used it to keep hold of the initiative. The Japanese could always retake an area a column swept through, but they could do little to stop another sweep coming back and killing another 100 men and capturing a few guns, neither of which Kimura could replace. They were simply overwhelmed.

Japanese doctrine was problematic too; to deny the enemy time to prepare, a commander was expected to attack with whatever was at hand as quickly as possible. The operation to retake Meiktila was under Katamura as 15th Army commander first, but his hands became increasingly tied by what the Japanese considered the main offensive around Mandalay. He effectively devolved command of the Meiktila operation to the divisional commanders, ordering them to coordinate, and left them to it. Even after Honda took over, communication problems meant coordination was never really achieved. The distances, difficulty moving in daylight, and the heavy equipment of Naganuma Force, meant the operation was disjointed. This played directly into Cowan's hands, who could send his columns out to the disparate Japanese units and destroy them, Slim's primary objective. If there was one battle that required a methodical approach, and time to build up two divisions with very heavy artillery for this size of operation, it was this one. Cowan never gave them a chance to even try.

As the broken remnants of Kimura's Burma Area Army pulled back to make a stand in southern Burma, Slim's attention turned to the skies above. Capturing Mandalay and Meiktila was a complete success, but it had taken slightly longer than hoped due to fierce Japanese resistance. There was barely a month before the monsoon was due. On 8th April, Slim issued an order of the day: 'We have advanced far towards final victory in Burma, but we have one more stage before it is achieved. We have heard a lot about the Road to Mandalay: now we are on the Road from Mandalay'.[46] Slim had fired the starting gun for the race to Rangoon.

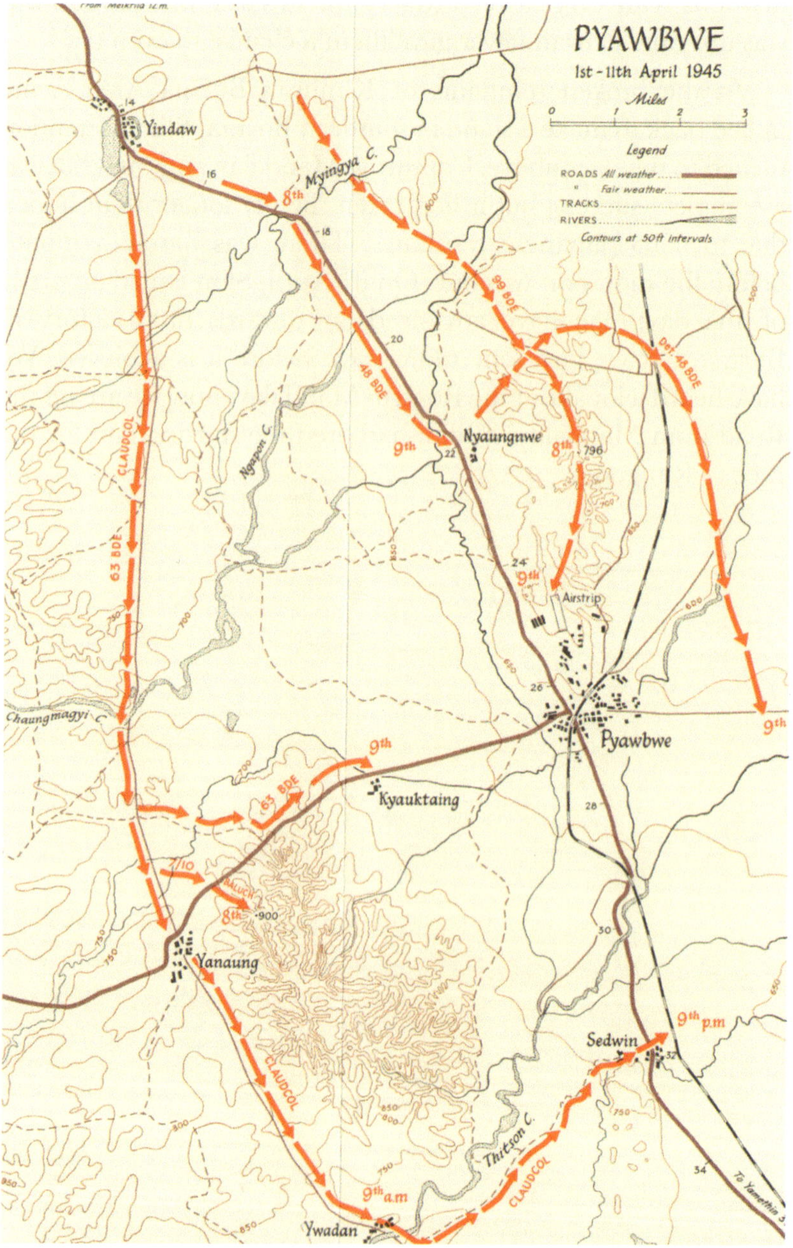
PYAWBWE
1st - 11th April 1945
Miles
0 1 2 3
Legend
ROADS All weather
" Fair weather
TRACKS
RIVERS
Contours at 50ft intervals
Yindaw
Myingya C.
8th
99 BDE
48 BDE
Det. 48 BDE
9th
Nyaungnwe
8th
796
Ngapon C.
CLAUDCOL
63 BDE
Airstrip
Chaungmagyi C.
Pyawbwe
9th
63 BDE
Kyauktaing
7/10
BALUCH
8th
900
Yanaung
Sedwin
9th p.m
Thitson C.
CLAUDCOL
9th a.m
Ywadan
To Yamethin

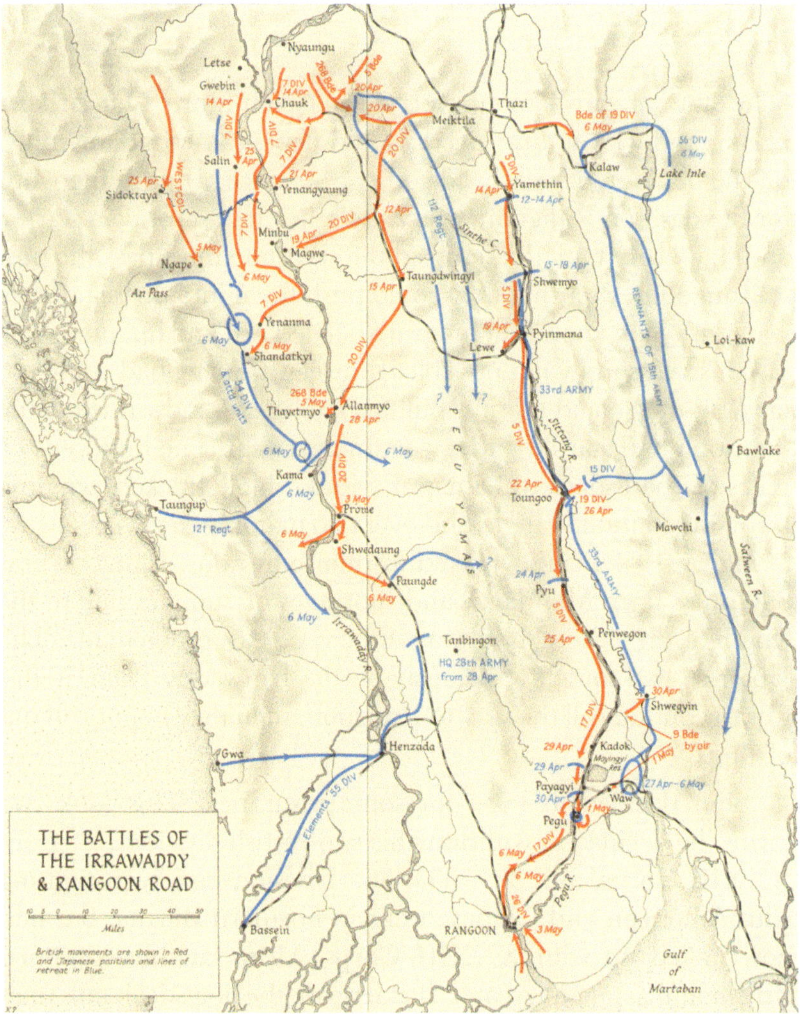
THE BATTLES OF THE IRRAWADDY & RANGOON ROAD
Miles
British movements are shown in Red and Japanese positions and lines of retreat in Blue.
Nyaungu
Letse
Gwebin
Chauk
Meiktila
Thazi
Salin
Yenangyaung
Sidoktaya
Minbu
Magwe
Ngape
An Pass
Yenanma
Shandatkyi
Taungdwingyi
Lewe
Yamethin
Kalaw
Lake Inle
Shwemyo
Pyinmana
Loi-kaw
Thayetmyo
Allanmyo
Kama
Prome
Taungup
Shwedaung
Paungde
Toungoo
Bawlake
Mawchi
Pyu
Penwegon
Tanbingon
HQ 28th ARMY from 28 Apr
Shwegyin
Kadok
Henzada
Gwa
Payagyi
Waw
Pegu
Bassein
RANGOON
Gulf of Martaban
PEGU YOMAS
Irrawaddy R.
Sittang R.
Salween R.
Pegu R.
Sinthe C.
WESTCOL
33rd ARMY
REMNANTS OF 15th ARMY
121 Regt
112 Regt
Elements 55 DIV
54 DIV & attd units
56 DIV
Bde of 19 DIV
9 Bde by air
17 DIV
26 DIV
20 DIV
5 DIV
7 DIV
268 Bde

14
The Race to Rangoon

'The state of our armour worried me even more. Our striking power, and with it, our speed, would depend, beyond anything, on the armoured spearheads of our advance…I gave the word for the dash on Rangoon, every tank they had must be a starter, and that every tank that crossed the start line must pass the post in Rangoon. After that they could push them into the sea if they wanted!'[1] Slim knew that his tanks needed rest and maintenance, but this was simply not possible. Fourteenth Army had come too far now, they could not just pull back to the Chindwin when the monsoon had started and try again next year. The hundreds of miles of roads back to Dimapur, mostly single tracked, winding through mountain ranges and over two major rivers, were always at high risk of being wrecked in monsoon rains. Rangoon was 390 miles from Mandalay, and shortages of supplies due to the length of the existing road was at the very least problematic. The Japanese had fought ferociously on the Irrawaddy Plain, if this was to continue all the way to Rangoon, then they might run out of time.

Slim decided to take out some insurance. This took two forms: he decided to withdraw his two British divisions, 2nd from XXXIII Corps, and 36th. The 36th Division had been fighting with American and Chinese units in northern Burma, but had now linked up with XXXIII Corps. More lavishly equipped British units put a greater burden on the logistical tail than Indian ones, and troop replacements from Britain always lagged behind demand, so it made sense to withdraw those divisions. As the fighting for Meiktila reached its climax near the end of March, Slim also asked Mountbatten to revive Operation Dracula, the seaborne invasion of Rangoon. By early April they were able to put a date on it: 5th May. This alleviated a big concern for Slim: the agreement to keep the bulk of US aerial supply forces from the Chinses front meant Slim would lose those aircraft when the monsoon started.

Slim also reshuffled his pack to suit the coming operation. 5th Indian Division had been mechanised while in reserve during early 1945, barring 9th Brigade who had flown into Meiktila in mid-March. They were now assigned to IV Corps, swapped with 7th Indian Division who would go to XXXIII Corps. 17th Indian Division was now completely mechanised: 5th Indian Division, 17th Indian Division, and 255th Indian Tank Brigade. These formations would be the main effort and be supplied entirely by air as they drove on as rapidly as possible. They would strike southeast following the railway line from Meiktila to Pyawbwe, 25 miles away at the head of the Sittang Valley, then head south through Toungoo, Pegu, then head southwest for Rangoon. Meanwhile, XXXIII Corps lost 19th Indian Division, which became Slim's reserve, having gained 7th Indian Division. 20th and 7th Indian Divisions with 254th Indian Tank Brigade would push down the Irrawaddy valley in a reverse of the 1942 retreat. They would seize the oilfields at Yenangyaung, then destroy the Japanese in the valley, and stop as many of them crossing the Pegu Yomas mountains into the Sittang Valley to reinforce resistance against IV Corps.

Kimura, on the other hand, had to make the best of a bad situation. Most of his divisions were at half strength and he had used his last reserves in the Battle of Meiktila, losing most of their vehicles and guns in the process. 15th Army, so badly mauled since 1944, was withdrawn to Toungoo to regroup. 33rd Army were to defend Pyawbwe and block entry to the Sittang Valley, then make a fighting retreat to Toungoo once 15th Army was reorganised. 33rd Army's three divisions were so understrength that they were barely the size of two regiments now, the equivalent of two British or Indian brigades. They were about to face two mechanised divisions (three brigades each) and a tank brigade. Lastly, there was 28th Army, which was to defend the Irrawaddy valley at Prome, and give time to withdraw the remains of 54th Division from Arakan. Kimura's best hope was to force a stalemate in the two river valleys, then rebuild his strength through the monsoon whilst Slim's dissipated through the difficulty of supplying his two corps over tenuous roads and inundated airfields. The clock was ticking.

The rear echelons for 255th Indian Tank Brigade, with vitally needed heavy repair equipment, finally moved forward from the Irrawaddy and got to work in the first few days of April. The race to Rangoon began on the 4th when they set out and found their first obstacle at Yindaw the next day. Yindaw proved to be an inauspicious start to the final phase of the Burma Campaign. With speed being the main factor now, there was no detailed reconnaissance of the village. All they could see was the high earth bund, topped with trees, and a moat on three sides, the only entry suitable for tanks was on the north side over two causeways on the moat. Infantry from the 6/7th Rajputs was to gain a foothold in the causeways, then sappers would clear the mines they assumed would be there, so the tanks could come up to support. Tanks and artillery gave supporting fire, and the infantry made it over facing only sniper fire. The sappers were called forward, when the opposition increased, light machine gun fire drove them and the infantry back, having only removed one mine from the left causeway. Spirited bayonet and grenade charges were put in, and Jemadar Sarup Singh's tank risked the mines to get across one causeway up to a roadblock and poured fire into the village, but it was to no avail. Unable to see enemy positions due to the high bund, and trees felled across the mined causeways, the tanks could do little to help. The day gave the first warning of the coming monsoon, with a very heavy thunderstorm and strong wind. This reminder of the timescales meant Yindaw was isolated, and the force would move on, the Japanese garrison slipping away in the night.

Yindaw was supposed to be 255th Indian Tank Brigade's base for the operation to take Pyawbwe, but now they shifted south to Kanbya. From here 48th Brigade would attack Pyawbwe from the north, 63rd Brigade from the west, 99th Brigade from the east, and a column from 255th Indian Tank Brigade would skirt the town south and attack it from the Rangoon road. This column was named Claudcol after 255th Indian Tank Brigade's commander Brigadier Claude Pert, and consisted of Probyn's Horse, A Squadron of 11th Cavalry for reconnaissance, 6/7th Rajputs, elements of 4/4th Bombay Grenadiers, 7/10th Baluchis, plus engineers and artillery.

As Claudcol set off on its flanking manoeuvre to the west of Pyawbwe, Smeeton was reminded of their role at the end of February. 'We were through as in the first days of our advance to Meiktila, driving across country and catching the enemy by surprise wherever we went'.[2] They smashed through remnants of 53rd Division at Yanaung, overrunning unsighted guns where the Japanese had no time to construct defences before Claudcol fell on them on the 8th April. Whilst in leaguer that night a Japanese tank with its headlight on came towards them. Some sappers manning the roadblock had recently been given new Hawkins mines and had laid them on the road. The sappers now panicked that these were friendly vehicles and ran out to stop the tank. The Japanese must have seen the Shermans looming in the murk beyond the roadblock and, realising their mistake, turned tail and ran while Smeeton and his men dropped their beers and ran to the Shermans. The tank had switched its light out and fired a single shot towards them but missed wildly. In a sign of the high morale of the troops Smeeton remarked 'a single ineffectual shell, which brought a shout of laughter from the Indian soldiers, as if it had touched their own particular sense of humour…down at the roadblock the sappers mumbled angrily together, and we went back to our beer'.[3]

Claucol now struck east across the dusty countryside after clearing Ywadan and neighbouring Okpo. They cut the road south of Pyawbwe on the evening of the 9th in the area of a pagoda on some high ground west of the Rangoon road. They were now sitting on the main supply route for 33rd Army in Pyawbwe, and still the Japanese did not seem to realise they were there. That evening a convoy of eleven Japanese lorries came up the main road towards Pyawbwe carrying reinforcements, with headlights blaring and completely unaware of Claudcol's presence. Smeeton's men had plenty of warning from their position above the road and manned the tanks. As the lorries drew level with them the tanks opened fire. There were no mines on the road, so they managed to drive on, the second lorry burst into flames almost immediately, as did the third and fourth. 'As the tracer from the tanks had ruled its straight bright lines across the road and then leapt at odd angles up into the sky, shouts and cries of alarm could be heard in spite of the noise of the Brownings'.[4] The infantry in the next two lorries abandoned their vehicle and made off, while the others turned sharply heading back the way they had come.

Just as Smeeton and his men were settling back into some food, they heard the distinctive whine of Japanese tanks, this time coming south from Pyawbwe. These were the last three tanks left in the 14th Tank Regiment, apparently withdrawing. The men jumped back to their tanks, this time more urgently with men taking whichever seats they saw available. One of Smeeton's troop leaders, Bahadur Singh, took the gunner's seat. Singh, the future Maharajah of Bundi, and one of the men who was key to clearing Oyin all those weeks earlier, and had snipers hit his turret 40 times that day. 'He was the best game-shot in the regiment and had knocked out his first tiger long ago in his teens. He was used to shooting at night, but not at tanks'.[5] The first tank saw the burning lorries and hesitated, then decided to carry on, Smeeton wondered whether they assumed the damage had been done by air attack earlier in the day. The tanks drove on 'as it came opposite us, I leant forward and touched Bahadur Singh's shoulder. A dagger of flame shot from the barrel of his gun, the enemy tank glowed redly, and immediately with a great belch of flame blew up'.[6] The next tank charged at the line of Shermans on the hill, silhouetted against the burning lorries on the road. The gunners in their turrets tried to depress their guns, but it was too low. The Japanese tank now ran across the line of tanks, but none could get a clear shot. The Japanese driver made a final, fatal error. Cutting back towards the road to escape, the Shermans got the angle back, and fired. The tank was hit and caught fire, rolling on and overturning in a ditch. The last tank turned back and raced off towards Pyawbwe as fast as it could, until it overshot a bend just before a bridge over a dry *chaung*. The tank careered over the edge, and landed in the bottom upside down.

On the 10th Claudcol now charged north towards Pyawbwe. Lieutenant-General Honda, commanding 33rd Army, was eating with his staff in a vineyard where he had his HQ for the battle. To the south they saw a cloud of dust approaching, and soon the guns opened fire. The officers and men panicked and began to flee as their staff cars and lorries were hit and caught fire, there was little cover and the men scattered. Honda and some of his staff managed to slip away whilst the tanks played havoc with the vehicles and HQ that had been set up amongst the vines and buildings, their importance unbeknown to the British and Indian troops. An opportunity to capture Honda and his staff was missed.

Claudcol also caught out some Japanese tanks, one on the right of the road, and two more dug in as pillboxes. There was a brief exchange of fire, and all three were destroyed. Major BH Mylne, the adjutant for Probyn's Horse, was interested to note

330   Forgotten Armour

that 'no attempt was made whatsoever to manoeuvre them in any direction'.[7] This typified the poor use of armour by the Japanese army in Burma. They were no more than mobile pillboxes for supporting the infantry, which was just about possible in the first half of the war in Burma. But now, modern manoeuvre warfare had reached them on this dusty, final corner of the central plain, and they could not cope. The last remnants of 14th Tank Regiment were tamely destroyed in situ, barely raising more than a sentence in the war diaries and official histories. Armour was a neglected part of the Japanese military that firmly placed the Imperial Japanese Army in the 1930s. This was not least due to Japan's now starved industrial base, caused by American submarine operations intercepting merchant shipping carrying raw materials to the home islands. That night the tanks withdrew, allowing the rest of 17th Indian Division and the Deccan Horse to finish Pyawbwe off the following day.

The fighting in and around Pyawbwe tore 33rd Army apart. Around 1,000 Japanese soldiers were killed, with Claudcol estimating, probably slightly optimistically, around half that number between 8th and 10th April. On top of this they destroyed six tanks of the very few left in Burma, dozens of guns, including the 150mm and 105mm guns of the former Naganuma force from Meiktila, and 60 lorries and staff cars destroyed or captured. While the Deccan Horse had grinded with the infantry to the north, supporting them with now classic and well-oiled bunker busting methods, Claudcol had played havoc with the enemy's rear.

As planned, 5th Indian Division now took over the advance after an operational pause, with 17th Indian Division to mop up any last pockets of resistance before catching up again. On the 15th April the tanks moved off with 5th Indian Division, Probyn's Horse rode transporters after their exertions in Claudcol, with the Deccan Horse further up ready to support the infantry. The advance sped up with the 33rd Army truly broken, catching Japanese columns retreating south in disarray, even overtaking them cross country, and capturing bridges and laying on ambushes. This was turning into a literal reverse of the dark days of 1942, that now seemed so long ago. On the 21st April, as they approached Toungoo, the going became difficult and tanks occasionally bogged down in pre-monsoon showers. Toungoo was captured the next day, where 17th Indian Division took the lead again, heading for Pegu, just 50 miles from Rangoon.

XXXIII Corps had also made good progress, clearing the area west of Meiktila, capturing the oilfields at Yenangyaung by 26th April, and continued the drive south down the Irrawaddy valley. The going was not all easy, the Japanese were still fighting. The men of the 3rd Carabiniers were tired, they had been in action almost continuously since the middle of March 1944. This was not helped by the knowledge that they were not the main thrust. In late April 1945 there was no grand prize awaiting them, just a slog in support of someone else's glory. Malcolm Connolly reflected later 'the tank losses were not good for morale, which was now at rock bottom, and it is my opinion that the squadron was to say the very least war weary'.[8] They had been living for so long out of mess tins, in holes in the ground, or slowly baking inside their tanks for whole days, jostling, lurching, and bouncing. He recalled a song they sang reflecting how much fighting they had seen from Imphal, through Mandalay and now into the Irrawaddy valley: 'Divs may come and Divs may go, but the Carbs go on forever'.[9] A few days later, in early May, one of the Lees from 5 Troop, C Squadron was destroyed by an AT gun and killed the entire crew. When they overran the position, they found it was a captured British 25-pounder field gun. 'The tank and its crew had not stood a dog's chance, this disastrous event had killed some of the most experienced crew members of the squadron, men who were well liked and who at this stage of the campaign would be very difficult to replace'.[10] XXXIII Corps' advance was not the priority, and so spares and replacement tanks were at a premium. In the final weeks of fighting, Connolly's C Squadron had lost seven tanks out of their last eleven, and the guns were practically smooth bore now, barely accurate over 100 yards. Despite Connolly and the Carabiniers' low morale, they were playing an important role, destroying 28th Army, and stopping it from making IV Corps job harder. There is no doubt that this supporting role must have made it hard for the men to keep going, but they had a fine reputation, and the Carbs did indeed go on for what felt like forever.

IV Corps' drive continued down the Sittang Valley. They reached Pegu on 29th April, just over three years since 7th Armoured Brigade arrived in the same town to try and halt the invasion after the Sittang Bridge disaster. Another Japanese stand was to be made, and the bridges across the river were blown. They were back amongst the bamboo and jungle that had so troubled 17th Indian Division in 1942 and were held up on mined roads and by ambushes on the riverbanks, severely slowing the advance at the worst possible moment, so close to Rangoon. They had advanced 250 miles since Meiktila in just twenty days. Once they cleared Pegu, they began the move southwest towards Rangoon, the prize they were all after. It was not to be. On 2nd May, the monsoon struck. The race was over.

The decision had been made earlier. First slipping out from Akyab and Ramree Islands on the 27th April, the 26th Indian Infantry Division and A Squadron of 19th Lancers took to sea. After a parachute landing in the early hours of 1st May, the force landed south of Rangoon, on the western side of the estuary. After a short fight at 4pm, they rested for the night. Earlier that day, the famous flight of Wing Commander AE Saunders, CO 110 Squadron, RAF, had flown to the deserted Rangoon in his Mosquito on 2nd May, and landed at Mingaladon Airfield, avoiding craters in the runway as best he could. He did not get back to HQ, travelling by sampan down the river, until the 3rd May, by which time 26th Indian Division was loading back onto landing craft. The lack of Japanese resistance and other rumours had made it back, and they sailed down the river and unloaded at Rangoon harbour at 4pm on the 3rd May, on the same wharves where 7th Armoured Brigade unloaded. The Japanese had started evacuating the city ten days earlier, the last of the garrison leaving on night of 29th April, making their way east, and crossing into Tenasserim, then Thailand. The same route taken during the invasion in 1942, their flank protected by the last stand at Pegu.

To many in IV Corps this was disappointing. George MacDonald Fraser remembered his older comrades, those who had fought since 1942, and their reaction to the fall of Rangoon by amphibious assault. 'The old division that had endured the retreat three years before, had been in the thick of the great battle that stopped Jap at the gates of India, and had led the way south, was denied the ultimate prize at the last minute…it seemed like a betrayal, and hit them [his comrades] harder than their commanders ever knew. It may seem a small, selfish thing; the taking of Rangoon was what mattered, not who took it. But soldiers have a strong primitive sense of fairness: no one had promised them Rangoon, but they felt there had been an understanding and it had been broken'.[11]

The final convulsion of the Japanese in Burma took place when the remnants of 28th and 33rd Army tried to evacuate across the Irrawaddy, across the Pegu Yomas mountains and then across the Sittang, from late June to early August 1945. Rangoon was already being transformed in preparation for further operations against Malaya and Japan, but there were tens of thousands of Japanese troops scattered throughout Burma. Kimura wanted to concentrate them to the east of the Sittang Valley in the Salween river north of Moulmein, the first town to fall in 1942. These plans were discovered at the beginning of July so IV Corps and guerilla movements like Special Operation's Executive's Force 136, who had done so much to disrupt the Japanese attempts to reinforce units opposing the race to Rangoon, made their own plans. Fourteenth Army set up multiple ambushes, many of them very heavily armed with artillery and air support laid on as the Japanese followed the captured plans to the letter, losing some 14,000 men. The tanks had been withdrawn now the monsoon had begun, and Smeeton had been promoted to the staff in 63rd Brigade. 'Ambushed on the road, harried from the air, sought out and attacked when they tried to resist, with guerrillas skulking at their heels…every day we counted the bodies as they floated down the Sittang'.[12]

The race to Rangoon and the final operations had been an unqualified success. Disappointing maybe to the old sweats of 17th Indian Division, Kimura's Burma Area Army had been utterly destroyed by the height of the monsoon in early August. The tanks themselves had been a huge part of that success. In IV Corps' report on their operations of 1944-45 they were unequivocal. 'There can be no doubt that the armour was the decisive factor in IV Corps' swift advance from the Irrawaddy to Pegu. The Jap had no effective defence against it and suffered appalling casualties in consequence. At the same time our own casualties were insignificant in comparison'.[13] The subsequent momentum built up from Oyin in February, through Meiktila in March, Pyawbwe in April, and to Pegu in May was irresistible, as each successive Japanese position was destroyed. There was never any let up as the inexorable march of Fourteenth Army used the heavy cocktail of air power, armoured manoeuvre, mechanised infantry, and towed and self-propelled artillery. They destroyed their enemy, many of whom passively waited for them in their bunkers as per their orders. They offered resistance against the infantry, before being blown away by superior firepower, frequently coming from the 75mm barrel of a Sherman tank. With each operation, the potential for further resistance weakened as Kimura's men's lives were frittered away hopelessly, with few opportunities to fight back effectively. What was notable in the final stages was the unprecedented number of prisoners taken in the final weeks of the war: 740. Furthermore, Japanese soldiers were seen running far more often than usual, especially in the face of armour. Many were cut down as they fled.

The tanks and the logistical system behind them had been incredible. 255th Indian Tank Brigade had covered 800 miles since 14th February until they reached Pegu at the beginning of May. Almost every single day there was at least one squadron in action. In Pegu, 90% of those battered and bruised tanks, who had carried men into battle, and then brought most of them out alive, were in fighting order. A testimony to the men, especially of REME and IEME and their machines. The tanks had been a priority, with the men of IV Corps on half rations for 34 days, but never short of war stores, especially fuel and ammunition, averaging 1,845 tons per day. Planes were sent overloaded, beyond their maximum hours before engine servicing, and at their maximum distances to keep the advance going. More and more airfields were built by the sappers, 50 tactical airfields were built between Imphal and Rangoon.

In August, Connolly, and the 3rd Carabiniers, were waiting for their orders for the next chapter. 'Then came the bombshell: the war was over! A new type of bomb had been dropped on Japan and they had surrendered unconditionally but for some unknown reason this did not create any great show of emotion among the other ranks in my squadron, only talk of repatriation and how soon we all might be on our way home'.[14]

Epilogue

The Burma Campaign had been fought in some of the worst terrain imaginable regardless of which arm soldiers fought. Jungle, hills, mountains, near-desert, coastal zones, flood plains, and paddy fields, in stifling heat and humidity and the incessant rains in monsoon. This was not a place to fight. Yet British, Indian, Gurkha, Chinese, Canadian, American, Australian, Nigerian, Ghanaian, Sierre Leonean, Kenyan, Burmese, and more did just that against a brave, committed, tenacious, vicious, and sometimes cruel enemy. The Burma Campaign was a disaster for Japan in the end. Between 144,000 and 165,000 Japanese soldiers lost their lives in Burma, many to disease and starvation that, while useful to the Allies, was in part caused by poor leadership and preparation. The Allies, on the other hand, lost 14,326 dead, almost 10% of the Japanese total, and the same as Japanese losses in their final breakout attempt between late June and early August 1945. This was the single greatest defeat of Japanese land forces in the Second World War, in the longest land campaign undertaken by the Western Allies*.

The tanks of the British and Indian armies had played a decisive role, despite the manner in which they were undermined in the interwar period. There are significant lessons from the 1930s that have clearly been forgotten in the modern day, especially by politicians. The British and Indian armies were unprepared for a large-scale war despite the obvious warning signs, and when the risks of doing too little were so great. This affected the whole army, not just the armour in the Indian Army. Failure to invest in the right kit at the right time, to penny-pinch, led to poor early designs, and shortages of better designs when

---

*The only campaigns of any arm that were longer were the Allied Bombing Campaign, the Battle of the Atlantic, and the Second Sino-Japanese War.

the war came around. US industrial might bailed out British and Indian tank units by being able to produce enough tanks and logistical vehicles to equip them relatively quickly as both armies expanded rapidly. As the 7th Armoured Brigade showed, tanks could have an impact, there were just not enough of them in Burma in 1942 to help bridge the gulf between the poor training of the 'milked' infantry units and Japanese tactical success in that period. Infantry often broke off engagements at a time of their own choosing under the cover of tanks and broke through roadblocks again and again. General Alexander was not wrong when he said that it was 7th Armoured Brigade that rescued Burcorps in 1942.

The Indian Army was particularly good at adapting itself. The army had so many different roles that the ingrained culture of adaptability was crucial, surviving the expansion of the army from 200,000 to 2,500,000 by the end of the war. When the war began, the Indian Army continued its normal roles, and also had to learn how to fight against powerful enemies in desert, then jungle, and then on desert-like plains for a new breed of manoeuvre warfare. This was done using the cast-offs of the North African and European campaigns; however, this was adequate for the enemy they faced. Japanese AT methods and use of armour were woefully poor, relying on older technologies which were then badly handled. The Imperial Japanese Navy and air power were the priority for Japan, and so their army suffered, taking mostly 1930s tanks and AT guns against 1940s armour. Furthermore, the homeland and its industrial base was hammered and strangled by the USA's bombing campaign and submarine blockade, limiting the ability to fix the problem.

Those cast-offs reflect one of the key features of the campaign. Compared to the western theatres' troops lavish scales of equipment, British and Indian Army units had to make-do. They had the resources and manpower to have a local advantage over the Japanese, such as during the Battle for

Imphal, and in 1945, although this was never overwhelming. Success was therefore built on the logistical system across diverse terrain and through a difficult climate, to shift forces where they were needed, and apply the sheer firepower that could be brought to bear. The key method of delivery of that firepower came through the barrels of 7th Armoured Brigade and 50th, 254th and 255th Indian Tank Brigades once it was proven in Arakan at the Tortoise and Battle of the Admin Box. Artillery and aerial bombing were too inaccurate to deliver decisive firepower at the key moment: when infantry needed to close with formidable Japanese bunkers. This explains why so much logistical effort was made to get tanks to the front, then keep them there through innovative maintenance methods and aerial resupply. Risks were taken, with aerial resupply aircraft overloaded and overused when the men of IV Corps were on half rations during the race to Rangoon. The food of the men was a lower priority than the fuel and ammunition for tanks and other vehicles. This is why tanks were used in every terrain, and always had an impact. Slim said swamp was the only terrain where tanks could not operate, yet through combined operations at Kangaw, tanks eventually found a way through the swamp to help defend Hill 170 and take Ramree Island. The ability for tanks to appear somewhere unexpected, Nunshigum and the tennis court for example, were absolutely decisive to those battles. Their ability to make their rapid sweeps in 1945 around Meiktila broke the Burma Area Army's back despite being surrounded and outnumbered.

The reconquest of Burma should be the stuff of British and Indian Army legend, just as well-known as Dunkirk, the Battle of Britain, and Overlord. Were something similar to have happened in a western campaign, or had been carried out by the *Wehrmacht*, it would be celebrated as one of the most incredible feats of arms in all military history. IV Corps' operations from Nyaungu in February to the end of the Battle of Meiktila in late-March 1945 is the greatest exemplar of modern manoeuvre warfare in the Second World War. What this came down to is the Japanese inability throughout the war to challenge the tanks they faced, relying on outdated weapons and suicidal infantry tactics. The obvious thing to do in any conflict is to use your advantages against your enemy's disadvantages. The lesson of 1942 to early 1944 was that Japanese troops were vulnerable to tank assaults, so long as the tanks were working in close cooperation with infantry. A symbiotic relationship true in any theatre but was crucial in the Burma Campaign because if tanks and infantry worked together perfectly, they *overwhelmed* their enemy not through mass, but by tactical nous.

None of this is to downplay the role of infantry. I began this book with the National Army Museum's website and the stereotype most people have of the Burma Campaign. All stereotypes have their element of truth. The infantry war in Burma was far more unnerving, violent, horrific, and so on, compared to that of the men in tanks. Whilst the men from both arms would frequently say they did not covet the other soldier's role, in Burma, a tank *was* a safer place to be. They rarely suffered the same kind of casualties, although the potential to be burned to death brought a special kind of hell to the fighting in the minds of tankmen everywhere. At night, tanks and their men usually could pull back into their harbours, although they still suffered from jitter raids and other night-time stresses, they did so far less often, and far less intensely than the infantry. The infantry spent longer fighting, through monsoon conditions most obviously, tanks only did so in the specific circumstances of 1944.

The point to remember is that the extremes of jungle fighting were a means to an end. Throughout the campaign the point of most operations was to engineer an opportunity to get the Allied superiorities in air power, armour, artillery, and logistics to the most advantageous places possible. In 1942, 7th Armoured Brigade was at its most effective on the central plain, 1944 Slim deliberately pulled back to the Imphal Plain to fight there, and Operation Capital and Extended Capital were about fighting an army-sized battle to destroy the enemy on the Shwebo and Irrawaddy Plains. This book hopefully shows the reader that the tanks did not win the war on their own. What they did was make the decisive contribution in major battles, changing the equation when it came to assaulting Japanese positions. Tanks sped up the destruction of Japanese bunkers, reduced casualties in the infantry during assaults, and provided the mobility in the final year of the campaign to destabilise and then destroy the Japanese in Burma. Smeeton felt the way tanks reached anywhere they were needed meant that no one would believe them: 'if it wasn't for the rusting hulls buried in the jungle…I wonder who sees them now, who even knows of them, and what strange tales are woven round them'.[1] Victory was only possible due the hard work of the entire British and Indian armies in theatre, the sappers, lorry drivers, gunners, pilots, aircrew, infantrymen and tankmen. Only through bravery, determination, and cooperation could the Forgotten Army wield with such success their Forgotten Armour.

What of those men who served in, with, or behind the tanks in the Burma Campaign? Val ffrench Blake who endured the lackadaisical progress of modernisation and the early tanks fought with the 17th/21st Lancers in North Africa until he was shot in the neck and arms in 1942. He returned to Britain and became involved in the Staff College then at Sandhurst, retiring from the army in 1949. He became an author and expert in dressage and horse breeding. Ralph Younger, who had witnessed the eventual mechanisation of the Indian Army, had fought through the entire campaign. He fought with the 7th Hussars in the retreat in 1942, commanded the 3rd Carabiniers through Imphal in 1944, and then became second in command of 255th Indian Tank Brigade until May 1945, when he was appointed brigade commander. After the war he continued with the army rising to major-general before retiring in 1958. Elephant Bill Williams, after a lifetime overseas, mostly working with elephants, retired to a garden in Cornwall. David Atkins wrote a wonderfully funny two volume memoir* of his time driving up and down the roads between Dimapur and Imphal between 1942 and 1945. He became a chartered accountant after the war in Southern Rhodesia, now Zimbabwe, but returned to Britain in 1953 and grew apples. John Henslow, perhaps the hero of the Irrawaddy crossing, persevering through the administrative jungle, continued in the army, and fought in the Malayan Emergency before retiring from the army.

Gordon Heynes recovered from his wounds and was preparing with the rest of the 25th Dragoons to use Sherman DD tanks in the invasion of Malaya when the war ended. After he was sent home, he returned to his banking career. John Leyin remained with the 25th Dragoons too and became an internal auditor in London after the war. He learned to skydive in his 50s, making five jumps. Tom Grounds was in the Victory Parade on the 8th June 1946 in London, riding in the Comet tank leading the Army Mechanised Column. He became a solicitor after the war. Arthur Freer ended up as the Intelligence Sergeant of the 3rd Carabiniers on the Northwest Frontier before he returned home. He worked in marketing before retiring to his garden to paint and keep bees in Peterborough. The war did not leave him though, his nephew Simon Welburn told me about an event shortly after Freer returned home. He was out shopping with his mother, when the sound of a backfiring motorbike made him leap to the floor. Malcolm Connolly, whose First World War veteran father had waved him off in his Home Guard uniform, who had found the end of the war so hard, returned to Britain in 1947 and was a successful businessman. His father had died before Connolly returned home, whilst serving in the RAF.

The Reluctant Major, and *The Forgotten Major: in the siege of Imphal*. Be warned, they are also very much of their time and Atkins's generation.

Gerry Waterhouse and his crew continued to serve throughout the rest of the Burma Campaign after Kohima, making it through despite some near misses. When he came home, he returned to his job at the Distribution Office for Columbia Pictures in Leeds and became the office manager. He did have contact with one of his crew, Jack Gill, later in life, and with Lou Morris, another Leeds man from the 149th RAC. He also corresponded with Geoffrey White of 2nd Dorsets after he published his book, which recounted the battle for the tennis court. His experiences returned to him at least once, in hospital in the late 1970s. His daughter, Janet Fox, told the author via email: 'Myself, my brother and my mother were there with him. In effect he had a flashback to the battle. He was fighting us and cowering on the bedroom floor. He was reliving the battle. He was shouting for his comrades and telling them that the Japanese were coming at them again and to get ready to fight. In particular he was shouting for Brad. He also spoke of not having any water to drink. We listened to him in horror, as did one of the doctors at the hospital. She came out of the cubicle to talk to us, and he was still reliving the battle and fighting them before they were able to calm him. I remember her in tears saying, "What that man has gone through". When he came round later, he did not remember anything about the episode. However, I did ask him who Brad was. He and my mother told me that Brad was his youngest crew member… My mother and her sister wrote to Brad throughout the war as he did not receive letters from home'. Waterhouse rarely spoke about his experiences, like so many who lived through the war. He remained proud of his achievements on that famous day on the tennis court, for which he should be far more recognised.

John Prendergast, who fought alongside tanks on Mandalay Hill remained in the army until 1960, taking posts all over the world. He returned to India each year with his wife to explore the country in a motorhome. John Masters survived being 'Pete' Rees's Chief of Staff and also continued to serve after the war, before moving to the USA, eventually becoming a full-time writer. Bahadur Singh became Maharajah of Bundi before the end of the war, when his father died in April 1945. Singh was still fighting down the Sittang Valley with Probyn's Horse and was immediately flown home to Bundi to take up his new role. He remained the titular head of Bundi after partition. Miles Smeeton, always in the thick of the action, and a real adventurer, left the army in 1947. He was reunited permanently with his beloved wife Beryl to a farm in British Columbia, Canada. Their adventures continued, selling the farm in 1955 and sailing all over the world, writing about their experiences. All of these men have since passed, a generation almost gone, I hope I have done them all justice.

I deeply regret my failed efforts to find more Indian tank men's voices, although I have tried to tell their story where I can. The histories and memoirs have primarily been written by British servicemen and historians. Unfortunately, post-war, and especially post-partition India and Pakistan was not the ideal environment for old soldiers to record their stories. I hold a tiny hope that this book may help bring some of these men or their families forward.

For the men who did not make it, they would have their own far-off corner of a foreign field. There are so many men, many of them volunteers, who paid the ultimate price to play their part in stopping the growth of the Empire of Japan, halting it's cruel and murderous march. The unnamed driver in Atkins's unit, Clive Branson, Gordon Barnes, and Frank Myers of the 25th Dragoons, Edward Sanford and the other tank commanders on Nunshigum in 3rd Carabiniers, Dayal Singh, Reginald Anderson, and Desmond O'Beirne-Ryan of Probyn's Horse. Every man deserves to be remembered.

John Prendergast put this well and rather presciently, despite the habit of newspapers then, and indeed now. The men who fought the Japanese in India and Burma were surely the most diverse army put into action in history. 'All of them fought bravely, but the Indian and Gurkha units took the lion's share of it, being on a ratio of two units to one British. And now the gallant Indian Army of those days is forgotten, and cuttings I still have, have gone yellow with age'.[2]

When Connolly was preparing to ship home, the men of the 3rd Carabiniers had to leave their tanks. 'Saying goodbye to these worn-out pieces of machinery was like losing a good old friend, the Lee had never faltered and earned a special place in their hearts'.[3] The tanks had been home, protector, and saviour to these men. On the sail home, Connolly, had a lot of time to himself looking at the sea stretching out before him. 'Many different thoughts passed through my head of past experiences that would stay with me for the rest of my life but also of a world before the war, when as a boy my mother would say to me if I had been hurt in some way or other that "soldiers' sons don't cry." But Mother was wrong: soldiers' sons do cry, but they try hard not to show it'.[4]

Acknowledgements

This book, like so many of the early 2020s, owes its origins to what started as a lockdown project. Confined to my home in the first lockdown, I started to make model tanks, like I had done with my Grandpa in my childhood. Whilst I lost myself in the minutiae of this world, my soundtrack was the superb *We Have Ways of Making You Talk Podcast*. This, and the livestreams that soon started as part of the Independent Company (IC, no.151), helped get me through the long days. I found myself having opinions(!) on the discussions being had, and it inspired me to look for a Master's course I could complete online part time. I found one at the University of Wolverhampton, which I happily worked away at each evening after a day teaching in secondary school for two years. When the *We Have Ways Festivals* began, I spoke to Rob Lyman about my ideas for a dissertation on mechanisation of the Indian Army, and he said it would be hard, but I should go for it.

As my course went on, I expanded my interest after reading a few bits here and there, where tanks were occasionally mentioned popping up in important places during the Burma Campaign, but there was never any detail about what they did, or the men who fought in them. I proposed it as my dissertation, my course leader Dr Howard Fuller encouraged me because it was so original and managed to get me Dr John Buckley as my supervisor who was also enthusiastic. As I was finishing the dissertation, *We Have Ways* put out the call to have IC punters take part on the fringe *Arsenal* stage at *WHWFest Drei*, I emailed in my idea, Forgotten Armour: Tanks in Burma. I finished my dissertation, gave the talk, and both were very well received. Al Murray saw my result on Twitter and asked to read my dissertation. I emailed it to him, and to my surprise in the next livestream, Al and James Holland spent twenty minutes praising my work. Twitter was incredibly kind and told me how interesting my work sounded, and people saying they would love to read a book on the topic. The idea rolled around in my head, along with the fact that the only previous book on the topic, *Tank Tracks to Rangoon*, was published in 1978, and was missing a level of depth I knew could be found after writing the dissertation. Stuart Leasor of Chiselbury Publishing approached me, and the rest is literally history.

There are therefore lots of people to thank. These are people who have done so many things to help me, however, any mistakes in the text are of course, my own. Firstly, thank you James Holland for the foreword to this book and alongside Al Murray and Tony Pastor, they allowed me to give war waffle in the first place. That decision has, without being too dramatic, changed my life. James and Al championed my work, James lent me a book and helped with advice and guidance. The WHW community in general is a wonderful thing that I am proud to be a part. Similar thanks go to Rob Lyman, who has also helped me immeasurably with advice and contacts, but mostly for being the person who encouraged me to study this specific topic in the first place. Huge thanks to Christopher Jary, who put me in contact with Gerry Waterhouse's daughter Janet Fox, for whom I owe so much, sending me private correspondence between Gerry and 2nd Dorsets commander Geoffrey White. To Arthur Freer's nephew Simon Welburn, for information and pictures, and Neal Bircher, Gordon Heynes's grandson, again for pictures. Chris Camfield who sent me some SEAC AFV technical reports from the Canadian Archives, Mary Coles and Jo Pearson too for sharing their research about their relatives after I reached out on the WW2 Burma Research Facebook page. Stuart Leasor has been a staunch supporter of the project from day one and is a pleasure to work with, and David Roy for his high praise when editing the book. I also wish to thank Alex Churchill and Alina Nowobilska on *History Hack* and Paul Bavill on *History Rage* for interviewing me to promote the book as it was being written, and Paul Woodadge on *WW2TV* on YouTube for having me on twice!

I also want to thank all of my friends for their support and encouragement. My IC/history friends Jimmy Bagnall, Waitman Beorn, Mary Buckman (we'll always have Kew), Ally Campbell-Grieve, Simon Errington (RedFive), Paul Hicks, Robert Lock, Tony Rowntree, and many, many more! My work colleagues at The Astley Cooper School, who knew everything I went through to get this book written, Minali Alwis, Becky Waters, Craig Hardy (geographers doing all their colouring in), Ellie Piper, Ian Tilbury, and most of all Eddie Gaynor, for whom we always shared a love of history, talking at length about the Second World War in particular.

Some of my best cheerleaders have been my students. All my 2023-24 students deserve a mention who were with me all the way, but in particular legends like Teagan, Finlay, Christian (the class's pet half-German), Kenzie, Olti, Harry, Hyed, Xander, and Alicia. I could never forget Roasty, Jack, Jake, and Berti (despite himself!). Gibbo, who gave me a beautiful painting of a sea of poppies, a gift that meant the world to me on my last day at ACS. Lastly, my amazing Y13s, Alina and Nyle, the Austrian 'twins' (not actual twins). Mia, Tegan, Felicity, Chloe, Gabriel, and Jodie, the last seven years teaching you from 11-18 years old has been an honour, and I wish you all the best for the future. You all wrote me such wonderful messages when I left, you really have been a special group to me, I know you will all go far. Thank you for everything and remember to travel – the best link to the past is to go to the places you read about.

My family are a huge part of my interest in history. My wife's family, the bunch of maggots, have always been huge supporters of me. Annie and Jon, pushing me on, helping with books, and always taking an interest in my achievements. My Mum Jacqui has always supported anything that I have tried to achieve, indulging my interest in military history for as long as I can remember. My Dad Neil who has also indulged my interest in military history, taking me to the Biggin Hill air show for many years growing up. My brother Mark, who helped when I was first offered the book deal. Not to mention other family, Denise, Nigel, Sam, and Henry.

My grandparents deserve a special mention, Grandma Pat who inspired my first history writing when she showed me a picture of her grandfather in the 4th Hussars in the First World War. I went away and researched him, and wrote a short history of his service just for the family. My Nan and Grandpa were two of the most important people in my life. When my mum had to work and when she went to university, my Nan and Grandpa looked after me. This was my real induction into history. Whilst Nan made sure we had everything we needed, Grandpa shared with me his own love of military history. His time as a steam locomotive driver, and especially his National Service in 11th Armoured Division driving Sexton self-propelled guns immediately after the Second World War was an inspiration. Many of his NCOs and officers had fought in the war, and he passed on their stories. We watched war films together, especially *A Bridge Too Far*. The VHS we recorded it on ran out before the end. I thought XXX Corps made it. He took us to historical sights, most impactfully to Vimy Ridge one year, then we stayed in a Dutch holiday camp and drove up Hell's Highway to Arnhem another year. When I broke my leg at eight years old, he brought in Second World War Airfix models that I made from my bed because I was in traction. By the time I was a bit old for them, I had 50 or so hanging from my bedroom ceiling. If it was not for my Grandpa – Gunner William Botten – I would not have written this book. I miss him terribly.

Finally, my wife. Alex (Alby) and our two cats Jenson and Sabrina. If there are any typos, they are likely to be when one or the other has walked across the keyboard. Alex drew the base map for the Tennis Court diagram, showing me her drafting skills, and allowed me to create a bespoke map that shows something quite complicated – there was no one map that I could find, until she said she could do it. Alex has been an absolute rock. She knew I was into history when we met at university, little did she know what she was getting herself into. She has supported me through some pretty difficult moments in my life during illness, whilst I did degrees part time whilst working full time, a career change, and now in my work as a historian. I am always onto some other project, which I am sure is infuriating, but she never waivers. This is despite the fact she is a frontline NHS worker. I have written about men in this book who answered their country's call, that many would consider heroes, who risked their lives and experienced things no person should ever have to see or endure. Yet my wife, answered her country's call during COVID, risked her life, and experienced things no person should ever have to see or endure. All the while supporting me in everything I have done. She is *my* hero.

Image Acknowledgments

Photographs are listed in order of appearance. Those from the Imperial War Museum and Alamy incude their reference number. Every effort has been made to trace copyright holders who are not credited below. Those that have been overlooked are invited to contact the publisher. All maps were either from Alamy or produced by the author.

1. Personal. John Henslow, A Sapper in the Forgotten Army, Portia Press Ltd 1986
2. Uncredited
3. IWM MH 10151
4. Author's collection
5. IWM KID 611
6. IWM HU 73815
7. Uncredited
8. WM KF 289
9. Alamy 2N935RP
10. Personal. JH Williams, *Elephant* Bill, The Reprint Society Ltd, 1951
11. Uncredited. David Atkins, The Reluctant Major, The Toat Press 1986
12. Uncredited. David Atkins, The Reluctant Major, The Toat Press 1986
13. Alamy PDR3GT
14. TNA WO 172/4593
15. Personal. Clive Branson, British Soldier in India The Communist Party London 1944
16. The Heynes/Bircher Photo Collection

Image Acknowledgements

17. Uncredited. John Leyin, Tell Them of Us, Lejins Publishing 2000

18. Personal. John Leyin, Tell Them of Us, Lejins Publishing 2000

19. Uncredited. Tom Grounds, *Some Letters from Burma* Para Press Ltd, 2006

20. TNA, WO 172/4593

21. IWM MWY 24

22. The Welburn/Freer Photo Collection

23. Royal Scots Dragoon Guards Museum facebook page (April 12 2019)

24. IWM MWY 24

25. Alamy 2T1MG20

26. Alamy 2MG751M

27. Pathe – Film ID 1980.11 INVASION SCENES FAR EAST (1944)

28. IWM MWY 23

29. IWM MWY 23

30. Alamy 2WY6KBM

31. Alamy 2T1FX4E

32. Alamy 2T1MG2P

33. Uncredited. John Henslow, A Sapper in the Forgotten Army, Portia Press Ltd 1986

34. Personal. John Prendergast, Prender's Progress, Cassell Ltd, 1979

35. Uncredited. John Masters, Chindit Affair, Pen & Sword, 2011

352   Forgotten Armour

36. IWM SE 3474.

37. IWM SE 3496

38. TNA, WO 203/541

39. Alamy 2T1FWWH

40. Alamy 2NDFMAJ

41. Alamy 2T1MF67

Notes

PROLOGUE

[1] Field Marshall Viscount Slim, Defeat into Victory, Pan Books, 2009, p452
[2] John Henslow, A Sapper in the Forgotten Army, Portia Press Ltd, 1986, p116
[3] Ibid, p117
[4] Ibid p121
[5] Ibid
[6] Ibid p122
[7] Ibid p123
[8] Ibid p131
[9] Ibid
[10] Lt Gen. Geoffrey Evans, The Desert and the Jungle: An Eyewitness Account of Five Decisive Battles, William Kimber and Co. Ltd., 1962, p155

INTRODUCTION

[1] https://www.nam.ac.uk/explore/far-east-campaign accessed 14/04/2024
[2] Slim, Defeat into Victory, p163
[3] Ibid, p335
[4] Ibid, p339
[5] Ibid, p437
[6] Jeffrey, Alan, and Rose, Patrick (eds.), The Indian Army, 1939-47: Experience and Development, Routledge 2016, p138
[7] Ibid, p132
[8] Major HW Howell, Report on Assaults by Infantry Supported by Tanks, Artillery, and Air on Japanese Positions in Razabil Area of Arakan 26-28 January 1944, TNA, WO203-1175, p27. Emphasis in original.

1 – THE FAILURE TO MECHANISE

[1] Major General Sir Louis Jackson, quoted in Sir Richard Dannatt and Dr Robert Lyman, Victory to Defeat: The British Army 1918-40, Osprey Publishing, 2023, p141
[2] Conrad Wood, Oral History of Robert Lifford Valentine ffrench Blake, IWM 946, 1977, Reel 1
[3] Val ffrench Blake, quoted in Roger Salmon, The Management of Change – Mechanizing the British Regular and Household Cavalry Regiments 1918-1942, PhD Thesis, University of Wolverhampton, 2013, p287
[4] Ibid
[5] Ibid p306
[6] David G Lance, Oral History of Ralph Younger, IWM 913, Reel 1
[7] Ibid
[8] Ibid

[9] Basil Liddel Hart, quoted in Salmon, The Management of Change, p83
[10] Brigadier RJ Collins, quoted in Report on the Staff Conference at the Staff College, Camberley, 14-17th January 1929, TNA, WO279/65
[11] Sergeant James Randall, quoted in Salmon, The Management of Change, p83
[12] Interim report of the Cavalry committee, WO32/2841, 23rd November 1926
[13] David G Lance, Oral History of Rupert Harding-Newman, IWM 834, Reel 7
[14] Brigadier John Blakiston-Houston, quoted in Report on the Staff Conference, WO279/65
[15] ffrench Blake, quoted in Salmon, The Management of Change, p308

2 – THE WAR AGAINST JAPAN

[1] Miles Smeeton, A Change of Jungles, Rupert Hart-Davis, 1962, p27
[2] Ibid, p28
[3] Ibid, p18
[4] Lieutenant John Smyth, quoted in Basil Liddell Hart, History of the Second World War, GP Putnam, 1970, p216
[5] Lieutenant John Smyth, quoted in Robert Lyman, A War of Empires, Japan, India, Burma and Britain 1941-45, Osprey Publishing, 2021, p85

3 - 7TH ARMOURED BRIGADE ARRIVE IN BURMA

[1] Lance Corporal Umeo Tokita quoted in Kazuo Tamayama and John Nunneley, Tales by Japanese Soldiers, Weidenfeld and Nicolson, 2001, p67
[2] Ibid
[3] Ibid
[4] Ibid, p68
[5] Ibid
[6] Ibid, p69
[7] Ibid
[8] Ibid, p70
[9] Ibid
[10] Ibid
[11] General Sir Archibald Wavell, Despatch on Operations in Burma, December 1941 – May 1942, TNA, WO106/2666, 1st July 1942, p11
[12] Ralph Younger, quoted in Brigadier GMO Davy, The Seventh and Three Enemies: The Story of World War II and the 7th Queen's Own Hussars, The Naval and Military Press Ltd, 1952, p218
[13] Lt GSB Palmer quoted in Bryan Perrett, Tank Tracks to Rangoon: The Story of British Armour in Burma, Pen and Sword, 2014, p35

4 – THE RETREAT FROM BURMA

[1] Lt Col Tony Mains, Soldier with Railways, Picton Publishing Ltd, 1994, p56
[2] Ibid, pxiii
[3] Ibid, p60
[4] FSV Donnison, Summary of the Census of Burma 1941, https://www.networkmyanmar.org/ESW/Files/1941-Census-Summary.pdf accessed 14/1/24
[5] Mains, Soldier with Railways, p58
[6] Ibid, p60
[7] Ibid, p61
[8] Capt Marcus Fox quoted in Perrett, Tank Tracks to Rangoon, p36
[9] HQ 7th Armoured Brigade Group War Diary, TNA, WO172/560
[10] Lt Geoffrey Palmer quoted in Perrett, Tank Tracks to Rangoon, p38
[11] Ibid, p39
[12] Ibid
[13] Ibid
[14] Lt Col Tony Mains, The Retreat from Burma: An Intelligence Officer's Personal Story, W Foulsham & Co Ltd, 1973, p62
[15] Ibid
[16] Major Llewelyn Palmer quoted in Davy, Seventh and Three Enemies, p257
[17] Palmer, quoted in Perrett, Tank Tracks to Rangoon, p48
[18] Slim, Defeat into Victory, pp70-1
[19] Ibid, p76
[20] Ibid
[21] Ibid, p75
[22] Ibid, p80
[23] Lieutenant Toshiro Matsumura quoted in Tamayama et al, Tales by Japanese Soldiers, p67
[24] Ibid
[25] Ibid
[26] Alan Barber, correspondence to DEKHO! The Journal of the Burma Star Association, No. 103, 1987, p37
[27] Ibid
[28] Ibid
[29] Ibid
[30] Slim, Defeat into Victory, p121
[31] Wavell, Despatch on Operations in Burma, p12
[32] Alexander, quoted in Davy, Seventh and Three Enemies, p257

5 – LAYING THE FOUNDATIONS

[1] JH Williams, Elephant Bill, The Reprint Society, 1951, p163
[2] Ibid p164
[3] Nobby Knowles quoted in Roger Annett, Drop Zone Burma: Adventures in Allied Air Supply 1943-45, Pen and Sword, 2008, p145

[4] John Henslow, A Sapper in the Forgotten Army, Portia Press Ltd, 1986, p43
[5] David Atkins, The Reluctant Major, The Toast Press, 1986, pp2-3
[6] Ibid, p50
[7] Williams, Elephant Bill, p177
[8] Ibid
[9] Henslow, A Sapper in the Forgotten Army, p44
[10] Malcolm Connolly, Soldier's Sons Don't Cry, Kindle edition, 2012, loc. 585
[11] Ibid, loc. 587
[12] Atkins, The Reluctant Major, p32
[13] Ibid
[14] Henslow, A Sapper in the Forgotten Army, p32
[15] Ibid

6 – ARAKAN: LESSONS LEARNED

[1] Slim, Defeat into Victory, p163
[2] Corporal Wedburn account attached to 146th RAC War Diary, TNA, WO172/4599
[3] Trooper Cooke account attached to 146th RAC War Diary, TNA, WO172/4599
[4] Sergeant Seago account attached to 146th RAC War Diary, TNA, WO172/4599
[5] Captain Da Costa's report in 146th RAC War Diary, TNA, WO172/4599
[6] John Predergast, Prender's Progress: A Soldier in India 1931-47, Cassell, 1979, p173
[7] Robin Schlaefli, Emergency Sahib: Of Queens, Sikhs and the Dagger Division, RJ Leach, 1992, p81
[8] Gordon Heynes, I Felt No Sorrow, This Was War, N&G Bircher, 2019, p16
[9] Slim, Defeat into Victory, p257
[10] Connolly, Soldier's Sons Don't Cry, loc. 1012
[11] Arthur F Freer, Nunshigum: On the Road to Mandalay, The Pentland Press, 1995, p48
[12] Heynes, I Felt No Sorrow, p27
[13] Ibid, p24
[14] Clive Branson, British Soldier in India: The Letters of Clive Branson, The Communist Party London, 1944, p115
[15] John Leyin, Tell Them of Us: The Forgotten Army – Burma, Lejins Publishing, 2000, p127
[16] Ibid, p127
[17] Branson, British Soldier in India, p116
[18] Heynes, I Felt No Sorrow, p31
[19] Ibid
[20] Ibid
[21] Major HW Howell, Report on Assaults by Infantry Supported by Tanks, Artillery, and Air on Japanese Positions in Razabil Area of Arakan 26-28 January 1944, TNA, WO203-1175
[22] Ibid

[23] Ibid emphasis in original
[24] Ibid

7 – 'I FELT NO SORROW' - BATTLE OF THE ADMIN BOX

[1] Frank Messervy quoted in Tom Grounds, Some Letters From Burma: The Story of the 25th Dragoons at War, Parapress, 1994, p62
[2] Patrick Hobson quoted in Grounds, Some Letters From Burma, p60
[3] Heynes, I Felt No Sorrow, p37
[4] Patrick Hobson quoted in Grounds, Some Letters From Burma, p65
[5] Ibid, p64
[6] Leyin, Tell Them of Us, p143
[7] Ibid
[8] Lieutenant-General Geoffrey Evans, The Desert and the Jungle, William Kimber and Co. Ltd, 1962, p99
[9] Leyin, Tell Them of Us, p147
[10] Heynes, I Felt No Sorrow, p38
[11] Leyin, Tell Them of Us, p151
[12] Heynes, I Felt No Sorrow, p39
[13] Ibid
[14] Tom Grounds, Some Letters From Burma, p85
[15] Leyin, Tell Them of Us, p159
[16] Heynes, I Felt No Sorrow, p43
[17] Ibid
[18] Heynes, I Felt No Sorrow, p42
[19] Ibid
[20] Ibid
[21] Antony Brett-James, Ball of Fire: The Fifth Indian Division in the Second World War, Naval and Military Press, 2014, p291
[22] Second Lieutenant Satoru Inazawa quoted in Tamayama et al, Tales by Japanese Soldiers, p148
[23] Leyin, Tell Them of Us, p161
[24] Heynes, I Felt No Sorrow, p46
[25] Ibid
[26] Evans, The Desert and the Jungle, p112
[27] Leyin, Tell Them of Us, p183
[28] Tom Grounds, Some Letters From Burma, p111
[29] Ibid
[30] Leyin, Tell Them of Us, p175
[31] Heynes, I Felt No Sorrow, p47
[32] Ibid, p178
[33] Ibid, p177
[34] Ibid, pp177-8
[35] Leyin, Tell Them of Us, p183
[36] Smeeton, A Change of Jungles, pp73-4

[37] Colonel IM Stewart, Note on Visit to Fourteenth Army and XV Corps, 5-15 March 1944, TNA, WO203/1897 emphasis in original

8 - ON MOUNTAINS AND PLAINS: THE BATTLE OF IMPHAL

[1] Peter Bray quoted in Annett, Drop Zone Burma, p112
[2] Ibid, p113
[3] John Hart quoted in Annett, Drop Zone Burma, p110
[4] Jot Ram, quoted in Perrett, Tank Tracks to Rangoon, p103. Jot Ram's recollections were translated from Urdu by Colonel Barlow and described in the first person.
[5] Ibid, p104
[6] Ibid
[7] Ibid, p107
[8] Ibid
[9] Ibid, p108
[10] Ibid
[11] Ibid
[12] Ibid
[13] Ibid
[14] Connolly, Soldier's Sons Don't Cry, loc. 1179
[15] Ibid, loc. 1180-2
[16] Ibid, loc. 1190-2
[17] Ibid, loc. 1198
[18] Ibid, loc. 1232
[19] Ibid, loc. 1305
[20] Ibid, loc. 1310
[21] Ibid, loc. 1326
[22] Ibid, loc. 1327
[23] Lt. Gen. Geoffrey Evans and Antony Brett-James, Imphal: A Flower of Lofty Heights, Macmillan & Co Ltd, 1962, pp218-9
[24] Richard McDonagh, Oral History of Arthur Francis Freer, IWM 19822, Reel 4
[25] Report on Action on Nunshigum, 3rd Carabiniers War Diary, TNA, WO172/4595
[26] Evans et al, Imphal, p222
[27] Ibid
[28] Richard McDonagh, Oral History of Arthur Francis Freer, IWM 19822, Reel 4
[29] Ibid
[30] Evans et al, Imphal, p222
[31] Richard McDonagh, Oral History of Arthur Francis Freer, IWM 19822, Reel 4
[32] Ibid, emphasis in original
[33] Ibid
[34] Ibid

[35] Lieutenant FA Shepherd, Account of the attack on Potsangbam on the 8th May 1944, 3rd Carabiniers War Diary, TNA, WO172/4595
[36] Ibid
[37] Ibid
[38] Freer, Nunshigum, p109
[39] Ibid, p110
[40] Ibid, p114
[41] Evans et al, Imphal, p287
[42] Jap Reaction to our Tks, in Report of Imphal Operations 1945, TNA, WO203/1901

9 - CLEARING KOHIMA

[1] Major E Rhodes, OC B Sqn's report on action 5/6 May 44, 149th Regiment, RAC War Diary, TNA WO172/4599
[2] Ibid
[3] Ibid
[4] Ibid
[5] Ibid
[6] Extract from Chief Royal Engineer, 2 Div, RE Lessons from the Battle of Kohima, 149th Regiment, RAC War Diary, TNA WO172/4599
[7] N Figg, correspondence to DEKHO! The Journal of the Burma Star Association, No. 114, 1993, p31
[8] Geoffrey White, quoted in Leslie Edwards, Kohima: The Furthest Battle, The Story of the Japanese Invasion of India in 1944 and the 'British-Indian Thermopylae', The History Press, 2013, p623
[9] Ibid, p624
[10] Lintorn Highett, quoted in Edwards, Kohima, p635
[11] Sgt Waterhouse, Report on Operation: DC's Bungalow and Tennis Court Bunkers, 149th Regiment, RAC War Diary, TNA WO172/4599
[12] Ibid
[13] Ibid
[14] 2nd Battalion, Dorsetshire Regiment War Diary, TNA, WO172/4875
[15] Norman Havers, quoted in Edwards, Kohima, p636
[16] Ibid
[17] Ibid
[18] Figg, quoted in Dekho No114, p31
[19] Waterhouse, 149 RAC, TNA WO172/4599
[20] Henslow, A Sapper in the Forgotten Army, p79
[21] Ibid, p80
[22] Ibid, pp80-1
[23] Lieutenant-General Kotoku Sato, quoted in Robert Lyman, Japan's Last Bid for Victory: The Invasion of India 1944, Praetorian Press, 2011, p214
[24] 7 Div Operation Note No. 13 Use of Tanks, 149 RAC, TNA WO172/4599

10 CAPITAL INVESTMENT: ENGINEERING AND LOGISTICS

[1] Connolly, Soldier's Sons Don't Cry, loc. 1753
[2] Ibid
[3] Ibid, loc. 1768
[4] SEAC AFV Report 1 September 1944, Library and Archives, Canada, RG-C-2 Vol. 9377, File 38, Tech-LIA 5, p10
[5] Williams, Elephant Bill, p228
[6] Henslow, A Sapper in the Forgotten Army, p79
[7] Ibid, p100
[8] David Atkins, The Forgotten Major in the siege of Imphal, The Toat Press, 1989, p109
[9] Ibid
[10] Freer, Nunshigum, p177
[11] Ibid, p179
[12] Maj. Gen. Cameron Nicholson, quote in 3rd Carabiniers War Diary, TNA, WO172/4595

11 – COMBINED OPERATIONS IN ARAKAN

[1] Unreferenced anonymous eyewitness account, in Perrett, Tank Tracks to Rangoon, p199. This account is possibly Major JG Pocock, who wrote the 19th Lancers official history The Spirit of a Regiment (1962), which this author was unable to obtain. This is the only 19th Lancers source that Perrett cites in the bibliography.
[2] Ibid, p200
[3] Brigadier KRS Trevor, Three Quarters of A Century Or 75 Not Out, extract from https://burmastarmemorial.org/archive/stories/1405841-the-battle-for-hil-60?q= accessed 14/3/2024
[4] Lieutenant-General Philip Christison, quoted in Perrett, Tank Tracks to Rangoon, p201
[5] Lieutenant-Colonel CAC Sinker, The History of the First Battalion the Lincolnshire Regiment in India, Arakan, Burma and Sumatra September 1939 to October 1946, Keyworth & Sons, 1949, p53

12 CROSSING THE IRRAWADDY AND THE ROAD TO MANDALAY

[1] Slim, Defeat into Victory, p437
[2] Major-General Nicholson letter of 30/12/1944 extract in Freer, Nunshigum, p190
[3] Slim, Defeat into Victory, p495
[4] Geoffrey White, Straight on For Tokyo: The Second Battalion, The Dorsetshire Regiment (54th Foot), Semper Fidelis Publications, 2016, p237
[5] Appendix P for Feb 1944, 3rd Carabiniers War Diary, TNA, WO172/7339
[6] Appendix C for March 1944, Ibid
[7] Ibid

[8] John Masters, The Road Past Mandalay, Cassell, 2002, p292
[9] Ibid
[10] Ibid, pp292-3
[11] Slim, Defeat into Victory, pp447-8
[12] Schlaefli, Emergency Sahib, p127
[13] Entire exchange detailed in Masters, The Road Past Mandalay, p302
[14] Prendergast, Prender's Progress, p218
[15] Ibid, p218
[16] Ibid, p220
[17] Ibid, p222
[18] Schlaefli, Emergency Sahib, p129
[19] Ibid
[20] Masters, The Road Past Mandalay, p308
[21] Prendergast, Prender's Progress, p224
[22] Ibid
[23] Masters, The Road Past Mandalay, p308
[24] Freer, Nunshigum, p222

13 THUNDER RUN TO MEIKTILA

[1] Smeeton, A Change of Jungles, p79
[2] Ibid, p80
[3] Henslow, A Sapper in the Forgotten Army, p107
[4] Report of IV Corps Operations, TNA, WO203/2679, Part II, p1
[5] Evans, The Desert and the Jungle, p145
[6] Wilfred Miles, Life of a Regiment: Gordon Highlanders 1919-45 Vol 5, Warne, 1980, p386
[7] Evans, The Desert and the Jungle, p147
[8] Henslow, A Sapper in the Forgotten Army, p149
[9] Evans, The Desert and the Jungle, p153
[10] Henslow, A Sapper in the Forgotten Army, p152
[11] Smeeton, A Change of Jungles, p85
[12] Major Stewart, Appendix J2 Action by B Squadron at Oyin 22nd February 1945, 5th Probyn's Horse War Diary, TNA, WO172/7347
[13] Ibid
[14] Smeeton, A Change of Jungles, p89
[15] Ibid, p88
[16] Ibid, p90
[17] Major Arkinstall, Appendix J3 C Squadron Engagement at Oyin 22nd February 1945, 5th Probyn's Horse War Diary, TNA, WO172/7347
[18] Major Benard Lorraine-Smith, Appendix J1 Action at Oyin 22nd February 1945 by A Squadron 5th Probyn's Horse and C Coy 6/7 Rajputs, 5th Probyn's Horse War Diary, TNA, WO172/7347
[19] Smeeton, A Change of Jungles, p91
[20] Ibid, p90
[21] Ibid, p92

[22] Major BH Mylne (ed.), An Account of the Operations in Burma carried out by Probyn's Horse During February, March, & April 1945, The Naval and Military Press, 2006, p8 – it should be noted this was originally printed in October 1945 whilst the regiment was still in Rangoon.
[23] Captain E Halliwell, Appendix J5, 5th Probyn's Horse War Diary, TNA, WO172/7347
[24] Smeeton, A Change of Jungles, p93
[25] Ibid, p94
[26] Ibid
[27] Ibid
[28] Slim, Defeat into Victory, p511
[29] Ibid, p513
[30] Ibid, p514
[31] Ibid, pp514-5
[32] Ibid, p515
[33] Appendix J22, Action by 'A' Sqn Probyn's Horse at Meiktila on March 1st and 2nd in support of 63rd Ind Inf Bde, 5th Probyn's Horse War Diary, TNA, WO172/7347
[34] Smeeton, A Change of Jungles, p99
[35] Mylne, Probyn's Horse, p26
[36] Smeeton, A Change of Jungles, p99
[37] Ibid
[38] Ibid, p100
[39] Mylne, Probyn's Horse, p27
[40] Smeeton, A Change of Jungles, p100
[41] Ibid, p101
[42] Ibid
[43] Ibid, p104
[44] Ibid, p106
[45] Operations: IV Corps, Oct 44 – May 45, TNA, WO203/2679
[46] Slim quoted in Annett, Drop Zone Burma, p149

14 THE RACE TO RANGOON

[1] Slim, Defeat into Victory, p511
[2] Smeeton, A Change of Jungles, p107
[3] Ibid, p108
[4] Ibid
[5] Ibid, p109
[6] Ibid
[7] Mylne, Probyn's Horse, p52
[8] Connolly, Soldier's Sons Don't Cry, loc. 1846
[9] Ibid
[10] Ibid, loc. 1850
[11] George MacDonald Fraser, Quartered Safe out Here: A recollection of the War in Burma, Harper Collins, 2000, p236

[12] Smeeton, A Change of Jungles, p111
[13] Operations: IV Corps, Oct 44 – May 45, TNA, WO203/2679
[14] Connolly, Soldier's Sons Don't Cry, loc. 1898

EPILOGUE

[1] Smeeton, A Change of Jungles, p79
[2] Prendergast, Prender's Progress, p228
[3] Malcolm Connolly, 'Tanks were in the Lead', in DEKHO! The Journal of the Burma Star Association, Issue No. 158, 2008, p28, https://burmastarmemorial.org/archive/dekho/dekho-the-journal-of-the-burma-star-association-issue-no-158-year-2008/1476186?q=connolly, accessed 6/4/2024
[4] Connolly, Soldier's Sons Don't Cry, loc. 2058

Bibliography

Published Sources
Secondary Sources

Allen, Louis, *Burma: The Longest War, 1941-45*, Pheonix Giant, 1998

Arnett, Roger, *Drop Zone Burma: Adventures in Allied Air-Supply 1943-45*, Pen and Sword Aviation, 2008

Aubin, Nicolas, Vincent, Bernard, Guillerat, Nicolas, Lopez, Jean, *World War II Infographics*, Thames and Hudson, 2018

Callahan, Raymond A. and Marston, Daniel, *The 1945 Burma Campaign and the Transformation of the British Indian Army*, University Press of Kansas, 2020

Dear, ICB, and Foot, MRD (eds.), *The Oxford Companion to World War II*, Oxford University Press, 2005

Dunlop, Graham, *British Army Logistics in the Burma Campaign 1942-1945*, PhD Thesis, University of Edinburgh, 2006

Dunlop, Graham, *Military Economics and Logistics in the Burma Campaign, 1942-1945*, Pickering and Chatto Ltd, 2009

Edgerton, David, *Britain's War Machine*, Penguin Books, 2012

Edwards, Leslie, *Kohima: The Story of the Japanese Invasion of India in 1944 and the 'British-Indian Thermopylae'*, Spellmount, 2009 (Kindle Edition)

Ellis, John, *World War II Databook: The Essential Facts and Figures for all the combatants*, BCA, 1993

Fennell, Jonathan, *Fighting the People's War: The British and Commonwealth Armies and the Second World War*, Cambridge University Press, 2019

French, David, *Raising Churchill's Army*: The British Army and the War Against Germany 1919-1945, Oxford University Press, 2000

Grehan, John and Mace, Martin (eds.), *Despatches from the Front, The Battle for Burma, 1943-1945*, Pen and Sword, 2015

Harris, JP, *Men, Ideas, and Tanks: British Military Thought and*

Armoured Forces, 1903-1939, Manchester University Press, 2015

Holland, James, *Burma '44: The Battle That Turned Britain's War in the East*, Corgi Books, 2016

Jeffrey, Alan, and Rose, Patrick (eds.), *The Indian Army, 1939-47: Experience and Development*, Routledge 2016

Jeffrey, Alan, *Approach to Battle: Training the Indian Army during the Second World War*, Primus Books, 2019

Latimer, John, *Burma: The Forgotten War*, John Murray Publishers, 2004

Lyman, Robert, *A War of Empires: Japan, India, Burma and Britain, 1941-45*, Osprey Publishing Ltd, 2021

Lyman, Robert, *Japan's Last Bid for Victory: The Invasion of India 1944*, Praetorian Press, 2011

Lyman, Robert, *Slim, Master of War: Burma and the Birth of Modern Warfare*, Robinson, 2004

Lyman, Robert, *The Generals: From Defeat to Victory, Leadership in Asia 1941-45*, Constable, 2019

Mansoor, Peter, and Murray, Williamson (eds), *The Culture of Military Organizations*, Cambridge University Press, 2019

Marston, Daniel, *The Indian Army and the End of the Raj*, Cambridge University Press, 2014

McLynn, Frank, *The Burma Campaign: Disaster into Triumph 1942-45*, Vintage, 2011

Moreman, Tim, *The Army in India, and the Development of Frontier Warfare 1849-1947*, Palgrave, 2020

Moreman, Tim, *The Jungle, the Japanese and the British Commonwealth Armies at War 1944-45: Fighting Methods, Doctrine and Training for Jungle Warfare*, Routledge, 2013

Overy, Richard, *Why the Allies Won*, Pimlico, 2006

Perrett, Bryan, *Tank Tracks to Rangoon: The Story of British Armour in Burma*, Pen and Sword, 2014

Salmon, Roger, *The Management of Change – Mechanizing the British Regular and Household Cavalry Regiments 1918-1942*, PhD Thesis, University of Wolverhampton, 2013

Tamayama, Kazuo, and Nunnelly, John, *Tales by Japanese*

Soldiers of the Burma Campaign 1942-1945, Weidenfeld and Nicolson, 2001

Tooze, Adam, *The Wages of Destruction: The Making and the Breaking of the Nazi Economy*, Penguin, 2007

Yamamura, Kozo, Chapter 9: Success Illgotten? The Role of Meiji Militarism in Japan's Technological Progress, in Pomeranz, Kenneth (ed.), *The Pacific in the Age of Early Industrialization*, Routledge, 2009

Memoirs

Atkins, David, *The Forgotten Major: in the siege of Imphal*, The Toat Press, 1989

Atkins, David, *The Reluctant Major*, The Toat Press, 1986

Branson, Clive, *British Soldier in India: The Letters of Clive Branson*, The Communist Party London, 1944

Evans, Lieutenant-General Sir Geoffrey Evans, *The Desert, and the Jungle: An Eyewitness Account of Five Decisive Battles*, William Kimber and Co. Ltd, 1962

Evans, Lieutenant-General Sir Geoffrey, and Brett-James, Antony, *Imphal: A Flower on Lofty Heights*, London Macmillan & Co. Ltd, 1962

Fraser, George MacDonald, Quartered Safe Out Here: a Recollection of the War in Burma, HarperCollins, 2000

Freer, Arthur F, *Nunshigum: On the Road to Mandalay*, The Pentland Press Ltd, 1995

Grounds, Tom, *Some Letters from Burma: The Story of the 25th Dragoons at War*, Powerpress Ltd, 1994

Henslow, John, *A Sapper in the Forgotten Army*, Portia Press Ltd, 1986

Heynes, Gordon, *I felt no sorrow, this was war*, Neal and Gary Bircher, 2019

Leyin, John, *Tell them of us: The Forgotten Army – Burma*, Lejins Publishing, 2000

Mains, Lieutenant-Colonel AA, *A Soldier with Railways*, Picton Publishing, 1994

Mains, Lieutenant-Colonel Tony, *The Retreat from Burma: An Intelligence Officer's Personal Story*, Foulsham and Co. Ltd, 1973

Masters, John, *The Road Past Mandalay*, Cassell, 2002

Prendergast, John, *Prender's Progress: A Soldier in India 1931-47*, Cassell Ltd, 1979

Schlaefli, Robin, *Emergency Sahib: Of Queen's, Sikhs, and the Dagger Division*, RJ Leach and Co., 1992

Slim, Field Marshal Viscount, *Defeat into Victory*, Pan Books, 2009

Smeeton, Miles, *A Change of Jungles*, Rupert Hart-Davis, 1962

Williams, JH, *Elephant Bill*, Reprint Society Ltd, 1951

Official Histories

Anonymous, *Black Cat Division: 17th Indian Division*, The Naval and Military Press Ltd, 2023

Brett-James, Antony, *Ball of Fire: 5th Indian Division in the Second World War*, The Naval and Military Press Ltd, 2014

Davy, Brigadier GMO, *The Seventh and Three Enemies: Seventh Queen's Own Hussars 1939-45*, The Naval and Military Press Ltd, 2014

Kirby, Maj. Gen. S. Woodburn, *The War Against Japan: Vol. II, Indian's Most Dangerous Hour*, Naval and Military Press Ltd, 2004

Kirby, Maj. Gen. S. Woodburn, *The War Against Japan: Vol. III, The Decisive Battles*, Naval and Military Press Ltd, 2004

Kirby, Maj. Gen. S. Woodburn, *The War Against Japan: Vol. IV, The Reconquest of Burma*, Naval and Military Press Ltd, 2004

Mylne, Major BH, (ed.) *An Account of the Operations in Burma carried out by Probyn's Horse During February, March, and April 1945*, The Naval and Military Press Ltd, 2006

Prasad, Bisheshwar, *Official History of the Indian Armed Forces in the Second World War 1939-45: The Reconquest of Burma Volume I June 1942-June 1944*, Pentagon Press, 2014

Prasad, Bisheshwar, *Official History of the Indian Armed Forces in the Second World War 1939-45: The Reconquest of Burma Volume II June 1944-August 1945*, Pentagon Press, 2014

Prasad, Bisheshwar, *Official History of the Indian Armed Forces in the Second World War 1939-45: Expansion of the Armed Forces and Defence Organisation*, Orient Longmans, 1956

Rissik, David, *The DLI at War: The History of the Durham Light Infantry 1939-45*, The Naval and Military Press Ltd, 2006

White, Lieutenant-Colonel OGW White, *Straight on for Tokyo: The War History of the Second Battalion The Dorsetshire Regiment (54th Foot)*, Semper Fidelis, 2016

Journal Articles

Borton, Major NRM, The Fourteenth Army in Burma: A Case Study in Delivering Fighting Power, *Defence Studies*, 2007

French, David, The Mechanization of the British Cavalry between the World Wars, *War in History, Vol. 10 No. 3*, 2003

Roy, Kaushik, Dennis Showalter and the history of armour during Second World War, *War in History, Vol. 29 No. 1*, 2022

Roy, Kaushik, Expansion and Deployment of the Indian Army During World War II: 1939-45, *Journal of the Society for Army Historical Research, Vol. 88, No. 335*, 2010

Online Sources

Connolly, Malcolm, 'Tanks were in the Lead', in *DEKHO! The Journal of the Burma Star Association, Issue No. 158*, 2008, p28, accessed via https://burmastarmemorial.org/archive/dekho/dekho-the-journal-of-the-burma-star-association-issue-no-158-year-2008/1476186?q=connolly,

Donnison, FSV, *Summary of the Census of Burma 1941*, https://www.networkmyanmar.org/ESW/Files/1941-Census-Summary.pdf

https://www.nam.ac.uk/explore/far-east-campaign

Palmer, Robert, *50th Indian Tank Brigade: A concise history of the 50th Indian Tank Brigade during the Second World War between 1942 and 1946*, British Military History, 2022, accessed via https://www.britishmilitaryhistory.co.uk/wp-content/uploads/sites/124/2022/11/50-Indian-Tank-Brigade-V2_2.pdf

Trevor, Brigadier KRS, *Three Quarters of A Century Or 75 Not Out*, accessed via https://burmastarmemorial.org/archive/stories/1405841-the-battle-for-hil-60?q=

Unpublished Sources
Archive Documents

2nd Battalion The Dorsetshire Regiment War Diary, TNA, WO172/4875

3rd Carabiniers 1944 War Diary, TNA, WO172/4595

3rd Carabiniers January-May 1945 War Diary, TNA, WO172/7339

5th King Edward VII 's Own Lancers (Probyn's Horse) October-December 1944 War Diary, TNA, WO172/4608

5th King Edward VII 's Own Lancers (Probyn's Horse) January-June 1945 War Diary, TNA, WO172/7347

7th Armoured Brigade War Diary, TNA, WO172/560

9th Royal Deccan Horse October-December 1944 War Diary, TNA, WO172/4610

9th Royal Deccan Horse January-May 1945 War Diary, TNA, WO172/7350

19th King George V's Own Lancers War Diary, TNA, WO172/4612

25th Dragoons War Diary, TNA, WO172/4593

146th Royal Armoured Corps War Diary, TNA, WO172/2261

149th Royal Armoured Corps War Diary, TNA, WO172/4599

Howell, Major HW, Report on Assaults by Infantry Supported by Tanks, Artillery, and Air on Japanese Positions in Razabil Area of Arakan 26-28 January 1944, TNA, WO203-1175

Lessons from the Burma Campaign 1942, TNA, WO203-5716

Report of the Expert Committee on the Defence of India, 1938-39, TNA, T192993

Report on IV Corps Operations Oct 1944 – May 1945, TNA, WO203-2679

Report on Imphal Operations 1944, TNA, WO203-1900

Report on Imphal Operations 1945, TNA, WO203-1901

Report on Operations – Fourteenth Army, TNA, WO203-1897

Report on the Staff Conference at the Staff College, Camberley, 14-17th January 1929, TNA, WO279/65

SEAC AFV Report 1, September 1944, Library and Archives, Canada, RG-C-2 Vol. 9377, File 38, Tech-LIA 5

SEAC AFV Report 3, January 1945, Library and Archives, Canada, RG-C-2 Vol. 9377, File 38, Tech-LIA 5

Supply and Maintenance Casualty Analysis AFVs, TNA, WO203-541

Wavell, General Sir Archibald, Despatch on Operation in Burma December 1941 – May 1942, TNA, WO106-2666

Private Papers

Blackater, Jim - papers

Hopton, Harry – papers

Waterhouse, Charles Gerard 'Gerry' – letters

IWM Sound Archive

Lance, David G, Oral History of Ralph Younger, IWM 913, 1977

Lance, David G, Oral History of Rupert Harding-Newman, IWM 834, 1976

McDonagh, Richard, Oral History of Arthur Francis Freer, IWM 19822, 1999

Wood, Conrad, Oral History of Malcolm Leonard Connolly, IWM 19049, 1999

Wood, Conrad, Oral History of Robert Lifford Valentine ffrench Blake, IWM 946, 1977

Index

A

ABDA Command 43
Abyssinian crisis 32
Admin Box 133, 139–144, 146, 152–154, 158, 160, 162, 173, 177, 191, 200, 249–250, 338
aerial resupply 93, 103, 137, 145, 158–159, 164, 193, 248, 256, 259, 293, 307, 338
Afghanistan 24, 37
Akyab Island 103–104, 115, 153
Alexander 47, 57–58, 65, 68–69, 71–73, 75, 81, 88, 91, 337, 355
Allenby, Edmund 26
Allied Formations
    11th Army Group 110
    Burcorps (Burma Corps) 57, 75, 79–80, 86–90, 110, 161, 337
    Eastern Army 11, 103, 110, 249
    Eighth Army 98
    Fourteenth Army 1–2, 6, 11–12, 17, 110, 121, 136–137, 160–161, 192, 197, 235–237, 239–240, 245, 248, 260, 262, 265, 280, 286, 303, 311, 324, 334, 358, 368, 370
    IV Corps 3, 5–6, 115, 159–163, 165, 176–177, 183, 196, 239–240, 244, 264–265, 271, 280, 284–286, 289, 291, 293, 325, 332–335, 338, 361–363, 370
    XV Corps 104, 109, 115, 136–137, 139, 144, 240, 248, 251, 260, 358
    XXXIII Corps 5–6, 185, 196, 220, 235, 239–240, 244, 248–249, 262–265, 270–272, 280, 285, 303, 319, 324–325, 331–332
Ammunition Hill 139–140, 147, 149
Amritsar Massacre 33
An Pass 248, 251, 256, 259
Anstice, John 53, 55, 77
Aradura Spur 216–217, 266
Arakan 16, 18, 93, 103–105, 109–115, 121, 136, 139, 152–154, 162, 164, 198, 200–201, 248–252, 259, 283, 326, 338, 353, 356, 360, 369
armoured cars 31–33, 35, 71, 219, 300–301, 311–312
Armoured Fighting Vehicle (AFV) School, Ahmednagar 114
Army Council 21, 31

Artillery Hill 139, 147–148, 154
Assam 94, 100, 200
Atkins, David 95–96, 99, 161, 341, 356, 360, 366
Auchinleck Committee 25
Auchinleck, Claude 25, 34, 110
Australia(n) 89, 98
Ava Bridge 87

B

B echelon 52, 70, 74, 91
B-24 Liberator 117, 256, 278
B-25 Mitchell 117, 256, 291, 307
Bailey bridge 6, 266
Bengal 94, 115, 252, 270
Bilin 45, 54–55
Bishenpur 169, 185–187, 191–192, 196, 198
bithess 97
Bombay 21, 98, 141, 255, 272
Borneo 41, 43
Brahmaputra Valley 94, 200
Branson, Clive 116–117, 152, 356, 366
Bray, Peter 158–160, 250, 358
Brett-James, Anthony 146, 357–358, 366–367
British Army
    1st Cameronians 58
    1st Gloucesters 72, 76
    1st Lincolns 257
    1st Royal Tank Regiment 32
    1st Royal Welch Fusiliers 206
    1st West Yorks 300
    2nd Division 193, 196, 201–202, 206, 214, 216–218, 220, 244, 246, 262–263, 265–266, 270–271, 279, 294, 317
    2nd Dorsets 207–214, 221, 266–267, 342, 346
    2nd Durham Light Infantry 204, 268
    2nd Royal Berkshires 277
    2nd Royal Tank Regiment 49, 52, 58, 65, 68, 72, 81–83, 85–86, 90
    2nd South Lancs 291
    2nd Suffolks 194
    2nd West Yorks 141, 147, 173–174
    3 Commando Brigade 250–253
    3rd Carabiniers 113–114, 164, 169, 172, 177, 183, 185–186, 192–193, 196–198, 202, 220, 235–

237, 244, 246, 262–263, 267–269, 284, 331, 335, 340–341, 343–344, 358–360, 369
4th Brigade 215, 256
4th Royal West Kents 213
5th Brigade 204, 266, 268
6th Brigade 205, 207
7th Armoured Brigade 12, 14, 36, 47, 49, 52–57, 61, 65, 67, 69–70, 72, 74–75, 81, 83–84, 86–88, 90–91, 99, 103, 110, 112, 146, 161, 168, 197, 235, 244, 266, 332–333, 337–339, 355, 369
7th Hussars 26–27, 53, 55–59, 64–71, 74, 79–82, 86–87, 90, 164, 284, 340
7th Worcesters 266
9th Borders 300
11th East African Division 235, 241, 244, 284, 286
17th/21st Lancers 19, 21–22, 36, 340
25th Dragoons 1, 112–120, 134–138, 140–143, 147, 152, 154, 191, 202, 250, 283, 341, 343, 357, 366, 369
26th Hussars 98
28th East African Brigade 286
36th Division 324
77th Field Company, Royal Engineers 5, 287, 290
81st West African Division 152, 249, 251
82nd West African Division 249, 254, 256
116th Regiment, Royal Armoured Corps (Gordon Highlanders) 283, 288
146th Regiment, Royal Armoured Corps 106
149th Regiment, Royal Armoured Corps 201, 359
150th Regiment, Royal Armoured Corps 164
387th Company (Amphibious) RASC 266–267
414th Battery (Essex Yeomanry) 52, 64, 69, 73, 76–77, 79, 85
414th Battery (Essex Yeomany) 52
No. 1 Commando 252, 254–255
bunker busting 113, 119, 121, 140, 146, 154, 183, 191, 198, 207, 249, 278, 280, 296, 309–310, 330
Burma Campaign 18, 67, 99, 109, 326, 336, 339–340, 345, 364–366, 369
Burma Command 45, 54
Burma National Army (BNA) 262
Burma Road 41, 43, 45, 100
Bushido 269, 299
Buthidaung 116, 119, 148, 152, 250, 283

C

C-47 Dakota 7, 158, 301
Calcutta 7, 9, 94, 114, 270
canister shot 15, 142, 166
Carden Loyd Tankette 35
Ceylon 54–55
Chatfield Committee 25, 34
Cheduba Island 256, 259
Chettle, Clive 209–210, 213
Chevrolet 99
Chibi bomb 51

Chiefs of Staff 14, 54, 57, 264, 311
Chin Hills 93–94, 169
China 9, 38–43, 55, 75, 87, 265, 271
Chindits 163
Chindwin River 87–88, 160
Chinese Army
    5th Army 75, 80, 87
    6th Army 75
    38th Division 83–86
    66th Army 75, 83
    Chinese Expeditionary Force 75
Christison, Philip 137–139, 248, 250–251, 256, 259–260, 360
Churchill, Winston 28, 364
Clark 267
Clark, Hugh 267
Claudcol 327–330
Clear the Line 292, 313–315
Combined Operations 18, 251–252, 259–260, 338
Connolly, Malcolm 98–99, 113, 173–176, 331–332, 335, 344, 356, 358, 360, 362–363, 368, 370
Corduroy road 97
Cornaby, Hubert 268
Cowan, David 'Punch' 57, 187, 192, 304, 306–307, 311–312, 315–321
Craddock, William 179, 181, 183
Critchley, Gerald 249–250
Curse of Scotland 89, 266
CV/33 Tanketter 64–65

D

D8 Bulldozer 194–195, 255
Daingbon Chaung 252
DC's Bungalow 201, 203–204, 207–210, 212–214, 359
Delhi 22, 95, 114, 133
Detail Issue (DIS) Hill 204
Dhond 44
Dimapur 94, 96, 161, 164, 172, 176, 185, 200–202, 204, 213, 262, 324
DUKW 266–267
Dunkirk 34, 69, 338
Dutch East Indies 39, 41, 43

E

Egypt 26–27, 52, 54
Evans 142, 147, 177, 181
Evans, Geoffrey 10, 139, 182, 195, 288, 290

F

ffrench Blake, Valentine 19, 21–23, 26, 36, 340, 353–354, 370
Field Supply Depot (FSD) Hill 204
First World War 13, 22, 24, 26–27, 38, 41, 45,

Index

67, 92, 104–105, 133, 152, 348
Force 136 334
Fort Dufferin 274, 277–278, 280, 317
Forward Observation Officer 69, 179–180, 183, 186, 194, 250
France 28, 38, 41, 69, 246
Fraser, George MacDonald 333, 362, 366
Freer, Arthur 114, 177–182, 184, 190–191, 263, 279, 356, 358–361, 366, 370
French Indochina 41

G

Gangaw 285–287
Garran Tribunal 24
Garrison Hill 201–206, 208
Gazala 133, 271
General Staff 28–29
GHQ India 111
Giffard, George 110
GPT Companies 96, 99, 161
Grant Tank 14–16, 121, 202, 214, 218
Grounds, Tom 134, 142, 148–149, 152, 357, 366
Grover, John 217
Guam 41–42

H

Hafiz VC, Abdul 176
Hawaii 42
Henslow, John 5–10, 95, 97, 100, 215–216, 287, 290–291, 353, 356, 359–361, 366
Heynes, Gordon 112, 115, 117–118, 135, 141–143, 145, 147, 150, 152, 154, 356–357, 366
Highett, Lintorn 'Snagger' 209–210, 212, 359
Hill 170 252, 254–256, 260, 338
Hlegu 57, 65, 68–71
HMS Prince of Wales 43
HMS Repulse 43
Honda, Masaki 317, 320, 329
Hong Kong 35, 41, 43
Hopton, Harry 266–267, 370
Hundred Days Offensive (1918) 24
Hurribomber 195
Hurricane 137, 145
Hutton, Thomas 35, 45–46, 54, 57, 61, 65, 72–73, 104

I

Imperial Japanese Army (IJA)
    2nd Tank Regiment 66
    14th Tank Regiment 169, 319, 328, 330
    15th Army 44, 121, 136, 161, 196, 220, 235, 239, 251, 263–264, 312, 320, 325
    15th Division 162, 164, 169, 172, 185, 193, 197, 279
    16th Regiment 266, 294
    18th Division 44, 74, 80, 312–313, 316–317
    28th Army 121, 136, 138, 248–249, 251, 254, 259–260, 317, 326, 332
    31st Division 162, 164, 200, 216–217, 219–220
    33rd Army 263, 317, 325, 328–331, 333
    33rd Division 46, 56, 71–73, 80, 86–87, 89, 162, 164, 169, 185, 187, 192, 244, 300
    49th Artillery Regiment 318
    49th Division 244, 303, 312, 317–319
    51st Regiment 176
    53rd Division 327
    54th Division 251, 255–256, 326
    55th Division 44, 56, 65, 72, 75, 80, 87, 117, 153
    55th Regiment 318
    56th Division 75, 80
    59th Independent Field Company 100
    60th Regiment 279
    112th Regiment 65, 87, 146
    121st Regiment 256–257
    122nd Regiment 72
    143rd Regiment 65, 117
    153rd Regiment 293
    168th Regiment 303, 312
    213th Regiment 90, 104
    214th Regiment 71, 73, 81–82, 192, 288, 300
    215th Regiment 82
    Burma Area Army 5, 240, 285, 303, 311, 321, 334, 338
Imperial Japanese Navy (IJN) 41, 337
Imphal 12, 88, 91, 94, 100, 114–115, 136, 153, 158–164, 169, 171–172, 175–176, 183, 185, 187, 192–193, 195–198, 200–201, 203, 207, 212, 215–217, 220, 251, 262, 280, 283–284, 286, 301, 304, 331, 335, 338, 340–341, 358–360, 366, 370
Imphal Main Airfield 193
Imphal Plain 12, 158–160, 163, 172, 184–185, 193–194, 196, 340
Imphal-Kohima road 172, 185, 193, 198, 215, 217
Indian Armoured Corps 99
Indian Army
    1/3rd Gurkhas 190
    1/4th Gurkhas 186
    1/7th Rajput 107
    1/10th Gurkhas 22, 174, 190, 309
    1/15th Punjab 108, 272–274
    1/17th Dogras 177, 196, 220
    1st Burma Division 35, 56–57, 73, 75, 80–86
    2/1st Punjab 106
    2/5th Gurkhas 114
    3/2nd Punjab 319
    3/4th Bombay Grenadiers 141, 276
    3/9th Jats 176
    4/4th Bombay Grenadiers 327
    4/4th Gurkhas 276

4/5th Gurkhas 288
4/7th Rajput 117
4/8th Gurkhas 143
4/10th Gurkhas 266
4/12th Frontier Force Regiment (FFR) 279, 309
4/14th Punjab 288
5/10th Baluchis 276
5th Indian Division 147, 164, 319, 367
6/7th Rajput 295, 299, 326–327
7/10th Baluchis 327
7th Indian Division 5, 9–10, 116, 119, 137–140, 153, 162, 201, 215, 217, 222, 285–286, 288, 292–293, 317, 319, 325
7th Light Cavalry 14, 89, 164–165, 266, 272, 275–276
8/12th Frontier Force Regiment (FFR) 279
9/14th Punjab 170, 187
9th Brigade 146, 317–318, 325
9th Royal Deccan Horse 283, 369
11th Cavalry 327
11th Sikhs 272
13th Brigade 85
14th Indian Division 105–106, 108–109
16th Brigade 44–45
16th Light Cavalry 301
17th Indian Division 6, 35, 44–46, 54–57, 61, 63, 65, 69–70, 72, 75, 81–82, 86, 168–169, 185–187, 192, 235, 280, 284–285, 292–293, 303–304, 307, 309, 325, 330–332, 334, 367
19th Indian Division 265, 270–271, 317, 325
19th Lancers 250–251, 253–255, 259, 332, 360
20th Indian Division 169–172, 185–186, 265–266, 271, 317
23rd Indian Division 185
25th Indian Division 250–251
26th Indian Division 250, 256, 333
32nd Brigade 185, 192
33rd Brigade 144, 215–217, 290
37th Brigade 164
44th Brigade 44
45th Brigade 44
45th Cavalry 217
47th Brigade 109
48th Brigade 44, 67–70, 81, 187, 192, 293–294, 300, 304, 306–308, 310–311, 319, 327
49th Brigade 163
50th Indian Tank Brigade 368
50th Parachute Brigade 163
51st Brigade 253
54th Brigade 254
62nd Brigade 272
63rd Brigade 68, 73, 187, 192, 293–294, 300, 304, 308–311, 318, 327, 334
64th Brigade 272–273, 276
71st Brigade 256–257
74th Brigade 251, 255
89th Brigade 134–135

98th Brigade 272, 276
99th Brigade 284–285, 292–293, 303, 311, 318, 327
114th Brigade 288–290
123rd Brigade 164, 177, 181, 193, 195
161st Brigade 200, 202, 215
254th Indian Tank Brigade 89, 160–161, 164, 177, 197, 325
255th Indian Tank Brigade 6, 280, 283–285, 287–288, 292–293, 300, 302–304, 307, 309, 311, 316, 325–327, 335, 340
309th General Purpose Transport Company 96
590th Tank Transporter Company, RIASC 287
Deccan Horse 287, 293–294, 300–301, 304, 306–307, 309–310, 313, 318–319, 330–331
Frontier Force Regiment 72, 259, 309
Indian Electrical and Mechanical Engineers (IEME) 287, 335
Indian Engineers 10, 187, 198, 272
Lushai Brigade 286
Probyn's Horse (5th King Edward VII's Own Lancers) 152, 283, 292–295, 299–301, 305, 309–310, 312–313, 318–319, 327, 329–330, 343, 361–362, 367, 369
Indian General Hospital (IGH) Spur 202
Indian Mutiny/Rebellion 25
Indian National Army (INA) 262
Industrialisation 39
Iril Valley 172, 176, 185, 193
Irrawaddy Plain 264, 288–289, 311, 324
Irrawaddy river 5, 49, 52, 81
Isolationism 39
Italy 41, 111

J

Jackson, Sir Louis 21, 353
Jail Hill 215–216
Jenkins, Vernon 269
Jessami 201
Jotsoma 201

K

Kabaw Valley 164, 169, 286–287
Kaing 90–91
Kaladan River 152
Kaladan Valley 250–251
Kalapanzin River 151
Kalewa 88, 90–91, 266, 270
Kangaw 248, 251–256, 338
Kangla Airfield 176
Kanglatongbi 164, 172, 174, 185
Katamura, Shihachi 251, 263–264, 312, 317, 320
Kellogg-Briand pact 28
Kimura, Heitaro 5, 263–265, 285, 293–294, 303, 310, 312, 317, 319–321, 325–326, 333–335

Index

Kinde 318–319
Kohima 94, 96, 114, 153, 161–162, 164, 172, 175–176, 185, 193, 195–198, 200–202, 204, 207–208, 215, 217, 251, 266, 280, 359, 364
Kokkogwa 49, 81
Korea 38
Kuki Piquet 204–206
Kunming 41
Kyigon 304, 311

L

Lake Myindawgan 312
Landing Craft Tank (LCT) 115
Lee tank 268, 275, 277
Lend-Lease 14, 173
Ley, Hugh 119, 140
Leyin, John 113, 116–117, 134, 136, 140–141, 144, 146, 148–149, 151–152, 356–357, 366
Liddell Hart, Basil 354
Light Aid Detachment (LAD) 173, 176
Lion Box 172–174, 176, 193, 197
Lloyd, Wilfrid 105
Locarno Treaty 28
logistics 12, 17, 93, 137, 162–163, 264, 339
Loktak Lake 169, 185–187

M

Mahlaing 300–301, 304, 312, 314–315
Mains 62
Mains, Tony 61–63
Malaya 35, 41, 43–44, 54, 74, 100, 110, 161–162, 333
Manchuria (Manchukuo) 40
Mandalay 5, 10, 12, 58, 61–63, 75, 80, 87, 103, 248, 262, 264–265, 270–272, 274, 276–278, 280, 284–285, 293, 303, 306, 311–312, 315, 317, 319–321, 324, 331, 356, 361, 366–367
Mandalay Hill 274, 276–278, 280, 317
Manipur 94, 160, 164, 200, 248
Masters, John 'Jack' 270–271, 273, 278, 361, 367
Matsu Detachment 254
Maungdaw 116, 138
Maymyo 63
Mayu Peninsula 103, 105, 152–153, 249
Mayu Range 103, 116, 118, 137–138, 146–147
mechanisation 16, 21–22, 24–29, 31, 35, 340, 345
Meerut 22
Meiktila 6, 9, 12, 86–87, 264–265, 271, 279–280, 283–286, 292–293, 299–304, 306, 308, 310–313, 315, 317–321, 324–325, 327, 330–332, 334, 338, 362

Messervy, Frank 133–139, 154, 288–289, 292, 307–308, 357
Middle East 34–35, 37, 44, 53, 91, 92, 95, 98, 100, 104, 110–111, 173
milking 34
Mk II Tank 22
Mk III Light Tank 32
Mk IV Light Tank 32
Modbung 193, 195
Mohmand Uprising 24
Molotov cocktail 70
Moreh 92, 169
Moulmein 44–45, 54, 333
Mountbatten, Louis 110, 164, 248–249, 264, 324
Mutaguchi, Renya 121, 136, 161–162, 164–165, 187, 196, 200, 216–217, 251
Myebon Peninsula 251, 256

N

Naga Hills 200
Naga Village 204
Naganuma Force 312–313, 316–317, 320
Nanking Massacre 40
National Army Museum (UK) 11, 339
Nazi Germany 41
Netherlands 42
New Zealand 98
Ngakyedauk Pass 118, 136–139, 143, 146, 151–152, 154
Ngazun 265–266, 268
Nicholson, Cameron 246, 263, 360
Ningthoukhong 186, 193
North Africa 35, 53, 55, 98, 133, 252, 340
Northwest Frontier 28, 32, 45, 98, 270
Nunshigum 176–178, 181, 183–185, 190, 198, 280, 338, 356, 358–361, 366
Nyaungu 285–286, 289–290, 292, 294, 303, 317, 320, 338

O

O'Beirne-Ryan, Desmond 318–319
Operation Capital 248–249, 260, 262, 264, 284, 340
Operation Dracula 248, 260, 324
Operation Extended Capital 248, 264, 271, 284
Operation Ha-Go 136, 160, 249
Operation U-Go 136, 161–162
Operational Research 114, 119
Oyin 294, 296, 298, 300, 302, 306, 328, 334, 361
Oyster Box 174, 195–196

P

P-38 Lightning 159

P-47 Thunderbolt 256, 278, 291
P-51 Mustang 159
Pacific 40, 42, 366
Pakkoku 288–289
Palel 100, 161, 169, 172, 196, 285
Palestine 26, 31
Palmer, Geoffrey 59, 68–70, 76–77, 354–355, 368
Panay incident 40
Payathonzu 65, 67, 69, 71–72
Pegu 56, 58, 61, 65–68, 75, 325, 331–335
Pegu Yomas 75, 325, 333
Pert, Claude 283, 316, 327
Philippines, the 38, 41–42
PIAT (Projector Infantry Anti-Tank) 259, 319
Pin Chaung 82
Point 315 143, 152, 154
Point 860 304, 306
pole charge 167, 211–212
Potsangbam 186–188, 190–192, 216, 359
Prendergast, John 108, 273–276, 278, 361, 363, 367
Priest self-propelled gun 295
Prome 57, 62–63, 69, 73–76, 78–80, 251, 326
Pyawbwe 325, 327–330, 334

Q

Quetta Staff College 152

R

Ram, Jot 165, 358
Ramree island 256
Ranchi 113, 283–284
Rangoon 41, 45, 52, 54–57, 61–62, 64, 68–69, 71–75, 86, 91, 103, 159, 248, 259–260, 264–265, 286, 312, 321, 324–328, 331–335, 338, 346, 354–355, 358, 360, 362, 365
Razabil 116–117, 119–120, 138, 152, 154, 353, 356, 369
Razabil Fortress 116–117, 119
Rees, Thomas 'Pete' 270–273, 275–276, 278, 280
Rhodes, Ezra 204–207, 359
Royal Engineers 5, 7, 18, 32, 46, 88–89, 95, 203–204, 214–215
Royal Marines
    42 Commando 252
    44 Commando 252
Royal Navy 24–25, 30, 248, 252, 258
Royal Tank Corps 23, 27, 29, 31
Russo-Japanese War 39, 41

S

Sakoku policy 38
Sakuma Force 312–313
Sakurai Force 138
Sakurai, Shōzō 46, 73, 90, 121, 136, 248, 250–251, 259–260
Sakurai, Tokutaro 138
Sanford, Edward 'Dizzy' 177–181, 184
Sangshak 163, 172, 201
Sappers 208, 217
Sato, Kotuku 200–202, 216–217, 219–220, 359
Sawumbung 172
Schlaefli, Robin 111, 272, 277, 356, 361, 367
Scoones, Geoffrey 163, 165, 169, 172, 177, 181, 185
Shan States 75, 80, 86
Shenam Saddle 172, 185, 193, 196, 198
Sherman Tank 14–16, 249, 253, 255, 275, 283, 291–292, 298, 300, 313, 320, 335
Shojiro, Iida 44
Shwebo 12, 159, 246, 262–263, 265, 271, 340
Shwebo Plain 12, 159, 262–263, 265, 271
Shwedaung 76, 78
Shwegyin 88–90, 266
Silchar Track 185–186, 192–193, 196, 198
Singapore 25, 35, 43, 54–55, 80, 161
Singh, Bahadur 298, 328
Singh, Bharat 167
Singh, Chunni 298
Singh, Daval 296
Singh, Piara 255
Singh, Ranbir 183
Singh, Sarup 326
Sinzweya 18, 135, 139
Sittang Bridge 46, 56–57, 61, 63, 87, 165, 332
Sittang River 46, 56
Sittang Valley 73, 75, 80–81, 86, 325, 332–333
Slim, William 'Bill' 6, 11–12, 57, 75, 81, 90–91, 104–106, 109–110, 113, 115, 121, 133, 137–138, 153–154, 160, 163, 172, 185, 196, 200, 262–265, 271, 280, 285–286, 307–308, 310–311, 320–321, 324–326, 338–339, 353, 355–356, 360–362, 365, 367
Smeeton, Miles 37–38, 152, 283–284, 292, 294–296, 298–300, 302, 305–306, 313–316, 318–319, 327–329, 334, 340, 354, 357, 361–363, 367
Smyth, John 45–46, 54, 56–57, 354
South-East Asia Command (SEAC) 110, 164, 346, 360, 370
Soviet Union 38, 40–41
Spitfire 137, 145, 159
Stiletto Force 272–277
Stopford, Montagu 270
Stuart tank 53, 64, 249, 266, 283

T

Ta-Dan hollow-charge shell 313

Taketi M2 Rifle Grenade 195
Tamu 92–93, 96, 100, 161, 169, 286
Taukkyan 63, 69, 71, 73, 91
Taungdwingyi 49, 80
Taungtha 293–294, 299–300, 303–304
Taungup 248, 251, 259
Tenasserim 45, 54, 333
Tennis court 201, 203, 207–215, 266, 280, 338
Thabutkon 293, 300–301, 303, 311
Thabutkon Airfield 300–301, 303
Thailand 44, 74, 333
Thazi 317
Third Arakan 18
Tiddim 161, 165, 168, 187, 192, 196, 198
Tiddim Road 165, 168, 187, 192
Tokita, Umeo 49–52, 81, 354
Tomekichi, Kasuya 303
Torbung 187, 192
Tortoise 116, 338
Toungoo 56–57, 61, 73, 75, 79–80, 325, 331
Treasury Hill 213
Treaty of Versailles 39
Tripartite Pact 41
Tuker, Francis 110–111
Type 95 Ha Go Tank 66

U

Ukhrul 161, 172, 185, 193, 196
Universal Carrier 170

V

Valentine Tank 14, 106–107, 187–188, 191, 353, 370
Vickers 29–30
Victoria Point 44
Viswema 218–220
Vultee Vengeance 177

W

Wake Island 42
War Office 30
Waterhouse, Charles 'Gerry' 207–215, 218, 346, 359, 370
Waziristan 24
weapon independence 39
Western Desert 67, 271, 313
White, Geoffrey 208–209, 212, 266–267, 346, 368
Williams, James 'Elephant Bill' 92–93, 96, 164, 355–356, 360, 367
Worthington-Evans, Sir Laming 21, 29

Y

Yamamoto Force 169, 185, 196
Yamauchi, Masafumi 162
Yanbauk Chaung 256–257
Ye-U 88, 263
Yenangyaung 52, 74, 80–81, 87, 293, 325, 331
Yindaw 326–327
Younger, Ralph 26–27, 53–54, 56, 64, 68, 164, 177–178, 181–182, 184, 283, 340, 353–354, 370